CRITICAL PERSPECTIVES ON LUSOPHONE LITERATURE FROM AFRICA

CRITICAL PERSPECTIVES ON LUSOPHONE LITERATURE FROM AFRICA

Compiled and Edited by Donald Burness

3€P

An Original by Three Continents Press

First Edition

ISBN 0-89410-015-7
ISBN 0-89410-016-5 (pbk)
LC 80-53348

Cover Art by Tom Gladden

Three Continents Press
1346 Connecticut Avenue N.W., Washington, D.C. 20036

S.h.
11/82

ACKNOWLEDGMENTS

I wish to thank the following individuals and publications for permission to print essays which appear in this book. Every effort has been made to contact copyright holders, but in a few cases this has proved impossible.

Richard Preto-Rodas and the University Presses of Florida for chapters from *Negritude as a theme in the Poetry of the Portuguese-Speaking World.*

Russell Hamilton and the University of Minnesota Press for chapters from *Voices from an Empire: A History of Afro-Portuguese Literature.*

Norman Araujo for parts of his book *A Study of Cape Verdean Literature.*

Gerald Moser and the Pennsylvania State University Libraries for "Castro Soromenho, an Angolan Realist," which appears in *Essays in Portuguese-African Literature.*

The Gulbenkian Foundation for "Luandino Vieira: o anti-apartheid" by José Martins Garcia and "Da dor de ser negro até ao orgulho de ser preto," by Manuel Ferreira, which appeared respectively in *Colóquio-Letras* no. 22 (Nov. 1974) and no. 39 (Sept. 1977).

Manuel Ferreira and Seara Nova for extracts from *No Reino de Caliban* - Vols. I and II.

Ba Shiru for "The Art of Luandino Vieira" by Tomás Jacinto.

I would also like to give particular thanks to Manuel Ferreira and Gerald Moser, who courteously provided me with necessary information.

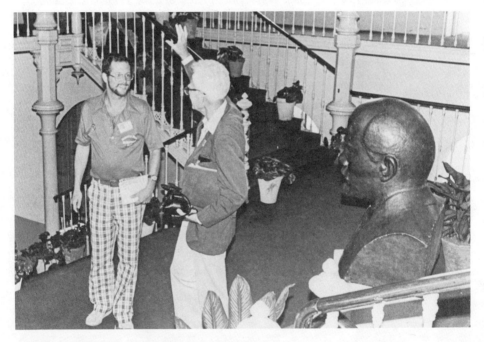

Donald Burness (l) and Gerald Moser.in lobby of
Conference Hall for Sixth Conference of Afro-Asian Writers,
(Luanda, Angola: 26 June - 1 July 1979)

For

Carroll Yoder

and

Jean Sarocchi

INTRODUCTION

This collection of essays provides a variety of critical perspectives on Lusophone African writing of the nineteenth and twentieth centuries. There has been in recent years, particularly in Portugal, the Soviet Union, and the United States as well as the African countries themselves, a growing interest in the literatures of Angola, Cape Verde, Mozambique, Guiné-Bissau and the twin islands of São-Tomé-Principe. Scholarly books, articles, and bibliographies inform us of the development and history of written African literatures in Portuguese and also focus on the achievements of individual writers. Nevertheless, because of limited translations and the fact that in non-Portuguese speaking lands, the Portuguese language is not studied extensively, Lusophone African writers have not reached as wide an audience both within and outside the African continent as their Francophone and Anglophone counterparts. Much work remains to be done so that we can have a greater understanding and appreciation of the contribution of Lusophone writers to the literature of sub-Saharan Africa.

The essays in this anthology are in English and Portuguese. I decided to include some Portuguese essays so that readers in Portugal, Brazil and Lusophone Africa might find the book useful. I have selected essays in Portuguese which for the most part deal with themes or writers that have not been explored sufficiently by critics in English speaking countries. This is particularly true of Manuel Ferreira's studies on sundry literary journals devoted to Angolan culture and literature. These Portuguese essays (in part two or three), I believe, give a more complete picture of Lusophone African writing. Each Portuguese language essay is preceded by a précis in English.

I have chosen to keep the essays in English separate from those in Portuguese. This has presented a dilemma of sorts: The English essays on the literary journals *Claridade* and *Raízes* might well have been placed with the essays on journals in Portuguese.

Although most of these essays have previously been published, several of them (including those dealing with post-independence writing) are appearing in print for the first time. In this way this collection is not merely eclectic; it hopes to provide new insights as well. Moreover, Professor Moser's essay on Castro Soromenho includes corrections (an errata section) for the originally published version reproduced in this volume.

The first two essays in English are general in nature and provide substantial historical information. The remaining essays in Part One are for the most part devoted to individual countries and writers. There is a greater emphasis on Angolan and Cape Verdean writing for two reasons: the quality and quantity of the literature from these lands is superior to that of Mozambique, Guiné-Bissau and São-Tomé-Principé; and there have been considerably more articles devoted to writing from Angola and Cape Verde than to the other Lusophone African countries. I have included, however, two essays on Mozambican literature and another which is concerned with the negritude poets of São-Tomé-Principé. The literature of Guiné-Bissau is discussed in two essays, Gerald Moser's "The Lusophone Literatures of Africa Since Independence" and Russell Hamilton's Cape Verdean Poetry and the PAIGC."

The essays I have selected do not necessarily conform to a single point of view. Particularly in the case of Cape Verde, there has been much criticism of the generation of the thirties, the generation of *Claridade,* by the younger or New Generation. Both sides are presented in this anthology. The essays on individual writers are devoted to literary figures of particular import. I could not, of course, in a book such as this include studies on all major figures, so I have had to limit myself to a few principal voices.

By selecting Mário António's essay on Cordeiro da Matta, the nineteenth century Angolan poet, linguist and historian, I have chosen to pay attention to the important contribution of Lusophone African writers and scholars of that time. Along with his San Tomesian contemporary Caetano da Costa Alegre, Cordeiro da Matta's influence on African letters cannot be neglected. I have chosen Gerald Moser's study of Castro Soromenho and two essays on Luandino Vieira to illustrate not only the impact these writers have had and the excellence of their art, but also to point out that in Portuguese speaking Africa, white writers, white *African* writers, have articulated the aspirations and the frustrations of Africans living under an oppressive colonialism. António Jacinto, David Mestre, João Grabato Dias, António Cardoso—these white voices, like those of Soromenho and Luandino, do distinguish African literature of Portuguese expression from the literatures of Francophone or Anglophone areas. (Of course there are major white writers in South Africa, but they have not been accepted as spokesmen by the oppressed African peoples.)

The third part of this collection concerns itself solely with six literary journals which have played an important part in the development of Cape Verdean and Angolan literatures from the 1930's to the early 1970s. These journals have not only explored and articulated literary and cultural goals; they also were forums where young, unknown writers returned to their cultural roots in order to reassert their Africanness. In the past two years new journals have been born. Gerald Moser alludes to several of these fledgling journals in his essay "The Lusophone Literatures of Africa Since Independence." I have provided a list with addresses of contemporary journals at the conclusion of the Selected Bibliography.

One final point: there are only a handful of recognized scholars who write in English on African literatures in Portuguese. That explains the inclusion of two or more essays by a single critic-scholar.

Donald Burness
August 20, 1980

CONTENTS

Part Two: Essays and Articles in Portuguese
With English Précis

Part Three: Essays on Six Portuguese
Language Journals—With English Précis

Angola

Cape Verde

List of Illustrations

PART ONE

Essays and Articles

(in English)

Portuguese Africa
Toward Mutual Assimilation

—*Richard A. Preto-Rodas*

U NLIKE HIS COUNTERPART in Brazil and the South Atlantic islands, the Negro in Angola and Mozambique is not a member of a long-established national or local community cast in a European mold. Until recent years, Portuguese influence was limited to the small minority and a tiny black elite living in a few coastal centers. With very little racial fusion, Portuguese Africa never witnessed the social and cultural "mulattoization" of Brazil, and one would seek in vain for a gradual awakening of racial consciousness. For the masses of Negroes the situation has been typical of sub-Sahara Africa, viz., a tribal society divided by a large number of local dialects.

The appearance of Negritude both in Angola and Mozambique has been limited to the educated African immersed in a culture essentially if not exclusively European. He accordingly feels no less alienated from the surrounding indigenous society than he does from the European world which is prepared to accept him only to the extent that it can forget that he is an African.[1] Like the literate, French-speaking Negro, he, too, has attended schools which teach him of others' ancestors involved in historical events not even remotely connected with his own land and people.[2] Inspired by the recent affirmation of racial origins by Antilleans, Afro-Brazilians, and French-speaking Africans, a rising chorus of Angolan and Mozambican poets has sought to establish a rapport with their past and with the very real African world about them. For them the line between Negritude and Africanitude becomes indeed tenuous. Their numbers have grown as the Lisbon government expands its influence economically and culturally. The

1. Moser, "African Literature . . . Last Discovered," pp. 79–83. See also Chilcote, pp. 28–30.
2. Cf. Moore's reference to African children reciting history lessons concerning "Our Gaulish ancestors" in *Seven African Authors*, p. 2.

result is a clash between opposite value systems involving Negritude and the equally visionary attitude comprising the traditional Portuguese policy in Africa. At present, both provide programs whereby two hostile elites attempt to mobilize the mass of Africans caught up in the vast changes of the last twenty years.

Several students of Portuguese Africa have pointed out the remarkable continuity of the traditional Lusitanian mystique which seeks to assimilate all colonial peoples into a multiracial Portuguese family. Extending back to the sixteenth century and continuing to the present day the goal has been to "fulfill the historic mission of colonization in the lands of the discoveries."[3] Like all families, the Portuguese multiracial family is not intended to be a partnership of equals, and its paternalistic character is clearly stated in the regime's plan "to Christianize and educate, to nationalize and civilize."[4] Moreover, it is a family where the "uncivilized" (i.e., non-Europeanized) child reaches maturity very slowly if ever, if one may draw any conclusions from the tiny percentage (0.5 per cent) of the total African population which had been "assimilated" by the late 1950's. Equally constant has been the Portuguese view regarding the alternatives to their colonization: a withdrawal would invite ideologies alien to the Christian West, whether under the sign of the crescent in the sixteenth century or of the hammer and sickle in the twentieth.[5]

Also a traditional, albeit less ethereal, trait of the Lusitanian presence has been the exploitation of the native as a cheap source of manpower.[6] Descriptions of the sad lot of Guineans being loaded into slave ships date back to the sixteenth century, and as recently as the beginning of this century dark rumors circulated concerning the prevalence of forced labor.[7] Until the present decade some form of obligatory work played an important part in reminding the indigenous element of its civic duties as a junior member of a national family.[8] With recent economic developments, a labor shortage has resulted leading to enormous shifts of the population and a consequent collapse of tribal structures. Additional large numbers have chosen to forsake the much touted racial harmony of Portuguese

3. See Duffy, pp. 171–81; Chilcote, pp. 46–47.
4. See Duffy, pp. 171–72; Chilcote, pp. 14–17.
5. Duffy, pp. 217–18.
6. See Duffy on "The Absolute Necessity to Work" and "Brotherhood for the Few," pp. 182–89.
7. Duffy, pp. 134, 136.
8. Duffy, pp. 184–89; Chilcote, pp. 11–13.

Africa in a search for adequate wages in the mines of South Africa and the sisal fields of Tanzania.[9]

For almost a century there has been a significant parallel reaction to the Portuguese policy in the form of intermittent warfare in the interior and an increasing reference to native customs in urban circles. Throughout much of the nineteenth century, as Portugal was obliged to develop the African interior or suffer the loss of its claims to other European powers, successive military campaigns engaged tribal chieftains in combat. The especially violent 1880's and 1890's also saw the birth of several newspapers edited by black Angolans.[10] While not openly calling for revolt against the European administrators, there was clearly a determination to maintain ties with native dialects and customs. In 1882 a bilingual weekly, *O futuro de Angola* (The Future of Angola), appeared in Luanda. Printed in Portuguese and Quimbundu, the local language, the newspaper was devoted to articles of topical interest.[11] At about the same time the self-taught black Joaquim Dias Cordeiro da Matta dedicated himself to compiling Quimbundu proverbs and translating them into Portuguese "to encourage the study of Quimbundu and Angolan traditions." His work was published in Lisbon in 1891 with the title *Filosofia popular em provérbios angolenses* (Popular Philosophy in Angolan Proverbs).

Such attempts to give substance to the official cant of a multiracial family were subsequently discouraged. The white minority was hardly receptive to local cultures and preferred that the educated African abandon his past entirely in exchange for a thoroughly Portuguese outlook. Thus, the promising start of the 1880's soon died out as censorship throttled what was considered a threat to European hegemony. When, in 1934, a volume of memoirs appeared describing life in Luanda at the turn of the century, the Negro author António de Assis Junior was promptly arrested and imprisoned in Lisbon where he died. His book *O segredo da morta* (The Dead Woman's Secret) aroused the same suspicious reserve of black intellectuals which we have seen in Viana de Almeida's contemporary account of São Tomé.[12]

9. Margarido, "The Social and Economic Background," pp. 63–70.
10. Chilcote, pp. 71–74.
11. Moser, "African Literature . . . Last Discovered," p. 80.
12. The author lamented that the official culture was "imposed through intimidation and fear rather than persuasion and reasoning. . . ." See Moser, "African Literature . . . Last Discovered," pp. 79–83. A similar, contemporary view is

Shortly after the Second World War a multiracial group of writers, Associação regional dos naturais de Angola (Regional Association of Native-born Angolans) launched a movement designed to provide a regional program which would include the racial, cultural, and geographic factors peculiar to the territory. Rallying to the motto "Vamos decobrir Angola" (Let us discover Angola), the members acknowledged their debt to the inchoate nationalism discernible in Matta's proverbs and in the turn-of-the-century bilingual press. The group published a journal, *Mensagem* (Message), which was suppressed after three issues owing to its separatist tendencies.[13] However, the ardor with which the young writers embraced the concept of a truly composite culture including—and here one is reminded of the Brazilian *Semana de arte moderna*—a distinctively Angolan-Portuguese literary style set the tone for subsequent intellectuals. As the official refusal to recognize local aspirations became more obvious several of the founders joined secessionist movements, a trend which continues as is indicated by the large number of exiled or imprisoned writers.[14]

Such a writer is Mário de Andrade, co-editor (with Francisco José Tenreiro) of the first anthology of Afro-Portuguese poetry and a former president of an independence movement, *Movimento popular de libertação de Angola* (MPLA). A physician as well as a poet and a writer fluent in at least three languages, Andrade has commented at length on the role of the "assimilated" Portuguese-speaking Negro. His dispassionate manner often angers his fellow revolutionaries as much as it does the most despotic colonial official. Thus, he reminds the latter that, bureaucratic rhetoric aside, there is no special bond uniting immigrant peasants from Portugal and Angolan farmers. Even minimal communication is possible only to the extent that the African learns the European's language, which, of course, destroys any a priori mystique. Since the assimilation is entirely one-sided, the much vaunted Lusitanian community is simply an imposition by a minority of European social, political, religious, and cultural standards on a majority whose own values are scarcely considered. Moreover, the small number of mixed bloods is not enough to constitute a new so-

found in a recent novel by another black Angolan. See Santos Lima, *As sementes da liberdade* (Rio de Janeiro, 1965).

13. Margarido, "The Social and Economic Background," p. 64. According to Chilcote only two issues of *Mensagem* appeared before it was banned. See p. 30.

14. For example, of the eighteen poets included in *New Sum*, only three have not been imprisoned or exiled at some time.

ciety; and the mixture, when it occurs, hardly affords a stable social base, since it almost universally entails concubinage between white men and native women.[15]

Andrade also questions the attempt by some Negroes to resurrect a pristine African culture. The *engagé* writer should not ignore the fact that his intellectual outlook, his literary medium, and even some of his values are the result of his incorporation into a Portuguese cultural framework. Andrade does not predict the future of the Portuguese language in Angola, but for the moment he considers it the only linguistic unifier in a country of four major languages and numerous dialects. Accordingly, he echoes Sédar Senghor's strategy of using the colonist's tools, including his language, to oppose him, thereby assimilating without becoming assimilated. The Angolan writer, he holds, should therefore address himself in Portuguese to the growing numbers of black students, reminding them of their inferior position in a society officially inclined to eradicate any identity with an African past.[16]

Andrade's view of Negritude is obviously a pragmatic one. While admitting that the movement is essential for "investigating positive currents in our African past and for taking stock of our condition" and that it may therefore "be offensive to the sensibility of Occidental esthetes," he would also regard it as a provisional means to racial rehabilitation. As such, it is a temporary program which may eventually allow for the cooperation of whites and mulattoes interested in the unique character of Angolan traditions. The primary responsibility for leadership, however, rests with the black elite, a class presently as divorced from the ordinary Africans as it is from the European ruler. Like Aimé Césaire, Andrade calls for an end to the pretense to be white with all the humiliating accoutrements, from hair straighteners to stilted Portuguese, and encourages unflagging dedication to the basis of Negritude, i.e., "championing the scandalous pride of being a Negro while protesting the equally common bond of past and present humiliation."[17]

---

15. See Andrade's introduction to his *Antologia:* "Cultura negro-africana e assimilação," pp. vii–xvi. After I completed my study, I discovered a short summary of Afro-Portuguese poetry by Mário de Andrade entitled "La poésie africaine d'expression portugaise: Evolution et tendances actuelles" in *Présence Africaine,* 65 (1965), 51–84.

16. See "Littérature et nationalisme en Angola," *Présence Africaine,* 41 (1962), 91–99.

17. Andrade, "Cultura," p. xiv.

Even politically submissive Angolan writers have tended to implement Andrade's message. Thus, the mixed blood Mário António Fernando de Oliveira, currently professor of African languages at Lisbon's Graduate Institute of Social Sciences and Overseas Politics, frequently invokes themes basic to Negritude along with his more numerous poems dealing with conventional lyrical themes.[18] Writing under the pen name Mário António, he often invokes his African ancestors such as in "Avó Negra" (Negro Grandmother) when he wonders whether his maternal grandmother sincerely broke with the "velha tradição" (old tradition).[19] The poet implies that cultural and biological assimilation has led to a spiritual loss. Thus, in "Donas de outro tempo" (Ladies of Another Time) he mourns the lost innocence of female Negro converts to Christianity, since they thereby forfeited for themselves and their descendants an animistic unity with nature.

The same elegiac tone pervades "Deuses" (Gods) when he mourns the heroism of African women harried and heroic in their silence, their hair straightened, and dressed in European hand-me-downs: "sapatos velhos, meias rotas" (old shoes, torn stockings). A more personal note appears in "Enfermaria" when he recalls "O Negrinho na minha infância perdida..." (the little Negro [that I was] in my lost youth).

Mário António's childhood camaraderie with the non-European is made difficult by his adult status as a mulatto socially if not psychologically integrated into European colonial society. Unlike some who might consider such a step a conquest, he gives a sarcastic self-portrait in "Anti-heróica" (Anti-heroic): "Bem-falante, educado, Bem-vestido" (Polished speaker, educated, well-dressed). His self-disparagement becomes guilt in several poems dedicated to his land such as "Pedologia africana" (African Pedology) where he begs the "chão sagrado" (hallowed ground) to pardon him for acquiescing to the ravages which have followed the economic exploitation of recent years. Echoing the theme of cosmic harmony between Negro and nature, Mário António finds peace only in love when, rejecting the veneer of the Christian ethic, he senses the living force of earth, river,

18. See João Alves das Neves, "Encontro com Mário António," *Estado de São Paulo Suplemento Literário*, March 4, 1962, p. 1.
19. *100 Poemas* (Luanda, 1963), p. 7. The examples from António's work which I cite are all from *100 Poemas* (in the order in which I cite them), pp. 108, 113, 57, 160, 105, 24, 22, 39, and 46.

and forest in a physical passion described as "pura, forte e selvagem" (pure, strong, and savage).

Less mystical is the very real bond which he feels with Negroes and other mulattoes everywhere by virtue of their common slave past and their present status as grudgingly accepted members of a white-dominated society. For Mário António even the briny smell of low tide is enough to conjure up a feeling of rot and decay, which, in turn, sparks an atavistic horror of manacles and the fetid holds of slave ships ("Mar" [Sea]). Similarly, in "Três desejos para a noite" (Three Wishes at Nightfall) a chance encounter with a Cape Verdean immigrant, a child of Africa like himself, suggests the archipelago's melancholy dirges, expressions of "Nossa saudade bela e nua" (Our own stark though lovely reveries). The universal brotherhood of race appears also in "Canto de farra" (Chant for a Spree) when the poet goes awenching with the Negro hero of Jorge Amado's *Jubiabá*. As in the Brazilian novel, the Angolan poet endeavors to capture a flavor of colloquial spontaneity, thus reproducing the breezy style of the Portuguese spoken by the nonwhite adventurers in the native quarters around Luanda: "Quando li *Jubiabá* / Me cri António Balduíno" (When I read *Jubiabá*, I thought I was António Balduíno).

A subsidiary theme in the poetry of the mulatto Mário António, Negritude is central in the writing of the Negro Geraldo Bessa Victor. A lawyer currently practicing in Lisbon, Bessa Victor expresses an idealistic humanism involving a partnership between white and black in his native Angola. His hesitant optimism, however, does not blind him to social inequalities, and he presses the African to affirm his dignity in the face of European attempts to establish a hierarchy along racial lines. While not making common cause with the separatist Andrade, Bessa Victor's poetic treatment of an uncompromising cultural Negritude has won him the acclaim of many foreign poets and critics in Brazil, France, and Italy. All note his wide range of tone, from the immediacy of an overheard conversation to the impassioned cry of the lover and the poignant lament of the martyr.[20]

As an example of Bessa Victor's conversational style we may consider his "Lamento de Maricota" (Maricota's Lament).[21] From a cas-

20. His *Cubata abandonada* (Braga, 1966) has a preface by Manuel Bandeira. There are endorsements by the Brazilian Catulo da Paixão Cearense, the Frenchman Roger Bastide, and the Italian Giuseppe Carlo Rossi in *Mucanda* (Braga, 1965). An anthology of Bessa Victor has been published in French under the title *Poèmes Africains*, tr. Gaston-Henry Aufrère (Braga, 1967).

21. *Cubata*, pp. 47–48.

ual street encounter between a middle-aged Negro woman and her former European lover, Bessa Victor distills the personal tragedy implied in concubinage. Snubbed by the "respectable" citizen, the indignant woman reminds him of the old days when, as a penniless immigrant youth, he shared bed and board with her while saving the fortune which now permits him to act the role of the decorous bourgeois. A far cry from today's perfumed gentleman married to a Lisbon lady was the laborer whom she would remind to bathe, "Vai tomar banho, José!" The dramatic monologue ends with a hurt query as she calls out to the retreating figure: "Aiué, Senhor José, / para que fazer assim...!" (Goodness, Mr. Joseph, / why carry on like that?).

Maricota's hurt confusion is shared by the young black man of "Canção de um negro com alma de branco" (Song of the Negro with a White's Soul).[22] Raised by a charitable white godmother, the Negro youth is repelled by her daughter when he confesses his love. Before the unexpected rebuke "Seu negro!" (You black), he can only stammer: "Mas eu tenho alma branca..." (But I have a white soul . . .). His error was allowing the kindness of *noblesse oblige* to lull him into a false security. In a society tainted by racial superiority, Bessa Victor regards the assimilated black who pretends to be white as an inhabitant of a fool's paradise.

The ideal, of course, is the child's carefree lack of awareness. Like other Afro-Portuguese poets already mentioned, the Angolan poet devotes many of his poems to lyrical evocations of childhood: "Só crianças, que não têm raça, que não têm côr" (Just children without race or color).[23] But the sad truth is that such a state is an ephemeral one. In his best known poem, "O menino negro não entrou na roda" (The Negro child did not join the circle), the poet tells of a group of European children happily dancing. When one invites a black child to join, he is scolded by his "zealous mama." One child is thus introduced to his elders' prejudice while the other, "Só, calado" (Alone, silent) is obliged to remember that he is black and therefore not a member of the circle.[24]

The solution which Bessa Victor proposes is love, both physical (i.e., racial mixture) and fraternal. In many of his poems he concre-

22. Victor, *Cubata*, pp. 27–29.
23. Victor, *Mucanda*, pp. 25–26.
24. Victor, *Mucanda*, pp. 13–14. The poem also appears in Andrade's *Antologia*, p. 55, and das Neves, "Poetas e contistas," p. 46. The remaining examples of Victor are from *Mucanda* (in the order in which I cite them), pp. 48, 37–38, 67–68.

tizes the union of European and African in hymenal odes which seek to realize the bureaucratic sloganeering regarding the formation of a new society:

> Ah, vem unir teus lábios onde provo tão bem
> O gôsto de cereja e da castanha quente
> Aos meus lábios que sabem perturbadoramente
> A goiaba e a dendém...
>
> (Ah, come join your lips on which I savor so well
> The taste of cherry and hot chestnut
> To my lips which taste excitingly
> Of guava and oilpalm fruit. . .).

The appeal is to the lovers' common humanity which overrides racial differences: "Sôbre a marca da negritude/há o sêlo do humano" (Over the sign of negritude there is the seal of the human). Unlike his social vignettes exemplified in "Lamento de Maricota," Bessa Victor is more rhetorical when treating of love, as though pleading for what is difficult if not impossible in present circumstances. His misgiving is clear in "Poema da fraternidade frustrada" (Poem to frustrated fraternity) where two poets, one black and one white, toast the end of racism. Their optimism is blunted against a background of sullenly silent members of both races.

Obviously, the Lisbon lawyer will not counter the persistence of white ethnocentrism with open hostility.[25] Even so, Bessa Victor often goes beyond his appeals for a racial rapprochement which would recognize the worth of both parties, and gives cautious reign to the "anti-racist racism" of a more refined Negritude. Thus, the reader finds frequent allusions to the color bond uniting Negroes, whether Angolan, Guinean, or Brazilian. In "Terras de Guiné" (Lands of Guinea) he exults in "minha raça negra.../a comunhão de sangue, amor, e fé..." (My Negro race, the communion of blood, love, and faith).[26] In Brazil or São Tomé, the Negro treads land which he has sown and irrigated with "pranto, sangue, e suor" (lamentation, blood, and sweat).[27] In a less impassioned mood, the Catholic Bessa Victor

25. For a view of Bessa Victor's fraternal Negritude which seeks rapprochement with Portuguese culture, see João Alves das Neves, "Hughes, Cullen e a 'Negritude'" in Estado de São Paulo Suplemento Literário, May 21, 1966, p. 1.
26. Cubata, pp. 79–80.
27. See "Na ilha de São Tomé" in Cubata, pp. 65–68.

will not hesitate to meditate on his pre-Christian unity with the elements and his pagan ancestors. Here his verse becomes hushed as the spirits of Queen Ginga and the warrior Gunjango pass through the wind-swept clouds and over the forested hills. The sense of primeval solidarity in a lost Eden becomes "A mensagem das Áfricas" (The Message from the Africas) which he hopes to take to the European world. For Bessa Victor, as for most exponents of Negritude, the whites sorely need the sound of marimba and drum to offset the clangor of the technocratic age.[28]

Bessa Victor's wavering hope for a synthesis between Portuguese and Angolan is rarely found in the angry verses of other notable examples of Angolan Negritude. So intent are they upon decrying the colonial system that they rarely transcend anguish and revolt to the more tranquil heights of racial mysticism and universal humanism. One detects, therefore, little desire for integration into existing society. Such representative poets as Viriato da Cruz, Agostinho Neto, and António Jacinto construe Negritude primarily as a call for transforming their society by rejecting the European and consigning for the moment to a minor position any reconstruction of native cultural values.

The regional scene and popular customs are, however, effectively used as a background by the journalist Viriato da Cruz who has been called the pioneer of a nationalistic Angolan literature.[29] In "Serão de menino" (Children's Evening Hour),[30] for example, he recalls a village of conical huts where children listen wide-eyed as their grandmothers tell Bantu fables around the fire. In a few disconnected verses, da Cruz provides a glimpse into the world of folk tales where animals, who live closer to the wisdom of nature than humans, serve as the paradigms of behavior:

> Matreiro o cágado lento
> Tuc... tuc... foi entrando
> Para o conselho animal...
> ("Tão tarde que êle chega!")

28. *Cubata*, pp. 77–78.
29. See Andrade, "Littérature et nationalisme en Angola," p. 97.
30. *Poetas e contistas africanos*, pp. 44–45. The first and still major compilation of native folk tales which are the background of da Cruz' poem is the work of the nineteenth-century Swiss missionary Héli Chatelain. See the recent bilingual edition *Contos populares de Angola* (Lisbon, 1964). The tiny bibliography devoted to Quimbundu language and oral literature is indicative of the scant official interest in native cultures. See pp. 105–8.

(The astute turtle slowly
Tuc ... tuc ... approached
The animal council ...
["He takes so long to arrive!"]).

The poet's sensitivity to such a session is evident in the onomatopoeic description of the tortoise's plodding pace, the deliberate prolongation of the suspense, and the excited expectancy of the enthralled children. But something more than a timeless lesson is implied in the wily tortoise's counsel to a doe who has been robbed by a lion, and the fable's conclusion is a call to battle: "–luta ao Mal! Vitória ao Bem!" (Struggle against Evil, Victory for the Good).

In addition to theme and structure, the aura of local customs is also conveyed in the poet's uses of native words and musical rhythms. In the same poem, the storm-tossed night is alive with ghostly sounds. The thrashing of leafy boughs and the samba beat of flapping doorway coverings are captured in such phonetically suggestive verses as "e [o vento] ramos xuaxualha de altos mulembas / e as portas bambas batem em massembas." On such a night the children fear a visit from ancestors' spirits, the *Casumbi*, but their elders, busily shucking grain for the next day's market, reassure them. Here again, the poem's immediacy is lessened by da Cruz' too obvious rhetoric as he attributes a righteous purpose to the zombies who harm "only those who have no love" while holding the promise of Happiness *(Felicidade)* for those who must live in the black night.

In a society where poets, white or black, often betray their elitist background, at least one Angolan, António Jacinto, has been singled out as the writer most aware of the daily realities of his ordinary countrymen.[31] In a moment of childhood revery similar to what we have seen in Bessa Victor and others, but more graphically specific, Jacinto ponders the fate of the neighborhood group who used to play soccer. His poem "O grande desafio" (The Big Game)[32] is a powerful indictment of the failing of the colonial social system.[33] In the rigorously stratified society imported from the Metropolis, yesterday's team captain is today's aloof college graduate who pretends not to recognize his former black schoolmates: "passa, passa, que não cumprimenta / -doutor não conhece prêto de escola" (he goes by and

31. See Andrade's article, "Deux expressions de l'Angolanité," *Présence Africaine*, 42 (1962), 76–81.
32. *Desafio* may also mean "challenge" which suggests an added dimension.
33. Andrade's *Antologia*, pp. 49–52.

doesn't even say hello / degree-holders don't know blacks from school days).[34] Another teammate is dying of tuberculosis, and the mascot is a gigolo whose woman supports him with the money she receives from white men. The partiality of the law resulted in the imprisonment of a fourth member of the team who attempted to defend his mother against a policeman's insults, and a fifth, unable to prove regular employment, has been sent to São Tomé as an indentured laborer. Jacinto unites nostalgia and hope in a prophetic conclusion with unmistakably revolutionary implications as he foresees another day when they will all be once more equal to play another game.

The wistfulness of "O grande desafio" is absent in the same poet's "Monangamba" (Contract Laborer) where violent, throbbing free verse underlines all the anger, outrage, and despair resulting from a cardinal precept of colonial policy: the black's obligation to work for a white man's economy.[35] A common theme among Negro poets in Portuguese Africa, "Monangamba" stands out in its feeling of immense scope which the poet attains by addressing a dramatic monologue to an unspecified number of listeners while invoking the testimony of the worker's surroundings, the untrammeled world of nature:

> Perguntem às aves que cantam
> Aos regatos de alegre serpentear
> E ao vento forte do sertão...

> (Ask the birds that sing,
> The brooks that happily zigzag along
> And the strong wind from the backlands . . .).

The charge which the African worker levels against the white overseer is that the fields are watered with the worker's sweat, the cherries ripen with his blood, and the coffee is toasted, crushed, and tortured to become as black as the worker himself. The unjust salary is described in an asyndetic torrent:

> fubá podre, peixe podre
> pano ruim, cinquenta angolares
> "Porrada se refilares"

34. In Portuguese society any college graduate is called "Doctor."
35. *Ibid.*, pp. 47–48, and translated in *Modern Poetry from Africa*, p. 147. The "brittle" character of Jacinto's verse recalls a similar style in French Antilleans. See Shapiro, "Negro Poets," p. 218.

(rotten corn meal, rotten fish,
shoddy cloth, fifty farthings,
"A beating if you answer back"
[the overseer's words]).

The body of the poem comprises a series of stabbing questions as the worker asks who makes it possible for the European boss to acquire machines, wives, and models of Negro heads in bronze to adorn the hoods of motorcars while enlarging belly and bank account. And nature responds "You, Monangamba." But nature's solidarity is small consolation, and Jacinto's despairing worker, overwhelmed by the injustice of his lot, seeks oblivion in the fumes of palm wine.

The same contrast between a free nature and its oppressed black child provides the structure of "Fogo e Ritmo" (Fire and Rhythm) by the physician Agostinho Neto:[36]

> Sons de grilhetas nas estradas
> cantos de pássaros
> sob a verdura húmida das florestas
> frescura adocicada
> dos coqueirais
>
> (Sounds of manacles on the roads
> bird songs
> in the moist undergrowth of the forest
> the sweet freshness
> of the coconut groves).

The absence of any verbs and a single conjunction in the entire poem result in a series of concrete, highly suggestive images united through a heavy beat. The repetition of three basic phrases—"fogo," "ritmo," and "estradas cheias de gente" (roads filled with people)—provides a thematic content which is the pendulum sway between suffering and the faint promise of deliverance. Thus, against the noonday inferno of work in the fields ("fogo no capim"), we find the counterpoint of

36. *Antologia*, pp. 39–40. For a study of such "conjunctive economy" as a reflection of a Bantu language base, see Sédar Senghor, pp. 164–65. A study of Neto's poetry including three poems translated into English has been prepared by W. S. Merwin, "Agostinho Neto—To Name the Wrong," in *Introduction to African Literature*, pp. 132–38.

crowded roads leading to, albeit, closed horizons, but (the only conjunction) roads nonetheless. And the day's scourge becomes the focal point at night for the dance around the fire when the blacks regain strength through the rhythmic flow of natural forces:

> Ritmo na luz
> ritmo na côr
> ritmo no som
> ritmo no movimento
>
> (Rhythm in light
> rhythm in color
> rhythm in sound
> rhythm in movement).

To be sure, the rhythm is kept by bare feet and broken fingers, but (again the only conjunction) it is still rhythm ("Mas ritmo/ritmo"), even when heard and felt in the "Vozes dolorosas de África" (the dolorous voices of Africa).

Maintaining his repetitive, rhythmic style, though with less economy than in "Fogo e Ritmo," Neto's "Adeus na hora da partida" (Farewell at the hour of parting) is a resolution to reject the defensive resignation which we have seen thus far.[37] The poet parts company with his stoical Negro mother who has always "waited patiently during the difficult hours" and cries out against the hardships of a schoolless youth, forced work, humiliation, poverty, and neighborhoods where "powerlines do not reach." Neto's shame for his uncomplaining elders is balanced by a new confidence which, as we read in "Aspiração" (Aspiration), is rooted in the birth of a racial pride not confined to his native Angola but extending to all "soul" brothers in "o Congo... Georgia... Amazonas."[38] The unity of a distinct group experience involving suffering and degradation is cemented by emotional ties: "algemas de amor nos caminhos paganizados do amor" (handcuffs of love on pathways made pagan in love). As with most *engagé* Angolan poets, Neto's Negritude obviously remains even here virtually synonymous with lament and anger. Other characteristics of the movement such as an emphasis on the African's superior rhythmic sense and his sensitivity to an emotionally respon-

37. *Antologia*, pp. 41–42.
38. *Antologia*, pp. 43–44.

sive nature, though constantly present, are less developed than in the poems of a Césaire or Tenreiro.

Several important factors with socioliterary implications are evident in any comparison between Mozambique and Angola. Situated on the eastern coast of the continent, Mozambique has always been less accessible to Portuguese influence than Angola which, along with Brazil and the Metropole, for centuries was a part of the "Atlantic triangle" of the Portuguese world. In the case of isolated Mozambique, however, native opposition to the European presence even in coastal areas required military activity as late as 1918. Subsequent to this date and until the outbreak of guerrilla warfare in the sixties, there were several sporadic revolts during the 1930's, 1940's, and 1950's, leading to mass arrests, executions, and deportations to São Tomé.[39] When one adds to the territory's remoteness the corollary of a small European immigration, one can readily understand why Portuguese East Africa has been even less favorable than Angola to the official mystique of cultural synthesis. Contributing to the cleavage between European and African ways of life is the strong influence which neighboring South Africa exercises on the dominant Portuguese structure. Besides acquiring a taste for Scotch whiskey, the urban Portuguese of Mozambique tend to reflect certain other Anglo-Saxon values which clash noticeably with their claims to a tradition of racial blending. Consequently, social realities are at wide variance from the official view of the closely knit Lusitanian family.[40]

Like Angola, however, Mozambique differs from the tradition-bound South Atlantic islands in its recent dramatic emergence into the economic and industrial developments of the contemporary era. The resulting social changes and shifts in population have accelerated the disintegration of tribal society. Thus, as in the case of the educated Negro in Angola, the literate black Mozambican is increasingly aware of the confrontation between African and European and the consequent subordination of the former to the latter. For him the dissemination of European culture implies the disappearance of indigenous values except for their shadowy existence consonant with the subjugated state of the ordinary native: "over-whelmingly illiterate,

39. See Chilcote, pp. 117–19.
40. Margarido points out that if racial awareness is more recent than in Angola, it is also more sharply defined. See 'The Social and Economic Background," pp. 71–74, and "Panorama," pp. 488–90.

carefully isolated against provocative news from abroad, subject to corporal punishment and deportation at the whim of the European authorities, [his] thoughts [are] never expressed, [his] real voice [is] unheard. . . ."[41] But for a single bilingual newspaper, *O brado africano* (The African Cry), which was founded in 1918 by João Albasini, a Xironga-speaking native, Mozambique never experienced anything like Angola's brief though rich editorial activity. Even this one exception is, however, carefully censored as are all Portuguese newspapers.[42]

As a result of Mozambique's colonial way of life and marked racial polarization there has appeared a local expression of Negritude thematically as complete as it is recent. With a scant literary tradition of their own, Mozambican poets tend to rely heavily on their predecessors writing in French and Portuguese. Additional influences have been the example and works of American Negroes such as Langston Hughes and Countee Cullen and the poetry of the Afro-Cuban Nicolás Guillén. Also significant has been the precedent set by socially committed Portuguese neo-Realists, some of whom belong to Mozambique's white community. However, the latter influence is an indirect one, since their preoccupation with social inequalities is not primarily focused on the African's plight. In fact, notwithstanding its own internal conflicts, white society is inclined to coalesce with respect to the black, and the downtrodden peasant immigrant from Europe is often an arrogant overseer to the even more demoralized African.[43]

It is hardly surprising that poetic examples abound of the first phase of Negritude: the note of angry revolt against European exploitation. In "Xangano, filho pobre" (Xangano, the indigent child) by Marcelino dos Santos, there appears a typical black child, "The poor son of a rich land."[44] He bears the present moment in the hope that "de nôvo eu serei rei" (once again I shall be king). The poet, who often writes under his African name Kalungano, treats the same theme in "Aqui nascemos" (Here We Were Born) where he invokes the help

41. Marvin Harris as quoted by Chilcote, p. 110.
42. Moser, "African Literature . . . Last Discovered," pp. 92–93.
43. See Moser, pp. 87–88; Margarido, "The Social and Economic Background," p. 72. Two outstanding examples of Mozambican neo-Realism which provide much towards an appreciation of racial and political frictions are Agostinho Caramelo, *Fogo* (Mozambique, 1964), and Guilherme de Melo, *As raízes do ódio* (Lisbon, 1965).
44. The examples of Kalungano's poems are all from *Antologia*, pp. 74–87.

of his African ancestors, living on in nature, to regain his lost inheritance. In both poems the forebears are one with nature, and their example merges with the earth's fertility to confer the necessary moral resilience necessary for the African to resist. Like the mythical Antaeus the black poet remains close to the earth, whether physically as in "Terra-Mãe" (Earth-Mother) or in spirit. The latter contact is required when he is in danger of losing his identity with his past in the steel and concrete world of the European in the new cities of his native Mozambique or in France where Kalungano lives in exile. A sparse statement of alienation comprises "Onde estou" (Where I am):

> Eu vivo
> perdido nas ruas
> de uma civilização
> que me esmaga
> com ódio
> sempre

> (I live
> lost in the streets
> of a civilization
> which crushes me
> with hatred
> always).

Like Kalungano, the poetess Noémia de Sousa—also known by the African name Vera Micaia—transcends the geographical limits of her country to attain unity with her suffering people everywhere. In "Deixa passar meu povo" (Let My People Go), for example, she is moved by the American Negro spiritual as interpreted by Paul Robeson and Marian Anderson.[45] Although they are strangers in a distant land, she calls them her brothers, "do mesmo sangue e da mesma seiva amada de Moçambique" (of the same blood and beloved life flow of Mozambique). As she listens to her radio the immediate present and its zinc-covered house under a tropic sky vibrating to the distant beat of marimbas takes on a universal character. The day's despair with its "barred windows, separated families, and cotton fields" is less a burden when shared in the lament of "Let my people go,/Oh, deixa passar o meu povo."

45. *Antologia*, pp. 92–93.

A common example of the bondage whose anguish permeates so much of Mozambique's poetic Negritude is provided by the figure of the *magaíça*, the laborer who leaves home and family to work in the diamond mines of South Africa. Noémia de Sousa dedicates at least one of her poems to the *magaíça*'s odyssey from the moment when he is beguiled by the company recruiter in his village to the day, many months later, when he steps off the train, grotesquely attired: "Um ser deslocado / embrulhado em ridículo" (a misfit wrapped in ridicule).[46] Yesterday's ragged duffel bag crammed with dreams has been exchanged for a valise stuffed with "O falso brilho / dos restos da falsa civilização do compound do Rand" (the fake sparkle / of the leftovers of the Rand compound's fake civilization). Along with his illusions, the *magaíça* has also lost his youth and his health, and all so that a few "stars" may twinkle "no decote de qualquer lady / nas noites de qualquer City" (on some lady's décolletage / in the nights of some City).

In "Sangue negro" (Negro Blood) the poet affirms the racial bond which unites her with all Negroes from *magaíça* to Marian Anderson.[47] In her affirmation, Noémia de Sousa provides a clear instance of Negritude as a defense which is consciously espoused by a Europeanized Negro. Thus, the poet confesses that she was once inclined to be assimilated by Europe's values rather than to assimilate them into her own experience as an African. As a result, she was in danger of becoming a tourist in her own land, wandering "por estas ruas de cidade engravidadas de estrangeiros" (through these city streets bourgeoning with foreigners). When, however, she was reminded by the "foreigners" that she is an African, she decided to convert the social stigma into a proud banner. Like Césaire's well-dressed black on a Paris streetcar, she has since sought to return as a prodigal child ("filha tresvairada") to a "Mother Africa" and her pagan mysteries, her tom-tom pulsations, and her suffering children, the poet's brothers all, united in "work, love, and song."

Despite her frequent protests of racial identification, Noémia de Sousa does not entirely avoid the dilemma which stems from her privileged position as a member of an African elite in a colonial society dominated by whites. There is something ironic in this "pagan" daughter of Mother Africa who sympathetically responds to hymns which she hears on her radio and translates from one European language to another. In any case, it is a situation hardly predicable of a

46. *Antologia*, pp. 88–89.
47. *New Sum*, pp. 468–69.

typical Mozambican black. One is left with the impression that, like Bessa Victor, Tenreiro, and other poets we have seen, Noémia de Sousa also views Negritude as a provisional attitude until the day when she may take full part in a truly multiracial society without having to feel apologetic for her color.[48] Indeed, in "Let My People Go" she refers to an idealized blue-eyed friend who encourages her to express her revolt. Like many other Afro-Portuguese poets she sees a prelude to such a society in her childhood which she recreated in "Poema da infância distante" (Poem of a Distant Childhood).[49] In the crowded neighborhood of her youth with its black, mulatto, white, and Indian children all playing in carefree fellowship, she finds hope that perhaps the eclecticism of the child will be emulated in the adult world. Thus, while in no way tempering the ardor of her militant stance and her solidarity with her people's suffering and vibrant sensuality, Noémia de Sousa longs for brotherhood, "Not just a pretty word . . . in the dictionary on the shelf" but as a social system "even when epidermis and scenery are so different."

From the ideal of universal brotherhood to the mystique of an African consciousness and from a mere hint of alienation to the rage of revolt: these are the basic variations on the very elusive theme which is Negritude. As a convenient summary of the theme in Mozambique we may mention the extremely vivid poetry of another Mozambican, the journalist José Craveirinha. A dark mulatto, the son of a Tombasana tribeswoman and a swarthy *algarvio* from the south of Portugal, Craveirinha feels the clash between Europe and Africa perhaps more keenly than a black African and certainly more so than even the least ethnocentric European settler.[50] As a European by education and an African in appearance, he is ruefully aware of the abyss between the West's technology and tradition of Christian humanism and the social realities of the African in Mozambique. Except for Tenreiro, few Afro-Portuguese poets have so explicitly countered the European presence while identifying with the indigenous substratum.

48. This seems to confirm our opinion regarding Negritude's transitory character as expressed in Chapter 1. See Fanon's remarks on "National Culture" in *The Wretched of the Earth*, pp. 206–27.

49. *New Sum*, pp. 465–66. Margarido points out that the theme of childhood, "the inauthentic paradise," is especially common in Mozambican Negritude. See "Panorama," pp. 490–91.

50. See Rui Knopfli regarding Craveirinha in Nuno Miranda, *Epiderme em alguns textos* (Lisbon, 1966).

Drawing of José Craveirinha

Craveirinha has written several poems which may be classified as "first level" Negritude where the subject and tone derive from the African's subjugated state. In such a poem, "Cântico a um deus de alcatrão" (Canticle to a Tar God), the writer presents the Negro as a machine *(máquina)* whose endless drudgery is captured in a series of verse-fragments where anaphora, the absence of articles, substandard grammar, and the frequent appearance of the nasal "-ão" as a final syllable combine to give a feeling of plodding despair:[51]

> Máquina começou trabalhar
> com sol
> com chuva
> com farinha e feijão
> Máquina começou abrir chão
>
> (Machine began to work
> with sun
> with rain
> with flour and beans
> Machine began to break ground).

The same devices appear in "Subida" (Price Rise) and "Grito Negro" (Black Cry) though with different effects. In "Subida" a despairing note persists in the refrain which joins the seven stanzas enumerating the African litany of woes: "Ai, a passividade animal" (Oh, the animal passivity!).[52] In "Grito," however, the poet draws the strength for future revolt from the Negro's present dehumanization. Using to full advantage a single metaphor identifying the African with coal, the poet calls attention to the native's color, his unity with his land, his exploitation, and his strength once he becomes "ignited": "Tenho que arder/queimar tudo com o fogo da minha combustão" (I have to flame,/burning everything with the fire of my combustion).[53] Once again we find a percussive background in the use of "-ão" at the end of all but two verses.

---

51. *Antologia*, p. 73.
52. José Craveirinha, *Chigubo* (Lisbon, 1964), pp. 24–25. The book is one of several by African authors published by Casa dos Estudantes do Império in Lisbon. Unfortunately the Casa was closed in 1965 by the police, and the publications are at present unavailable. See Chilcote, p. 20.
53. P. 29, translated into English by Moser in "African Literature in the Portuguese Language," pp. 289–90.

In his rehabilitation of the African, Craveirinha shows a ready familiarity with all the elements which comprise the mystique of Negritude. In "Poema Manifesto" (Manifesto Poem), for example, he chooses a Whitmanesque free verse to extol the solidarity of his race in a powerful creation of the symbolic African.[54] With not a single complete sentence or inflected verb form to detract from the passionate outburst, the long poem is a series of exultant cries beginning with: "Oh/meus belos e curtos cabelos crespos/e meus olhos negros" (Oh,/my beautiful short crisp hair/and my black eyes). In this African "Song of Myself" we find praise for each of the racial characteristics once considered inferior: thick lips, flaring nostrils, black skin, and loud, lusty laughter. Throughout, the exuberant verse-form underlines the pulsating sensuality and oneness with a fecund nature. To add to the pronounced rhythm and "savage" beat, the poet invokes a dozen exotic tribes and their tattooed, naked women dancing to "a bárbara maravilha eurítmica das negras ancas sensuais" (the barbarous, eurhythmic marvel of sensuous black hips).

In "Poema Africa" Craveirinha attacks the civilization which the European has tried to impose upon him.[55] While assuming a more offensive attitude he implies that the mechanized West has much to learn from the "primitive" African: "Mas já não ouvem a sutil/voz das árvores nos ouvidos surdos do espasmo das turbinas" (But they [i.e., the whites] no longer hear the subtle/voice of the trees with their ears deafened with the spasm of turbines). He points an accusing finger to the dogmatism of missionaries who "love me with the intolerant love of their gospels" while depending on

> A mística de suas missangas e da sua pólvora
> a lógica das suas rajadas de metralhadora
>
> .   .   .   .
>
> e canções das suas terras que eu não conheço
>
> (The mysticism of their glass beads and gunpowder
> the logic of the bursts of their machine guns
>
> .   .   .   .
>
> and songs from their lands which I do not know).

54. Pp. 5–7.
55. P. 65. Cf. Césaire's ironic "J'ai laissé la patience des missionaires / insulté les bienfaiteurs de l'humanité..." in *Cahier*, p. 50.

For all their efforts, Craveirinha sees little gained aside from a substitution of the "tin ovals" of Catholic medals for native amulets.

The poet expands his African rejoinder to the Portuguese (and European) cultural system to include the absurdity of schools where Negro children learn "only of the grandeur of their [i.e., European] heroes / the glory of their stone cities and their Rolls Royce." And while implementing a new morality which tries to "civilize my chaste African immodesty" with the "kiss" of bullet and tear gas, the new bureaucracy introduces social shame with "birth certificates for the child of unknown father." With perhaps no more oversimplification than one finds in European accounts of African "barbarism" the poet rounds out his indictment of the "civilized" world by referring to such doubtful contributions to humanity as the electric chair, the efficiency of Buchenwald, the Inquisition, the Ku Klux Klan, Hollywood and Harlem, and "o pássaro que fêz o chôco/sôbre o ninho morno de Hiroxima" (the bird which hatched an egg/on the warm nest of Hiroshima).

Anger, revolt, racial mysticism, and a rejoinder to the European's smug superiority—all these facets of Negritude appear in Craveirinha's poems without, however, resolving his sense of personal conflict as a nonwhite imbued with a European culture and sired by a European father. As is the case with Noémia de Sousa and other Afro-Portuguese poets, his Negritude is provisional. In an elegy to his father ("A meu pai")[56] Craveirinha suggests that the ideal may yet lie in a cultural fusion: "ibéricas heranças de fados e broas / se africanizaram para sempre nas minhas véias" (Iberian legacies of *fado* and cornbread have been africanized forever in my veins). For the present, though, Negritude is his way to affirm an identity in a society which scorns his African past. Neither present marginality nor a pristine pre-European state are possible solutions for the alienated African. In his self-portrait "Poema do futuro cidadão" (Poem of the Future Citizen) our poet looks forward to a new society with none of the present's antagonisms between races and cultures: "Eu! Homem qualquer/Cidadão duma nação que ainda não existe..." (Me! Just a man,/a citizen of a nation which does not yet exist).[57]

56. *New Sum*, pp. 476–79.
57. Craveirinha, p. 11. Translated into English in *African Writing Today*, ed. Ezekiel Mphalele (Baltimore, 1967), p. 315. Other poets that I have discussed who are included in Mphalele's anthology are Kalungano and Agostinho Neto.

The Lusophone Literatures
of Africa Since Independence

A sound multinational reality,
looking forward to a bright future

Manuel Ferreira
*Literaturas africanas de ex-
pressão portuguesa*, Lisbon,
1977, vol. II, p. 103

1. The Setting

In April 1974, a military coup, the direct result of war in Africa, overthrew an almost fifty-year old dictatorship in Portugal. It initiated a political revolution which under the slogan of "decolonization" had to concede independence to five new African states: the Republic of Cape Verde, the Republic of Guinea-Bissau, the Democratic Republic of São Tomé and Príncipe, the People's Republic of Angola, and the People's Republic of Mozambique. In all five of these territories, writers had been active before 1974. What has happened to literature since then?

When the guerrilla wars of liberation broke out in 1961, first in Angola, next in Guinea, then in Mozambique, a tidal wave of terror and counter-terror threatened to drown the tender shoots of a neo-African literature expressing itself in Portuguese. Even when the fighting moved away from the more densely populated areas, the African patriots continued to be silenced within the Portuguese empire. Some of their writings were printed outside the empire's borders, reduced to small anthologies of translations into other languages, while the original texts remained largely unknown. Inside Portuguese Africa, a few daring souls, mostly intellectuals of wholly or partly European descent, began once more to work towards the goal of furthering national consciousness through an Angolan literature, a Mozambican one, a Cape Verdean one. In poetry, their more or less camouflaged activity was possible, poetic language being vague by nature. When political independence became a reality all of a sudden, the Pandora's box of fear, hatred, inhumanity was reopened, as another, this time fratricidal struggle for power, pitted elements of the African population against one another while throwing the Portuguese colonials into a panic. The struggle was brief, except for the richest prize, Angola. But the disarray was general. It seemed as if no room would be left for artistic creation, whether in Portuguese or in any other language.

A trip to Portugal in the summer of 1977 gave me an opportunity to talk with a dozen writers from the Cape Verde Islands, Angola, and Mozambique. They confirmed what I had begun to suspect for months: literature surfaced as the five new states were being consolidated. I asked five questions:

1. In what language is literature being written now?
2. Has independence led to a burst of cultural activity, and of literature in particular?
3. Can authors write as they please, now that the Portuguese censors have departed?

4. Where do authors write and where do they publish? and
5. Who reads them?

I received tentative answers. The account that follows is based on them. The answers not only defined the evolving situation of the past few years since independence; they also offered clues as to future development.

2. The Language Question

As in the case of the former European colonies in the Americas, almost all of the former European colonies in sub-Saharan Africa, including those of Portugal, remain firmly attached to the languages of their erstwhile masters. The five new states are no exception. Portuguese remains their official language, and we can properly refer to a *lusophone,* that is to say Portuguese-speaking, Africa even now, after Independence. Portuguese continues to be the medium of teaching, of law, of administration, and also of communication between ethnic groups of different speech within each state. Consequently books, especially text books, have to be written in Portuguese as before. What is new is the spirit and thus the viewpoint, so that the new history texts, to take the most obvious example, reflect the African perspective from which history is now taught: history begins with the past of the particular African country, say Mozambique, instead of starting with the rise of the Roman empire or of medieval Portugal.

In contrast to neighboring parts of Africa, especially Zimbabwe (Southern Rhodesia) and the Republic of South Africa, whose peoples began developing written literatures in their own languages early in the nineteenth century, the former Portuguese colonies have yet to produce one individual author who would write and publish in an African vernacular. The one exception is Cape Verde, but only in part; for the Creole language of the islanders is a regional variety of Portuguese possessing few purely African features. Moreover, books in Creole are rare; almost all the literature of the Islands is written in standard European Portuguese, colored by a smattering of local expressions. It is true that the use of written Creole, especially by poets, has increased in this century. Curiously enough it was a writer from Portugal, Manuel Ferreira, who, having lived in the Islands and having married a Cape Verdean, has gone the farthest in bending Portuguese prose in the direction of Creole speech. He did this in 1971 when he published his novel *Voz de prisão* (under arrest.")

In the Cape Verde Islands, as elsewhere, standard Portuguese is bound to prevail as long as national unity has to be protected against centrifugal ethnic or regional forces. For precisely that reason, all the leaders in the struggle for liberation, most explicitly Amilcar Cabral in Guinea-Bissau, insisted on retaining Portuguese as the official language, in spite of their opposition to Portuguese domination.

On the continent, writers have begun to modify standard Portuguese consciously, by introducing Africanisms into it. The goal and the problems to be solved were stated by an Angolan ethnologist, who is also a poet. He told his Portuguese publisher in the course of a conversation they had in Lisbon in November 1975, where he stopped on his way home to an Angola that had just obtained its independence: "I transmit my poetry in a language which is colonial, and I cannot forget that. It ought not to become the only language spoken by the Angolan people That would be a horrible cultural genocide. Therefore, since I am ignorant in this respect, not knowing the languages of Angola well enough, I at least try to africanize the colonial language by giving it contents that are our own. As a matter of fact, the common people are doing so already, and poets follow their lead at last. The African languages have been capable also of a most beautiful *oral* poetry. Why wouldn't they be as capable of a most beautiful *written* poetry? It's simply the poets who have been lacking in capacity, and the Angolan people should not forget it." (Arlindo Barbeitos, in *Angola Angolâ Angolema,* Lisbon, Sá da Costa, 1976, pp. 7-8. The English translation is mine.)

3. Literary Activity since 1974

a) A chance to publish older works at last

A curious thing happened. It had been assumed that once the dictatorship of Salazar and his heir Caetano had been swept out of power, including its secret police and its ubiquitous informers and censors, the writers would take advantage of their regained freedom, especially since most had been opposed to the regime. No doubt, they would now publish numerous works which had gathered dust by having to be kept in the desk drawer, as the Portuguese say. But in Portugal proper nothing of the sort happened! Instead of poems, stories, plays, in short, creative works, it was political, economic, and sociological literature that filled the bookstores, much of it translated from other languages.

In Africa the picture was different. The majority of the African authors came out into the open with works they actually had written during their years in exile, in jail or in labor camps. Their *committed* poetry and prose fiction appeared now side by side with historical works reflecting an African and usually Marxist point of view. Thus one really can speak of a burst of activity; for the long suppressed works appeared in quick succession. New writings were very few at first; too many urgent tasks claimed the full attention of the small intellectual contingent.

Writers became at once active in three regions: the Cape Verde Islands, Mozambique and Angola.

Before 1974, most writers in the Cape Verde Islands had published at long intervals and then only short works that steered clear of such dangerous subjects as self-determination, economic reform, or pan-Africanism. If at all, they touched upon them in Aesopian language. The rhythm of publishing could not be accelerated as long as the islanders were poor and backward. However, some exiles came forward with daring writings. Such was the case of Gabriel Mariano, a member of the Lopes da Silva clan, which has produced more Cape Verdean intellectuals than any other family. He was to publish *Capitão Anselmo* ("Captain Anselm") in 1975, a poem in praise of the martyred leader of a popular revolt during one of Cape Verde's cyclical famines. Under the dictatorship, the long poem had circulated underground in a cassette recording. Its author, a judge, had been removed to the tiny, stagnating tropical island off Mozambique, on the east coast of Africa, to which he and his family were confined for six years. At the end of 1976, Mariano followed the earlier work up with *Vida e morte do João Cabafume* ("John Cabafume's Life and Death"), a collection of stories also composed during the dictatorship. The tale which gave its title to the volume was about a penniless Cape Verdean laborer who refused to be treated like a dog and paid for it with his life.

Another exile, the biologist João Varela, who lived first in Belgium, then in France, could at last visit his island home. While there, he published his first long poem on a Cape Verdean subject in 1975, *O primeiro livro de Notcha* ("The first book of Notcha"—Notcha being his father's *nominho* or nickname.) It dealt with what had been taboo topics until then, the undernourishment, starvation and disease that were endemic among the majority of the islanders. According to the dateline on the last page, Varela began the poem in 1961 and completed it in 1972 while he was in Berne, Switzerland.

Luís Romano, another exiled writer, trained as an engineer, who lived in Brazil after living in Morocco, also returned temporarily. Upon rejoining his family in Brazil, he edited in 1976 some poems written by the great political rebel Amilcar Cabral in his youth. However, *Morabeza* ("Lovability"), his little Cape Verdean journal came to a halt in 1976. Romano had been editing it in Rio de Janeiro with a friend, the poet Artur Vieira. Nor has Romano been able yet to find a publisher for the two anthologies of Cape Verdean literature he has been preparing for years.

Several Mozambican poets who had identified themselves with the armed struggle for liberation waged by Mondlane's and Machel's Frelimo movement published volumes of poetry that had been withheld a long time. One of them, Orlando Mendes, belonged to an older generation and was born of European parents in Mozambique in 1916. He is the rare Mozambican author who has been publishing books regularly since 1940. In 1974 he was ready to publish a collection of poems under the title *Adeus de gutucumbuí* ("The parting call of the gutucumbuí"). The poems, written all before March 1971, made public what had had to remain "soliloquies instead of impossible dialogues during sleepless nights" (lines from "Successão dos dias"—successive days, pp. 23-24). The monologues spoke of solidarity with Africans who acted submissive during the day but resisted at night, "even though it was in vain" (from the poem "Aluguer," for hire, p. 100).

The most electrifying event on the literary scene was the resurgence of popular José Craveirinha, who had been jailed and then harassed during the final years of Portuguese rule for Frelimo sympathies. During those years, nothing written by him circulated, aside from some articles on folklore in periodicals of small importance and a few poems that appeared in the short-lived little magazine which bore the telltale name *Caliban* (1971/72). Then, in 1974, Craveirinha could publish what was only his second book of poetry, *Karingana ua karingana* ("Story of stories," the formula in ba-Ronga which introduces the telling of a story). The poems in the volume had been ready since 1963! At that time, he dedicated verses to an indigenous Chopi musician that went as follows:

"I shall compose for you this year (. . .) the full beauty of the sound/ and the full feeling of the fury/ of this my rebellions/ my unpoetic poetry" ("Msaho," Chopi song, p. 109). In the same book, he reprinted one of his best remembered poems, "Quero ser tambor" (I want to be a drum), in which he said that he wanted to be the drum for the nocturnal dances of his people, and not the river, the flower, the spear—not yet the spear!—, nor anymore the poetry of despair (see pp. 105-106).

Since prose narrative had been little cultivated in Mozambique, no fiction of significance came to light. Luís Bernardo Honwana's collection *Nós matámos o cão-tinhoso* ("We've killed the mangy-dog") could be reedited in Mozambique in 1975 when the author returned from exile.

A much greater editorial activity developed in Angola. That country's older and larger nuclei of European colonisation had given rise to broader contacts between the races, more intermarriage, and readier access to schools and the printed word. As in Mozambique, intellectuals with European training dominated cultural activities at the outset. For example, there was Dr. Orlando de Albuquerque, a physician in Lobito, who had studied in Coimbra, Portugal. For a while, he was successful in keeping his monthly *Cadernos Capricórnio* ("The Capricorn Booklets") free from political entanglements. In it he published besides his own, writings by authors of different political and ethnic backgrounds. The experiment floundered when civil war engulfed Lobito. In July 1975, he published booklet no. 33, the last, containing a sociological essay by Lopo do Nascimento, a member of the embattled MPLA movement and of the transitional government. Soon thereafter, appalled by the ferocity of the combatants, who did not spare the sick patients in his clinic, Albuquerque abandoned Angola and started life over again in Portugal.

However, there were many Angolan intellectuals who, unlike Albuquerque and the vast majority of their counterparts in Mozambique, chose to remain in Africa. One reason may have been that the MPLA which came to power in Angola had a more interracial and intellectual character than liberation groups elsewhere. Suffice it to mention that the leader of the MPLA at the time of independence was a doctor and poet, "Angola's offbeat leader," as an astonished Washington Post reporter called him.

The Portuguese Revolution enabled this man, Dr. Agostinho Neto, and the other prominent intellectual personality in Angola, José Luandino Vieira, the country's foremost prose writer, to publish their works again. Both had been punished with jail, forced residence and exile for their political activities. Collections of Dr. Neto's poems appeared in many countries before they could be read in his own. His *Sagrada esperança* ("Sacred hope") was published in 1974 in Lisbon, his *Poemas* in August 1975 in Angola, as one of Albuquerque's booklets. A Brazilian edition, based on the latter, appeared during the same year with an introduction by no other than Jorge Amado, the most popular living writer in Brazil.

José Luandino Vieira had more unpublished manuscripts to offer than any other Angolan. After the Revolution, works of his became available that had only been printed in small, pirated editions or in translation. And so, in 1974, Lisbonese publishers issued one after another—his *No antigamente na vida: estórias* ("Life in the olden times: tales"), then *Velhas estórias* ("Old tales"), next a third edition of *Luuanda*, followed by *A vida verdadeira de Domingos Xavier* ("Dominic Xavier's real life." the tale best known through its film version "Sambizanga," but written in 1961 already and first published in a French translation in Paris, 1971). Topping the other volumes, there appeared Vieira's first novel, written in a new Angolan literary idiom, *Nós, os do Makulusu* ("We, the boys from Makalusu"). The "narrative," as he modestly called it, dated from 1967 when he had been confined to the penal colony at Tarrafal, on the largest of the Cape Verde Islands.

In 1975, Vieira added another collection of older stories, *Vidas novas* ("New lives," reedited in 1976, an obscure French edition having appeared in 1968).

Poetry also emerged in volumes by authors that had been unavailable before: Viriato da Cruz (posthumously in 1974), Costa Andrade (1975), and a rising star, the ethnologist Arlindo Barbeitos, whose *Angola Angolê Angolema* of 1976 conveyed the feeling of life as it had been lived deep in the eastern bush country during wartime:

"In the velvety night/ scary stories are no longer told:/ of headless wild dogs/ their gaping throats barking at wax bearing caravans./ In the velvety night/ they now are telling/ stories of us making history" (p. 46).

The new freedom gave an opportunity to another young writer to publish an experiment in a genre rarely tried before in Angola, the historical novel. Dealing with the biography of an extraordinary black queen of the seventeenth century, who had fought the Portuguese during most of her reign, Manuel Pacavira wrote the novel *Nzinga Mbandi* while languishing, like Vieira, in a Cape Verdean camp, which is to say in 1967 or soon thereafter. In the work, he consciously identified the old queen with the modern guerrilla fighters, and her struggle with the war for national independence. The book appeared in 1975 or 76.

The colonial war itself has not yet received appropriate literary treatment. Too little time for reflection has elapsed since its end. However, the beginnings of the war have found a narrator in Manuel dos Santos Lima, which he, an accomplished novelist, wrote on the basis of his own experience. It brings home the difficulties involved in transforming a poorly armed, uneducated peasantry into a force able to withstand an army equipped with airplanes, napalm and other sophisticated tools of destruction.

The publication of an autobiography spanning the progress of Angolan self-confidence since the first World War was an event that has largely escaped notice. Óscar Ribas, the blind Mestizo ethnographer, folklorist and story writer, published his memoirs in 1975 giving them the title *Tudo isto aconteceu: romance autobiográfico* ("All this has happened: an autobiographical novel"). He told the story of his black Angolan mother's and white Portuguese father's happy married life, of his own travels, tribulations and joys in Portugal and Brazil, of his career in Angola, and of the trying war years. Not mincing words about past slights suffered by blacks and mestizoes in Luanda, he narrated the turmoil in Angola between April and October 1974 in the final chapter. Nevertheless, the memoirs end on a plea addressed to Africans, not to scorn the Portuguese, "whose language and culture have become Angola's heritage ; and a plea to the Portuguese settlers to stay in Africa, but on terms of "perfect equality, without racism or a bitter heart" (p. 609). The pleas fell on deaf ears in 1975.

As an ethnographer, Ribas published a second, considerably enriched edition of one of his major works in the same year of 1975. It concerned Angolan beliefs in, and practice of, magic: *Ilundo: espiritos e ritos angolanos* ("Ilundu: Angolan spirits and rites"). The practices and beliefs were illustrated with stories, as well as with factual accounts. Another contribution to the tribal history and lore of Angola came in 1977 from a woman who was probably the first black African scholar to carry out field work in the country. Maria Helena de Figueiredo Lima, a Mozambican by birth, who teaches in Brazil, published *Nação ovambo* "(The Ovambo nation"), based on research undertaken among the Ovambos, who straddle the border region between Angola and Namibia to the south. No doubt, the search for roots and rebirth will inspire other African scholars and thereupon men of letters to follow the example given by those two ethnographers. In literature, the trend has begun with Pacavira in Angola, Craveirinha in Mozambique, Mariano and Romano in the Cape Verde Islands, to name a few authors.

Nothing has been mentioned about writings in the other two territories which gained their independence from Portugal, the twin islands of São Tomé and Príncipe in the Gulf of Guinea and on the other hand, the small triangle of Guinea-Bissau, to the northwest of them. The two islands had produced several respectable poets before 1974, foremost among them Francisco José Tenreiro, who introduced the affirmative concept of négritude into Portuguese African writing during the late nineteen forties, inspired by the writers of the Harlem Renaissance. But Tenreiro died prematurely in Portugal.

Guinea-Bissau had barely begun to be equipped with its first official schools before

1974. It had no written literature to speak of, and its oral literature falls outside the Portuguese language.

The nature of the works written and published since 1974

It will take some years before we will know if the optimism of Papiniano Carlos, a Mozambican living in Portugal, was justified. Carlos stated in February 1976, in his preface for an anthology of Mozambican poetry, that "poetry (and in fact, literature generally) could fulfill its role as the medium of discovery, privileged to communicate collective exaltation, radiating in every direction the victorious song of the new man that is being born, once all the creative energy of the people has been liberated by the Revolution." Is all creative energy being released, let alone harnessed? Perhaps the verdict will not be in until the first peacetime generation has matured.

At the present stage, one can detect hopeful signs of new life in a few works conceived and published since 1974. A great outpouring of literature seems not only unlikely but impossible. The authors who are writing now differ widely in viewpoint. Roughly speaking, they fall into four categories, depending less on literary or aesthetic positions than on circumstances, such as ancestry, political and economic background, and the war experience. Racial identity has not been a decisive factor in the formation of those categories.

A first category consists of former colonials who have never been able to identify with Africa to the degree of conceding a leadership role to black Africans. For them, there is no such thing as a national African literature in Portuguese, but only an exotic or assimilatory extension of Portuguese literature into Africa. All such writers either chose emigration or were forced into it. I shall omit them therefore, although the *retornado* ("returnee") literature they have produced offers psychological and historic angles that deserve attention.

Then there is the category of those whose allegiance belongs undoubtedly to Africa, although they continue to live and work outside the continent, even after independence. They have adopted a wait-and-see attitude, principally for economic reasons, and partly for political ones.

A third category comprises a group of intellectuals who have committed themselves wholeheartedly to the political and social reshaping of their countries in a collectivist and nationalist direction, tied to the socialistic or communistic regimes on other continents, whether of Algeria, Cuba, Mainland China or the European Soviet block.

A fourth, heterogeneous category includes individuals who had been part of the third group but find themselves in exile or hiding because they have come into conflict with the ruling faction.

Those who adopted the wait-and-see attitude of the second category because they had grown roots elsewhere are few in the case of Angola, many in the case of Cape Verde. Two Angolan writers more or less fit the definition, poets both who double as cultural historians, Geraldo Bessa Victor and Mário António (Fernandes de Oliveira). Both have lived in Lisbon for many years and apparently burned their bridges when they accepted crumbs from Salazar's table. Especially in Victor's case, concentration on the study of history signified escape. Victor has not published poetry or prose fiction since 1973 when his *Monandengue* ("The younger child") appeared, a series of poems resulting from a nostalgic visit to the land of his birth. Mário António has failed to publish poetry or fiction since 1970, the year when he produced a collection of poems with the revealing title *Coração transplantado* ("Transplanted heart").

The category of emigrants who return only for brief visits is numerous only among the Cape Verdeans. For generations, they have had to seek a livelihood or a higher education abroad, while maintaining close ties with the families left behind on the Islands. This situation has been perpetuated by the economic weakness of the new regime in Cape Verde. Some writers are producing new works in the diaspora, especially poets, among them "Sukre d'Sal" (F.A. Tomar) and "Tacalhe" (A.V. Silva), both of whom have studied in Lisbon. Their verse has only found its way into anthologies and periodicals so far. A promising development in the Islands has been the creation in 1977 of a new literary review, *Raízes* ("Roots"), which appears in Praia, the capital of the young republic. Its keynote seems to be continuity of culture. It has called on all Cape Verdean intellectuals to contribute, on the young and the old, on the emigrants and on those at home. Since *Raízes* might serve as a model for reviews elsewhere, a summary of the contents of its first issue will be enlightening.

The issue is divided into three principal sections, along the lines of literary genres; essay, prose fiction, and poetry. Among the essays, one is new. It was presented as a paper in Dakar, Senegal, in October 1976 by the Angolan Mário de Andrade, now active in Guinea-Bissau, in collaboration with Arnaldo França, the Cape Verdean editor of the review. Their paper deals with the role culture should play in national liberation and development, according to the ideas of Amílcar Cabral, the late leader of the PAIGC. The other essay, by the late Jaime de Figueiredo, defines the poetry of the Cape Verdean António Nunes, also deceased, and dates from 1945, having been found among Figueiredo's papers.

In the second section, prose fiction, there are stories by the two most prestigious authors of the older generation, the teachers António Aurélio Gonçalves ("Biluca," a character study) and Baltasar Lopes ("Nocturne de D. Emília de Sousa," concerning an old maiden lady and her faithful manservant, who remains by her side when she falls on evil days.) In addition, one finds three lyrical prose sketches by thirty-year old Osvaldo Osório ("3 histórias de amores de rua"—three stories of love in the streets). Osório had published a booklet of "poems about the struggle" in 1975, *Caboverdiamadente construção meu amor* (The Cape Verdean construction of my love").

In the third section, poetry, nine authors rendez-vous. Here the younger revolutionary ones predominate. Corsino Fortes, born in 1939, calls for revolution instead of waiting for miracles. Mário Fonseca, born also in 1939, sends love poems of a fisherman from Dakar. "Tacalhe," born in 1943, pictures Poetry bleeding until the oppressed will have ceased to cry out. Arménio Vieira, born in 1941, writes of decay, mystification, oblivion—the old themes—, while João Carlos Fonseca, born about 1950, multiplies inebriating rhapsodies to freedom, love, poetry and the future:

"Behold Poetry/ powerful/ lashing time/ galloping unbridled/ on the red turn/ covering frontiers."

These poets appear in the company of three elders, "Osvaldo Alcântara" (i.e. Baltasar Lopes), born in 1907, Pedro Duarte, born in 1924, and Ovídio Martins, born in 1928. They remember too vividly the misery and the struggles. Martins cries out:

"Victorious over despair/ we desperately overcome."

Three issues of *Raízes* have been published so far. While the editor found it impossible to keep the original deadlines, he has maintained a remarkably high artistic level, independent from narrowly drawn ideological directives. Numbers 2 and 3 each contain poems by half a dozen young men on a wide spectrum of themes, reaching from terror in South Africa ("In the south," by Arménio Vieira) to boyhood days in Cape Verde ('Ballade des compagnons du temps jadis," in French, by Mário Fonseca). Both issues reproduce unknown poems by Jorge Barbosa, the neo-realist pioneer of social poetry in the Islands. The second number also contains a masterly chapter from a forthcoming novel by another older writer now living in Portugal, Henrique Teixeira de Vasconcelos. It tells about the passing of the semi-feudal society of Fogo Island. The novel will be all the more significant as it will correct the pessimistic appraisal of the literary situation by Ovídio Martins, made at the end of 1977. In the preface to an anthology of works by poets who had participated in the "Floral Games" of 1976 *(Jogos florais 12 de Setembro 1976),* he stated that no fewer than twenty-seven poets from almost all of the ten islands took part, presenting some excellent verse, whereas the stories, prose sketches and articles submitted to the jury could not be accepted under the terms of the contest. "It is too bad," he concluded, "that this should have been so, since the proposed themes—the struggle for national liberation, national reconstruction, and African values in politics and culture—surely deserve their rightful treatment in all genres, not just in poetry" (p. 4).

Thanks to the review *Raízes,* writers of the second and third categories have been able to cooperate.

Among the committed writers of Guinea-Bissau, the poetic vein seemed to flow most easily. In January 1977, the first post-independence anthology of fourteen Guinean poets appeared under the title *Mantenhas para quem luta!* ("Hail to the fighters!"). Its preface touched upon the problem of language in Guinea-Bissau, where Cape Verdeans have played an important role for centuries: "What determines the quality (of poetry) is its function, the social value it may represent. Although this poetry is at present written in Creole and Portuguese, we have before us the task of committing it to the national tongues, the depositaries of the true African values," (cited after Manuel Ferreira, *Literaturas africanas de expressão portuguesa,* Lisbon, 1977, vol. I, p. 91). Literature seems to look towards the future in another West African territory, the Islands of São Tomé and Príncipe, but on a very elementary level: A. Pinto Rodrigues edited an anthology in 1977 which was destined for its schools, the *Antologia poética juvenil de S.Tomé e Príncipe.*

The writers of the third category have been very active in Angola. Among the intellectuals involved in reconstruction, a bright new talent has appeared in the person of Ruy Duarte de Carvalho. His first volume of poetry, *Chão de oferta* ("Ground for offerings") had already appeared in 1973. He has developed the difficult style, stripped of non-essentials, which David Mestre introduced. Carvalho came out with a second volume in 1976, *A decisão da idade* ("The decision of the age"), which contained a long symphonic poem for several voices, "Noção geográfica" (Geographic notion), written in October 1974. The poem falls short of drama; after a prologue, spoken by the "offstage voice" of the author himself, a shepherd, a hero, a king, a woman and a sorcerer are heard as they join in celebrating the historic oneness of Africa. In the poet's words, these voices represent "threads of an inscrutable, mythical weaving of time" (p. 67). They have come to life again in order to kindle the "resolve of the (present) age . . . in the breasts/ of the humiliated race/ which is great and preserves/ the strength to life/ the voice of the present/ face to face with the past/ in an outcry with the flaming/ assurance of having/ to give to the future/ the grand glory/ of the voice of victory" (p. 96, final lines). Since then, Carvalho has published a volume of three tales, *Como se o mundo não tivesse leste* ("As if the world had no east," 1977), in which he, a white man, born and raised in Angola, participates, as far as possible, in the world of the black herdsmen of southern Angola, among whom he had lived. One part ends upon programmatic words: "Look at man, able to rule the world, understand its depths, organize its march. Look at God's altar: the earth. Look at its priest: man" (p. 114).

A small number of Angolans belong to the fourth and last category of displaced revolutionaries. One of them is Manuel dos Santos Lima, who lives in self-imposed exile in Canada. His latest work is his first attempt at play writing, *A pele do diabo* ("The devil's skin," 1977), a three-act drama on racial conflict in the United States. A second writer in this category is Mário (Pinto) de Andrade, now serving the government of Guinea-Bissau as an educator. He has begun to publish his newest anthology of the lusophone African poets that helped prepare the minds for liberation. A first volume, *Na noite grávida de punhais* ("In the night pregnant with daggers," a title taken from a poem by the Cape Verdean Ovídio Martins) appeared in 1975. He is also the author of historical essays on the colonial wars in Angola and Guinea-Bissau which were published in 1974. More recently, in 1977, new essays of his, such as "Literatura africana e consciência nacional" (African literature and national conscience), appeared in Cape Verdean periodicals.

A third writer of this group is Nito Alves, who published his *Memória da longa resistência popular* ("Memory of the people's long resistance," 1976) while he was still a powerful member of the present Angolan government. Now he is in hiding, after having led an unsuccessful coup. His poems, composed between 1966 and 1976, express a fanatical devotion to the revolutionary cause as he understands it. At the same time, they document his experiences as a guerrilla leader, who will not forget what his dead comrades fought for. He wrote doctrinaire, exhortatory verses, with titles such as "Razão da intransigência" (The reason for intransigence), a poem which ends in this fashion:

"We resisted/ resisted/ resisted./ The people's war/ in its impetuous dramas/ changed our nerves to hard rock/ intransigent/ against reaction/ against counter-revolution.// Are there some who don't understand us?/ We believe absolutely.// It does not matter/ that men/ today/ do not understand.// History/ history will understand/ and do us stern justice/ however far away/ that day may be" (p. 22).

What, however, has happened to the militant writers in Mozambique? In June and July of 1974, only weeks after the Portuguese Revolution, Grabato Dias (i.e. António Quadros) composed a long poem of great expectations in the first flush of enthusiasm. It was published under the punning but confident title *Pressaga pré-saga saga/press* (1974). He called on all fellow poets in the country to join him in a grand, difficult epic enterprise:

"Now is the time to open one's eye, sharpen one's tooth and prepare/ the great common poem in a cheap pocket book/ at the level of simple minds, which we have not/ and the perception of children, which we have not yet forgotten/ and this after all is what we're afraid of: it's hard./ (. . .)

Pronto! this is the dream on today's schedule. Other dreams will come/ others will come and other needs" (p. 16).

After that call to action, why did a sudden stillness descend over Mozambique?

4. Freedom of the Press?

Did independence lead to a restoration of the freedom of the press, which had been withheld during a dictatorial, colonial regime that lasted for forty-eight years, from 1926 to 1974? The answer is: no. Whereas this freedom can now be fully exercised in Portugal itself, the five newly independent nations have, in plain words, been muzzled by tightly organized marxist minorities. Feeling embattled, they brook no opposition. Those intellectuals who have chosen to remain in Africa belong for the most part to these revolutionary organizations. A few non-political authors encounter no difficulties because of their international reputation in a non-literary field, as is true of the Mozambican ethnologist A. Rita-Ferreira or of the Angolan Oscar Ribas.

The importation and sale of printed material is limited and supervised by the governments of Mozambique (since 1976) and Angola (since 1977). Presumably the same holds true for the other three nations.

5. The Publication of Books and Periodicals

Most of the writings by African authors whose language is Portuguese continue to be published in Portugal after 1974, with the essential difference that the Portuguese government no longer decides what may be published or what should be blacklisted and suppressed. As a result of the involvement of all Portuguese in African events, of the sympathy of some, and, on the part of the previously forbidden African authors, of the desire to be printed at last, new publishing houses were anxious to include African books in their lists. One example among many is the small Limiar firm in Porto, which is editing the Angolan poets Carvalho and Monteiro dos Santos. A few older publishers, such as Francisco Franco in Lisbon, whose authors included Henrique Calvão, and the Libraria Cruz in Braga, which used to issue the works that won prizes in the official contest for colonial literature, publish a diminishing number of new writings by returnees from Africa, such as Orlando de Albuquerque, Rodrigues Júnior, and António Pires. Others, notably Sá da Costa in Lisbon, encourage the best writers inside Africa. Sá da Costa started a series, *As Vozes do Mundo* ("The Voices of the World"), in 1974, which is reserved for them exclusively. It opened with a volume of Agostinho Neto's collected poems and has run to seven volumes so far. Another publishing house in Lisbon, Edicões 70, started in 1970, has undertaken the publication of the complete works of a living author, the Angolan José Luandino Vieira. It also initiated a series, *Autores Angolanos* ("Angolan Authors"), with a novella by Pepetela in 1976. A third House, África Editora, specializes entirely in African literature. It is about (in 1978) to launch a periodical with its name, *África*, to be edited by Manuel Ferreira, the first professor of lusophone African literatures at a Portuguese university.* Such a periodical has not existed in Portugal since 1964 when little *Mensagem* was suppressed. Most general literary journals have been shortlived because they were organs of cliques. Even those of longer duration published African authors or articles about them infrequently. Only one, *Colóquio/Letras* in Lisbon, dedicated a special issue to lusophone African writing in September 1977.

Political reasons may have prevented Brazilian publishers from taking advantage of the natural ties between Brazil and Africa.

*The first number appeared in July, 1978.

In the new African states of Portuguese speech, several publishing houses were still active during the transitional period between the end of the colonial war in 1974 and the transfer of power during the following twelve months. Among them was the Académica in Maputo, the former Lourenço Marques. But these private businesses have disappeared, and it is not clear what has taken their place. The PAIGC of Guinea-Bissau and the Frelimo of Mozambique publish their own books, chiefly, perhaps exclusively, in the field of current events and politics. The official presses, which continue to function as before 1974, rarely find time for belles-lettres. Government agencies, in Cape Verde for example, placed orders for textbooks—in Portuguese—with East German printers. But Cape Verde also created an Instituto Cabo-Verdiano do Livro ("Cape Verdean Book Institute), which published the poetry anthology of the Floral Games of 1976 in 1977. The official União de Escritores Angolanos ("Union of Angolan Writers") sponsored the publication of the *Escritores Angolanos* series in Portugal in editions of 3 to 5,000 copies.

Immediately upon independence, a new literary journal, *N'goma* ("Drum"), was launched in Luanda, Angola, with the poet João-Maria Vilanova as chief editor. But *N'goma* folded after the first number, and Vilanova went to Portugal. The União de Escritores Angolanos is making efforts to create another journal. In Cape Verde, a notoriously difficult terrain for any sustained effort, the journal *Raízes* made its debut, as noted above, in February 1977.

6. The Readers

For whom is the lusophone author in Africa writing today? He cannot communicate yet with the broad mass of the population which, with the single exception of the Cape Verdeans, had been kept illiterate. In the nineteen sixties, opportunities for education were even further reduced. Many of the mission schools, which had educated several future leaders of the independence movements, had been forced to close during the last years of the colonial regime.

Nevertheless, an African public exists, small as it may be at present. According to a letter written in 1977 by José Luandino Vieira, five books that had been published each in editions of 10,000 copies went out of print in Angola within two months. One must remember that there exists an illiteracy rate of 85% among the population of five million, according to Vieira's optimistic estimate.

Outside their own countries, the African writers can also count on readers in Portugal. But on how many? I found deep pessimism on the part of some knowledgeable people there, for example Dr. Orlando de Albuquerque. He pointed out that the middle class which formerly was the chief buyer of books could no longer afford them so that sales of books of poetry and fiction in particular have slumped since 1974, while the public has been saturated with works on current events, political doctrine and economics. Other intellectuals, such as Egito Gonçalves, who has his own small publishing house in Porto, were optimistic because of the increasing number of interested university students. Their interest is reflected in the multiplication of courses on African affairs, including the literatures of the continent, ignored by the four Portuguese universities until 1974 (Lisbon, Coimbra, Porto and Braga.) The first course on lusophone African literatures, was introduced in Lisbon by Manuel Ferreira during early 1976. Since then, a chair of African literature of Portuguese expression was created in Porto in the same year, and the first course was offered in 1976/77. It included analyses of three literary works, i.e. Manuel Lopes' Cape Verdean novel *Chuva braba* ("Heavy rain"), L. B. Honwana's Mozambican tales in *Nós Matámos o cão-tinhoso*, and J. Luandino Vieira's Angolan stories in *Vidas novas*. Porto also offered a course in francophone African literature. Similar courses were planned in Coimbra and Braga.

In one respect, the situation has not yet changed. Lusophone Africans, like Portuguese and even Brazilians, generally speaking, lack readers in the countries of the self-styled "western world." Aside from some outdated anthologies, published while the guerrilla wars aroused curiosity, hardly any translations have been published. This contrasts with a certain continuing interest, not for purely aesthetic reasons either, on the part of the so-called "socialist" countries—Soviet Russia, Czechoslovakia, Hungary, Romania, East Germany. Thus, an anthology of the "Poetry of the struggle," translated from Portuguese and Creole into Russian, appeared in 1976 in Moscow, and 10,000 copies of it were distributed. But even this cannot match the reading public of the African writers who work in French or English.

To sum the matter up, it is estimated that four fifths of the copies of books by lusophone African writers are now purchased in Africa.

7. Conclusions

One hesitates before drawing conclusions on the basis of incomplete evidence about developments that have been set in motion a mere four years ago. Only a few simple observations can be made with some assurance.

1. The authors in the five countries that had been Portuguese colonies can be expected to continue to write in standard Portuguese during the foreseeable future.

2. The Cape Verde Islands represent a special case. Their population is as alienated from African origins as are the black and mixed populations in the Americas, and for the same reasons. The attempted union between the Islands and mainland Guinea-Bissau, which seemed so logical and desirable to Amílcar Cabral and the other leaders of the PAIGC around him, is apparently resisted by many Cape Verdeans and Guineans alike so that it has been postponed for the time being. The attempts to stimulate writing in Creole, instead of standard Portuguese, are not making headway, although there are signs that the vocabulary and to some degree the syntax of written Portuguese are gradually being modified, as is happening also in Angola. Such a trend will no doubt become stronger with the development of a national conscience. However, the Cape Verde Islands are peculiar in maintaining close relations with Portugal and western Europe as a whole, since so many of their nationals live there.

3. Because an unusually large number of leaders of the independence movements have been writers, they have established a model for militant intellectuals. Others have followed it, for example José Luandino Vieira and Ruy de Carvalho in Angola, Luís Romano and Corsino Fortes in Cape Verde, Óscar Mendes and José Craveirinha in Mozambique. Literary activity has thus acquired a connotation of participation in public affairs. By the way, this had been already traditional in Portugal.

4. The relative position of the different literary genres within the lusophone literatures of Africa reflects the initial stage of these literatures as expressions of budding nationalities. Lyric poetry ranks highest, while dramatic works are almost nonexistent. Perhaps the high prestige accorded the lyric poet in Portugal and Brazil is partly responsible; perhaps the relative scarcity of long narrative fiction and especially of plays

is due to the present lack of a sufficiently numerous public that has been educated to read or see long works.

African literatures in Portuguese are most cultivated in two areas, the Cape Verde Islands and Angola. Literary creation has not come up to unrealistic expectations. For many reasons, an artistic flowering may only occur when the new states have had time to coalesce, prosper, and multiply their schools. First they have to overcome the disarray caused by the mass flight of an active part of their literate population. In this sense, the "struggle continues" for all writers.

Gerald M. Moser

The Pennsylvania State University
University Park, Pennsylvania

PRESENTATION OF THE DELEGATION OF THE ANGOLAN WRITERS UNION

"The Use of Oral Traditions in Literature of Portuguese Expression"

Our subject is quite rich and it has merited the most passionate attention of writers and students of literature in Africa as well as in Latin America, Asia and Europe.

I believe that by oral tradition we mean here that kind of culture expressed even today by peasants or those of peasant origin among African populations. Sometimes this tradition is called *ORATURE*.

The insertion of this type of literature into Africa's modern literature, produced by persons of petty bourgeois origins or background, is generally understood as one of the richest and most valid forms of lending a more meaningful, dynamic, and original character to modern African literature.

I do not believe that it is a question of returning to origins or of a denial of culture of European origin. This is because, from a formal point of view, and one also based on content, we are headed for a kind of universal culture.

From the formal point of view, that is, from the point of view of creative processes and the expression of ideas, the literature produced today in Africa is taking on a universal character. The insertion of oral traditions, beyond its strictly aesthetic-literary enrichment, would also bring about a content enrichment as a means of bringing writers of petty bourgeois origins or background closer to the mentality and way of life of the peasants and workers.

I don't believe that this is either a new problem or one exclusive to Africa. It has arisen to an extent everywhere from the times in which the development of the productive forces brought about by the development of capitalism progressively promoted a separation and divorce between culture of popular origin and so-called learned culture.

To give some universal comparisons, we might cite the examples of Hans Christian Anderson and other Nordic writers, or we might mention the Russian Alexander Pushkin. Those of us educated in the Portuguese literary tradition might recall Almeida Garrett who, in the *Popular Song Book,* presents a vast collection of his country's popular literature.

I believe that if we measured the global weight of the oral tradition on the literature of diverse countries their contribution is greater in the Asian countries than in those of Africa and even greater than in Latin American countries. This is because the cultural forms of the Asian countries assumed a more developed and robust character which allowed them to offer greater resistence to the impact of European culture. African culture, because of its more fragile forms, was obliged to give in, to a great extent, to the colonizing impact.

We have had little opportunity to look into the collection and recreation, in modern literary form, of oral tradition in countries like Guinea-Bissau or Mozambique. We know, however, that there has been work carried out there during colonial times and after National Independence.

In Angola, we can say that the concern with the insertion of oral tradition dates from the beginnings of our literary activity, although it never became a dominant form.

If we were to think of our great writers of the 19th century, we would have to mention Joaquim Cordeiro da Matta who, in a now famous plea to Angolan intellectuals, exhorted them to develop *their* literature. By "their literature" we are to understand in part, a literature in which, besides the use of Angola's national languages, traditional culture is used and developed. We refer specifically to proverbs, riddles, tales, etc.

Thus Angolan writers of the turn of the century created a bipartite literature. This is to say that within the prose or poetry written in Portuguese writers have used expressions, proverbs, and thoughts in the Kimbundu language precisely when they wanted to express something more intimate or profound. However, their use of a relatively vast knowledge of oral tradition did not constitute a new process of literary creation but rather a juxtaposition of two modes of expression. Also, this use of the oral tradition was relatively moderate and never became dominant in the various literary modes of the time—i.e., journalism, novels, poetry.

The novel *O Segredo da Morta* (The Dead Woman's Secret) by the Angolan Antonio de Assis Junior and the novella *Nya Muturi* by the Portuguese Alfredo Troni date from the first decades of this century. These works, especially the first, contain descriptions of social gatherings in which African oral culture figures. The characters, by means of stories, narratives, proverbs, and riddles, express a type of philosophy, heavily imbued with religiosity; that reflects an African world view often in conflict with the concepts and moral values of European culture. Nevertheless, these European culture values usually end up imposing themselves.

In the 1940's and 1950's Oscar Ribas's works began to appear. This relatively prolific writer oscillates between the simple ethnographic collecting of oral tradition and the literary creation based on the stories and expository techniques of this tradition. It is in *Ecos da Minha Terra* (Echoes of my Land) that the literary creation gains momentum. In the *Misoso, Jisabu,* etc. the collection to which the author attempts to lend a framework that does not turn out to be entirely scientific, is one of the richest by an Angolan ethnographer since the time of Cordeiro da Matta.

Presently, we can speak of Uanhenga Xitu who in several novellas and stories has brought to literary expression the way of life of a small community of peasants in the region of Catete, in the hinterland of the State of Luanda. The day-to-day oral tradition expressed by this community appears here as part of the way of living, of being, or of reflecting the world of this community of peasants, not necessarily as a process or form of literary creation in itself.

In poetry, the use of national languages as the medium of expression has met with some successful attempts. From the poem "Muinhu Ia Sabalu" (Sabalu's song) by Mário de Andrade, which constitutes the first great attempt at creating poetry in national languages, to those more contemporary poets, like Bernardo de Sousa, who has fashioned quite good poetry in the Kimbundu language. It is necessary to note here that the writers we have been speaking of are from the area of Kimbundu influence in the north-central part of Angola where oral tradition is expressed principally in prose.

The Angolan peoples who create poetry are the pastoral peoples of the South. Clan poetry, short and synthetic poems about the rains and agrarian life replete with metaphors and images. Although there is poetic expression from the Maiobe forests of the extreme northern enclave of Cabinda to the extreme south, it is the Kwanya-wa of southern Angola who can truly be called poets. Their creations have already attracted the attention of some poets of the most recent generations, like Arlindo Barbeitos and Ruy Duarte de Carvalho.

By means of a careful study of the roots of this poetry, these poets, who write in Portuguese, have sought to capture the plastic forms and the imagistic richness of the popular poets. They have incorporated this richness into Portuguese poetic discourse either as aesthetic valuation or as a position taken with respect to national problematics.

The use of oral traditions has thus been over the years one of the vectors of development of Angolan literature—not the dominant or most influential vector, but one that has always found those capable of using it.

Either as bilingual literature, with respect to end of the century writers, or as a reflection of the life and psyche of peasant communities, as in the case of Uanhenga Xitu, or as a repository of literary forms and the sources of research for new literary forms and new modes of interpreting reality as in the case of Arlindo Barbeitos.

With writers of the 1960s and 1970s, the literary treatment and modes of speech from the Kimbundu language have been incorporated into Portuguese discourse that's giving greater plasticity and expressiveness to the prose of Luandino Vieira, Jofre Rocha, and Jorge Macedo despite the fact that the general syntax of their writing is that of Portuguese.

Finally, we should stress that the Angolan writers should not use oral tradition just to be using it, or tell traditional stories just for the telling because the influence would take on a weak and ambiguous character, as occurs in some of Oscar Ribas's stories.

To tell while recreating, to create in order to tell something new, to create something that enriches life itself and that contributes to modify life is what needs to be done during this phase in which the Angolan people are debating problems related with the edification of socialism, of national independence, and of economic emancipation.

Today we have knowledge more through the gathering of traditions over time, and not always with the most correct perspective, carried out by ethnographers, and which are relatively extensive and rich, than through direct contacts with the populations themselves (contacts that are always difficult and usually best left to specialists).

To bring this to a close and to touch on a related theme, I would like to refer to different categories of oral tradition arranged according to an ethnographic conception that is broadly accepted in Angola.

The first category consists of fiction, known in Kimbundu as *mi-so-so*. These stories are generally to entertain more than to instruct. Often they contain elements of the fantastic and the supernatural.

Fables and stories about animals are common to many regions of Africa and they reveal the great homogeneity of Bantu culture. Of great interest are the stories about monsters heard in the South and about huge birds heard in the East. In general these recreations are highly symbolic and imaginative stories based on true occurrences.

The second category consists of stories about everyday life and true happenings. These stories are called *maka*.

The third category is made up of the *ma-lunda* which consists of chronicles of the tribe or Nation. These are stories preserved and transmitted by the chiefs or elders of the community, and they are part of the latter's political history.

The fourth category contains the proverbs, or *ji-sabu,* which reflect philosophy, not properly religious or metaphysical, but more precisely moral.

The fifth is poetry, and it embraces several styles: epic, satirical, idyllic, religious, etc. While in the first three categories expository techniques are accompanied by theatrics, in the fifth category poetry and music are combined, and, in the fourth, one notes the beginnings of poetic metrification.

The sixth category is made up of the *ji-mongongo,* these being riddles which, besides serving as a pasttime, also serve to awaken the memory and the intelligence.

Scholars have referred to the marvelous symbolism of the proverbs of Cabinda (the northern enclave), to the philosophic sense and spirit of observation in the stories of the Kiokos, to the imagistic force of Kwanyawa poetry, and to the dramatic force of many of the stories of Angola and of Bantu Africa in general, all of which reveals a strongly ontological psychism.

How to incorporate this cultural richness into a literature destined to serve a constantly changing modern world? I would like to hear the opinions and critical comments of the illustrious participants who were kind enough to listen to me.

Uanhenga Xitu
Ruy Duarte de Carvalho
Henrique Guerra

Luandino Vieira

Luanda: Musseque against skyscrapers

ANGOLAN WRITING—AN ARM OF LIBERATION

It is perhaps axiomatic that the nature and substance of Angolan writing in the past twenty to twenty-five years reflects the conscious struggle of an African people to rid themselves of colonialism. While in the late 1950's and early 70's African countries colonized by the French and English were granted independence, Angola like Mozambique, Cape Verde, Guinea-Bissau and the islands of São Tomé and Príncipe had to struggle another decade and a half before achieving their independence. Angolan poets, essayists and novelists both as artists and as freedom fighters have participated actively in the long struggle which actually began five centuries ago when the Portuguese first settled in Angola. Among the more celebrated contemporary writers many, including Viriato da Cruz, Mário de Andrade, Manuel dos Santos Lima, Manuel Pacavira, Luandino Vieira, António Cardoso, Costa Andrade, António Jacinto and Agostinho Neto have been members of the Movimento Popular para a Libertação de Angola, the MPLA. Most of these men spent years of their lives in prisons—in Tarrafal in Cape Verde, in Bié in the center of Angola, in Aljube and Caxias in Lisbon.

Their writings naturally manifest a thematic and philosophic oneness—love of the motherland or in some cases such as that of Luandino, the adopted motherland; a will to create a free, just, human society; respect and pride for those heroes from Rainha Ginga—the celebrated guerilla queen of the 17th century to Comandante Kwenha killed in battle in 1973; a triumphant faith in the future; a shared suffering and a shared joy. The theme of racism is all but nonexistent in this literature, for in fact a Luandino, a Costa Andrade, a Jacinto, a David Mestre are white men. Jacinto today is Minister of Education in the government of President Neto—and the words of both these poets put to music by Rui Mingas were sung by guerilla fighters marching through woodlands and fields. It is not within the scope of this paper to explain this phenomenon, but no one can argue that the fourteen years Luandino spent in prison because of his commitment to Angolan people in any way makes him less an Angolan than those black men such as Mário de Andrade and Manuel dos Santos Lima who spent most of the war years in the comfortable confines of Western capitals.

I do not wish to suggest that Angolan writing is mere propaganda, mere patriotism. Each of the writers is unique; each contributes a personal voice that echoes throughout the cities and the villages, the mountains and the rivers. Viriato do Cruz, one of the founders of the MPLA, who died in 1973, wrote the following lines in the early 1950's in his poem "Mama Negra"—(Canto de esperança):

Pelos teus olhos, minha Mãe
Vejo oceanos de dor
claridades de sol posto, paisagens
roxas paisagens
dramas de cam e Jafé...
Mas vejo também (oh se vejo...)
mas vejo também que a luz roubada aos teus olhos ora esplende
demoniacamente tentadora—como a Certeza...
cintilantemente firme—como a Esperança...
em nós outros teus filhos,
gerando, formando, anunciando

—o dia da humanidade
O DIA DA HUMANIDADE...

In your eyes, My Mother
I see oceans of grief
reflections of the setting sun, landscapes
purple landscapes
dramas of Cam and Jafé...
But I also see (oh if I see...)
but I also see that the lost light of your eyes now shines
demonically tempting—like Certainty...
scintilatingly firm—like Hope...
in us your sons,
begetting, forming, announcing
—the day of humanity
THE DAY OF HUMANITY...

The identification of the beloved mother with the entire black race and with Angola in particular will be repeated by Neto in "Adeus à hora da Largada" (Farewell at the time of departure) in the final stanza:

Nós vamos em busca de luz
os teus filhos Mãe
(todas as mães negras
cujos filhos partiram)
Vão em busca da vida.

We are going in search of light
your children Mother
(all black mothers
whose children left)
are going in search of life.

The struggle for liberation is painful and difficult. Men die; mothers weep. And there are many dangers. In an animated modern folk-tale by Luandino, "Estória da Galinha e do Ovo" (Tale of the Hen and the Egg), we are presented with a social vision divorced from, to use a phrase of Soyinka, "the superstitious accretions of unworkable African tradition" and unacceptable European control. Two neighbors squabble about the ownership of an egg. Nga Zefa claims the egg is hers because the hen Cabíri that laid it is hers. Corpulent Bina claims the egg is hers because not only did she feed the hen, but the egg was laid on her property. After Dona Bebeca, the old lady of the village, fails to resolve the conflict, various "wise men" are brought in to present their opinions on the subject. Sô Zé says the egg actually should belong to him, for he provided the grain that fed it and has not yet been paid for it by Bina; Azulinho, the young religious scholar, advises that what is Caesar's should be rendered unto Caesar and what is God's should be rendered unto God, but that the egg belongs neither to Caesar nor to God; o Vitalino from whom Bina rents her home, claims the egg is his since it is his property on which the egg was laid; O velho Lemos, a former legal assistant, regularly kicked out of his home by his wife, Rosalia, so she can earn some needed money as a prostitute, offers a solution—a legal hearing. But his plan is rejected once he demands legal fees from all concerned in order to buy a drink or two. In the end, Bina keeps the egg; Nga Zefa keeps her hen and the police who break up the public gathering are foiled in their attempt to keep the hen for themselves.

"Estória da Galinha e do Ovo" is a modern parable in which Luandino employs qualities of traditional oral storytelling. The theme of the trickster, the use of symbolism and proverbs, and a surprise resolution of the conflict can be found in the oral literature of many African societies. But this amusing tale does not present an affirmation of traditional wisdom. "Estória da Galinha e do Ovo" must be seen as a satire of society in the musseques or suburbs of Luanda and throughout Angola. Bebeca, Sô Zé, Azulinho, o Vitalinho and the old man represent respectively in this contemporary allegory traditional wisdom, the merchant class, the "enlightened" church, the land-owners and the legal profession. Each fails in his attempt to contribute to the solution of the dilemma of the egg (the future of Angola). The arrival of the police (an obvious symbol of Portuguese colonial presence) precipitates a sudden climax. The egg is no longer the sole issue; the ownership of the hen (Angola herself) is at stake. Throughout the story two boys, Xico and Beto, have been playing with the hen while the elders' debate continued. When they see that their gallinacious friend Cabíri is in the hands of the police sergeant, Beto loudly imitates the crowing of the rooster, a trick he learned from a local resident; a frenetic Cabíri, responding to the call, flies from the group of her alien captors; harmony is restored. Luandino is saying that it is the youth of Angola who must determine the future of their country, for the older generation has failed to recognize that without flexibility and creative innovation, traditional wisdom cannot deal effectively with certain modern problems. Moreover, personal selfishness and dishonesty will help neither the individual nor the society as it seeks to live in a new age with new and different problems.

The stories and novels of Luandino Vieira constitute a major contribution to Angolan and in fact, African literature. Luandino, a committed writer, avoids the pitfalls of sloganism, sentimentality and political dogma that can mar political literature. But his is only one voice. Costa Andrade is the poet of guerrilla warfare. His notebooks composed during his own years as a freedom fighter have recently been anthologized by Sá da Costa in the Colecção Vozes do Mundo under the title *Poesia com Armas* (Poetry with Arms). António Jacinto writes in "Monangamba" (Worker) of black men who sweat under an Angolan sun in coffee fields, and in "Carta dum Contratado" (Letter from a man working under forced labor), of men who are carried away to São Tomé. In the latter poem the alienated and lonely worker realizes his letter will never reach his beloved:

> "Mas ah meu amor, eu não sei compreender
> por que é, por que é, por que é, meu bem
> que tu não sabes ler
> o eu — oh! desespero — não sei escrever também!

> But ah my love, I cannot understand
> why it is, why it is, why it is, my beloved
> that you do not know how to read
> and I — oh! despair — do not know how to write either.

The final sad line is also an indictment of the Portuguese who unlike the French failed to establish schools in the interior of the land they colonized. In the schools they did set up the use of African languages was forbidden so that a writer like Agostinho Neto, for instance, does not speak an African language—he speaks only Portuguese. Unlike Chinua Achebe or Kofi Awoonor whose respective knowledge of Igbo and Ewe permits then as Achebe says in his essay "The African Writer and the English Language"

Postal Poem / Bernardo de Sousa

Postal Poem / Manuel Rui

Postal Poem / David Mestre

to write a "new English, still in full communion with its ancestral home," the Angolan writer has been alienated linguistically from his ancestral home. But writers like Luandino and Manuel Pacavira, writing in a European language, refuse to write Portuguese as it is written in Lisbon or Coimbra. The Portuguese language itself is revitalized by these writers into an Angolan Portuguese, a Portuguese that reflects the rhythm and pulse and diction of Angolan life. So that one can safely say that Angolan writing is not only an arm against colonial oppression, but also an arm against the tyranny of a European language over African thought and expression. Syntactic transfiguration, neologisms, altered phonetic spelling to reflect the word as it is actually spoken in the musseques—these are some of the devices used by Angolan writers to free themselves from the constraint of the language of Camões and Anthero de Quental.

The dream of independence has been realized. From Cabinda to the Cunene the dream of a better day can become a reality. There is a great optimism among the leaders of the government for the future of Angola. In his Independence Day speech on 10 November, 1975, President Neto, paying tribute to the heroes who fell in five long centuries of resistance, claims that the struggle for freedom and justice is not over: "the struggle continues; victory is certain." For the Angolan writers, too, new opportunities are present, opportunities to explore African languages like Kimbundu, opportunities not only to project a social vision, but to recapture the Africanness of their country that has yet to be fully comprehended.

Donald Burness

poesia

ONZE DE NOVEMBRO

No rosto intranquilo
do camarada caído em missão
não há assombro
nem perguntas desnecessárias.

No rosto intranquilo
do camarada ceifado no escuro
floriu com o alvoroço da manhã
uma certeza.

E de Cabinda ao Cunene
das entranhas dos homens
e das feras
dos guerrilheiros insepultos
na morte já derrotada
pelo amor da sua luta
e do seu sangue
surgiu o mesmo grito:

INDEPENDÊNCIA!

Novembro/75
JOFRE ROCHA

11 DE NOVEMBRO

Um mastro nú
Entre outros engalanados.
Depois lentamente
A bandeira foi subindo
(Instantes de respiração suspensa)
E tímida ao princípio
Chegada ao topo
Drapejou ao vento.
Então
Foi a explosão
Do grito do riso do choro.
Gerado e parido na dor
Um filho
Um filho de todos
Acabara de nascer.

Dezembro de 1976
ANTERO ABREU

BANDEIRA (LEITURA 2.ª)

Não chores bandeira de Novembro
faz dessa lágrima um rio de protesto
entre o vermelho e preto
margens do silêncio interrogado
que desfraldas

Não chores bandeira de Novembro
o guia está na pátria que legou
e onde era uma jornada voluntária
com a catana cortaremos mais
onde era a emulação da classe operária
com a roda dentada emularemos mais

Não chores bandeira de Novembro
limpa essa lágrima com a voz do chefe
para que a estrela amarela brilhe mais.

1979
MANUEL RUI

Two-page spread, pp. 8-9, Lavra & Oficina No. 14, Nov. 1979

REFLEXÕES SOBRE CULTURA, CULTURA POPULAR, CULTURA DE MASSAS

Largo é o caminho a percorrer no domínio da cultura de massas. A exploração colonialista caracterizou-se também por uma brutal agressão cultural. Cultura, diziam eles, vinha no modelo estrangeiro, português. Necessariamente se negava a existência de uma cultura africana. Sabemos como o nosso povo resistiu ao domínio estrangeiro. E resistiu porque resistiu culturalmente. O início da luta armada desencadeada pelo M.P.L.A. veio trazer um grande contributo à nossa independência, por realizar essa luta em termos novos: luta nacionalista e luta popular. Foi pois a luta armada um acto de cultura do nosso Povo, de tipo novo porque nacionalista, porque popular.

Lutámos para libertar.

Libertámos para construir.

Os tempos novos, um país novo, um homem novo, requerem, e determinarão, uma cultura nova.

Mas a cultura não é algo de abstracto e que se fabrique artificialmente. A cultura corresponde a um estágio económico-social, corresponde a uma realidade e a um tempo concreto. Gera-se e exerce-se no seio do povo.

Os camaradas vão levar daqui a noção de que as nossas actividades culturais terão de ter o **apoio** do Povo. Mas não só isso; não basta o **apoio**. É necessário, sobretudo e essencialmente, a **participação** do Povo. Sem essa **participação**, activa e massiva, não estaremos satisfeitos com o trabalho que viemos a desenvolver. Esta filosofia de **participação popular**, para além do apoio popular, é filosofia já bem experimentada pelo nosso Partido. A chave do êxito está precisamente nessa participação.

Falamos bastante de cultura popular. Há em verdade nas nossas designações erros de linguagem. Que se entende por cultura popular? Devemos falar apenas em CULTURA. E devemos aqui fazer uma prevenção e acautelar erros de linguagem.

Na verdade criámos Centros de Cultura Popular, quando deveríamos indicar Centros Populares de Cultura, para melhor precisar nossa intenção.

Há quem distinga a cultura popular como a cultura cultivada pelo povo, atribuindo-lhe um certo cunho de **inferioridade**. E uma cultura erudita, intelectual ou intelectualizada, atribuindo-lhe um cunho de certa superioridade. Sempre a cultura transporta uma marca de classe. E a classe dominante intenta dar **superioridade** à sua cultura, que permite a dominação, relegando a cultura da classe dominada para um plano de **inferioridade**. Não é isso que se pretende na República Popular de Angola. Emendaremos o lapso linguístico para evitar confusões. Nós pretendemos locais e organismos populares, onde o povo tenha acesso, para divulgar e criar cultura. Divulgar a nossa cultura e os valores grandes da cultura universal, que são património da humanidade e, consequentemente, também nosso património. Como expressava Lenine, devemos dar oportunidade aos operários e camponeses de conhecer os grandes valores culturais da humanidade. Devemos dar também oportunidade ao povo para expressar e criar a sua cultura. Buscar não só o **apoio** do povo, mas a sua **participação** às actividades culturais.

Para isso, e com os ensinamentos agora colhidos, levai a obrigação de **educar as massas**, mas também, e essencialmente, a de **ser educado com e pelas massas**.

As massas devem expressar os seus valores culturais em plena liberdade. E não se trata aqui só de regressar ao passado. Uma situação nova impõe uma realização cultural nova, como já foi dito. O M.P.L.A. - Partido do Trabalho definiu o aproveitamento de quanto for válido na nossa cultura tradicional. Mas só do que for válido para a etapa que estamos vivendo no sentido da criação de uma sociedade nova e socialista. Teremos de observar, analisar, verificar o que é válido na verdade e só então corrigir, ou interferir, com habilidade, com inteligência e com segurança. Mas nada de passos falsos, ou incorrectos.

O trabalhador da cultura, hoje, no nosso país não pode ser um mero funcionário demasiadamente preso a todas as peias burocráticas. Se assim for, tornar-se-á mais um «pequeno burguês» inútil que a própria revolução se encarregará de anular. Deve ser atento e consciente. Deve orientar-se correctamente pelas orientações políticas do Partido. Deve ser dinâmico e dar expressão à livre iniciativa.

Nada se fará num dia. Nem num seminário. Teremos de ser perseverantes. Teremos de respeitar as orientações correctas. E os resultados surgirão. Em cultura o caminhar é mais lento, mais subtil, mais delicado. E os resultados surgem, por vezes, e quase sempre, a longo prazo.

(Extracto de um discurso de ANTONIO JACINTO).

4 | CASTRO SOROMENHO, AN ANGOLAN REALIST

Revised version of an article first published in *Africa Today*, Denver, Colorado, vol.15, no.6 (December 1968/January 1969), pp. 20-24.

Since a prose literature written by individual authors arose in Portuguese Africa only about the turn of the present century, one cannot expect to find in it even belated manifestations of such literary movements as Romanticism and Realism, which belong to an earlier age. The term "realism" can only be applied to writers of our time when speaking of their honesty in observing and describing the circumstances of present-day life, stimulated perhaps by readings in the social sciences. Castro Soromenho achieved the reputation of being the first Portuguese writer to do justice to the African, to have seen him as he "really is," instead of accepting the image in which the conqueror unconsciously sees the conquered in order to justify his actions. He was so successful in his interpretation of African customs and ways of feeling that Léopold Senghor, we are told, was astonished to learn that this writer was not a black African. The compassion with which he looked upon the African as a full if unfortunate member of the human community may have been the result of personal sensitiveness molded by two early contacts. One was the loving care of a Negro nurse from a village that was to be destroyed by Portuguese troops; to her he dedicated some of his earliest stories: "Nothing remains of your village and of its wild scrubs," he wrote. "And of the arms that rocked the white boy, and of the breast which you gave him, taking the milk from the black child, nothing remains either. Only the longing of your white boy was left between your nonbeing and his living, Nurse, *black mother*, this longing, reaching back more than thirty years, now invokes your memory, upon the conclusion of this book about your unhappy race."[1]

The other contact came through his first job as a recruiter of African contract labor for a powerful mining company in Northeastern Angola. It was to give him ample opportunity to observe the changes in the traditional African village economy by the requirements of western industrialism.

But in addition, Castro Soromenho had to have models to express his experiences in an adequate literary way. The models presented themselves to him in two trends which changed Portuguese literature in the 1930's and 40's. Prose fiction then turned away from subjective caricaturing of the types and passions of Portuguese middle class society that had been practiced by two masters in the nineteenth century, Camilo Castelo Branco and Eça de Queiroz. Under the influence of such foreign psychological and social novelists as Tolstoy, Anatole France, André Gide, and Dostoevsky, some Portuguese writers began to explore the individual psyche. Others investigated the human geography of their country city by city, region by region, with an ear attuned to the speech of the people, eager to publicize the conditions under which the humble majority of their countrymen had to live — fishermen, workers, sharecroppers, shepherds, and miners. Some, associated with the reviews *Presença* and *Revista de Portugal* (Coimbra) laid stress on craftsmanship and psychological insight and "authenticity." Others, reacting against the political evolution towards military dictatorship about 1930, chose to commit their writing to the service of social protest, having learnt a good deal from Dos Passos, Steinbeck, and the Brazilian novelists "of the Northeast." In Portugal they were called Neo-Realists, and Castro Soromenho was considered one of them. They also had several native mentors, notably Raúl Brandão, from Porto, the first to write proletarian fiction and drama; Aquilino Ribeiro, who created a genuine peasant novel with roots in the rocky uplands of central Portugal; and Ferreira de Castro, who told about the hardships of the poor Portuguese emigrant from personal experience. In Castro Soromenho we find the same sense of social justice, but he was not satirical, wordy, or sentimental as they frequently were.

The other literary trend of Castro Soromenho's times, also furthered by the *Presença* group and the Neo-Realists, led away from a picturesque and self-conscious travel literature, exemplified in books on Holland, Egypt, Japan, North Africa, etc. As World War I decisively interrupted the flow of trade and migration between Portugal and Brazil and threatened Portugal's hold on Africa, it spurred interest in the Dark Continent. The result was an outpouring of "colonialist" publications, written by soldiers, administrators, adventurers and journalists (but not by missionaries, since most of them were not Portuguese at that time). They were spinning dreams of new Brazils to be developed and settled in Portuguese Africa. They viewed Africa as an exotic place inhabited by wretched, childlike savages waiting to be civilized by the Portuguese. An additional factor determining the new literature about Africa was the development of anthropological and folklore studies in Portugal from the 1880's on. They were undertaken by philologists and historians of literature, first in Portugal proper, then in the Azores. Later on, but still at a rather early date, they were extended to the African possessions, where a black Angolan, Cordeiro da Matta, was one of the pioneer collectors. Castro Soromenho studied African folklore on the spot in Angola before he turned to the writing of fiction. This study, unspoiled by any feeling of white superiority, was to provide him with a solid basis of a truly African flavor.

The details of Castro Soromenho's literary apprenticeship remain unknown. Perhaps out of modesty, he never seems to have written about his own career as a writer, nor to have been interested in theoretical discussions. All we can say is that the circumstances of his life offered him firsthand experiences from which he, a born storyteller, could choose themes for writing about Africa like an African. Even the little we know of the exterior circumstances of his life is merely what he disclosed to publishers, editors, and his academic employers. Fortunately, his widow, Dona Mercedes de Castro Soromenho, has kindly filled in many details never mentioned by her late husband, such as the names of his parents.

Fernando Monteiro de Castro Soromenho, who signed everything he wrote with his last two family names, was born on January 31, 1910, in the coastal town of Chinde, the port of the Sena Sugar Estates company in Zambezia, one of the provinces of Portuguese East Africa or Mozambique. His parents belonged to the upper middle class. His father, Artur Ernesto de Castro Soromenho, had been district officer for the Portuguese Congo

(Cabinda), of Huila, Bié and Moxico before becoming governor of the Lunda Province, all of which are in Angola. His mother, Stella Fernançola de Leça Monteiro de Castro Soromenho, was the daughter of a judge on the Supreme Court in Lisbon. How their children happened to be born in Mozambique remains a mystery.

His childhood was spent in Angola, to where his parents took him as a baby in 1911. In his sixth year he was sent to Portugal for his education in elementary and secondary school. He returned to Angola in 1925 when he was fifteen and remained there until he was twenty-seven, i.e., until 1937. During these decisive years he was first employed by "Diamang" as a recruiting agent of African labor. "Diamang," the Diamond Company of Angola, is the most powerful mining company in the country. Now, as then, it operates in the northeastern inland region of Lunda, so named after the large Bantu nation that lives on both sides of the border with the formerly Belgian Congo.

From there Castro Soromenho went back to school in Huila, to be trained as a colonial administrator in the *Escola Superior Artur de Paiva*. Upon completion of his studies he served for many years as a *chefe de posto* in various interior districts. In the course of this work he became interested in the Bantus' way of life, and thus, in 1932, gathered materials in the Dala District (Lunda) for his study of the circumcision and initiation rites for boys of the Quioco (Chokwe) tribe. Finally, perhaps tired of the isolated life in the "bush," like the officials in his novels, he gave up his administrative career, moved to Luanda, the fast-growing capital of Angola, and became a journalist, joining the staff of the *Diário de Luanda*.

He still was a journalist when he moved to Lisbon in 1937 and began to edit the weekly *Humanidade* there, with the collaboration of two well-known members of the *Presença* group, Adolfo Casais Monteiro and João Gaspar Simões. By the end of that year he took a trip to Brazil as a special correspondent, interviewing Brazilian writers for Portuguese periodicals, but also writing for Brazilian publications, such as *Dom Casmurro* in Rio de Janeiro. In 1943 he gave up his second career, journalism, and turned to publishing. But before he started his own publishing house, first the *Sociedade de Intercâmbio Luso-Brasileiro,* then the *Edições Sul,* he made another extended trip overseas, to Brazil and Argentina. While he was in Rio de Janeiro he gave a lecture at the new National University, which was sponsored by Arthur Ramos, then the foremost specialist in Afro-Brazilian studies. While he was in Argentina, he fell in love with a charming Argentine, Mercedes, and married her.

Following his move to Europe and his first stay in Brazil, he had published *Nhári,* his first collection of African stories. Although it appeared in 1938 in faraway Luanda, it gained him immediate recognition in Portugal and was the first of several of his works to be awarded the "Prize for Colonial Literature" with which the Portuguese government of the time sought to stimulate overseas writing in Portuguese. In a somewhat flamboyant style, Castro Soromenho dedicated these stories "to all those men who opened trails across the Black Continent, trails which I trod, in the service of humanity, accomplishing missions under great hardships" (p. 7).

Aside from several other ethnographical studies, he published works of prose fiction, all of which dealt with what he was most familiar with, the Lunda Province, relatively unspoiled by European colonists. His last work was a novel published in 1959, *Viragem* (Turn), in which he described the relations between the Negro villagers and their traditional chieftains on the one hand, and the Portuguese district officers — *chefes de posto* — their assistants, womenfolk, and native constabulary on the other. He did so in an uncompromising, uncomplimentary fashion which understandably annoyed the authorities in Lisbon. His previous novel *Terra morta* (Dead Land), ready in manuscript since 1945 but published only in 1949 and then in Brazil, had been banned in Portugal because it dealt with the process of "pacification" from inside knowledge and in the same unwelcome spirit. Now, in 1960, life in Lisbon was made unbearable for the author, whose opposition to the ruling dictatorship was well known. When the government prevented further distribution of its titles, his publishing house was ruined and with it Castro Soromenho's livelihood. Warned of imminent arrest, he fled to France, choosing exile although both he and his wife were in poor health, and there were three young children to be supported.

For the rest of his life he wandered from country to country — from France to the United States, where he taught for half a year (1961) at the Portuguese Center of the University of Wisconsin in Madison, helping to compile anthologies, and back to France. Shortly before his return to Paris, he wrote in a letter of June 5: "Madison is lovely in the spring. Everything is green and peaceful. It hurts me to leave this country before having had a chance to tour it extensively, but life imposes its conditions, and for an exile they are harsh ones." In Paris, he worked as

Portuguese and Spanish reader for the publishing house of Galli-mard, contributed to the reviews *Présence Africaine* and *Révolu-tion*, and did research for the African Section of the *Musée de l'Homme* under the direction of Michel Leiris.

Brazilian and Portuguese friends brought him to São Paulo, Brazil, in December 1965, enabling him to eke out a meager living by giving sociology courses at the State University in the city and its branch campus in Araraquara. Now and then he wrote an article on an African topic for Brazilian papers. What had happened to his creative vein? Quietly, slowly, he was com-pleting a new novel, *A chaga* (The Wound), a sequel to *Vira-gem* and the second part of a projected trilogy. Just when his new career as a university lecturer was at last promising to give him economic security, his heart failed him and he died of a brain hemorrhage in São Paulo on June 18, 1968.

His name remains indissolubly linked to Angola, the theme of all his writings. To this day he is the foremost writer to be born in Portuguese Africa of European parents who could interpret the "souls of black folk" convincingly. "He penetrated most deeply into true knowledge of African humanity, without superfluous lyricism or ethnological erudition," wrote Pierre Hourcade, then Director of the French Institute in Lisbon and a good judge of literature.[2] Fernando Mourão remarked that in his re-creations of African folk tales, "Castro Soromenho shows that he knows the mentality of the Negro so well that he makes us think some-times of the traditional storyteller who accompanies his words with mimicking."[3] Castro Soromenho characterized himself at the end of *Terra morta* with sly humor, where a conversation be-tween the district officer and his secretary turns to the subject of a certain Monteiro:

"All sorts of crackbrained fellows show up around here. Just look at that officer in Caluango, that Monteiro fellow, who in-stead of collecting taxes and dispatching men to the mines spends his time going into the native villages to find out how the blacks live and to listen to their stories. What on earth can anyone see in the stories of those savages! The fool! I have never seen so many crackbrains as now. What do they think they are doing? I'd like to have seen them in the olden days when I came here. They would have changed their notions fast. You bet your life they would have!"

"A couple of days ago (the secretary rejoined) I came upon Monteiro in a village of the Luita district. There he was, sitting with the niggers around the fire, deep in conversation. I even pointed out to him that it was not a thing to do for a white man. It sure isn't, sir. Makes you feel uncomfortable."

"It's one reason, among others (said the officer) why the niggers are emboldened and get uppity. People like that fellow are no good in these parts, Valadas. What's wanted here are tough men, hard-working men."[4]

Since none of Castro Soromenho's stories have been translated into English so far, it will not be amiss to give some idea of each of his works of fiction. Special attention will be paid to the realistic elements in them, i.e., elements based on the author's own experience.

Nhári, like the subsequent works, dramatizes African life as a struggle for survival against droughts, starvation, the chieftains' cruelties, raids by other tribes, spells cast by sinister witchdoctors or malignant spirits. Nhári gets its title from the last and longest of the five tales of the Lunda country which form the first part of the volume: it is the name of a young slave girl who was sold by her own uncle to a vicious old man. The other tales tell of tribal wars and the misfortunes of defeated chiefs, of a witchdoctor who changes into a crocodile and the hold of superstition over "these poor black people who are always sad" (p. 52). There is also a story of a black Oedipus, unwittingly committing incest and then hanging himself, and a story of a black Bathsheba, in which the ghost of the deceived husband can only by witchcraft be stopped from haunting the guilty chief. The second part of the work consists of five legends, including a first version of Queen Lueje's tale, the tale of the "Land of Friendship," a myth about the origin of the warlike Quioco (Chokwe) tribe in the rebellion of ferocious Quinguri against the rule of his sister Lueje, Queen of the peaceful Lundas. Another legend which recurs in the author's works explains the origin of a lake, in this instance the Dilolo Lagoon in Moxico, where a village had once stood. Like Sodom and Gomorrah, the village perished from wickedness. In this case it refused hospitality to a miserable leper woman. Its inhabitants were turned into black ducks.

Each of the stories is told about definite tribes and specific places with which the author had been familiar. At this point of his career, he still wrote awkwardly, trying too hard to be literary. There are too many adjectives, too many ready-made phrases, detailed descriptions of nature, and the traditional touch of sensual exoticism, as in this passage of the second story: "Already the tamtam and the songs — songs which are ripples of sensuality — caused the voice of the jungle to echo, now vibrantly, now mournfully, but always tinged with mystery, like the exotic life of the black man" (p. 26). Even so, this first work already revealed Castro Soromenho's chief quality: his empathy with the emotions of those black people, not only in the original tales but in the folk legends as well. Here and there a mood is suggested with poetic intensity:

> "Faraway, a *quissange* is moaning.
> The hour of melancholy.
> The child of the jungle who is strumming the *quissange* seems to be crying tears of longing for a distant love. . .
> The nostalgic voice of the barbarian rent the silence of the night. He was singing the song of the slaves" (p. 56).

These lyrical moments were to become rarer, and a word like "barbarian," a remnant of European pride, would disappear from the author's vocabulary.

In short, the stories in *Nhári* did not yet represent a clear-cut break with the colonial mentality.

Castro Soromenho made the break in his second work of fiction, the novel *Noite de angústia* (Night of Anguish), in which he strove to bridge the gap between black and white ways of thinking. It is a tale of witchcraft and terror among the Lundas. Young people are mysteriously dying off in the neighboring villages of old *soba* (chief) Xandumba and of his vassal, the crafty *sobeta* Salema, until at last the latter is unmasked as the culprit and must publicly drink poison. The readers are plunged into the Lunda world of superstitious fears, where night reigns, a night that terrifies the illiterate black man. The description of emotions fills pages, but they are no different from what all men feel. Even Ivenga, the slave woman who had been Salema's willing tool and with whose pitiful, lonely death the story ends, is shown to have emotions which we can share. In a single chapter, she thus passes from a disturbed mind (*alheamento*, p. 111) to discouragement (*desalento*, 111), to bitterness (*amargura*, 112), somber thoughts (*pensamentos sombrios*, 112) and fear (*mêdo*, 112), on to melancholy (*melancolia*, 113), chill (*frio*, 114), indignation (*indignação*, 115) and at last, despair (*desespêro*, 117). Just as the emotions accompanying the action are objectively noted by the author, so are the details of the natural environment, but only insofar as they can be generally recognized: the animal sounds in woods and fields, the changes in temperature, the alternation of dry and wet seasons, of day and night. Castro Soromenho, the "writer and journalist," as he styled himself, had succeeded to the satisfaction of his European readers in what had been the goal of generations of ethnographers, that is, comprehending the Negro soul, *a alma negra*. He saw it and imprisoned it in a tragic light, oppressed by custom and circumstance, a picture quite different from the happy darkies' world of (white) American folklore.

Aside from the details about the village way of life in Africa, particularly the ideas connected with death, the author's anthropological orientation is apparent in the information he gives about the relations between the various classes of village society, from slaves and servant boys to ordinary men and women up to the elders, the chiefs, the witchdoctors and the soothsayers. He does this unobtrusively, without interrupting the narrative flow. A few bits of traditional folklore literature are woven in: the song a villager composes for all to sing about a young man who had been killed by a lion (pp. 69-70) or the legend of the lagoon that covered a Lunda hamlet as a punishment for refusing a drink of water to a lost hunter (pp. 162-168).

Three years later, Castro Soromenho published another Negro novel, *Homens sem caminho*. It dealt with traditional slavery as it exists among the African tribes, for the "men without a trail" of the title are the slaves, who, figuratively speaking, have lost the ability to follow a path of their own choosing. The author maintains his objective reserve; he does not give any clue that could make us interpret the tale as either a demonstration that the Portuguese should not be held responsible for the past evils of the slave trade, or a camouflaged attack on "contract labor," the forced labor system of modern times, which was exposed by Cadbury and others in this century.[5] We are given a vivid picture of the horrors of captivity, as Djàlala, an escaped Lunda warrior, tries to impress his easygoing fellow tribesmen with what it means to fall into the hands of the brutal Quiocos, their arch-enemies (pp. 40-48 and 89-90.) His efforts are in vain; bitterly he concludes: "In our land, there are no free men left. Xanama handed the Lunda state to the Quiocos when he killed off its big men. We are slaves, all of us" (p. 162). Inexorably, as in ancient tragedy, the action moves towards the defeat of the beleaguered Lundas. Unfortunately, the masculine, heroic quality of the story of Djàlala's resistance is destroyed in the end, as the author piles misfortune on misfortune; within twenty-four hours a noble elder hangs himself from the sacred spirit tree, the decrepit chief throws the inherited insignia of his office into the fire, Djàlala's faithless wife has a stillbirth, and his only other son perishes in a violent storm that also fells the sacred tree, the symbol of the clan's prosperity. As in the first novel, an individual drama — the chief's seduction of Djàlala's wife during the latter's absence and captivity — is combined with the collective drama of the enslavement of a whole Lunda village by another tribe. Perhaps because the author wanted to endow his story with symbolic power, he overdramatized it. He also used many more folkloric elements than in *Noite de angústia*. The lagoon legend appears again (the legend of Lake Carumbo, pp. 11-12). Other folktales are added: that of Ilunga and Luegi, founders of the Lunda dynasty (pp. 122 ff.), the story of chief Xanama's revenge of his mother's murder (pp. 162-63), and punishments meted out to adulterous women (pp. 106-07). The stories are recapitulated in an enumeration of song themes (pp. 188-89). The first page presents us with a visual image, whose symbolism is evident: we see the watch fires of the besieged Lunda mountain refuge giving off a reddish glow in the "deep black night" (p. 9). Like most of Castro Soromenho's stories, this novel ends with the hero's death and the community's destruction, as if to symbolize the destructiveness of inhumanity.

Like the two novels preceding it, the collection of tales which Castro Soromenho named *Rajada* (Gust) deals exclusively with black Africans — Lundas, Quiocos, and Bângalas — who live in Northeastern Angola. It is named after the first and longest tale. Like the preceding works, most involve misfortunes, death and terror, with the same folk flavor, thanks to the mention of customs, beliefs, migration stories and legends. The tale "Rajada" resembles *Noite de angústia* in that it concerns the tragic deaths of many young people, in this case young boys who perish in the course of the rigorous circumcision rites, which were to be described by the author a year later in a detailed monograph. Once more we find him using the motif of the lagoon created by divine wrath in the story "O lago enfeitiçado" (The Haunted Lake). Still another story, "Samba," became a favorite. It told of the ancient auction of female slaves held at Cassange, through the individual fate of the homely Samba who, not having found a buyer, leaped to her death rather than let herself be killed. As good is the tale "A voz da estepe" (The Voice of the Steppe) which unfolds the character of Dumba-iá-Cuilo, "Lion of Cuilo," a Lunda hunter who because of some undisclosed misdeed was snatched by an alligator while hunting a jaguar with his men. We learn a great deal about the Lunda's way of hunting and the hunters' class in passing.

Two more stories were published in 1945 with the title *Calenga*. Both were based on old legends of the Lunda nation, beautifully retold and enlivened with individual characterizations of the protagonists as if they were people living today. One story tells of Calenga's childhood and rise to the chieftainship of the Calambas, a Lunda tribe, and his and their miraculous salvation by Luía, a river goddess and divine mother (*mãe de água*, "water mother"). As the Egyptian princess saved the babe Moses, Luía appeared on the river with calabashes in which the tribe could hide from its pursuers, submerging and floating away to safety. The other story is a new, extended version of the Lueji and Ilunga legend. Both combine accounts heard by the author with printed versions first given by the great Portuguese explorer Henrique de Carvalho. Carvalho's books are rare now, but his version of the Luía and Calenga legend was reproduced by J. Osório de Oliveira.[6] A comparison shows how skillfully Castro Soromenho elaborated it. He also made its plot more personal by introducing a portrait of the Luba chief Mutombo Muculo, father of the hunter Ilunga and a great storyteller himself. Midway in the story he adds a portrait of Lueji's father, the old Bungo chief and matweaver Iala Mácu, helping us to understand the quarrels between his children and especially the rebellion of his eldest son Quinguri. Equally vivid is the narrative of the progress of a devastating drought that leads to Ilunga's long journey to the Bungo territory. Castro Soromenho set himself an almost impossible task when he treated the legends psychologically. A contradiction subsists between the fundamentally epic and in a sense unreal character of the legends, with their supernatural elements (sidestepped in the Lueji story) and on the other hand, the nature of realism which favors the surface treatment of matter contemporary with the writer. Unquestionably, the realistic element of the psychological portrayals gives originality to Castro Soromenho's storytelling. He "re-created the legend by amplifying it with a [personal] knowledge of man," as he put it (p. 77).

During the same period, about 1945, he had turned to the past in other works of his, which dealt with the voyages of Portuguese explorers in Southern Africa. But after World War II had ended, he no doubt was hoping with many Portuguese intellectuals for changes in the direction of greater democracy, and so he decided on a realistic treatment of contemporary African society as he had known it in the Lunda region and in Luanda. As examples of literary realism the two novels that resulted are the most interesting.

In *Terra morta* (Dead Land) and *Viragem* (Turn) he pictured with compassion and indignation the relations between the backward African populations and the Portuguese officialdom that was sent to Africa to "civilize" them. The Portuguese found these works hard to stomach since hardly any noble Portuguese character could be found in them, but no one denied that they were well written.

Terra morta begins by introducing the reader to a quartet of minor Portuguese officials. Their diverse character traits are revealed as they are playing cards at the forlorn, decaying military outpost of Camaxilo where once a business community had flourished when rubber was king. The worst of the lot is a cowardly fellow by the name of Silva who tries to blackmail his colleagues; the best is Joaquim Américo, a young man who grew up in Brazil, took part in the São Paulo uprising of 1934 against Vargas' dictatorship, and had to leave the country. He and, one suspects, the author with him, has much more democratic ideas about Negroes and mulattoes because of his Brazilian experience. The time is 1935 or 1936.

Unlike Soromenho's earlier fiction, this novel and the next showed the Africans in contact with Portuguese traders and officials, their mixed offspring, and their auxiliaries, the black soldiery and constabulary. By means of a few flashbacks, e.g., in the mind of an old black *cipaio* ("sepoy"), we realize why these relations are scornful, resentful, or fearful on the Africans' part. We learn of the way in which the traders guided and abetted the soldiers when the countryside had finally been "pacified" (Chapter 3), of the way in which the officials and their constabulary used to take all able-bodied men away for one year's forced labor in the diamond mines (Chapter 5), or how the villagers were forced to mend the roads (Chapter 6). On the other hand, as the author has us listen in on the conversations between officials, we are not surprised that they find life at the post "nothing but wretchedness and dirty business" (p. 100) and believe that the blacks won't behave unless you teach them with lashes: *"Isto só a chicote!"* (p. 114). Two chapters are dramatic; in the ninth an old chief has the courage to stab a sepoy to death when his village is raided in search of fugitives from labor service, and to hang himself subsequently in order to spare his people the retribution of the Portuguese authorities. And in the thirteenth, Joaquim Américo intervenes in defense of a young mulatto whom Secretary Silva attacks with a whip for "insolence." The black bystanders are so surprised by the defense that they exclaim: "Folks, the heart of the white man has been born!" (p. 190).

The reading of *Terra morta* leaves the reader with grave doubts, however, as to whether European rule will bring anything but misfortunes to the African, in spite of the presence of a few sympathetic officials like Joaquim Américo. To make matters worse, Joaquim Américo quits government service as the novel ends.

The mutual lack of understanding between blacks and whites is even more pronounced in the second novel, *Viragem*. Like so many of Castro Soromenho's stories, it ends on a note of death: the return of a kindly but mortally ill district officer to his district, a walking corpse who had already been rumored to have died in the distant hospital. This return coincides with the drumming and dancing in honor of a dead African sepoy in the nearby village. The account is wrapped into an intrigue of seduction (in the district officer's absence his young mistress is seduced by his substitute, an impudent and incompetent young man). For the first time, white women are shown in the isolated interior of Angola. While they are not bad, they do not win the Africans' respect. In situation after situation negative attitudes are aroused in the Africans towards their white overlords, particularly against the bungling, arbitrary substitute official: annoyance, incomprehension, hate, anger, scorn, distrust, uneasiness (when they must express themselves in broken Portuguese), fear, indignation, disappointment (when permission to hold a village dance is refused), culminating in the public humiliation of a faithful veteran sepoy and his suicide (pp. 145-53, 161-68, 180.) Ending with the symbolic return of the dying official, the novel also begins symbolically: a violent storm breaks at night, during which the two frightened white women, the mistress and her grandmother, find themselves alone in the isolated residence of the district officer and hear knocks at the door. While the story rings true in its details, it loses dramatic impact because the Africans' misfortunes would not have been so great except for the fortuitous presence of one incompetent official, whose sordid little romance and comical flight detract from the main theme, the relations between the conquerors and the conquered.

As is generally true of realistic writing, Castro Soromenho's sympathy also went to the underdog; he, too, felt little concern about literary techniques. But he avoided their shallowness, did not blow ordinary, ignorant people up into great heroes, did not fall into the trap of a narrow regionalism. He restricted his subject matter to what he really knew well, finding the common denominator of human nature as well as the general precariousness of the human situation among the people of a little-known region in the interior of Africa.

Castro Soromenho's manner of writing underwent two noteworthy changes. One was pointed out long ago by a Portuguese critic, Franco Nogueira, who studied the revisions the author had made in the second edition of *Noite de angústia*. Having observed that the changes merely attenuated the defects of that early work, he analyzed the change in the wording of the dialogues between Africans. In the original version, "the dialogues were composed in current Portuguese speech, that is to say, in a language which, as the reader realized, was not that of the characters. [. . .] And the more extensive dialogues showed a logic in reasoning [. . .] which correspond entirely to the fully developed mental character of the white race. And yet the black race has its own ways of debating, a different mental process, specific arguments, a peculiar imagery, whose validity is lost if the white man's insistence on logic prevails."[7] In the revised edition Franco Nogueira noticed how the author had shortened and even suppressed many dialogues, replacing some with indirect speech,—"and not always with the greatest skill: in some passages the assertions passed from the characters to the author" (p. 57). But the critic had to admit that the veracity of the remaining dialogues was greater. For example, where a Negro had said in the first edition "Everything went very well. Soon there will be a meeting," this was changed in the second to "Everything turned out fine. Soon the old men talk with the *soba*." (*Ficou tudo direito. Logo os velhos falam com o soba.*) One might add that Castro Soromenho had given the Portuguese reader the impression of African speech by using the popular speech of Brazil (*ficar direito*, verbs instead of nouns, the present tense replacing the future). The critic noticed other changes tending toward greater psychological depth, "with the intent of giving us the African Negro as a moral being, with his conflicts, his dramas, his ambitions. [. . .] The hypocrisy of sub-chief Salemo; the ambition and desire for revenge on the part of Muaquife; the devotion of the slave woman Ivenga; the serene good sense of chief Xandumba; the integrity of Cagia — all these works of fiction interest more because of their contents and the author's stated or implied attitudes than because of the style or technique of the narrative. Yet, his manner of writing differs from old nineteenth-century realism. For example, he is too much a child of our impatient age to waste time on describing exterior appearances in detail, whether they be human ones — faces, bodies, clothes, ornaments — or the human environment — housing, villages, towns — or the natural surroundings — vegetation, relief. On the other hand, he is fond of short lyrical paragraphs that can suggest a mood, e.g., in the brief description of a sunset, or of the wildlife in the jungle, or of the woods at night in which a girl is waiting to meet a man for the first time. Considerable pain is taken to indicate and motivate the emotions, thoughts, actions of Africans, such as the feelings leading to suicide. Their beliefs and customs, even the harshest ones, like slavery, and the most repulsive ones, like cannibalism, are made understandable in the framework of tribal society. In this respect, Castro Soromenho's realism is modern, guided as it is by the objective methods of psychology, anthropology, and sociology.

The narrative is usually straightforward. It has been characterized as epic by more than one critic. Castro Soromenho uses few flashbacks, and then only in his last novels. He scorns the modern fiction writer's tricks of the trade. We always know who speaks to whom. There is no flow of consciousness, no simultaneity of several actions, no circular movement or psychological time, and none of the toying with metaphysical problems of man's place in the universe with which the masters of contemporary fiction intensify the impact of their stories. Nor is there any experimentation with vocabulary or syntax, not even a suggestion of genuinely African ways of speaking, barring a few exceptions, such as the passage of the birth of the heart of the white man in *Terra morta*. At bottom, Castro Soromenho remained a journalist who sought out the facts, with a flair for the dramatic, yet unsentimental, stating them in correct, plain language, accessible to average readers. It is remarkable how sparingly he used African terms so that he could dispense with the glossaries which burden so many works stressing local color. In his early stories, African words are more frequent, but their meaning is always made clear by the context.

Castro Soromenho has been linked to the Portuguese Neo-Realist movement, which corresponded more or less to the "social realism" of Marxist theoreticians. Like other Neo-Realists, he was influenced by the Brazilian novelists of the 1930's and 40's. His are perfectly delineated. And this is the more difficult as it is a fact that the white reader is not accustomed to such an attitude toward black humanity and its social and moral climate" (p. 59). Franco Nogueira concluded by stating that "the style is always compact, impetuous, virile; and the objectivity and bluntness of the prose make it extraordinarily accessible and expressive" (p. 60).

Another stylistic change is striking. Castro Soromenho made it after Franco Nogueira had written about him. Before, one finds the author pitying the black man, convinced that the latter is backward, superstitious, barbarous compared to the civilized part of humanity. Thus, in *Homens sem caminho* he wrote of the adulteress who had just been visited by the vision of her absent husband: "And she let herself be swept off to the black world of superstition, an abyss into which the life of the barbarian plunges every minute, prone as it is to the fatalism that enslaves the soul of his pitiable race" (2d ed., 1946, p. 27). In the revised version of 1960, terms such as pitiable *(miserando)*, barbarian *(bárbaro)*, race *(raça)*, savage *(selvagem)*, savagery *(selvagaria)*, apelike *(simiesco)*, joss *(manipanço)* have been removed or in a few cases replaced by objective words, such as clan *(clã)*, tribe *(tribo)*, forest dweller *(selvícola)*, and fetish *(fetiche)*. These simple changes reflect an evolution from an attitude of sympathetic, benevolent paternalism to a humanistic socialism that has abandoned all unscientific feelings of superiority. In this sense, Castro Soromenho became a realist of the highest order, in the best, rarely recognized Portuguese tradition, but going beyond the ideal of a mere assimilation of European civilization by Africans.

One of Castro Soromenho's French admirers, the sociologist Roger Bastide, attributed the changes in Castro Soromenho's thinking and writing to the evolution of Africa. According to him, the early tales and novels evoke a rural and tribal African society by means of a poetic style akin to ancient tragedy and medieval epic, while the Neo-Realist descriptions of his last works translate the "emotional pathology" of a traditional society in disarray, which is losing its homogeneity. "Ancient tragedy has been degraded to modern drama. Man no longer faces a jealous supernatural power. The black man has lost his gods and flounders in the void. The white man, away from his society and his civilization, is slowly sinking into some sort of slough, where he does not even have any courage left to struggle, to utter a cry — one single cry for help."[8]

The validity of Castro Soromenho's description of conditions in Angola is contested by some Portuguese (e.g., Amândio César) who think that it left out the constructive efforts made since the 1950's.[9] But it is significant that César, writing shortly after the publication of *Viragem* in 1957, expanded Castro Soromenho's absence from Angola from twenty to forty years. Castro Soromenho's view was pessimistic. But enough is known about the processes of colonization in Africa as elsewhere, its benefits and its evils, to see that he expressed psychological truths compassionately, and at last angrily.

BIBLIOGRAPHICAL NOTE
on Fernando Monteiro de Castro Soromenho
(b.   Chinde, Mozambique, 1910; d. São Paulo, Brazil, 1968.)

WORKS PUBLISHED BY CASTRO SOROMENHO

1. *Lendas negras.* Coll. Cadernos Coloniais, 20, Lisbon, Editorial Cosmos, 1936. 45 pp. (Perhaps identical with the second part of no. 2 of this list.)
2. *Nhári; O drama da gente negra.* Contos. Luanda, Livraria Civilização, 1938. 183 pp. "Prémio de Literatura Colonial," 1939. (Contents: 1. O último batuque 2. Gando—o feiticeiro! 3. Angústia 4. O milagre do Ganga 5. Nhári. Lendas negras: 1. Os embaixadores à Côrte do Além 2. Terra da Amizade 3. Para além da vida 4. Aves de além 5. A lagoa maldita.)
3. *Noite de angústia.* Romance. Porto, Livraria Civilização, 1939. 227 pp. 2d, revised ed., Lisbon, Inquérito [1943]. 234 pp. 4th ed., Lisbon, Ulisseia, 1965. 156 pp. *NB.* The third ed. is identical with no. 16 of this list (1960).
4. *Imagens da cidade de São Paulo de Luanda.* Coll. Cadernos Coloniais, 55, Edições Cosmos, [1938?]. 27 pp.
5. *Homens sem caminho.* Romance. Lisbon, Portugália, 1942. 238 pp. "Prémio de Literatura Colonial," 1942. 2d ed., Lisbon, Inquérito, 1946. 235 pp. 4th ed., Lisbon, Ulisseia, 1966. 211 pp. (Dedicated to his wife Mercedes.) *NB.* Reedited as part of no. 16 of this list (1960) which counts as 3d ed.
6. *A aventura e a morte no sertão; Silva Pôrto e a viagem de Angola a Moçambique.* Coll. Cládio, 11. Lisbon, Livaria Clássica Editora, 1943. 86 pp.
7. *Rajada e outras histórias.* Lisbon, Portugália [1943]. 179 pp. "Prémio de Literatura Colonial," 1943. (Dedicated "to my former companions in the Angolan interior, humble men, who met bitter fates in the portentous land.") (Contents: 1. Rajada 2. Os escravos dos deuses 3. A árvore sagrada 4. A morte da "chota" 5. O lago enfeitiçado 6. Samba 7. Perdeu-se no caminho. . . 8. A voz da estepe.) *NB.* Two of the stories were reedited as no. 14 of this list; all eight reappeared as part of no. 16.
8. *Sertanejos de Angola.* Coll. Pelo Império, 98. Lisbon, Agência Geral das Colónias, 1943. 37 pp. (Introduction: "Above the barbarity of the African backlands, a mere few dozens of adventurers raised their country's flag as a symbol of occupation. Those *sertanejos* [backwoodsmen] are known as *pombeiros* and *funantes* [African and European

itinerant traders.] Their history is yet to be written. Some of their traits and few of their names will be found here. Proudly they called themselves *sertanejos."*)

9. *Mistérios da terra; Mucanda-Cangongo.* Coll. Forum, Estudos Coloniais, 1. Porto, Editôra Educação Nacional, 1944. 83 pp. Illus. with 2 plates.

10. *A expedição ao país do oiro branco.* Coll. As Grandes Epopeias (Viagens e Aventuras), 15. Lisbon, Livraria Clássica Editora, 1944. 229 pp. (On Lacerda e Almeida's expedition to Cazembe.)

11. *Calenga.* Contos. Lisbon. Inquérito, 1945. 233 pp. Illustrated by Manuel Ribeiro de Pavia. (Dedicated to Arthur Ramos and Paulo Duarte. Dated "Parede—1944." (Contents: 1. Calenga e a lenda dos rios do amor e da morte 2. Lueji e Ilunga na Terra da Amizade.) *NB.* Both tales were reedited in no. 16 of this list (1960).

12. *A maravilhosa viagem dos exploradores portugueses.* Lisbon, Sociedade de Intercâmbio Cultural Luso-Brasileiro, 1946 (i.e. 1948). 391 pp. and 84 plates. Illustrated by Manuel Ribeiro de Pavia. 2d, revised ed. Lisbon, Editorial Sul, [1956]. 364 pp. and 33 plates. 3d ed. Lisbon, Arcádia, 1961. 476 pp.

13. *Terra morta.* Romance. Coll. Gaivota, 1. Rio de Janeiro, Livraria-Editôra da Casa do Estudante do Brasil, 1949. 228 pp. (Dedicated to Adolfo Casais Monteiro. Dated "Lisboa—Dezembro de 1945.") 2d. ed., Lisbon, Arcádia, 1961. 267 pp. (Banned upon publication.) French translation: *Camaxilo.* Trans. by Violante do Canto. Preface by Roger Bastide. Paris, Éditions Présence Africaine, 1955; 2d. ed., 1963. Also translated into Czech (1960), Russian (1962), German (1964), and Hungarian (1964).

14. *A voz da estepe.* Coll. Novela, 14. Lisbon, Fomento de Publicações, n.d. [1956]. (Contents: 1. A voz da estepe 2. Samba.) See no. 7 of this list.

15. *Viragem.* Coll. Atlântida, 1. Lisbon, Ulisseia [1957]. 218 pp. (Dedicated to his wife Mercedes.) 2d. ed. São Paulo, Edições Arquimedes, 1967. 181 pp. French translation: *Virage.* Trans by Marlyse Meyer. Coll. Du Monde Entier, Paris, Gallimard, 1962. Also translated into Italian (1965).

16. *Histórias da terra negra.* Contos e novelas e uma narrativa. With a study by Roger Bastide. 2 vols. Lisbon, Editorial Gleba, 1960. Illustrated by Alice Jorge and Júlio Pomar. (Contents: Vol. I, Contos e novelas: 1. Samba 2. Calenga e a lenda dos rios do amor e da morte 3. Os escravos dos deuses 4. Rajada 5. A morte da "chota" 6. A árvore sagrada 7. A voz da estepe 8. Perdeu-se no caminho 9. O lago enfeitiçado. Narrativa: Lueji e Ilunga na terra da amizade. Vol. II: Romances: 1. Noite de angústia 2. Homens sem caminho.) Slightly revised and corrected versions of nos. 2, 5, 7, and 11 of this list.

17. Portuguese translation of L. Tolstoy's *Sebastopol.*

18. "Wenceslau de Morais," *Perspectivas da literatura portuguesa do século XIX,* ed. João Gaspar Simões, vol. II, pp. 313-327. Lisbon, Ática, 1948.

NB. Castro Soromenho contributed articles to the *Diário de Luanda, Jornal de Angola* (Luanda), *Humanidade* (Lisbon), *Seara Nova* (Lisbon), *O Diabo* (Lisbon), *O Primeiro de Janeiro* (Porto), *Jornal da Tarde* (Lisbon), *Diário Popular* (Lisbon), *A Noite* (Lisbon), *Dom Casmurro* (Rio de Janeiro), *O Estado de S.Paulo* (São Paulo).

WORKS ABOUT CASTRO SOROMENHO

1. Bastide, Roger. *L'Afrique dans l'oeuvre de Castro Soromenho.* Paris, P.J. Oswald, 1960. 30 pp.

2. César, Amândio. *Parágrafos de literatura ultramarina.* (Lisbon), So-

ciedade de Expansão Cultural, 1967. (Review articles about *Viragem*, pp. 150-152, and the fourth edition of *Noite de angústia*, pp. 152-154.)
3. Margarido, Alfredo. "Castro Soromenho." *Estudos Ultramarinos* (Lisbon), 1959, no. 3, pp. 125-39. [Not seen.]
4. Nogueira, Franco. *Jornal de crítica literária (1943-1953).* Lisbon, Livraria Portugália [1954]. (Chap. II, "Castro Soromenho, romancista da África Negra," pp. 49-68.)
NB. Reviews of Castro Soromenho's books were published by numerous other critics.

UNPUBLISHED WORKS BY CASTRO SOROMENHO

Castro Soromenho announced the preparation of *No mundo dos negros* (an ethnographical essay, 1944), and *Desterrados* (a novel, 1945), perhaps published under different titles. In 1962, the author was reported by João Alves das Neves to be working on a new novel, *A chaga.* According to his widow, Senhora Mercedes de Castro Soromenho, he actually wrote this novel in 1964 while living in Paris. It was to be published posthumously by the Editorial Samambaia in São Paulo, Brazil.

Gerald Moser

Errata

p. 63, line 1: for "Argentina" read "Lisbon"

p. 66, line 33: for "disturbed" read "disturbed frame of"

p. 74, line 41: for "Salemo" read "Salema"

p. 76, line 16: for "Perhaps...list" read "Legends from Timor and Angola. Those from Angola are identical with the second part of no. 2 of this list."

p. 76, line 37: for "86 pp." read "88 pp."

p. 78, line 10: for "unpublished works" read "unpublished and posthumous works"

p. 78, lines 17-128: for "It was...Brazil" read "It was published posthumously by the Editora Civilizacao Brasileira in Rio de Janeiro, Brazil; 1970, with a preface by Ruy Coelho, dated 1968, (5) + 189 pp.

Geraldo Bessa Victor

The Art of
LUANDINO VIEIRA
Tomás Jacinto

Luandino Vieira (the pseudonym for José Graça) is one of the most gifted writers from Africa today. He is an ex-convict, now living under house arrest in Lisbon, Portugal. He has spent almost one-third of his life in one prison or another.

Vieira was sentenced to a 14 year term in 1963 by a military tribunal; his violation was the disclosure of secret certified lists of army deserters from the Portuguese armed services fighting in Africa. Vieira disclosed this information during a BBC interview. He was tried and convicted for, in his own words, "telling the truth." He was paroled in the summer of 1972, on the condition that he remain his Lisbon for five years. He cannot leave Portugal.

Vieira was also imprisoned because he is a talented short story artist whose works are well known in the Portuguese world. Although *Luanda*,[1] his finest published collection of stories, had no political intent, the realism that the stories convey is volatile— enough for it to have been prohibited from sale by Portuguese authorities in Portugal and Africa.

Vieira, a second generation white Angolan, is thirty-seven years old, and holds no bitterness against the Portuguese authorities. His only desire is to be free to write. But he is having trouble finding a publisher in Portugal.

The Portuguese authorities have had mixed feelings about permitting Vieira's *Luanda* to be published. The book has been prohibited from sale twice. On his release from prison in 1972, Vieira was allowed to publish a slightly amended third edition of *Luanda* in Lisbon. One month after being sold in the librarias in Lisbon, the remaining 25 copies of the 5000 printed were confiscated by the Portuguese censors. The book is currently banned.

Why is the book banned?

The answer can only be because it tells the truth.

Greatly influenced by the Brazilian writers Jorge Amado and Guimarães Rosa, Vieira's literary evolvement branches into three broad areas: a simplicity of narration, the usage of the common Portuguese speech of Angola and of Kimbundu, the Bantu language spoken around Luanda, and lastly, the re-representation of life as it was and is in Angola: or realism.

This paper will serve as an introduction to *Luanda* and Luandino Vieira. It will include four parts:

    1) Summary of the stories of *Luanda*,
    2) A structural analysis of one story, pointing out the similarities
       to oral traditions,
    3) Notes on the usage of Kimbundu and a word-list,
    4) A bibliography of works by the authors.

The term "Luuanda" is the Kimbundu word for Luanda, the capital of Angola. The three stories of the book *Luuanda* all have as a setting the musseques, or slums, of that city. The first story is entitled "Vávo Xíxi e Seu Neto Zeca Santos" (Grandmother

Xixi and Her Grandson Zeca Santos). It is the story about these two people in a musseque. Grandma Xíxi is old and tired. Her grandson, Zeca, cannot get a job, and the
two are reduced to abject poverty and hunger. Zeca attempts to find employment, but
he is black and uneducated. At one place he is whipped, because the proprietor knows
that Zeca's father is in jail, a convicted "terrorist." At another interview he is chased
away because his appearance is shabby, and because it is discovered that his family
was originally from "Icolo e Bengo," an area at which the Portuguese army had encountered guerrilla resistance in the early days of the war. Vávo Xíxi, starving, resorts
to eating dahlia roots, and when Zeca returns home without a job, she castigates him
for spending their last savings on a bright, new, yellow shirt.

But the new yellow shirt is, as Vieira so skillfully points out, important to Zeca's
life. If he has no money or no food, why not at least own a shirt that will attract a
woman's gaze? Thus, when Vávo Xíxi offers to cook the dahlia roots and a rotten
orange for her grandson, Vieira writes:

> E foi nessa hora, com as coisas bem diante da cara, o sorriso de vavó cheio
> de amizade e tristeza, Zeca Santos sentiu uma vergonha antiga, uma
> vergonha que lhe fazia querer sempre as camisas coloidas, as calças como
> sô Jaime só quem sabia fazer, uma vergonha que não lhe deixava aceitar
> comida. . . (p. 23)

> And it was at this time, with everything set in front of him, that Zeca
> Santos felt that old shame, a shame that always made him want
> colorful shirts, and pants that only Jaime knew how to make, a
> shame that wouldn't let him accept food. . .

Zeca would not accept hand-outs from his friends, or even allow his grandmother to
fool him. His shame is overwhelming and sincere. His great pride is the pride of the
poor.

And this is what Vieira is revealing in "Vávo Xíxi," that there exists great poverty
and hunger in Luanda, but that there are, amongst the poverty-stricken, the strong
ones. Zeca Santos, at the story's end, takes a backbreaking job at a cement factory at
slaves wages. He has no choice, for he must survive.

The story of Zeca Santos has no direct political implications. Nonetheless, the war
between the Angolans and the Portuguese serves as a "backdrop" to the events, a
backdrop that cannot be concealed. Why then is there so much fear amongst the
authorities and the establishment about terrorists? Or why is there so much distrust
among the people? And Vieira punctuates his stories with comments such as this:

> . . . os pequenos filhos de novembro estavam vestidos com pele de poeira
> vermelha espalhada pelos vanto dos jipes das patrulhas zunindo no meio
> de ruas e becos. . . . (p. 13)

> . . . the young November children (of grass) were dressed in skins of red
> dust, red dust spread by the wind of patrol jeeps roaring down the middle of
> roads and alleys. . . .

But Vieira has no intention of implicating the war or the presence, the ubiquitous
presence, of the Portuguese army. It is an expose of life as it is in Luanda.

The second story, "Do Ladrão e do Papagaio" (The Thief and the Parrot), goes
into greater character depth. It is the story of three "thieves," Dos-Reis, João Miguel
("Via-Rapida"), and Garrido, the latter of whom learns a lesson in friendship. The
three men are extremely different. Dos-Reis is black, a family man, Garrido is a mulat-

to with a lame leg, and João Miguel is a bachelor lost in the world of *diamba,* or marijuana, because he accidentally killed his best friend in a train accident.

The three plan a heist. But before the burglary materializes, Garrido and João Miguel have a vicious argument. João belittles Garrido because of his deformity, and Garrido confronts João with the fact that he hides in his *diamba* world. The two, once the best of friends, almost come to blows, but do not fight, João Miguel, hearing the truth about himself, leaves infuriated. Garrido, dismayed at what he has previously overheard his best friend say about him, also leaves. Only Dos-Reis remains, and he is later caught attempting to steal the ducks that night. he unjustly blames Garrido for his capture, and denounces him to the authorities.

As a subplot, Vieira explores the "love-life" of the crippled mulatto. Garrido goes to Inacia's house. She is a buxomy black girl who thoroughly dislikes Garrido. But the mulatto is in love with her. She mistreats him sorely, forcing him to walk on his hands with his crippled leg around his neck, in exchange for a kiss that she never gives him. Instead, she soothes her parrot Jaco, which sings "O Kamtuta, sung' o pe" or, "masturbator, pull your leg," in Kimbundu. "Kamtuta" is Garrido's nickname in the musseque, for it is known that he had never slept with a woman.

But Garrido is only a boy. He becomes infuriated with Inacia, and puts the blame on the parrot; he decides to kidnap Jaco that night. This Garrido does, but he mishandles the entire affair. When he returns home with the parrot, he cannot kill it. In the morning he is arrested on Dos-Reis' trumped-up charges.

Garrido is taken to jail, and there he confronts Dos-Reis, the informant. With the help of an old man, the two finally become friends again. Almost painstakingly, Vieira reveals in this story the honesty of friendship and its resultant problems. For as Garrido discovers, a friend is one who can forgive, and not one who continues to forget or hate or act unfairly (like João Miguel and Inacia).

The last story, "Estória de Galinha e do Ovo" (The Story of the Chicken and the Egg) will be discussed now with an analysis of its structure, rather than be summarized, since the plot will be made readily apparent in the analysis itself. However, a brief discussion on structure and oral traditions is first necessary.

Oral traditions are composed of structural building blocks, which Harold Scheub has called "expansible images." (These images are in turn composed of other structural items, all of which do not concern us here.) These expansible images may have similar settings, but have different characters. Frequently, the outcome, the resolution made in one image differs considerably from another. These differences among expansible images, whether they be in the type or role of character, in the plot or action, or in a mood or nuance, reveal the theme to an audience through a process of repetition of similar episodes with slight variances. It is through these differences that the theme of a narrative continues, and is eventually and fully revealed.[2]

The thematic impact in an oral narrative, then, is determined by the degree and quality of those differences among expansible images. As well, the theme is revealed, substantiated, and dramaticized through the juxtaposition of images (or groups of images), much like Eisenstein creates his theme through *montage.* We may call these images which embrace a central axis "expansible images."

These images exist in the oral literature of all lands. If taken far enough, one might venture to say that these patterns of images do not occur only in oral fictions, but in written fictions as well, that they are not simply a structure of fiction, but also a structure of the mind. Expansible images found may also be clearly seen in Vieira's story "Da Galinha e Do Ovo."

In an interview with Vieira at a cafe in Lisbon, he told me that he devised the idea of different mediators with a purely symbolic intent. Yet, the inherent structure of the story is apparent in what we call oral traditions. Also, this story contains another aspect of oral literature. When the egg-chicken controversy begins, the old Bebeca listen to both disputants, and then speaks this old proverb:

> A cobra enrolou murinque!
> Se pego a murinque, cobra morde.
> Se mato a cobra o murinque parte. (p. 160)

> The snake coils inside the water pot!
> If you save the pot, the snake will bite.
> If you kill the snake, the pot will break.

This exact proverb can be found in José Martins Vaz' *A Filosofia Tradicional dos Cabindas* (Lisboa, 1963), The existence of this proverb in Africa is most widespread.

Let us now proceed with the structural analysis. The story concerns the dispute in a musseque over an egg. One woman owns the chicken, another surrepetitiously fed it in her yard. The egg is laid in that yard, and the dispute soon begins.

Not including the introductory and concluding images, there are six parallel expansible images in "Galinha." The action occurs in one spot, on one "stage;" the setting does not change. Most of the characters remain in all six sets. The major differences among the parallel images concern the entrance and existence of a pivotal character (or group of characters), and the shift in mood in the final image.

In the first expansible image, the old lady Bebeca attempts to mediate the controversy. She becomes perplexed, and cannot decide.

Then in the second, Sô Zé appears. He is the white owner of the neighborhood *quitanda,* from which one of the disputants bought the corn to feed the chicken, the corn which produced the egg. Sô Zé decides that the egg belongs to him, because the corn had never been paid for. In a somewhat humorous mood, the women chase him away.

Next comes Azulinho. A religious schoolboy, the scholar, neatly attired in his all-season blue suit, he is a caricature of a candidate for *assimilação.* Azulinho decides that since the egg belongs to neither of the disputants, then as a matter of circumstance, it belongs to God, and that, in God's absence, the priest should have the egg. Azulinho is also chased away.

The owner of the *cubatas* (shacks), Sô Vitalino, is an old white man interested only in money and carnal desires. In the fourth image he is asked to find a solution, and, as expected, he decides that the egg belongs to him, since neither of the disputants have paid his current rent. As in the previous two images, the women "insult" him away. In the fifth image, Sô Arturo, "Vintecinco linhas," arrives. An ex-notary's aide, well-versed in law, Arturo is now a misbehaved drunkard afflicted with elephantiasis. The women bring the case to him, and he decides that since neither of the disputants have title to the property, he'll take the egg in exchange for arranging a trial. This plan is as ridiculous and unacceptable to the women as the other, and Sô Arturo, "Vintecinco linhas," is hounded away.

In these first five expansible images, the pattern remains the same. The women ask a newcomer to solve the dispute. The old lady, the *dono de quitanda,* the schoolboy, the landlord, the notary, all are asked to decide the case of the egg, and all fail to do so in their greed. The story progresses, thematically, from one image to another. In each image a societal facet is exposed. Who can help the people? Who can help them to decide the fate of the egg, or better, the fate of Angola?

Vieira is exposing these cultural stereotypes in order to establish their real worth in Angola. The traditional elder, the old buinessman, the *assimilado,* the church, the landowner, the legal profession, none can decide the fate of this egg. Who is left to decide?

Well, the army hasn't made its entrance, its try for possession of the egg. So, in the sixth image, a *polícia,* the army, arrives. The sergeant decides to take not only the egg, but the chicken as well. The people are startled, but there is nothing they can do.

The difference between this image and the others is obvious. In the others, the women can control the imbalances; they can chase off the mediators. And the mediators are humorous, or, at least, foolish. But in this last image, these aspects no longer prevail. The people are at the mercy of the police. There is no humor, There is a definite shift of mood.

In the entire story there exists a movement from harmony to conflict, to the resolution of that conflict. This movement is a *rite of passage:* a movement of separation, transition, and incorporation. The story begins with the harmony of the boys playing with the chicken, then the harmony is disrupted, the would-be mediators appear, and finally the boys solve the crisis. Within the six images there is also a movement from conflict to resolution. In each image, a minor conflict arises as each mediator attempts to take possession of the egg; each of these "conflicts within a conflict" are resolved. These minor conflicts correspond to a transition in the whole story.

But it is the entrance of the army, so clear from the analysis of expansible images, that becomes so different in comparison with the previous images. The previous mediators represent no real threat to the women. They can all be reckoned with, as in bygone days. On the other hand, the army is a different things. The women are faced with a hopeless situation. It is only right, then, that it is their children who save the egg, and resolve the conflict.

I have withheld, up to this point, any commentary on the introductory and concluding images. These too are, in a sense, parallel images, parallel to each other. In the introductory image, in harmony, the boys Xico and Beto play with the chicken Cabíri, talking to her; in the concluding image, they "play" with her again, imitating a cock's crow, so that she flies away from the grip of the sergeant. With the chicken lost, the egg is kept from the sergeant. The boys are instrumental in bringing harmony back to their society; they, the youth of Angola, are the ones, according to the story, who will determine the destiny of their country. It is only they, and not their elders, who can speak with Cabíri.

Vieira's comment is forceful. On the one hand, he exposes the greed and dishonesty of Luanda society, while on the other he emphasizes that the Angola youth accept their destiny. This is the major theme embedded in the structure of the narrative.

One of the most interesting aspects of Vieira's style is his usage of Kimbundu loan words in Portuguese. Over the centuries, the Portuguese language has been influenced greatly by the Bantu languages surrounding Luanda, especially Kimbundu. Like many of his contemporaries, Vieira employs local expressions in the popular vernacular, but unlike most, he uses pure Kimbundu occasionally. Indeed, Vieira writes the ways things are spoken in Luanda. In pure Kimbundu, Portuguese, and a mixture. His usage of Kimbundu extends to common speech, popular sayings, and even the reproduction of Kimbundu songs. He maintains this "Luanda speech" throughout the three stories. In the introductory note he quotes in Kimbundu from an oral narrative:

> Mu 'xi ietu ia Luuanda mubita ima ikuata sonii.
>
> In this our land of Luanda, there occur many shameful things.

Vieira includes in each story some pure Kimbundu, an aspect he expects to continue more elaborately in the future. For example, in the first story, Vávo Xíxi, when she hears of the white child being born to a black couple, exclaims:

> Mu muhatu my 'mbia! Mu tunda uazele, mu tunda uaxikelela, mu tunda uaksuka. . . (p. 32)
>
> A woman is like a pan, out of her comes white, black, or red. . .

In the second story, Vieira makes this comment; the orderly in the jail wakes everybody up;

> Nem *Uazekele kie-uazeka kiambote,* men nada, era só assim a outra maneira civilizada como ele dizia. . . (p. 70)
>
> Not even *Uazekele kie-uazeka kiambote,* or anything, it was only in the other more civilized manner that he spoke. . .

Uazekele kie-uazeka kiambote is the traditional Kimbundu good morning saying.

Or, in the third story, this is one of the songs sung by Cabíri, the chicken (sung, of course, in Kimbundu, giving an added symbolic depth to the chicken):

> Ngexile kua ngana Zefa
> Ngala ngo ku kalela
> Ka. . .Ka. . .Kakila.
>
> . . .ngejile kua ngana Bina
> Ala kia ku kuata
> Kua. . .Kua. . .Kuata

Estava en casa de nga Zefa (cackle of chicken).	I was living at nga Zefa's house (cackle of chicken).
Vim pra casa de nga Bina Ela está já agarrar-me (cackle of chicken).	I came from nga Bina's house She tried to catch me (cackle of chicken).

Unlike his contemporaries, Vieira is not adverse to reproducing the unique linguistic features that occur between languages. For example, the Portuguese language is able to easily adopt Kimbundu verbs: the verb *vuzar* was borrowed from the Kimbundu verb *kuvuza* which means "to pull out a person's hair." By dropping the KU- prefix of the Kimbundu verb, and adding the Portuguese suffix -AR, the loanword verb is then conjugated in the normal manner. Other verbs, which are used by Vieira, with their derivatives and meanings are as follows:

> Cambular — (kukambula) to catch a moving object
> Cassumbular — (Kukasumbula) to knock something out of one's hands, a child's game

Cocaiar — *(?)* to pick out lice eggs
Muximar — *(kumuxima)* to flatter
Muxoxar — *(*from the noun *muxoxo)* to show disdain for a person
    by making a sound with the tongue and teeth
Tunde — *(*Kimbundu only, from *kutunda)* to come out, leave
Xaxualhar — *(?)* to rustle (through leaves)
Ximbicar — *(kuximbika)* to wander about aimlessly
Xingar — *(kuxinga)* to insult
Xinguilar — *(kuxing'i'la)* to evoke the dead
Xuculula — *(kuxucula)* to look at with displeasure
Uatabaram — *(kutoba)* to belittle (In this verb, Vieira transcribed
    the Kimbundu subject prefix *U-*, and the Kimbundu
    preterite tense marker *-A-*, including them in the loan-
    word. Otherwise, he could have used simply *tobar*. For
    the Portuguese-ation he added the preterite suffix
    -ARAM.)
Vuzar — *(kuvuza)* to pull out one's hair

Vieira's concern, then is to reproduce as realistically as possible the Luandanese Portuguese. This makes the reading of *Luaanda* extremely difficult for the literary scholar. What follows is a word list of the other Kimbundu loan-words used by Vieira, with their Kimbundu derivatives in parentheses (where known), and their Portuguese and English translations:

Bitacaia — pulga livre; louse
Cabobo — *(kabobo)* desdentado; toothless
Cacimbados — de cacimbo (see next item)
Cacimbo — *(kixibu)* em Angola, a estação de nevoa e chuva; in
    Angola, the season of fog and rain
Cafofo — *(kafofo,* diminutive of *kofofo)* cenguinho; blind
Camuela — *(kamuelu)* sovina; pouco liberal, que da pouco;
    emprega-se em sentido humoristico; miserly
Candingolo — bebida de cana, aguardente; whiskey
Capanga — *(kapanga)* entre sovaco; armpit
Cariengue — homens que se alugaram para trabalhar; men who
    rent themselves out for work
Cassanda — *(assa)* branca ordinaria; ordinary white woman
Cazumbi — *(*diminutive of *muzumbi)* chuva que amanhece e se
    conserva até altodia; rain that begins in the morning and-
    continues until midday
Diamba — *(liamba)* marijuana
Fimba — mergulha; dar fimba; to dive, sink
Gumbatetes — *(ngumbatate)* vespa que construi ninho com barro;
    wasp that builds his nest with clay
Jindungo — pimenta, malagueta; Indian pepper
Jingunas — *(nguna)* formigas brancas; termites, white ants
Kabulu — lebre; have
Kam'tuta — masturbar-se; to masturbate
Luando — esteira de mabu (tipo de palmeira); mat made from a
    palm tree
Maca — *(maka)* conversa feia, palavras feisa; insults
Macutas — *(makuta)* embrulho pequeno, mealheiro; small sum
Makutu — mentiras; lies

Mangonheiro — (mangonia) fingimento de actividade de trabalho;
  preguiça, indolência; pretense of working
Maquezo — (makezu) fuito de arbusto; cola; Kola nut
Massambala — (mas'ambala) milho miudo; sorghum
Massuicas — (?) rocks making a tripod, housing the fire
Matacanha — (ditacaia?) pulga; louse
Mataco — (taku, mataku) madegas; buttocks
Matete — papas; breasts
Mauindo — ninho de pulga com ovos (Riuindo); louse's nest with
  eggs
Maximbombo — (madimbondo) autocarro velho; old "bomb" car
Marimbondo — (madimbondo) vespa; wasp
Monandengue — criança; child
Monangamba — (ngamba, mon' a ngamba) carregadores,
  servente; dock workers, freight handlers
Mulemba — grande arvore angolense, de raizes aereas,
  popularmente chamada "barbas;" large Angolan tree with
  aerial roots, called "beards"
Muringue — (muring'i) moringue; water pot
Mutopa — cachimbo com agua para fumar diamba; pipe for smok-
  ing marijuana
Nga — senhora; lady
Ngoma — (ngoma) drum
Ngueta — branco ordinario, pobre; poor white man
Pacassa — (pakasa) boi selvagem; buffalo, water buffalo
Piapias — andorinhas; swallows
Quileba — (kileba) alto; tall
Quimbombo — bebida feita de milho e fuba de bombo; alcoholic
  drink made from dry manioc
Quinda — (kinda) especie de cesto; tape of basket
Quinjongo — (kinjongo) gafanhotos grandes; large grasshopper
Quiquerra — (kikuera) farinha de mandioca com acuçãr natural e
  amendoins; manioc flour with sugar and peanuts
Quissemo — (kisemu) defeito; desdem; disdain
Quissenda — (kisende) calcanhar; pontape; kick
Quissonde — (kisonde) formiga brava; wild ants
Quitande — (kitande) feijão descascado; shelled beans
Quitata — (kitata) prostituta; prostitute
Sape-sape — árvore; tree
Salale — termite; termite
Sumauma — fibra de semente de árvore mufuma; fibre of the
  mufuma tree
Sungadibengo — (?) mulatto
Sung'p pe — (kusunga) to pull
Tuji — (tuji) excremento, esterco; excrement
Ximba — (ximba) gato do mato; wildcat

Words whose glosses and Portuguese equivalents are not available include cagunfas,
imbumba and plim-plaus.

Luandino Vieira's usage and reproduction of Kimbundu is unique in fiction and
narrative written in Porguguese (many Angolan poets, among them Tomas Vieira da
Cruz, Agostinho Neto, António Jacinto, and Viriato da Cruz have used Kimbundu in

their poems). Whether or not he will be able to continue to publish his works is a matter of question; however, there exists a German translation of "Vávo Xíxi," and an English translation of *Luuanda* is in progress. Doubtlessly, Vieira will have to publish outside of Portugal. A Bibliography follows, with those stories already published by Vieira:

A *Cidade e a Infância.* Colecção Autores Ultramarinos, 2. Lisbon, Casa dos Estudantes do Império, 1960.

Duas Historias de Pequenos Burgueses. Colecção Imbondeiro, 23. Sá de Bandeira, Imbondeiro, 1961.

"La Em Tetembuatubia." Em o jornal *Expresso.* 3 Marco 1973. *Luuanda.* Luanda, ABC, 1963.

"Os miudos do Capitáo Bento Albano." Em *Novos Cantos d'Africa,* 1962.

"Primeira cançáo do mar." Colecçáo Imbondeiro, 14. Sa da Bandeira, Imbondeiro, 1961.

Vidas novas. Contos. Casa dos Estudantes do Império, Lisbon, 1962.

Notes

[1] Luandino Viera, *Luuanda,* Edições 70, Lisbon, 1973, 3rd edition. All quotes are from this edition.

[2] Harold Scheub, *The Ntsomi: A Xhosa Performing Art,* Ph.D. dissertation, University of Wisconsin, 1969, and in "The Technique of the Expansible Image in Xhosa Ntsomi-Performances," *Research in African Literature,* vol. 1, no. 2, 1970.

Agostinho Neto

AGOSTINHO NETO AND THE POETRY OF COMBAT

DONALD BURNESS

Agostinho Neto is one of the few Lusophone African writers with an international reputation. He has spent much of his life in the struggle of his people to win independence. Whereas some Angolan intellectuals chose to live in Europe during the thirteen years of guerrilla warfare, Neto remained in his homeland organizing resistance to Portuguese domination. Moreover, Neto did not isolate himself from the great masses of Angolans living outside urban centers. He personally visited interior sections, eating with the people and frequently sleeping in their mosquito infested huts. For Agostinho Neto his own life has taken on meaning only in conjunction with the lives of the oppressed peoples of Angola.

Born in September, 1922, in the village of Kaxikane in the region of Icolo e Bengo about forty miles from Luanda, Neto was raised in a Christian household. His father was a Protestant pastor who like Neto's mother was also a teacher. After finishing his high school work in Luanda and working for a while in the Health Service, Neto went to Portugal in 1947 to study medicine at the University of Coimbra. He later transferred to the University of Lisbon. Like other African intellectuals, Neto quickly became involved in political activities. He was first arrested in 1951 and sentenced to three months imprisonment in Caxias, several miles west of Lisbon, for gathering signatures for the International World Peace Conference in Stockholm. He would return to Caxias in 1955, sentenced this time for two years. Neto's reputation as a poet brought particular attention to his case. Jean-Paul Sartre, André Mauriac, Nicolas Guillén and Diego Rivera were among those voices protesting his incarceration. Somehow, in between prison and writing poetry, Neto managed to complete his medical training and received his degree in 1958.

With his wife Neto returned to Angola where he was given a position of leadership within the M.P.L.A. When Portuguese authorities arrested him again in June 1960, and transferred him first to Cape Verde and later to Lisbon, protests were voiced from men and women who feared for his life. C. Day Lewis, Basil Davidson, Doris Lessing, John Osborne, Angus Wilson, Iris Murdock and Allan Sillitoe published a letter of protest in *The Times.* Penguin Books edited a book entitled *Persecution* by Peter Benenson in which Neto's case was examined. Moreover, International Amnesty became involved in the plight of Agostinho Neto. Bowing to such strong international opinion, Portuguese authorities released him in 1962 upon condition that he remain in Portugal. In July, 1962, Neto escaped and returned to Africa where in December of that year he was elected president of the M.P.L.A., a position he has held to the present time.

Neto's importance in Lusophone Africa has been compared to that of Léopold Senghor in Francophone Africa. Such a comparison is not without merit. Both Neto and Senghor are political figures who used poetry as a weapon in the struggle of African peoples to assert the originality, dignity and beauty of African cultures. Both négritude poets abandoned their literary careers, however, once they became political leaders. Neto and Senghor share a vision of a world of peace, love, brotherhood and harmony. Each man has received attention throughout Africa and much of the rest of the world. But there are marked differences as well between the two. Neto's prison experience and his activity in the resistance movement find no parallel in Senghor's life. Nor is the theme of political independence present in Senghor's négritude poetry whereas it constitutes a principal motif in Neto's poems of the late 1950's and 1960. Finally, the lushness of Senghor's imagery, the resonance of his line, is in contrast to the simpler, less descriptive language of Neto that ultimately moves us more by the message than by the rhythm of the poetry itself. It would be worthwhile for a detailed comparative study to be made on the poetry of these two men, but such an examination lies outside the scope of this book.

In 1961 Casa dos Estudantes do Império in the Colecção Autores Ultramarinos published a small volume of Neto's poetry under the title *Poemas.* A much larger selection appeared first in Italy in 1963 under the title *Con Occhi Asciutti (With Dry Eyes).* This book was later published in Yugoslavia, Russia and China. The first complete Portuguese edition came out in 1974 as *Sagrada Esperança,* (Sacred Hope), the title Neto preferred. It was awarded the Poetry of Combat Prize by the University of Ibadan in 1975. The forty-eight poems in this collection constitute nearly all of Neto's poetic work and cover a period from 1945 through 1960.[1]

The theme of night is dominant in Neto's early poems; it is not the vibrant exuberant African night that Senghor celebrates, but a somber time of ignorance, fear and death.

It is night when Manuel leaves his wife to be taken to São Tomé to do forced labor in "Partida para o contrato" (Departure for Forced Labor):

> *Não há luz*
> *não há estrelas no céu escuro*
> *Tudo na terra é sombra*
>
> *Não há luz*
> *não há norte na alma da mulher*
>
> *Negrura*
> *Só negrura. . .* [2]

> There is no light
> There are no stars in the dark sky
> Everything on earth is darkness
>
> There is no light
> There is no north star in the soul of the woman
>
> Blackness
> Only Blackness

The departing boat merges with dark sea and the dark sky which reflect the darkness in the soul of Manuel's wife.

At night in the musseque of Sambezanga, a district of black men and women, death comes in the form of a white policeman who beats a man mercilessly. The people seek an explanation for such murders and the taking of prisoners; the only answer is that they are black.

The poet is a prisoner of darkness. In the poem "Noite" (Night) he laments the misery of his condition:

> Eu vivo
> nos bairros escuros do mundo
> sem luz nem vida.
>
> São bairros de escravos
> mundos de miséria
> bairros escuros.
>
> Onde as vontades se diluíram
> e os homens se confundiram
> com as coisas. [3]

I live
in the dark quarters of the world
without light, without life.

They are slave quarters
worlds of misery
dark quarters

Where desires have been diluted
and men have been confused
with things.

The people of the musseques struggle to survive. The shopkeeper in
"Quitandeira" (Shopkeeper), sitting under a mulemba tree outside her
stall to avoid the direct rays of the hot sun, cries out to a passing lady
that the oranges she has for sale are good. But she has not spent her life
merely selling fruit—she has given up as well her spirit that has been
trampeled by her hard life.

Compra laranjas doces
compra-me também o amargo
desta tortura
de vida sem vida.

Compra-me a infância de espirito
este botão de rosa
que não abriu

E ái vão as minhas esperanças
como foi o sangue dos meus filhos

Aí vão as laranjas
como eu me ofereci ào alcool
para me anestesiar
e me entreguei as religiões
para me insensibilizar
e me atordoei para viver.[4]

Buy sweet oranges
Buy from me also the bitterness
of this torture
of this lifeless life.

Buy from me the innocent spirit
this rose bud
that did not open

And there go my hopes
like the blood of my own children

There go my oranges
just as I delivered myself to drink
to anesthetize myself
in order to become insensitive
and I made myself dizzy in order to live.

A rose bud that never opened, a life of fruitless sacrifice—the quitandeira need not feel alone. Another quitandeira in "Meia-noite na quitanda" (Midnight in the Shop) works beyond midnight to earn money so her son can pay taxes. Gathering her individual tostões (a tostão is worth ten centavos or approximately a quarter of a cent), Sá Domingas must earn ten thousand reis or one hundred escudos, about four dollars. So she sits outside calling out:

Cem réis de jindungo
Cinquenta réis de tomate
Três tostões de castanha de caju[5]

One hundred reis for pepper
Fifty reis for tomatoes
Three tostões for cashew nuts

Neto presents a gallery of victims in his early poems. Forced labor, hunger, loss of dignity, loss of hope, humiliation, even death, assault the body and spirit of the African living under colonialist domination. Life in the musseques is "ansiedade" (anguish). There is "saudade (nostalgia) dos dias não vividos" (of days never lived) in "Sábado nos musseques" (Saturday in the Musseques). But Neto does not despair. In the very first poem of *Sagrada Esperança*, "Adeus à hora da largada" (Farewell at the Hour of Departure), he asserts his faith in himself and the people to create a new destiny. Blind hope offers no hope; change can only be effected through individual and collective action:

Sou eu minha Mãe
a esperança somos nós[6]

I am my Mother
Hope—it is us

This is the sacred hope of an Angolan future in which justice and human dignity will replace bondage and excoriating humiliation. Neto identifies with the people. In "Sombros" (Shadows) shadows pass before him of manacled convicts who were dragged away to die; all the suffering of Af-

ricans who lived under imperialist domination in the past becomes shared
in the present. There is no "I"; there is only "we." Past and present are
merely paths leading to a certain future.

Neto recalls his childhood friend Mussunda in three of his poems, but
it is in "Mussunda Amigo" (Mussunda Friend) that he best captures the
quality of that friendship which is symbolic of the bond uniting all oppressed Angolans.

> Contigo
> Com a firme vitória da tua alegria
> e da tua consciência
>
>> O ió kalunga va mu bangele!
>> O ió kalunga va mu bangele-lé-lelé. . .
>
> Lembras te?
>
> E escrevo versos que não entendes
> compreehendes a minha angústia?
>
> Mas no espirito e na inteligencia
> nós somos!
>
> Nós somos
> Mussunda amigo
> Nós somos[7]

> With you
> with the firm victory of your happiness
> and your conscience
>
>> O ió kalunga va mu bangele!
>> O ió kalunga va mu bangele-lé-lelé . . .
>
> Do you remember?
>
> And I write verses you don't understand
> Do you understand my anguish?
>
> But in spirit and comprehension
> We are one!
>
> We are one
> Mussunda my friend
> We are one

Although Mussunda did not go to school and therefore cannot read
the poems of Agostinho Neto, in his spirit and in his thinking, he too

shares the vision of a better day. The Kimbundu phrase was spoken by Mussunda who recognized in his friend a potential leader or guide of the Angolan people. The first of the two lines is best translated "And you were created by destiny." The second line echoes the first but suggests that Neto's ideas of liberty and justice, which he voiced as a boy in conversation with Mussunda, are rooted in a distant past, the "lé-lelé" at the end of this line indicates a past more remote than the simple past tense of the first line. "Kalunga" has several meanings in Kimbundu—sea, death, or destiny; each one possesses the quality of being endless. "Kalunga" is frequently negative, but in "Mussunda Amigo" it is an affirmative destiny, ineluctable as death or the sea, a destiny of freedom and peace.

That "Kalunga" can also be destructive and cruel is apparent in Neto's short story "Nausea," which was first published in *Mensagem* in 1952 and later included in Fernando Mourão's anthology *Contistas Angolanos.* In this sad tale, velho João, the youngest son of a fisherman, who rejected his father's profession in order to gain more money hauling sacks for the white man in Luanda, comes to regret the choice he made. While visiting his sick brother on an island near Luanda, velho João escapes the stifling heat of his cubata in Samba Kimôngua where he lives in the suburbs. The clean air, the soft sand and the smell of the ocean bring him a sense of peace that he has not had in a long time. After a good lunch, he strolls along the shore with his young nephew.

The sea is kalunga, the sea is death. The endless sea with monstrous sharks that devour man has brought misery to many fishermen. The sea took his grandfather to another continent; the sea took the life of his cousin Xico who died when his canoe overturned and he drowned. But if the sea is kalunga, so also is it life for the African in Luanda:

> O trabalho escravo é kalunga . . . kalunga é a fatalidade . . .
> Trouxe o automovel o jornal a estrada. . . . A civilizacão
> ficou embora ao pé da praia, a viver com kalunga. E kalunga
> não conhece os homens. Não sabe que o povo sofre. So sabé
> fazer sofrer.[8]

> Slavish work is kalunga . . . kalunga is fate. It brought the
> automobile, the newspaper and roads . . . Civilization re-
> mained at the foot of the beach to live with kalunga. And ka-
> lunga doesn't know men. It doesn't know that people suffer.
> It only causes suffering.

The lures of urban life created by the Portuguese are like the lures of the sea. Beneath an attractive surface there is only inevitable suffering.

The happy mood of velho João vanishes. He feels nauseous. Looking away from the sea at the tidy asphalt road leading to the city, he vomits his lunch. His nephew helps him return to the house and thinks that his uncle has, like other old men he knows, drunk too much. The nephew does not understand the significance of "O mar. Mu'alunga!" When velho João spoke these words aloud, the boy silently listened, waiting for an explanation and when it did not come, he paid no attention to the utterings of the old man. How could he have known what life was like before Luanda had grown into a metropolis? How could he have known the disappointment that kalunga brought to velho João?

The fate of velho João cannot be changed, but the future of his nephew will not be so degrading. A new day is dawning. It is expressed in the tormenting rhythm of the tom-tom that beats out a clear message:

> Ninguém nós fará calar
> Ninguém nos poderá impedir
>
> Vamos com toda a Humanidade
> conquistar o nosso mundo e a nossa Paz.[9]

> No one will silence us
> No one can impede us
>
> We are going with all humanity
> to conquer our world and our peace.

These lines from "A reconquista" (The Reconquest) announce a renunciation of an African past that has been ravaged and raped by facades of democracy and Christian equality; they announce a victory over poverty that causes prostitution, over the intimidating weapons of the white colonialist, over a past in which everything traditionally African was denigrated.

A new day is suggested through images of flowers and fruit, springtime and birth. The rosebud that remained unopened in "Quitandeira" blossoms in "Mãos esculturais" (Sculptured Hands) and in "Um bouquet de rosas para ti" (A Bouquet of Roses for You). The roses are sweetness and freshness, happiness and friendship, strength and sureness, but most of all, life:

> Um bouquet de rosas para ti
> —rosas vermelhas brancas
> amarelas azuis—
> rosas para o teu dia
> e Vida! para o teu dia[10]

A bouquet of roses for you
—roses of red, white
yellow blue—
roses for your day
and Life! for your day

After a pan-African conference in Bamako, Mali, in 1954, Neto writes:

Bamako!
ali nasce a vida

Bamako!
fruto vivo da África
de futuro germinando nas artérias vivas de África

Ali a esperança se tournou arvore
e rio e fera e terra
ali a esperança se vitoria amizade
na elegância da palmeira e na pele negra dos homens[11]

Bamako!
there life is born

Bamako!
future fruit of Africa
of a future germinating in the live arteries of Africa

There hope was transformed into a tree
and river and heart and land
there hope applauds friendship
in the elegance of the palm tree and in the black skin of men

A new Angola, an Africa reborn cannot find inspiration in Europe; it must above all look to Africa's past, to Africa's traditions, to Africa's values to create a vigorous African future. Western civilization did not bring enlightenment but only slavery and misery. In "O verde das palmeiras da minha mocidade" (The Green of the Palm Trees of My Youth) Neto recalls his own childhood; the Cuanza river flows through his mind; he thinks of marvelous prophecies of the sorcerers and of objects transformed into gods. Images of mysterious secret sects and oral stories recounted around a fire dance before him. And then he remembers how he left this Africa to discover a world his friend Mussunda would never know, the world of Europe, of Beethoven. The alienated Neto seeks to return to the world he left when he came to Luanda. This feeling is best expressed in the stirring poem "Havemos de voltar" (We Must Return):

Às cases, às nossas lavras
às praias, aos nossos campos
havemos de voltar

Às nossas terras
vermelhas do café
brancas do algodão
verdes dos milharais
havemos de voltar

Às nossas minas de diamantes
ouro, cobre, de petróleo
havemos de voltar

Aos nossos rios, nossos lagos
às montanhas, às florestas
havemos de voltar

À frescura da mulemba
às nossas tradições
aos ritmos e às fogueiras
havemos de voltar

À marimba e ao quissange
ao nosso carnaval
havemos de voltar

à bela pátria angolana
nossa terra, nossa mãe
havemos de voltar

Havemos de voltar
À Angola libertada
Angola independente[12]

To the homes, to our tillage
to the beaches, to our fields
we must return

To our lands
red with coffee
white with cotton
green with maize fields
we must return

To our wealth of diamonds
gold, copper, petroleum
we must return

To our rivers, our lakes,
to our mountains, to our forests
we must return

To the coolness of the mulemba
to our traditions
to the rhythms and to the fires
we must return

To the marimba and to the quissange
to our carnival
we must return

To the beautiful Angolan homeland
our land, our mother
we must return

We must return
to Angola liberated
to Angola independent

This poem was written in Aljube prison in October of 1960. At that time many African countries colonized by the British and French were achieving independence. But the Portuguese were unwilling to give up their hold on Lusophone Africa. Neto can no longer be satisfied to speak merely of love and harmony and brotherhood; no longer can he think in terms of an undefined future. Dignity demands full political independence as quickly as possible. The hoisting of an Angolan flag, victory in the struggle that has gone on for five centuries, must be achieved.

The poems written in 1960 are poems of combat. The poet speaks of the impending battle. A sense of impatience and agitation is present. In "Depressa" (Immediately) Neto rejects one biblical posture—the turning of the other cheek—in favor of another—an eye for an eye, a tooth for a tooth!

e vindimem folhagens e frutos,
para derramar a seiva e os sucos sobre a terra húmida
e esborrache o inimigo sobre a terra pura
para que a maldade das suas vísceras
fique para sempre aí plantada
como monumentos eternos dos monstros
a serem escarnecidos e emaldicoados por gerações
pelo povo martirizado durante cinco séculos.[13]

and gather grapes, leaves and fruit
to scatter the sap and juices over the moist earth

and squash the enemy over the pure earth
so that his inner evil
may remain forever fixed there
like eternal monuments of monsters
to be scorned and cursed for generations
by the people made martyrs for five centuries.

Angolan heroes of earlier ages who fought the Portuguese are praised for their courage which is shared by those descendants who will not fear death, for individual death is but a path to new freedom for Angola. Ngola Kiluanji and Rainha Ginga, Kimbundu Legendary figures, stand side by side with the people who may be named Benge, Joaquim, Gaspar, Ilídio or Manuel. Wave upon wave will stand up against the enemy, for the land and the people together cry out—"Independência!"

"A Voz Iqual" (Equal Voice), the last poem in *Sagrada Esperança*, synthesizes the themes of Neto's poetry. The black man who built Western empires in Africa, the laborers who were sacrificed so Europe could plunder Africa's coffee, diamonds, oil—these men were given nothing in return except ingratitude and cruelty. Africa, which gave its rhythms to America and its bodies to the international athletic community, rejects a past in which Europe was glorified and Africa was debased. With independence a future of dignity and pride is to be created, nourished by the roots in the ancestral humus of Africa. A return to Africa's past is the best way to purify the continent of alien cultures and to reconstruct a modern African society. There will be a collective sharing of joys and sorrows, for workers will work side by side in the fields for the benefit of the entire community. Africa will take her place as an equal in the modern world. She will contribute her energies to create a harmonious world in which brotherhood among men becomes a reality.

The battle will be hard, but there will be no tears. With determination and a new found confidence the Angolan people will create their destiny. Like his first poem, Neto's final poem is a departure. From 1961 to 1976 he has been a military and political leader guiding the M.P.L.A. in the long and difficult battle for independence. The military successes of the guerrilla fighters in Angola as well as in Mozambique finally were rewarded. The Portuguese military, tired of a war they could not win and unwilling to continue fighting so a few wealthy people within Portugal could profit, revolted and on 25 April, 1974, the revolution suddenly overthrew the fascist Caetano government in Lisbon. On October 1, 1974, General Costa Gomes, the President of the Republic, declared that he would personally direct negotiations leading to the decolonization and independence of Angola. On November 11, 1975, Angola became an independent nation. And once again, there is another beginning for Angola.

The language of Neto's poetry is nearly always simple and direct. It is seldom colloquial, in contrast to the popular poetry of Jacinto. Occasional Kimbundu words and expressions do serve to create an African ambiance not merely in subject matter but in spirit as well. A call for courage in Kimbundu

> Xi ietu manu
> kolokota
> kizuua a ndo tu bomba
> kolokotenu[14]

> Our land
> courage
> a day will come in which
> the enemy will have
> to ask pardon of us

is a particularly African appeal. But Neto does not write in Kimbundu for several reasons. He himself is much more competent in Portuguese and those Angolans who can read are much more likely to know Portuguese than Kimbundu.

In his imagery, sparse as it is, Neto brings to his poems the people, landscape, trees and animals of different parts of Angola. Life in the musseques is recreated as well as life in the countryside. Those in the kinaxixi (public market place in Luanda), the women of Lunda, the Bailundos (an Umbundu people of the South around Sá da Bandeira), and the Kiocos (a vibrant people in the Northeast section of Angola famous for its diamonds) are brothers in the struggle. The umbundeiro trees, the valleys, the giboía (a cobra), the virgin forests of Maiombe— this is the Angola that Neto loves. Nevertheless, the poet cannot completely suppress that part of him that has been westernized. When Neto writes of the glorious struggle of the people which produces music in his soul, he entitles the poem "Sinfonia." An unconscious betrayal perhaps, but certainly African music could have provided a more appropriate title. He goes to Europe for an image in "Assim clamava esgotado" (Thus They Cry Out Exhausted) comparing African innocence drowned in slavery to Shakespeare's Ophelia, a victim not only of her innocence but her own betrayal of Hamlet. Such imagery does not seem appropriate, for few of Neto's Angolan readers would even know the sad story of Polonius' daughter.

The short lines of the early poems are replaced by much longer lines in some of the later poems, for in these Neto uses many more adjectives and adjectival phrases. Nevertheless, in nearly all his poems the rhythm is created by repetition of word or phrase. Like a drum beating out a message, the repetitious pattern of the sounds of the words gives the poem an internal unity of form. In "Havemos de voltar", the series of prepositional phrases beginning each stanza with "to the", accompanied by the beat of "havemos de voltar" at the end of the stanzas, creates a sense of urgency and discipline.

At times Neto can be lyrical, especially when he speaks of his beloved:

> Sonharei
> sonharei com os olhos do amor
> encarnados nas tuas maravilhosas mãos
> de suavidad e ternura.
> Sonharei com aqueles dias de que falavas
> quando te referias à Primavera:
> Sonharei contigo
> e com a prazer de beber gotas de orvalho
> na relva
> deitado au teu lado,
> ao sol-uma praia furiosa lá ao longe.[15]

> I will dream
> I will dream of your loving eyes
> incarnated in your marvelous hands
> of sweetness and gentleness.
> I will dream of those days in which you spoke
> when you thought of Springtime;
> I will dream of you
> and of the pleasure of drinking dewdrops
> in the grass
> lying at your side,
> in the sun—a savage coast there in the distance.

But Agostinho Neto does not often write of an individual love—that is a luxury; he writes about his love of his people, of his land and of liberty. And he writes primarily for his people. Unlike the Francophone Négritude poets whose voices were heard more in Europe than in Africa, men like Neto, Costa Andrade, and António Jacinto brought their words to their own market place where the Angolan people came to know them. Many of Neto's poems have been put to music by soldiers who would sing these hymns of Africa. Poems such as "Havemos de Voltar" and "Criar" (Create) are particularly well known. Ruy Mingas, among others, put out a record of Neto's poems and his songs can be heard in the streets of Luanda today, for in Neto's words the dreams of Angola are expressed.

Footnotes

1. I know of one Neto poem, "Fogo e Ritmo" (Fire and Rhythm), that is not contained in *Sagrada Esperança;* probably there are others.

2. Agostinho Neto, *Sagrada Esperança* (Lisbon, Livraria Sá da Costa Editora, 1974), p. 37.

3. *Ibid.*, p. 56.

4. *Ibid.*, pp. 49-50.

5. *Ibid.*, p. 53.

6. *Ibid.*, p. 35.

7. *Ibid.*, pp. 79-80.

8. Agostinho Neto, "Nausea" in Fernando Mourão, *Contistas Angolanos* (Lisbon, Casa dos Estudantes do Império, 1960), pp. 57-58.

9. *Sagrada Esperança*, p. 85.

10. *Ibid.*, p. 110.

11. *Ibid.*, pp. 92-93.

12. *Ibid.*, pp. 127-128.

13. *Ibid.*, p. 124.

14. *Ibid.*, p. 114.

15. *Ibid.*, p. 99.

Luis Bernardo Honwana

Mozambique's Modern Literature

Rui de Noronha, who died in 1943 at the age of thirty-four, left a collection of poetry called *Sonetos* (Sonnets), which was published posthumously in 1949 and apparently was considerably revised by the editors.This *mestiço* poet borrowed from a European tradition of Parnassian-like verse, and within the fixed metrics of his poetry he occasionally rose to heights of exhortation. This is exemplified in "Surge et ambula" (Arise and Walk), one of his most frequently quoted and anthologized sonnets in which he calls on supine and somnolent Africa to stand up and march shoulder to shoulder with the rest of the worlds. The Mozambican critic Eugênio Lisboa has written that Noronha is "a more or less mediocre poet, not because he is not very representative of a specifically African set of problems, but very simply because his poetry, as poetry, is little more than mediocre."[1] Lisboa is right on both counts, and more will be said presently on poetry as poetry, but the fact that Noronha did use an African thematic, of sorts, makes him historically important in the context of Mozambican literature.

It would be redundant, however, to evaluate Noronha's poetry, since technically and thematically it differs little from much of what can be considered representative of Angolan poets. His poem "Quenquelequeze" (a Ronga salute to the moon) has the same contrived exoticism found in many of Bessa Victor's pieces, to draw but one comparison. Bessa Victor achieved much of his exotic effect with Kimbundu words, while Noronha depended on the Ronga language for the same effect.

Similarly, João Dias, the black author of one book, *Godido e outros contos* (Godido and Other Stories, 1952), while of some historical significance in the development of Mozambican literature, exhibits the same technical defects as those of some Angolan writers. During his short life (1926-49) he experienced the frustrations of the black man in a hostile, white society. His stories contain a note of bitterness that will be observed as an important factor in the writings of several authors from the islands of São Tomé and Príncipe. In an autobiographical piece entitled "Em terras do norte" (In Lands of the North), the black protagonist disembarks from a train in rural Portugal to face the curiosity, derision, and even the animosity of the local villagers. He ruminates about the repulsion whites feel toward his color and then considers that when Portuguese mariners first reached Africa they reacted to the people's color with such envy that as a defense they assigned the negative label of black to the skin hue they in reality admired. The narrator then says, "Today, nobody seems to notice that our color is not black. 'Coal is black' the offended children of my neighborhood used to retort."[2] In the turgid prose of his essayistic stories Dias reveals a bitterness and sarcasm that reflect the hypersensitivity of a black Mozambican reared in a society where racism has generally lacked the veiled subtleties of São Tomé and Angola.

Dias's stories, like Rui de Noronha's sonnets, represent early manifestations of the types of tensions that would continue during the more recent decades in Mozambique. Although many parallels exist between Mozambique and the other regions of Portuguese Africa, Mozambique also offers a uniqueness of literary expression, both in the works of individual authors and in its polemical aspects.

Mozambique's Regional Consciousness

The move toward a regional, literary consciousness in Mozambique gained impetus in the early 1950s. One indication of a new literary and cultural awareness came in the form of a few pages of poetry published in 1952 under the title *Msaho* (a type of song of the Chope people); then in August 1957 appeared, in the Mozambican city of Beira, the first issue of a monthly magazine called *Paralelo 20* (the twentieth parallel passes very close to Beira) which was to continue until February 1961. These coordinated efforts by Mozambicans themselves signaled the beginning of a sometimes soul-searching consideration of the province's cultural autonomy. To *Msaho* eight poets each contributed one to three poems. Some of the contributors can be identified as genuine poets while others are first and foremost members of a generation which saw poetry as a valid means of participating in a heightened cultural and artistic awakening. Thus, *Msaho* can be said to have at least a symbolic importance.

From 1959 to 1963 the Casa dos Estudantes do Império published poetry anthologies from three regions of Portuguese Africa, including *Poetas de Moçambique* (Poets of Mozambique, 1962), which consists of poems published previously in such newspapers as *O Brado Africano, A Voz de Moçambique,* and *A Tribuna.* The anthology brings together samplings of the works of twenty-six poets; it also includes some traditional Chope songs as proof of the same interest in an African oral tradition displayed by the Angolans in *Poetas angolanos.*

Along with the anthologizing of poetry came, in *Paralelo 20* and in a special supplement of the Angolan journal *Mensagem,* articles and appraisals of the literary phenomenon in Mozambique. But it was Alfredo Margarido who set off a significant, and somewhat bizarre, debate with his appraisal of poetry in Mozambique.

Polemics and the Question of Poetry in Mozambique

Alfredo Margarido, who has written on all areas of Afro-Portuguese literature, applied, in his introduction to *Poetas de Mozambique,* a modified Marxist approach to Mozambican poetry. Among his several declarations is the assertion that "we therefore should enunciate some problems linked to Mozambique's socio-economic structure, because this poetry must have as its primary objective a didactic function, and in order to accomplish this end it has to structure and radicalize the needs of the masses so as to reveal, with its basis in these very elements, the essentially historical objectives toward which the social current flows."[3] Such statements could not help but elicit a reaction from those members of the Mozambican cultural and literary elite who considered poetry as an end in itself.

The white Mozambican poet Rui Knopfli issued a mild protest, without mentioning Margarido by name, in the arts and letters section of *A Tribuna,* a Lourenço Marques newspaper. Margarido in turn replied to Knopfli in the April 1963 issue of *Mensagem,* a journal published in Lisbon by the Casa dos Estudantes do Império and named after the then defunct Angolan cultural and literary review. To Margarido's sarcastic article, entitled "A poesia Moçambicana e os críticos de óculos" (Mozambican Poetry and the Bespectacled Critics), Knopfli responded with the first installment of a three-part essay published in *A Voz de Moçambique.* He made these major points: (1) too much importance has been given to the incipient phenomenon of Mozambican poetry; (2) anthologies and certain critics have limited themselves to problems concerning only the black man; (3) poetry anywhere is a specific aesthetic phenomenon and should be treated as such; (4) Mozambican poetry can only be defined in all its diversity as suggested in item two; (5) all other considerations, speculative or not, have to be approached and developed around the basic themes outlined in these points.[4] "A small oracle of Mozambican culture," Margarido termed Knopfli in "do poeta Knopfli à cultura mocambicana" (From the Poet Knopfli to Mozambican Culture), published in the June 1963 issue of *Mensagem*.

The debate was rapidly reaching the level of derisive comments and ad hominem attacks as Margarido and Knopfli assailed one another. Margarido, in a short note entitled "Outra vez o poeta" (Once Again, the Poet), defended the ranking of poets according to their importance as representatives of the praxis of black Mozambique. "Praxis," used in its Marxist sense, appears several times in Margarido's writings, and Knopfli makes it a point to ridicule him for his insistence on the word. Knopfli indeed has the last say in the controversy with his article "Ainda o diletante Alfredo Margarido" (Still the Dilettante, Alfredo Margarido), which appeared in *A Tribuna*. From the standpoint of wit and a compelling argument Knopfli emerged the victor in the protracted debate. Still, the major question remains unresolved: what can be considered Mozambican poetry, and who should be considered a poet of Mozambique? Knopfli himself admits to having engaged José Craveirinha, a fellow poet, in friendly debate on the matter, and, of course, the two differed on whom they would include in the category of poet of Mozambique.

Before attempting to reach some conclusion on the question of poetry in and of Mozambique, we must discuss another participant in the debate. Eugênio Lisboa, a perceptive and provocative critic, has contributed several articles on the subject of poetry in Mozambique. One such article is the preface to Rui Knopfli's 1969 collection of poetry *Mangas verdes com sal* (Green Mangoes with Salt). Lisboa supports and supplements Knopfli's main points on the subject with the contention that poetry is its own reality, its own universe. Like Knopfli, Lisboa quotes some European theorists to defend his basic thesis, but his most significant reference is to the Mexican poet Octavio Paz. In his book *El arco y la lira* (The Bow and the Lyre) Paz defines poetry, in very poetic prose, as multifaceted, involving many things that have to do with human experience. Poetry, he writes, is the "voice of the people," and Lisboa follows this up with the comment "voice of the people, collective voice—some beautiful poems by Craveirinha would fit this, also (if her language were up to it) would some of Noémia de Sousa's poems fit this. . . ."[5] Lisboa categorizes other Mozambican poets on the basis of Paz's definition: Knopfli, for example, belongs to the group of those who speak the "language of the elect."

In a later article, "A poesia em Moçambique" (Poetry in Mozambique), Lisboa states that poets such as Noémia de Sousa were "invented," meaning that her rhetoric and subject matter have given her a prestige out of proportion to her talent as a poet. (More will be said about Noémia de Sousa's poetry later.) But although Lisboa and Knopfli stand firm on what constitutes the language of poetry, they exhibit a frustration and impatience that occasionally result in flippancy when they attempt to demystify the literary situation in Mozambique. Lisboa wrote, for example, that "an infinite number of cartridges has been fired in Byzantine distortions: José Craveirinha is a Mozambican poet, Reinaldo Ferreira is a European poet, Rui Knopfli is a complicated mixture of the two. . . Rui Noronha is black in color but white in his sonnets, Fernando Ganhão is white of skin but black of content, Rui Nogar is somewhere in between."[6] Of course, all are poets born in Mozambique. Under the pretext of denying rigid classifications of poetry, Lisboa implies that categorization based on an African thematic or lack of it has no validity, although he himself talks about the "voice of the people" and the "language of the elect" as separate groupings. It seems even more likely and necessary to make these distinctions for an incipient poetic expression (good, bad, and indifferent) than for an established literature, and even more so in Mozambique where social and racial factors confuse and complicate the cultural scene. Angolans have wrestled with the problem of poetry of and in Angola, and in Mozambique the problem has been aggravated by the absence of a viable black and mestiço bourgeois elite. A relatively small group of white Mozambicans, led by Knopfli and Lisboa, has grappled with the philosophical and aesthetic questions inherent in the phenomenon of literary expression and culture, and in doing so their own exasperations have occasionally obscured some of the basic issues that by necessity relate the poetry of Mozambique to the social conditions there. Margarido erred mainly be relegating poetry to a position subordinate to its artistic value, and he left himself open to the censure of those who understand that form cannot be divorced from content.

There are many kinds of poetry, as the critic David Caute points out in his introduction to the English translation of Jean-Paul Sartre's *Qu'est ce que c'est la littérature?* (What is Literature: 1967). He takes issue with Sartre on some fundamental points concerning poetry:

> Prose, he [Sartre] argues, is capable of a purposeful reflection of the world, whereas poetry is an end in itself. In prose, words are significative; they describe men and objects. In poetry, the words are ends in themselves. It is doubtful whether Sartre's radical distinction is a tenable one. Many kinds of poetry exist, ranging from the communicative and discursive (as in 18th-century England) to the most "poetic" and symbolist (as with Rimbaud and Mallarmé). Although criticism of a poem must pay close attention to its immanent structure of words and symbols, it is obvious that the reader enters the poem through word associations and references which are linked, however indirectly, to everyday significative language.[7]

Lisboa indicates, in his enthusiasm for Octavio Paz's openended, inclusive description of poetry, that he too accepts the fact that there are many kinds of poetry. As was already mentioned, Knopfli maintains that poetry in Mozambique should be seen in all its diversity and not just in the assemblage of problems relating to the black man. The trouble is that even though Mozambique may also be the 150,000 or so whites who run the province, it is still valid to approach the question of Mozambican poetry from the standpoint of a literature of Portuguese expression that makes use of an African thematic. This approach will naturally exclude some of the more purely European poets, but it will include others who, often indirectly, enhance and give form to the phenomenon. Likewise, those black, white, and mestiço poets who sing, often discursively and even artlessly, of an African Mozambique deserve inclusion in the framework of a literature of Portuguese expression. Universal tenets and the primal cry of poetry notwithstanding, good, even excellent, poets such as Alberto de Lacerda and Reinaldo Ferreira warrant less attention than does, say, a lesser poet such as Noémia de Sousa. And, it is not so much that too much attention has been paid to Mozambican poetry, but rather that the individual poet, representative of this incipient movement, has been projected into a position of importance he does not fully deserve as an artist.

The black and mestiço poets who write from or within a black psychology and who assume a committed or militant stance constitute a category—obviously of significance to anyone interested in an African literature of Portuguese expression in Mozambique. White poets who attempt to write from an African perspective or who display a committed sense of regionalism form another group that can be further broken down into subdivisions, such as those who merely exteriorize and those who identify. If a poetry *of* Mozambique means everything, then those who consciously write from a European perspective, and who, for want of a better designation, are called Euro-Africans, play a role in our consideration only insofar as they take part in the two categories just identified. So, expanding on the allusion to Alberto de Lacerda and Reinaldo Ferreira, it can be said that they are poets who write almost exclusively within a European tradition and should therefore be viewed in the context of contemporary Portuguese poetry; on the other hand, that element in their poetry which reflects any discernible aspect of a Mozambican reality, even an acculturated or Europeanized one, does deserve passing commentary in this study. To contemplate briefly how the varied Mozambican reality affects a Euro-African writer, we might mention one white Mozambican critic's contention that the poet Rui Knopfli is presently going through an identity crisis. Presumbably, then, Knopfli does have ambivalent feelings toward the question of poetry *in* and of Mozambique. And Eugénio Lisboa is no less ambivalent than Knopfli when he implicitly rejects the idea that Knopfli is a mixture of the European and the African, if by mixture is meant a sensitivity to his place in the mainstream of European poetry and his conscious relationship to non-European thematic elements as represented in his art. Indeed, Knopfli has shown that he can be sensitive to the black reality around him even if he neither fully comprehends nor completely accepts it.

Northrup Frye has written that "in literature man *is* a spectator of his own life, or at least of the larger vision in which his life is contained."[8] This larger vision includes not only the universal but also the microcosmic immediacy of a regional experience. In the case of the Mozambican poet who aspires to capture the essence of the word, extraliterary factors conspire frequently to lend an artistic tension to his work. Subliminally or otherwise, some white Mozambican poets are aware of the so-called African praxis, and this awareness contributes to this tension in form and content. A white Mozambican intellectual has said that for some of his group there remains one of two alternatives: either to paint themselves black or to join the ranks of those in power, the latter being the ultraconservative wing that currently controls the destiny of the province. In its flippancy this remark neatly sums up the dilemma of the white intellectual who, while ideologically and philosophically opposed to the political and social status quo in Mozambique, does not see himself as expendable in any radical alternative. Such a situation may be at hand with the change of government in Portugal. For the time being, however, only the literary scene as it appears before April 1974 can be assessed.

No less ambivalent than his Euro-African colleagues, the *mestiço* poet José Craveirinha commands the respect and admiration of those who uphold the idea of poetry for poetry's sake. Craveirinha pays for this acceptance in that he must always be the protégé. The "clever black lad" has become a negative catch phrase for the paternalism of the colonialist mentality which is played out in the patronage of promising writers or artists by white intellectuals. Certainly, in the practical sense, the good offices of a white elite have afforded some blacks and *mestiços* an opportunity that the general racist structure of Mozambican society would ordinarily deny them. But the lack of a certain self-determination has the disadvantage of a kind of vassalage which means that when the non-white becomes more than just a clever black lad he represents a threat to the white fief. The painter Malangatana, the poet Craveirinha, and the short story writer Luís Bernardo Honwana have been at once the victims and the beneficiaries of this set of circumstances. Craveirinha has reacted with a certain bitterness to the offhanded racism of some of his colleague-protectors, and maybe his hypersensitivity makes him resent such relatively minor, but sociologically significant, incidents as the casual remark of a white friend that he had sent the "black" to get his suit from the cleaners; the black being the houseboy *(moleque)*. On the other hand, Craveirinha reacts to what is inherent in such otherwise innocent comments; he reacts to the fact that the black masses on the periphery of the white city have been depersonalized, even when they perform their function as domestics in the homes of Europeans.

Even more significantly, Craveirinha rejects the inclusion of a host of poets in the category of poets of Mozambique. And this brings us back to the basic dilemma of poets *in* and *of* Mozambique. Both sides of the issue present problems: to deal with only those poets who reflect an African thematic is to reduce the field to a very few, while to include those who display a strictly Western viewpoint is to blur the picture of an Afro-Portuguese literary phenomenon in Mozambique. The literary climate is confused and amorphous, but certain patterns have evolved to the point where some semblance of a direction can be seen.

Russell Hamilton

Footnotes

[1]Lisboa, "A poesia em Moçambique," p. 13.

[2]João Dias, *Godido* (Lisbon: Africa Nova, Edições da Secção de Moçambique da Casa dos Estudantes do Império, 1952), p. 97.

[3]Alfredo Margarido, ed., *Poetas de Moçambique* (Lisbon: Casa dos Estudantes do Império, 1962), p. 5.

[4]Rui Knopfli, "Considerações sobre a crítica dos poetas de Moçambique," *A Voz de Mozambique,* 15 June 1963.

[5]Eugênio Lisboa, preface to Rui Knopfli, *Mangas verdes com sal* (Lorenço Marques: Publicações Europa-América, 1969), p. 12.

[6]"A poesia em Moçambique," p. 13.

[7]David Caute, introduction to Jean-Paul Sartre, *What is Literature?* trans. Bernard Frechtman (London: Methuen, 1967), pp. vii-viii.

[8]Northrop Frye, *The Critical Path* (Bloomington: Indiana University Press, 1971), p. 129.

MOZAMBICAN LITERATURE:
CONTEMPORARY TRENDS AND PROSPECTS

Mozambique's combative literature parallels Angola's in that during the mid- and late-sixties a small number of militant poets wrote verse while in exile. However, no poet of the caliber of the Angolan Agostinho Neto has contributed to this phase of Mozambican literature. Mário de Andrade's anthology includes under the general heading of "War," selections by the Mozambican poets Sérgio Vieira, Armando Guebuza, and Jorge Rebelo. All three are members of the independence party FRELIMO. Vieira's "Tríptico para estado de guerra" (Triptych for a State of War) documents the cruelties of combat. Slogans are dispersed throughout his poem, such as the one at the end of the final stanza: "Frelimo e Moçambique/ Para que em povo viva/ e estado de guerra morra"[1]) FRELIMO and Mozambique/ So that a people might live/ and a state of war might die). As the title indicates, the poem is divided into three parts, and perhaps the poet means to suggest that the book of war should be closed just as the triptych tablets may be folded shut. Despite this "artistic" touch Vieira's poem has little to recommend it either aesthetically or as a combative poem. Guebuza's "As tuas dores" (Your Sorrows) has a better overall sense of technique but even more exhortative rhetoric than Vieira's verse, and Rebelo's "Poema de um militante" (Militant's Poem) gives just a hint of the aesthetic didacticism sometimes well developed in guerrilla theater.

Whatever our sympathies may be for the cause represented by Mozambican combative poetry, we must turn to that literature still being written and/or published in Mozambique for any cogent assessment of the future of that phenomenon. Writers such as Luís Bernardo Honwana, José Craveirinha, and Rui Nogar served prison terms as political dissenters; upon release they followed separate and necessarily cautious paths in their literary and cultural activities. Honwana presently studies law at the University of Lisbon, but he also plans to revise his *Nós matamos o cão tinhoso* and perhaps to publish a second book of stories. As mentioned previously, Craveirinha and Nogar continue to live in Lourenço Marques where they write and publish an occasional poem. More will be said shortly on the participation of both poets, particularly Craveirinha, in the recent literary effort.

The bizarre arrest and trial of Duarte Galvão (pseudonym of Virgílio de Lemos), because he wrote a poem which allegedly insulted the Portuguese flag and was therefore subversive, stand as proof of the sensitivity that attended the cultural and literary scene in Mozambique during the mid-sixties. Galvão's *Poemas do tempo presente* (Poems of the Present, 1960) includes "Poema à cidade" (Poem to the City) which he wrote in 1954. One reference in the poem irked the zealous authorities: "bayete bayete bayete/ à capulana vermelha e verde"[2] (*bayete bayete bayete/* to the red and green *capulana*). *Bayete* is a Ronga phrase equivalent to "long live!" and *capulana* is the long flowing robe worn by many African women in Mozambique. Red and green are colors of the Portuguese national flag, but during the trial it was pointed to the prosecution that colors also have a symbolic significance for the Ronga people.

Although Duarte was acquitted, the incident, besides its political implications, speaks to the problem of how ignorant many white Mozambicans are of African culture. But in the midst of this racist reality and during the period of relative calm that settled over the

PALAVRA DE ORDEM

Nesta terra batida por gerações
As cinzas vão no vento baixo
E são galinhas e são cabritos e são meninos
A ser o quase pouco mais que fumo de sombras
Só terra batida cinzas e vento
E na borda os camaradas olhando para dentro de si.

. . . .

Não vos soube explicar camaradas que estava orgulhoso:
Enquanto os paus de Missanha ficarem de pé
Está tudo de pé no nosso País
Porque este inimigo não conhece o seu inimigo
Tornou-se inimigo do capim porque arde depressa
Mas não sabe que este seu inimigo a mentir nasce depressa
E nem imagina quanto principalmente importante
É os paus de Missanha que estão de pé.

Um inimigo que não conhece o seu inimigo
É o seu próprio inimigo e deixa-me perplexo.
Palavra de Ordem: Ninguém vai explicar da Missanha a Kaulsa.

OPERAÇÃO DA GUERRA DE LIBERTAÇÃO

Esta árvore amiga é o inimigo
Destroncar esta árvore é uma operação contra o inimigo.

Escolhemos um inimigo, inimigo, à medida da nossa grandeza
Um inimigo do tamanho da nossa tarefa
Que vai dar muita chatice a cair, e táctica e estratégia
E vai servir derrubado melhor que em pé
Pois se que esta terra é boa para uma árvore tão alta
Há-de ser muito boa para dar machamba.

Vai ser ataque de serrote ou machada ou enxada na raiz?
Vai cair para o lado do vento?
Vai ser de cinto de fogo ou trotil mesmo?
Vai ser com as mãos fazendo força, camaradas?

Onde há uma árvore maior que a força do Povo?

Se vier o velho, a mulher, o menino, todos um e um e um
Riscar com a unha do dedo pequeno, lamber com a língua
Nove milhões de pequenas carícias e pouca força
Esta árvore cai mesmo.

Por onde passa o Exército de Libertação
Fica um rasto verde e cheiroso e o caminho aberto
Para passar a Liberdade e o Futuro.

É fácil ver quem passou aqui.

Two poems from *Eu o Povo: Poemas da Revolução* (Moçambique, 1975) literary and cultural world of Mozambique in the late sixties and early seventies, some scattered, but significant occurrences of a cultural, literary, and scholarly nature have given at least a hint of continuing activity. Newspapers such as *A Voz de Moçambique* and *O Cooperador* have continued to carry news of local cultural happenings. In 1971 *A Voz de Moçambique* reported on a unique event that caught the imagination of the intellectual and literary community: Lindo Hlongo, a young black man, had written a play which a Portuguese, Norberto Barroca, produced and directed in Lourenço Marques.

The play, *Os noivos ou conferência dramática sobre o lobolo* (The Newlyweds or a Dramatic Consultation on the Lobolo), treats a subject of cultural and economic importance to the African population. Similar to the *alembamento* in Angola, the *lobolo* is the practice whereby the groom compensates his father-in-law for marrying his daughter. In modern times hard cash has become the usual tender in such matrimonial transactions, and as a result certain hardships have been forced on the male who must often go to the diamond mines of South Africa to earn the necessary money. Social problems arise from the often long separation of the groom from his bride, and the play treats these questions as part of the general theme stated in the subtitle *A tribo em trânsito* (Tribal Life in Demise).

None of the actors in the productions had had any previous experience, but despite its overall amateurishness the play succeeded in conveying a message aesthetically clothed in social satire and musical folklore and comedy. The very naiveté of the acting frequently achieved a pleasing effect of slapstick and caricature that served to satirize the internal and external forces that had contributed to the general demise of tribal values. But tribute was paid to the tenacity of an African musical culture. Between every scene a traditional or popular dance was performed, and at the play's end the entire cast, including the director, danced the *marrabenta*.

The first performance of *Os noivos* took place on April 28, 1971, in a theater in the downtown area of Lourenço Marques. A note on the event published in *A Voz de Moçambique* makes quite a bit of the heterogeneous composition of the audience, which is considered revolutionary in a city where the races live separate and unequal existences. The writer of the note then thanks the playwright and praises the director who, as an outsider, has done more for theater in Mozambique than any native son. In May 1971 the performance was repeated in an East Indian-owned theater in the African suburb of Xipamanine before a larger black and *mestiço* audience.

The play has dubious importance in the development of theater in Mozambique; as a spectacle and a cultural event it has symbolic significance even though it may not quite herald an African renaissance in Lourenço Marques. Indeed, while there may be evidence of a renewed interest in things African on the part of a segment of the white intelligentsia and a reappraisal of their Africanness by black and *mestico* youth, much of what is expressed in literature is either relegated to the purely ethnological or viewed as purely decorative.

As an example of the decorative, in 1971 the first issue of a small poetry magazine called *Caliban* was organized by J.P. Grabato Dias and Rui Knopfli. The cover features an African mask from the region of Angoche in Mozambique, and on the inside cover is a quotation from Act I, scene 2, of Shakespeare's *The Tempest*. Caliban, the slave, tells Prospero: "You taught me language, and my profit on't/ Is, I know how to curse. The red plague rid you/ For learning me your language! . . . "[3] These lines and others spoken by the two Shakespearean characters are repeated by Janheinz Jahn in his development of theses originally put forth by O. Mannoni 'and George Lamming.[4] Grabato Dias and Knopfli obviously had in mind similar attitudes toward the language of the colonizer, but the contents of their magazine have a very cosmopolitan flavor. Besides a short article by Eugénio Lisboa on T.S. Eliot, there appears a translation of "Ash Wednesday" by Rui Knopfli, plus an anthology of poems by Jorge de Sena, José Craveirinha, Rui Nogar, Sebastião Alba, Jorge Viegas, Grabato Dias, and Knopfli. What for Jahn was a method of solving the aesthetic and stylistic, as well as psychological, problems of an African literature written in a European language has become for the organizers of *Caliban* the broader issue of the tension of poetic language per se. This tension seems to be the one unifying theme in the publication's four issues; but the Mozambicans' awareness of the more sensitive problem of an African awareness and their use of African masks as decorative illustrations constitute a kind of integration that perhaps reflects Knopfli's views on the question of poetry in and of Mozambique, and poetry anywhere for that matter.

A close-up of the facial portion of a *mapico* mask adorns the second issue of *Caliban,* and the cover of the combined third and fourth issue has on it the bulging headlights and the grillwork of an automobile, which the editors entitle "Land Rover Mask." Along with the humor they probably intended to represent traditional Africa and the technological West combined, and the meaning of the title is emphasized in the depiction of the savage Caliban in the grotesque beauty of the masks. The tension of poetic language is seen in the translations of the Polish poet Zbigniew Herbert and the American Marianne Moore, the original poems by a small number of mostly Euro-African poets, and the selection from Lindo Hlongo's play *Os noivos.* Translations, particularly of poetry, always pit one language against another, and in the case of *Caliban* they aid in giving the magazine an audacity under its seemingly sophisticated façade.

Jorge de Sena, one of the better contemporary Portuguese poets, has been a kind of distant mentor of Knopfli and Lisboa. His critical acumen has aided the Mozambicans in their efforts to demystify the literary situation in their province. A reading of Jorge de Sena's contributions to *Caliban* demonstrates to what extent he shows a sensitivity to the cultural signficance of language. Two of his poems in the first issue are in English, and another, in the joint issue, is called "Noções de linguística" (Ideas on Linguistics). De Sena's children, born to the Portuguese language but raised mainly in the United States, now prattle naturally in their adopted English. This observation leads to a reflection on the paradox of language, its durability, and its cultural inheritability:

> As línguas, que duram séculos e mesmo sobrevivem
> esquecidas noutras, morrem todos os dias
> na gaguês daqueles que as herdaram;
> e são tão imortais que meia dúzia de anos
> as suprime da boca dissolvida
> ao peso de outra raça, outra cultura.
> Tão metafísicas, tão intraduzíveis,
> que se derretem assim, não nos altos céus,
> mas na merda quotidiana de outras.[5]

(Languages which last for centuries and even survive/ forgotten in other tongues, die daily/ in the stammering of those who have inherited them;/ and so immortal are they that a few years/ can suppress them from the mouth fragmentized/ under the weight of another people, another culture./ So metaphysical, so untranslatable are they,/ that thus they mollify, not in the heavens on high/ but in the quotidian crap of other tongues.)

The poet speaks with irony of the vulnerability of languages and cultures, and he contrasts the idea of language as a purveyor of philosophical thought and untranslatable sentiments with the idea of insidiousness of an imposed language and culture. This poem relates obliquely, but not remotely, to the problem put forth in the Caliban-Prospero metaphor.

Other poems in *Caliban* relate even less directly to the problem of language and culture, but most selections in some way have a bearing on the magazine's unifying theme of integration and poetic tension. The magazine's co-editor adopts the Latinized name Frey Ioannes Garabatus and writes verse in the style and language of the sixteenth century. A kind of experimentation pervades the magazine, and even Rui Nogar contributes to the spirit of the sound and feel of language in his poem "Do himeneu vocabular" (Of Vocable Hymeneal) in which he says, "Eu amo a frescura das palavras adolescentes/ sinto prazar en desnudá-las/ sílaba a sílaba/ lentamente" (*Caliban* 1, p. 26) (I love the freshness of adolescent words/ I take pleasure in undressing them/ slowly/ syllable by syllable). The poet manipulates his words with sensual pleasure and a feel for their purity.

But it is José Craveirinha who best plays out the conflict of language in a manner which speaks to the problem of an African poetry of European expression. It has been seen how in his earlier poetry Craveirinha achieved an African stylistic through the use of words and rhythmic patterns. In the poems he contributes to *Caliban* he still demonstrates a preference for vivid, surrealistic images, but less of a concern with the ancestral element of an African thematic. Still, the angst and the escape into erotic dreams are characteristics in his phase of Craveirinha's development that present a portrait of the African confined to the European city. The poem "Escape" illustrates this theme:

> Na noite açulada de nervos
> as línguas
> uma na outra furiosas
> húmidas afiam-se os gumes no beijo
> e os ásperos mamilos
> dos teus seios masoquisam-me o peito.
>
> Ah, sonho!
> única maneira
> livre de existir
> enquanto ferozes as manhãs
> no langor das urbes
> sanguíneas florescem nas acácias
> (*Caliban* 1, p. 23)

(In the night incited by nerves/ our tongues/ one furiously on the other/ humidly whet their sharpness in the kiss/ and the rough nipples/ of your breasts rub masochistically against my chest.// Ah, dream!/ only way/ to cease to exist/ while ferociously the mornings/ in the languor of metropolises/ sanguineously blossom in the acacias)

A motif of violence comes out in the erotic, tactile imagery of the first stanza with its metaphor of the knife and the rough texture of the nipples, while in the second stanza the visual imagery dominated by allusions to the color red converts the violent eroticism into a passion of feeling. Awaking from the dream in the crimson light of dawn, the poet identifies this sentiment of escape with the freedom of nature—the crimson acacias—that covers the languid, stultifying city.

If the general cast of *Caliban,* as a cosmopolitan Mozambican magazine, is unilateral integration from a Euro-African point of view, then Craveirinha offers another direction to the multi-faceted litarary scene. White writers may make occasional forays into the black and *mestiço* suburbs and hinterland of Mozambique for the decorative or even for a suggestion of a cultural or psychological truth, but Craveirinha comes from that rural reality to meet the dominant group on equal terms. Symbolically, Craveirinha is Caliban, and his distortions of Prospero's language constitute an aesthetically formulated curse. The urbanized poet voices his denial of the city, not with romantic invocations of Mother Africa, but with totemic images; in this respect "Lustre à cidade" (Brightness Comes to the City) represents some of Craveirinha's best poetry:

> Velha quizumba
> de olhos raiados de sangue
> sorve-me os rins da angústia
> e a dentes de nojo
> carnívora rói-me a medula infracturável do sonho.
>
> E nas quatro costas
> do horizonte reaccionário das paredes
> uma exactidão de féretro tem precisamente
> as passadas infalíveis dum recluso.
>
> E a vida
> a injúrias engolidas em seco
> tem o paladar da baba das hienas uivando
> enquanto no dia lúgubre de sol
> os jacarandás ao menos ainda choram flores
> e de joelhos o medo
> puxo lustro à cidade.
>
> (*Caliban* 1, p. 22)

(Old *quizumba* [the hyena]/ eyes streaked with blood/ sucks my kidneys of anguish/ and with loathsome fangs/ carnivorously gnaws on the unbreakable marrow of my dreams.// And on the four coasts/ of the walls' reactionary horizon/ a coffinlike exactness has precisely/ the infallible footsteps of a recluse.// And life/ with its insults unflinchingly borne/ tastes of the slaver of hyenas screeching/ while on the gloomy, sunlit day/ at least the jacarandas still cry flowers/ and fear, kneeling,/ pulls brightness toward the city.)

A repulsive beast of carrion in the folklore of some African cultures, the hyena comes in the dark of night, with pusillanimous audacity, to eat defenseless creatures and decaying flesh. Craveirinha uses this element of African folklore along with images of darkness, loneliness, decay, and death to represent the anguish of the urbanized African; and in the last stanza combines the surrealistic image of the hyena with the idea of the indignation heaped on him by the city, which even in the sunlight contains gloom. Nature, in the form of trees "crying" flowers, and the poet's cautious apprehension bring the only ray of hope for his survival in the city.

Caliban in no way offers a comprehensive sampling of all that has occurred recently in Mozambican letters. On the other hand, the magazine's synthesis and integration, to say nothing of its high artistic standards, offer some sense of the general literary climate in Lourenço Marques where more than likely any future development in Mozambique will take place. For the time being, important writers and critics such as Lisboa, Knopfli, Craveirinha, and Honwana, to mention a few of the small elite, will constitute a viable base for whatever coordinated literary movement may develop in the future. But as is the case in Angola, the future is nebulous.

Russell Hamilton

Notes

[1]Mário de Andrade, *Literatura africana de expressão portuguesa.* I. 285.

[2]Duarte Galvão, *Poema do tempo presente* (Lourenço Marques: Published by the author, 1960), p. 65.

[3]J.P. Grabato Dias and Rui Knopfli, eds., *Caliban* 1 (Lourenço Marques: Published by the editors, 1971), p. 2.

[4]See ch. XV, "The Negritude School" (1. Caliban and Prospero), in Jahn, *Neo-African Literature*, pp. 239-242.

[5]*Caliban* 3/4 (June 1972), 81.

Russell Hamilton

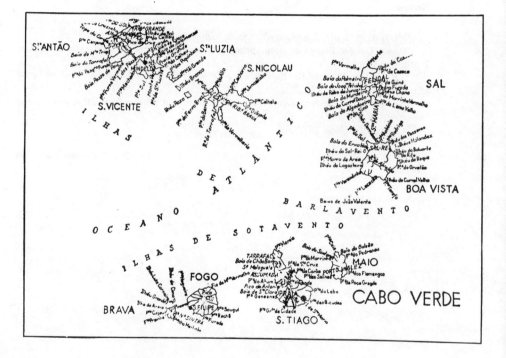

Cape Verde and São Tomé-Príncipe
A Search for Ethnic Identity

Richard A. Preto-Rodas

Situated midway on the maritime route between Portugal and Brazil, the Cape Verde archipelago is comprised of ten small, volcanic islands three hundred miles from the African coast. Uninhabited prior to their discovery by the Portuguese in the fifteenth century, they at present have a population of 200,000, mostly descendants of Portuguese, Genoese, and Africans who were settled during the fifteenth and sixteenth centuries. Owing to factors similar to Brazil's social development, such as a large slave population and widespread racial mixture, the majority of Cape Verdeans, perhaps 70 per cent, are of Afro-European ancestry with the remainder divided between whites (5 per cent) and blacks (25 per cent).[1]

In recent times the islands have provided a paradox of cultural sophistication and economic misery. With a literacy rate considerably higher than Portugal's, the Cape Verdeans continue to be plagued by severely limited natural resources and periodic, devastating droughts, a sad history scarcely alleviated by bureaucratic ineptitude.[2] The surrounding sea is both road to escape and jailer for the islanders who have emigrated by the tens of thousands to the Americas and to the Portuguese territiories in Africa and São Tomé. In light of the tradition of relatively high literacy and economic privation, the islands have supported a surprisingly rich literature which oscillates between the themes of grinding poverty and nostalgic pining for home and family. Throughout the present century the dominant theme has been epitomized in the following verses, written in 1916 and recently adapted as the epigraph of a best-selling Cape Verdean novel: "O

1. On the Cape Verde as ethnic precursor of Brazil, see Nuno Miranda, "Presença de Cabo Verde na literatura portuguesa e estrangeira," *Garcia de Orta*, 9 (1961), 144.

2. See Norman Araujo, *A Study of Cape Verdean Literature* (Chestnut Hill, Mass., 1966), pp. 17–24.

corpo que é escravo, vai/O coração que é livre, fica" (The body, which is a slave, goes away,/the heart, which is free, remains).[3]

Alone among the tropic lands where Portuguese is spoken, Cape Verde reveals little racial alienation between the literary elite and the masses, whether rural or urban.[4] Moreover, Cape Verdean writers frequently use the local Creole dialect, thereby further identifying with the popular culture while contributing to making the dialect a flexible and respectable tool for literary expression.[5] Thus, unlike the situation in Brazil, there has never been a social phenomenon similar to whitening. Except for one of the larger islands, São Tiago, the adverse agricultural circumstances have simply rendered a plantation economy impractical, and there is little of the vestigial master-slave relationship which survives as a social value in Brazil. Also, the lack of a clearly demarcated distinction between the races has not encouraged the open polarity of the Negritude characteristic of the French Antilles. The causes and character of Negritude in modern Cape Verdean poetry are, therefore, peculiar to the islands' special circumstances.

The literary roots of Cape Verde extend at least as far back as 1842 when the *Boletim oficial* published in the capital city of Praia began to include a supplement devoted to literary topics.[6] We must wait until 1894, however, before finding a literary reflection of the African constituent of local culture. Towards the close of the last century the diocesan seminary published an *Almanach Luso-Africano* "Dedicated to the youth of Portugal, Brazil, and the Portuguese colonies."[7] The publication, followed by a second and final number in 1899, contained a wide variety of headings, ranging from astronomy to telegraph service. As is evident from the very title, the non-European character of the islands was acknowledged and there are even some examples of dialogue and verse in "indigenous dialects." The general tone is subservient to classical Portuguese cultural and literary trends, however, and it is not by accident that the *Almanach's* organizer, Canon Teixeira, also translated the Lusitanian national epic, *The Lusiads*, into Creole Portuguese for the patriotic edification of his students.

3. The quote is from the works of Eugênio Tavares and is found in Baltasar Lopes da Silva, *Chiquinho* (São Vicente, 1947), p. 7.
4. See Gerald M. Moser, "African Literature in Portuguese: The First Written, The Last Discovered," *African Forum*, 2 (1967), 83.
5. See Miranda, pp. 151–53.   6. Moser, p. 80.
7. For references to the *Almanach*, see Araujo, pp. 26–28.

A similar penchant for classical orientation is evinced by the poets of the first half of the present century. In fact, reminiscent of the Luso-Brazilian Arcadian school in its detachment from reality is the work of the dean of Cape Verdean letters, José Lopes da Silva. A self-taught intellectual well versed in the major Western literatures, Lopes da Silva won honors from France, Brazil, and Portugal in the form of decorations and memberships in learned societies. Aside, however, from a single trip to Angola, the poet never left his islands. And yet, when referring to his homeland he has been described as "vague, uncertain, very fleeting."[8] The island scenes which he some-times depicts show a preference for the idyllic evasion of travel poster delights rather than the harsh realities of the Cape Verde and its un-usual social and cultural aspects. Lopes da Silva's serene ideal is a re-sult of his unswerving allegiance to the Parnassian dictum: "Meu verso é clássico, sempre bem feito / Não prostituo a língua de Ca-mões" (My verse is classic, always well turned, / I do not prostitute the language of Camões).[9]

Similar attempts to assimilate completely Portuguese literary norms of a bygone era set the tone for Lopes da Silva's colleagues. Such poets as Januário Leite and Mário Pinto, for example, wrote more like nineteenth-century rural European vicars than twentieth-century mulattoes living on remote, poverty-stricken tropic isles.[10] To be sure, even in the early years of this century there appeared an occasional sharp criticism of mismanagement of the islands' economy. An ex-pression of anger is unmistakable in the prose writings of Eugênio Tavares who inveighed against the ambitious, young Portuguese career diplomat biding his time with heart set on a more prestigious assignment. But the revolutionary implications of such stirrings of discontent had to wait to bear fruit until there was an ideologically more propitious atmosphere.[11]

It is only with the advent of the thirties and the repercussions of modern socioliterary movements in the outside world that a new spirit began to stir among the islands' writers. A primary influence was Brazilian Modernism insofar as it revealed a kindred world where a racially "new" people was struggling to define its unique character despite the continuing imposition of specifically European social

8. See Araujo, pp. 25–45.
9. Araujo, p. 31.
10. Araujo, pp. 45–52.
11. See Araujo's comments on Tavares, pp. 66–68.

values, language, and literary norms. The bond which young Cape Verdeans felt between themselves and the nonwhite characters of Jorge Amado and José Lins do Rêgo, so like themselves even in their use of Portuguese, served to remind them of their own cultural status as an appendage of a European world which had no place for the archipelago's African past. Europe, however, also aided in their self-discovery, especially in the form of Portuguese neo-Realism. Such novelists as Ferreira de Castro, dedicated to plumbing the depths of social injustice and class distinctions, encouraged island poets and writers to cast a scrutinizing eye on local conditions.[12]

Prompted by the new currents of social criticism and cultural renovation, the classically inclined poet Pedro Monteiro Cardoso decided to delve into the folk history of his people in an attempt to discover the unique character of Cape Verdean customs. The result, *Folklore caboverdeano* (Porto, 1933), is a mélange of factual prose and bilingual verse in Portuguese and Creole. Among the poems dedicated to island life the reader finds an unusually frank admission in Creole Portuguese of color differences and corresponding social and economic inequalities which had hitherto been ignored in Cape Verdean letters. In its stark statement of contrasts, the poem is strangely evocative of Caldas Barbosa's quartet of a century earlier:[13]

> Nhô ê rico mi ê probe
> Nhô ê branco mi ê preto;
> Calquer dés ê ca grandeza,
> Calquer dés ê ca defêto.
> Nhô crê nu rasgâ nós beia,
> Nu dixâ sangue corré.
>
> (You are rich and I am poor;
> You are white and I am black;
> Neither of these is grander,
> Neither is a defect.
> You want me to slash our veins,
> [And] let our blood run.)

12. For the influence of Modernism, neo-Realism, and other literary currents on Cape Verdean writers, see Araujo, p. 88; G. M. Moser, "African Literature in the Portuguese Language," *The Journal of General Education*, 12 (1962), 273–74. *Antologia da ficção cabo-verdeana*, ed. Baltasar Lopes (Praia, Cape Verde, 1960), pp. xviii–xxix. All point out that local forces were activated rather than created by external influences.

13. See Araujo, pp. 53–63. The translation is Araujo's.

Especially noteworthy is the reference to bloodshed between the races, a polemic stance only partially offset farther on by an allusion to mutual cooperation between white and black ("Branco ê papel mas sim tinta/Ê mudo êl ca ta papiâ" [Paper is white but without ink it is mute and does not speak]). While it would be anachronistic to detect an influence of explicit Negritude in Cardoso's poem, it is apparent that the poet arrived at the first stage of the movement in his lament of a black in a white-ruled society, albeit remotely so in the case of the Cape Verde. The sequence through revolt, racial solidarity, and the mystique of "soul" required further sharpening of the islanders' sense of cultural autonomy and a strengthening of ties with other non-European poets.

Consolidating these nascent developments and with a view to adapting to local conditions the critical view of the socially oriented writers of Brazil and Portugal, a group of Cape Verdean writers founded a review in 1936 entitled *Claridade*. Modeled in part on *Presença*, the organ of the Portuguese neo-Realists, *Claridade* represented an attempt to break away from academic preoccupations with poetic form and metaphysical speculations in preference for social themes. The *Claridosos*, as the founders were called, were above all encouraged by the remarkable success of a Brazilian regionalist like José Lins do Régo in conferring universal relevance on local situations. To capture the unique flavor of island life, they gave increasing importance to its African base along with discussing the familiar themes of isolation and the tension between the desire to escape and homesickness. Thus, the black origins of popular celebrations and customs were examined and sociological papers were published scoring the ascent of the mulatto in local bureaucracy at the expense of the previously unchallenged European administrators.[14]

As the nativist tone of *Claridade* became more pronounced, the note of social protest and black identity gradually grew louder. Jorge Barbosa, perhaps the review's most prominent poet, laments the far-off central government's lack of concern for its South Atlantic wards in "Crianças" (Children):[15]

> Sem remédios
> Sem escolas
> Sem brinquedos

14. *Ibid.*, pp. 77–98. See especially pp. 77–91.
15. See *ibid.*, p. 93.

>Ninguém sabe
>Ninguém dá por isso.

>(Without medicine,
>Without schools,
>Without toys;
>No one knows,
>No one is even aware.)

The focus narrows in "Pretinha" (Little Black Girl) where the crushing weight of daily hardship soon transforms the bright-eyed Negro child into a spiritless woman old before her time, a theme which appears again in "Moça-Velha" (Old Young Girl).[16] A similar cry is heard in "Casebre" (Hovel) where the poet relates the havoc of drought and famine when entire families die, their plight made even more poignant by the indifference of the outside world:[17]

>Tão silenciosa a tragédia das sêcas nestas ilhas!
>Nem gritos nem alarmes,
>Sòmente o jeito passivo de morrer!

>(So silent is the tragedy of droughts on these islands!
>Neither cries nor alarms,
>Just the passive knack of dying.)

In "Não era para mim" (It was not for me), Barbosa hints at revolt when he implies that much of the suffering could be alleviated by a more equitable distribution of wealth:[18]

Gente sem nada pedindo um pouco sòmente
do muito que sobeja nas searas e nos cofres
mas...
não sou eu que tenho a espada e a balança para fazer a divisão.

(People with nothing asking for just a bit
of the plenty which is left over in the harvests and vaults,
but . . .
it is not I who has the sword and the scale to make the division.)

16. *Ibid.*, p. 105.
17. Jorge Barbosa, *Caderno de um ilhéu* (Lisbon, 1956), pp. 27–28.
18. *Ibid.*, pp. 69–70. The poem is dedicated to "Dr. Marcelo Caetano," the present premier of Portugal.

The only immediate remedy is emigration, a motif which Barbosa consistently accompanies with Brazil as his destination. His reasons reveal a racial affinity in the Afro-Portuguese basis of both Cape Verdean and Brazilian cultures. Thus, in "Você, Brasil" (You, Brazil), he alludes to a common heritage grounded in "saudade antiga dos serões africanos..." (old longings for African evenings).[19] The poet finds the traits of such a heritage in the soft Portuguese spoken both on the islands and in Brazil, in their distinct rhythmic melodies, and—here one detects an echo of Negritude's mystical "soul"—a "natural poetry" and a "philosophy without erudition."

The rather hesitant Negro conciousness seen thus far in Cape Verdean letters reflects the position of nonwhites on the islands: they are neither subjugated to an all-white minority nor do they constitute a resentful minority. Rather, their recent recognition of an African past is largely an incidental consequence of political protest and accompanies a growing impatience with a central government historically unresponsive to their pleas. Increasingly mistrustful of their ties to Portugal, the Cape Verdean poets examined above have only gradually turned to non-European, especially African, cultural sources.[20] Even so, the *Claridade* movement, while undeniably a powerful force for the autonomy envisioned in Brazilian Modernism, still failed to develop fully the seeds of Negritude in its stress on the Portuguese substratum of the islands' linguistic, social, and literary history. The final step from inchoate valuation of blackness to an explicit avowal of Negritude was prompted in part by the example of Negro writers in other countries and in part by a short-lived journal, *Certeza*.[21] The latter's openly Marxist orientation indicated that some leading Cape Verdean intellectuals were rejecting Europe in preference for an unequivocal alliance with the emerging nations.

Just how far some contemporary Cape Verdean writers have come from the classic Lusitanism of José Lopes da Silva is suggested in an essay, *Consciencialização da literatura caboverdeana* (The Growing Self-Awareness of Cape Verdean Literature [Lisbon, 1963]). Its poet-author Onésimo da Silveira insists that the younger writers of his

19. *Ibid.*, pp. 57–60. Cf. "Carta para Manuel Bandeira" and "Carta para o Brasil," pp. 53–56.
20. See Manuel Ferreira, "As ilhas crioulas na sua poesia moderna," *Estrada Larga*, 3 (Porto, n.d.), 444–54; Alfredo Margarido, "The Social and Economic Background of Portuguese Negro Poetry," tr. H. Kaal, *Diogenes*, 37 (1962), 55–56.
21. Araujo, pp. 148–53.

islands be considered the exponents of a literary African regionalism.[22] A program as well as an analysis, the essay encourages Cape Verdean authors to further the cause of African consciousness by deriving their "spirituality" from the Negro or Negroid world. The author's openly anti-Portuguese attitude not surprisingly resulted in the book's seizure at the time of publication and in the author's flight and present exile. Whatever his political designs, however, his program is clearly non-Quixotic, for several serious critics have called attention to the recent rise of Negritude in Cape Verdean letters. Thus, an anthology of works of Portuguese-speaking poets from the Negro world pointedly excluded examples from the Cape Verde in its first printing in 1953 while its second edition, published five years later, includes no fewer than six poets from the archipelago.[23]

Perhaps the first poet to show the contemporary shift to a rediscovery of an African past is Aguinaldo Brito Fonseca, who takes upon himself the black poet's role of spokesman for his people.[24] Thus, in "Poeta e povo" (Poet and People) he describes his task as articulating "O grito do povo, o chôro do povo" (The cry of the people, the weeping of the people).[25] Their cry is for a new identity which will reconcile their particular status as neither African nor European. The poet skillfully fuses the notion of cultural alienation and geographic remoteness in "Taberna beira mar" (Sea-side Tavern) where he depicts the tavern as an anchored ship. Its clientele is a heterogeneous crew of rootless people: "Gente de todas as raças / gente sem pátria e sem nome"[26] (People of all races, / people without a country and a name). Again, in "Canção dos rapazes da ilha" (Song of the boys from the island), he likens the islander's lot to that of a marooned sailor who casts his fond hope of rescue into the sea, "Metido na garrafa bem rolhada" (Stuffed into a tightly corked bottle).[27]

22. See Moser's article in *African Forum*, p. 86; Margarido, p. 53. For a French version of "Consciencialização" which appeared after I completed my study, see Onésimo da Silveira, "Prise de conscience dans la littérature du Cap-Vert," *Présence Africaine*, 68 (1968), 106–21.

23. *Caderno de poesia negra de expressão portuguesa*, eds. Mário de Andrade and Francisco José Tenreiro (Lisbon, 1953). Its second printing is Andrade's *Antologia da poesia negra de expressão portuguêsa* (Paris, 1958). Also see Ferreira, p. 454.

24. See Ferreira, p. 452; Araujo, pp. 167–68.

25. Araujo, p. 162.

26. In Andrade's *Antologia*, pp. 3–4. An English translation is found in Moore and Beier's *Modern Poetry from Africa*, pp. 135–36.

27. *Poetas e contistas africanos*, ed. João Alves das Neves (São Paulo, 1963), p. 18.

One is reminded of Brazilian Negritude in "Herança" (Inheritance) where the poet suggests that his present ills are a legacy of his slave grandfather. Thus, yesterday's chains have become today's economic and political stagnation.[28] But the atavistic bonds comfort as well as distress, since they establish a link with an African past which creates an aura of permanence and stability. Moreover, the unity of anguish binding grandfather and grandson is a reminder of a more fundamental unity which binds the Negro of Negritude to the cosmic unity of all nature in a rhythmic whole. For example, in "Magia negra" (Black Magic) Brito Fonseca perceives his ancestor's laments against a background of throbbing drums dimly heard in the passing breeze and the rustling palm fronds. His anxieties assuaged by the comforting presence of his forbears, "O negro dorme / sonhando ser santo um dia" (The Negro falls asleep, / dreaming of being a saint one day). The same optimism based on the black's unity with a mystically sympathetic nature is found in "Mãe-Negra" (Black Mother) where a friendless old Negro woman happily espies a comforting hand waving from every distant star.[29]

The related themes of continued subjugation to alien directives and the bittersweet comfort of ancestral ties transmitted through primitive rhythms form the structure of António Nunes' "Ritmo de pilão" (Pestle Rhythm).[30] Like the tom-tom, the throbbing monotony of the large pestle as it grinds corn into flour evokes a past of slave ships and black nurses telling their white charges tales of "forests, animals, haunted houses." The modern use of the pestle also reminds one of dashed hopes as emancipation became modern economic bondage. The heavy, hopeless sound of the pestle is reflected in the poem's long verses which never end in a complete sentence but lunge onward, much like the weariness of the Cape Verdean's life: "luta dia a dia" (a day-to-day struggle). The future is glimpsed in "Poema de amanhã" (Tomorrow's poem)[31] when Nunes foresees a happy land which will belong to those who till it, "filhos do nosso esfôrço, frutos do nosso suor" (the children of our own effort, the fruit of our sweat). He also implies that present barrenness of his land might well be unnecessary and probably stems from the neglect and technical backwardness of officialdom.

28. Araujo, pp. 167–68.   29. Araujo, p. 167.
30. Araujo, pp. 170–71. The throb of the pestle is a common figure in Negritude. See Mélone's comments on "Fleurs de Laterité" by Francesco Nkitsouma, p. 66.
31. Araujo, pp. 171–73.

Other modern Cape Verdean poets stress the revolutionary aspect of Negritude, thereby exacting a high price for the faint optimism glimpsed in the works of their colleagues mentioned above. Certainly the most bellicose is Gabriel Mariano whose "Cantiga da minha ilha" (Song of my island) is a catalogue of past and present sufferings in the form of questions:[32]

> Quem é que chora de dia
> e morre podre de fome
> na ourela fina do mar?
>
> (Who cries by day
> and dies wasted with hunger
> along the slim shore of the sea?)

He answers each question with "Eu" (I). But he warns that he wreaks strength from his woes for some future day: "Depois, ninguém me acuse / de ter sido misterioso" (Then let no one accuse me / of having been mysterious). But even the most revolutionary pose seemingly allows for the persistence of the European element in a new social order. Thus, the theoretician of Cape Verdean Negritude mentioned above, Onésimo da Silveira, balances open revolt in "Lema" (Motto) with the incorporation of all races in a specifically Cape Verdean society as we read in "A Hora grande" (The Great Hour):[33]

> As crianças serão crianças!
> Negras e louras e brancas
> Serão pétalas da mesma flor...
>
> (Children will be children,
> Black, golden and white
> They will be petals of the same flower . . .).

Since the present sociopolitical system is bound to Europe, however, any reaction will continue to stress the African component of these unfortunate islands. Taken for granted by a distant metropolis, it is little wonder that their poets look for inspiration to the nearby African continent to which they are tied no less than to their European cousins. Despite the similarity of certain motifs, Cape Verdean

32. Andrade's *Antologia*, pp. 5–6.
33. See *New Sum of Poetry from the Negro World*, pp. 456–57.

Negritude is far more assertive than the Brazilian version in its insistence on an African past and less concerned with the simple fact of
skin color. With no established national culture to absorb them, as in
Brazil, the nonwhite poets of the islands seek an indigenous society,
one truly Afro-Portuguese. For the present, therefore, their program
is to define their character as shaped by past and present factors. In a
metaphor admirably expressive of Negritude's theme of the black's
physical union with his environment, Onésimo da Silveira looks forward to the day when[34]

... libertos do sal do nosso sorriso de enteados,
seremos frutos de nós mesmos
nascendo da barriga negra da terra...

(... no longer smiling the tearful [salty] smile of step-children,
we will be the fruit of ourselves
born of the black belly of the earth ...).

Like the Cape Verde, the twin islands of São Tomé and Príncipe
were unpopulated at the time of their discovery by the Portuguese in
the fifteenth century. Aside from this fact, however, they have little
in common with the Creole archipelago. Lying just north of the equa-
tor in the Gulf of Guinea, these hot, humid islands have always failed
to attract large numbers of white settlers, and their first inhabitants
were a motley group of exiles, traders, and recent, if unwilling, converts from Judaism.[35] Throughout the following centuries the bulk
of the islands' population has been comprised of slaves and, in modern
times, indentured black workers from the African mainland. As a result, the present social structure is unmistakably colonial: the 60,000
inhabitants include a small number of Portuguese-speaking whites
and a mass of blacks and mulattoes who speak either a popular Creole
dialect called *Forro* or the native tongues of their African homelands.

The constant influx of African laborers is a result of the fertile soil
and climatic conditions which are ideal for the widespread cultivation
of such luxury crops as cocoa and coffee. As recently as 1950, govern-

34. *New Sum*, p. 457. The same leitmotif runs through the Cape Verdean
Oswaldo Alcântara's "Mamãe-Terra" in Andrade's *Antologia*, pp. 11–12.
35. For an introduction to Portuguese Africa, see James Duffy, *Portugal in
Africa* (Baltimore, 1963), and Ronald Chilcote, *Portuguese Africa* (Englewood,
N.J., 1967).

ment statistics showed at least one-third of the population as "non-civilized" with general illiteracy. When it is remembered that approximately 10 per cent of the population owns 93 per cent of the arable land, then it becomes clear that the islands provide all the symptoms of a stratified class structure defined primarily in terms of color.[36]

A low level of literacy, cultural privation, and an agricultural economy based on the plantation system can hardly be considered factors favorable for literary creativity; and in fact, Príncipe and São Tomé lag far behind the Cape Verde with regard to the number of writers and works which have been produced. On the other hand, the clear distinction between European and African combined with the oppressive conditions which have regulated the lives of the latter are suited to the development of Negritude in its classic form: a reaction of a small, nonwhite elite determined to create a distinct ideology for a society separated by color from the ruling establishment, Hence, as we shall see, the recent rise of literary expression on São Tomé especially has provided one of the most complete expressions of Negritude in Portuguese. Its significance as a break with the past, however, requires a word regarding the gradual progression of racial awareness which can be detected in the very modest literary corpus produced on these two islands prior to the contemporary era.

São Tomé's first writer of note, Caetano da Costa Alegre (1844–89), was a mulatto. As in the case of some of the Brazilian poets mentioned above, it was because of his white father that this son of an African servant woman was able to attend university in Portugal. Unlike his contemporary Gonçalves Crespo, though, Costa Alegre never succeeded in winning the love of a sympathetic Portuguese woman during his short life. On the contrary, he was constantly reminded of his color by the ladies to whom he dedicated the romantic verses so popular with nineteenth-century Portuguese students. Stung by frequent rebuffs, the young poet set his talents to invoking the beauty of the dark island girls of his youth. Strangely enough, his carefully worked poems, which reflect both Symbolist and Parnassian influences, show no sign of an angry rejoinder to racial discrimination. Like many nonwhites of the nineteenth-century Luso-Brazilian world, the frustrated suitor accepted passively the prevailing standard regarding the races and looked upon his color as a sad fact of life. As a result, his posthumously published *Versos* (1916) show color in, at

36. Margarido, pp. 56–58.

best, an ambiguous light. Clearly, Costa Alegre looked upon his Negro origin as anything but a badge to be proudly displayed.[37]

As examples of the meaning of black for Costa Alegre we cite two poems which also show the poet's Symbolist-Parnassian tendencies. In "Visão" (Vision)[38] an island girl glimpsed from afar is compared to a walking statue of ebony. The poet is captivated by her strange beauty—a combination of aristocratic grace and an air of heavy mourning—but before he can draw nearer she disappears, again compared to an ebony statue: "Como uma estatura de ébano ambulante." The rapt observer becomes an impassioned lover in the longer "A Negra" (The Negro Woman). The poet comforts the grieving black woman who mourns her fall from a previous state of whiteness. She is a "singed star," and her "darkened skin" has been "burnt by the flame of love." Employing an Ovidian device, Costa Alegre alludes to his beloved's former state as "white snow" until she loved and lost a lily and was blackened by her unrequited passion. Referring to himself as a violet, he now begs for the love formerly lavished upon the white flower. If blackness in "Visão" was an exotic motif, in "A Negra" it is certainly a curse.[39] Like his Brazilian contemporary Cruz e Sousa, the poet betrays an awed reverence for whiteness even when describing his mistress. Thus, her lovely, coal-like exterior ("carvão mimoso e lindo") houses a crystal diamond while her breast nurses a glow which fairly absorbs the darkness of her skin: "luz,/Que aborve a tua escurecida pele."

After Costa Alegre little is found in the literary annals of São Tomé until the contemporary era. It would appear, however, that the unhappy poet might have met a different reception in the Portugal of a half century later if we may judge from a book of short stories by a fellow mulatto from the islands, Viana de Almeida. Among the narratives which comprise Almeida's *Maià Poçòn: Contos africanos* (Lisbon, 1937), the title tale concerns a young mulatto medical student who weighs the pros and cons of remaining in Portugal after his graduation. He foresees an ordinary bourgeois future should he remain in Lisbon: "I would reside in a modern part of town with some little Lisboner with nervous body and simple soul who

37. Margarido, p. 59. See also Margarido's article "Panorama" in *Estrada Larga*, III, 482; João Alves das Neves, "A poesia do mundo negro," *Estado de São Paulo Suplemento Literário*, June 28, 1967, p. 1; Moser, "African Literature . . . Last Discovered," p. 81.
38. Found in *Poetas e contistas africanos*, p. 29.
39. Andrade's *Antologia*, p. 29.

would be willing to join her destiny to mine, thereby compensating for my dark color with the prestige of a successful physician" (p. 13). But the difference in social attitudes revealed in Almeida's short story is merely one of degree especially regarding the position of the non-white intellectual who lived in São Tomé. In another story, "O ódio das raças" (Racial Hatred), he sardonically describes the opposition which returning nonwhite graduates encountered when they attempted to found a cultural society: "It was looked upon unfavorably by certain elements among the European colonists. They had the perspicacity to discern in the project heaven only knows what subversive and liberating designs. They took it as an insolent challenge to the supremacy which, in their opinion, the white ought to exercise over the black regardless of the situation in which they may find themselves" (pp. 50–51).

The preceding, faintly mocking appraisal of white attitudes is far removed from Costa Alegre's meek resignation fifty years earlier and clearly shows the revolution which was transforming the cultural outlook of the Luso-Brazilian world at the time. The transition from submission to unequivocal racial rehabilitation occurred a few years later in the poems of Francisco José Tenreiro (1921–63), another mulatto from São Tomé, who is universally acknowledged as the first and perhaps foremost exponent of Negritude in Portuguese. Sent by his white father to Lisbon to study, he subsequently earned a doctorate in geography and eventually became a respected scholar with dozens of books, papers, and articles to his credit. A deputy representing São Tomé and Príncipe in the Portuguese National Assembly, Tenreiro was also a talented poet, literary critic, and novelist in the neo-Realist tradition.[40]

Despite his years in Portugal and travels which took him to most of the countries of Western Europe, Brazil, and North Africa, he confessed himself forever bound emotionally to his native island and Black Africa where he traveled extensively during his final years. A testament of his emotional commitment is found in his poetry which is entirely devoted to the Negro and his world. His first collection of poems, *Ilha de Santo Nome* (Island of Holy Name), centers on São Tomé while the second volume, *Coração em África* (Heart in Africa), includes not only the islands but also such far-flung places as New York's Harlem, Brazil's Bahia, and the Sudan. Since the two books

40. For Tenreiro's biography and bibliographical production, see the edition of his poetry *Obra Poética* (Lisbon, 1967), pp. 9–31.

span Tenreiro's entire adult life—the first was published in Coimbra in 1942 and the second appeared posthumously in Lisbon in 1964—the writer's abiding love for Africa and the African is obvious.

Unlike the literal Negritude of some Brazilians, Tenreiro's inspiration encompasses far more than color and involves a search for African values. His views are stated in an article on African literature where the geographer-poet analyzes Negritude as an ambitious cultural movement initially sparked by the Afro-American Renaissance of the twenties and thirties and then continued by European, Latin American, and African writers and artists. All have been united in the common goal to construct "a humanist philosophy which will serve as a renewal and a stimulus in relation to Africa."[41] The Afro-Portuguese scholar echoes Césaire and Sédar Senghor as he proceeds to define the movement as one transcending sectional and political interests in its pursuit of a Pan-African awareness which might effectively combat the complacent ethnocentrism of Occidental culture. He sees the essence of such an awareness in the esthetic mystique of African art which portrays man as both an aspect of nature and a member of a community. Man's dual identity, then, as nature's child and society's citizen constitutes Negritude's *sagesse* (the poet's term). Tenreiro saw his task as helping to disseminate such wisdom by expressing it in his native tongue, Portuguese. That the means should be primarily poetic in form, though not essential, is in keeping with the value which the African places on the emotional aspects of human culture as opposed to the objective, scientific outlook of the European.[42]

Tenreiro's own pre-eminently European education and his official importance as a delegate to the Portuguese National Assembly probably account for the theoretician's silence regarding the anguish and revolt basic to Negritude and his emphasis on the movement's mystique. In fact, in his essay the author disavows the anticolonial aspects of modern Negritude. Nonetheless, in view of the paternalism which was criticized in *Maià Poçòn* and which, as will be shown in Chapter 4, still characterizes the Portuguese presence in Africa, it would be extremely unlikely if Tenreiro the poet revealed none of the Negro intellectual's reaction to the hegemony of the European in an African society. Accordingly, the writer displays a certain ambivalence

41. See Francisco José Tenreiro, "Acerca da literatura 'negra,'" *Estrada Larga*, III, 472–81.
42. Tenreiro, pp. 480–81.

between his emotional commitment to Africa and a black mother whom he never knew and his intellectual formation as the son of a European administrator and recipient of a highly technical education. Certainly he could not remain indifferent to the social circumstances implied in his origin as the product of a white man's use of an anonymous Negro woman to satisfy a momentary sexual need. One has only to read the dedicatory verses of *Ilha de Santo Nome* with their cry of personal and social alienation to suspect that the mulatto Tenreiro saw in Negritude something more than the philosophical outlook which he implies in his analysis of an African esthetics. An African in Europe and a European in Africa, his poignant address to his mother reads:[43]

> Mãe!
> Entre nós: Milhas!
> Entre nós: Uma raça!
> Contudo
> êste livro é para ti...
>
> (Mother,
> Between us, miles;
> Between us, a race.
> And yet
> this book is for you . . .).

The conflict which the poet feels within himself defines the social relations between white and black on his island and beyond. Rarely in Tenreiro's poetry does one glimpse the racial harmony which the statesman and scholar envisioned. For example, the European colonist is succinctly described in "Romance de seu Silva Costa" (p. 43) as a penniless immigrant who fattens on profits selling liquor, land, and the contracts of indentured workers. He seduces adolescent girls while driving the men beyond endurance to clear the bush in an unceasing quest for more arable land: "Os olhos do branco como chicotes/ferem o mato que está gritando" (The eyes of the white man like whips, lash the jungle which screams [p. 73]). While the white community spends the evening hours talking business over chilled champagne, the native huts "soluçam.../batidos dum luar sem sonho"

43. Tenreiro, *Obra*, p. 37. Further reference to this work is incorporated in the text.

(sob ... bathed in the sheen of a dreamless moon [p. 54]). In the title poem "Ilha de Santo Nome," Tenreiro leaves little doubt that the entire colonial system depends upon "a pólvora que o branco trouxe num navio escuro/... a espada" (the gun powder which the white brought on a dark ship [and] a sword [p. 80]). And the poet asserts what the politician would never dare say: "é terra do negro leal forte e valente que nenhum outro!" (it is the land of the sincere, strong, valiant Negro who has no equal).

In keeping with his pan-African concept of Negritude, Tenreiro, like Césaire, often goes beyond his island to other lands to attack the injustices which the black suffers in a white world. In "Epopeia," for example, he shows a prophetic wrath as he surveys the devastation of ancestral Africa with the advent of the European and the subsequent wholesale deportation of her people to the coffee fields of Brazil and the tobacco plantations of the American South. He finds especially revolting the exploitation at the hands of the "idealistic" Americans:

> Os homens do norte
> os mais lúcidos, cheios de idéias
> deram-te do que era teu
> um pedaço para viveres... Libéria! Libéria! (p. 59)

> (The men from the North,
> the most lucid and full of ideas,
> gave you—from what was yours—
> a piece for you to live ... Liberia, Liberia.)

Since Tenreiro's anger is obvious, the lack of a call for revolt seems inconsistent. As noted above, however, nowhere in his essay does he explicitly advocate open rebellion. The occasional note of violence is subdued as in "Fragmento de Blues" (A Fragment of the Blues). There is unmistakable racial pride in his panegyric of the American boxer Joe Louis: "Joe Louis bateu Buddy Baer/e Harlem abriu-se num sorriso branco" (Joe Louis beat Buddy Baer, and Harlem opened wide with a white smile [p. 91]). He maintains a defiant stand in the same poem by affirming the continuity of the Negro race, assimilation and racial dispersal notwithstanding:[44] "Ai, os negros não morrem,

44. In his *De la négritude*, Mélone points out that the Portuguese stress on cultural assimilation has had a corresponding effect on African poets who react by stressing the theme of racial immortality. See pp. 82–83. For the ambiguity of Tenreiro regarding revolt, see Margarido, "The Social and Economic Background," pp. 60–61, and "Panorama," p. 484.

nem nunca morrerão!" (Oh, the Negroes are not dying, nor will they
ever die), and declares his solidarity with them in "song" and "battle."
But he does not return to the theme of battle, preferring to find the
guarantee of Negritude in song, a lyrical dedication to the mystique
which lies at the heart of the movement's philosophy.

A major motif in *Ilha de Santo Nome* and *Coração em Africa* is,
accordingly, the fusion of black man and nature, thereby implying
that both will somehow survive despite their reduction to a dispos-
able state by European and Arab. The continent, like its Negro inhabitants, is a living creature; its maze of rivers and streams are so
many "-veias entumecidas dum corpo em sangue!" (swollen veins of
a bloody body [p. 59]). There is constant renewal, for both man and
land share an inexhaustible fertility which Tenreiro often describes in
frankly sexual imagery such as in this description of a breadfruit tree
in the rain:

> Cabeleira de folhas à chuva
> ternamente amolentando teu ventre
> de banana-pão
> que se desfaz em cachos fálicos
> símbolos da pujança da Terra (p. 123)

> (Leafy coiffure in the rain
> tenderly softening your belly
> of breadfruit
> which unfolds in phallic curls
> symbols of the Earth's vitality).

The same premise, cosmic unity, explains the Negro's oneness with
the rhythmic movement of natural phenomena which is expressed in
his "soul" or spontaneous love of life, his best defense against despair:

> Que a tua música
> seja o ritmo de uma conquista...!
> ... que a tua gargalhada
> de nôvo venha estraçalhar os ares
> como grito agudo de azagaia! (p. 62)

> (Let your music
> be the rhythm of a conquest ...
> ... let your laughter

once again rend the air
like the shrill cry of the javelin.)

In Tenreiro's adaptation of Negritude to São Tomé one often finds
the vibrancy of hearty laughter and barbed irony. In a poem inspired
by his own mixed parentage, "Canção de mestiço" (Mestizo's Song),
he alleges that his soul is doubly gifted, since it is "uma alma feita de
adição" (a soul composed by addition [p. 48]). He concludes the
same poem with a jocose flippancy calculated to infuriate a racist de-
tractor. When the white scornfully calls him a mulatto, he answers
that the term is an ambiguous one, and not without its advantages:

Quando amo a branca, sou branco...
Quando amo a negra, sou negro.
Pois é... (p. 49)

(When I love a white woman, I'm white . . .
When I love a black woman, I'm black.
That's how it is . . .).

His irony has a bitter edge in "Negro de todo o mundo" (Negro of
the Whole World [p. 68]) where he shows that the scorned Negro
is really an international model. The same whites who dismiss him as
sub-human "ape" (*macaquear*) his dances from Paris and the Folies
Bergère to the rooftop night clubs of New York and the showboats
on the Mississippi. The poet's wit shows an elfin touch in "Longindo
o ladrão" (Longindo the Thief) where a clever black thief appre-
hended *in flagrante* outwits his white victim by closing first one eye,
then the other, and then both, leaving the baffled European groping
in inky blackness while the sea in solidarity guffaws its derisive mock-
ery on a near-by beach (pp. 77–78).

But the tone of Tenreiro's Negritude is far more often a serious
one, since he seeks to emphasize the African's contribution to a cosmopolitan humanism. In his reverence for the feeling and spontaneity
embodied in the mystique of "soul" his poetic side often clashes with
the scientist in him. He puts aside his own technical proficiency when
he attributes man's ills to "civilization's ritual tray of poison" and the
"wisdom" which made possible the gas chamber and replaced the kiss
with a Freudian analysis ("Coração na vida" [p. 108]). The poet is
fond of observing that the Occidental world's divorce from the vital-
izing power of nature has led to its premature senility and distorted

values. Thus, a white "expert who knows everything about Africa" keeps a gullible audience enthralled with cheap exoticism and false analyses while his false teeth click "na caveira consumida de sabedoria" (in his skull shrunken by wisdom [p. 88]).[45] In the title poem of *Coração em África*, the poet walks along "joyless streets" in Portugal, lined with "carious houses" and seemingly filled with ragged newsboys. Against the dehumanized efficiency and poverty of Europe he invokes the African's world of religious sensuality in "Mãos" (Hands):[46]

Mãos prêtas e sábias que nem inventaram a escrita nem a rosa-
   dos-ventos

. . . .

Mãos que da terra, da árvore, da água e do coração tam-tam
criásteis [sic] religião e arte, religião e amor. (p. 90)

(Wise black hands which invented neither writing nor compass
   rose;

. . . .

Hands which created religion and art, religion and love
from the earth, from the tree, from the water and the tom-tom
   beat of the heart.)

Throughout the poem where the preceding verses appear, the poet maintains a throbbing beat by repeating the title twenty-five times at regular intervals, an effect heightened by internal rhyme and the inclusion of musical place names from his idealized Mother Africa.

Since Tenreiro and his fellow mestizo poets from the islands owe an African awareness to their black mothers, the "Mother-Africa" metaphor can be literally explained. Aside from its more fundamental significance as the mystical source of the movement's ethnocultural structure, the theme also suggests an innocent time of carefree childhood when questions of race and color were unimportant or at least did not assume the proportions they have in the adult world.[47] In

45. A similar mocking parody of the white "expert's" description of blacks ("les nègres-sont-tous-les-mêmes, je-vous-le-dis") is found in Césaire's *Cahier*, p. 58.

46. Cf. Césaire's reference to the white world, "horriblement las de son effort immense," in *Cahier*, p. 72. This is part of the contrived, negating character of Negritude mentioned in Chapter 1 and referred to as the "us-them" polarity by Norman R. Shapiro, "Negro Poets of the French Caribbean: A Sampler," *Antioch Review*, 27 (1967), 211–28.

47. For the significance of the theme of childhood in poetry from São Tomé and Príncipe, see Margarido, "Panorama," p. 485.

"Dona" (Lady), Tenreiro wistfully recalls a white woman (his father's wife?) who "nas tardes de então / passava na minha carapinha
duas maõs brancas e delicadas..." (in afternoons of yore would stroke
my kinky hair with two, white delicate hands... [p. 30]).

Idealized childhood also occurs in the poems of Tenreiro's island
compatriot Alda do Espírito Santo. As a schoolteacher, she sees in her
charges a bittersweet reminder of happier days: "As crianças brin-
cam e a água canta... / Velam no capim um negrito pequenino" (The
children romp and the water sings as they keep watch over a tiny
Negro child on the grass).[48] In "Descendo o meu bairro" (A Stroll
down Neighborhood streets)[49] she reconstructs ("vou recordar") a
poor quarter teeming with the sights, sounds, and smells of a festive
time like carnival or a Sunday soccer match. In retrospect she finds
an underlying unity in the heterogeneous crowds of mulattoes and
blacks from diverse lands in the form of a racial sympathy concretized
in an African homeland not found on any map:

> ... o nosso bairro...
> filho da população heterogênea
> brotado pela conjuntura duma
> miscelânea curiosa
> das gentes das áfricas mais díspares
> da África una dos nossos sonhos
> de meninos já crescidos
>
> (... our neighborhood...
> offspring of the heterogeneous population
> that has sprouted from the juncture of a
> curious miscellany
> of people from the most disparate africas
> of the single Africa of our dreams
> as grown-up children).

A sister colleague from Príncipe, Maria Manuela Margarido, invokes the dimly remembered image of her mother in "Memória da
Ilha do Príncipe" (Memory of Prince Isle). The vaguest contours of
scenes long past are limned in a series of synesthetic patches where

48. See "Lá na água grande" in Andrade's *Antologia*, p. 23. But this idyllic
view is shattered in "Para lá da praia" on pp. 34–35 where the children are a
ragged lot with distended bellies and carry smaller brothers strapped to their
backs.
49. See *New Sum*, p. 492.

physiognomy and island background coalesce to provide a surrealistic effect,[50] e.g., "a fragrant lilac face wreathed in cocoa leaves." A voice, a feeling of warmth, and little else unite her to the all-but-forgotten past and her distant mother:

> E ambas nos lançamos
> nas grandes flôres de ébano
> que crescem na água cálida
> das vozes clarividentes

> (And we both cast ourselves
> into the great ebony flowers
> which grow in the warm water
> of clairvoyant voices).

These references to childhood notwithstanding, both women, like other contemporary devotés of Negritude in São Tomé and Príncipe, generally prefer to direct their attention to the social situation of the Negro on their islands. As a result, their work is more impassioned and immediate than the more universal Negritude of the prudent Tenreiro.[51] Espírito Santo, for example, counterbalances her image of adolescent independence with the less attractive aspects of family life. Thus, her children's mother is a harried woman who must leave her family to work from dawn to dark, "Na luta da vida / ... na faina do dia" (in life's struggle, in the daily toil).[52] The most common work is selling the fish which landless fathers catch in the sea, "remando, remando no mar dos tubarões/p'la fome de cada dia" (rowing through shark-filled seas for their daily hunger).[53]

With the bloody suppression of a native rebellion in 1955, the anger has grown, spilling over into such fiery poems as Espírito Santo's "Onde estão os homens caçados neste vento de loucura" (Where Are the Men Hunted Down in This Wind of Madness) and Margarido's "Vós que ocupais a nossa terra" (You Who Occupy Our Land).[54] The "us-them" polarity characterizing the revolutionary phase of Negritude is as basic to these poems as it is in Margarido's "Sócòpe."

50. *Poetas e contistas africanos*, p. 31.
51. See Margarido, "The Social and Economic Background," pp. 61–63.
52. In "Para lá da praia," pp. 34–35.
53. See "Angolares" in *New Sum*, pp. 496–97.
54. In *New Sum*, pp. 495–96, 499–500.

The latter takes its title from a popular dance step whose percussive rhythm provides a temporary substitute for the islanders' smoldering resentment: "monótono se arrasta / até explodir na alta ânsia de liberdade" (it shuffles along monotonously until it explodes in the heady desire for liberty).

Given the continuation of present conditions, it seems likely that the first level of Negritude will maintain the attention of nonwhite poets from São Tomé and Príncipe. Even the rare examples of Europeanized blacks may be expected to reflect the rising tide of African awareness as symbolized in Negritude. The ethnocentric colonial policy whereby Europe provides the cultural model is, therefore, increasingly challenged as it passes from the unquestioning acceptance of a Costa Alegre to the ambivalence of Tenreiro; and it falters even more when it pretends to supplant indigenous values entirely. In "Meu canto, Europa" (My Chant, Europe),[55] the Thomense physician Tomás Medeiros juxtaposes the mechanized world which has absorbed him and the fast-disappearing world of his African past. In twenty-seven brittle verses shot through with an insistent urgency achieved by frequent repetition and combining to form a single question, the poet epitomizes cultural alienation. For him the meeting of Africa and Europe has resulted in a new order where the telephone and Morse code replace his people's tom-tom. By caricature and force, European ways have apparently supplanted local traditions and folk customs, but the poet wonders about the wisdom of this experiment in shaping an African into a European:

> Agora
> Agora que me estampaste no rosto
> os primores da tua civilização
> eu te pergunto, Europa
> Eu te pergunto:
> AGORA?
>
> (Now
> Now that you've imprinted on my face
> the glories of your civilization
> I ask you, Europe
> I ask you:
> NOW WHAT?)

55. In *Poetas e contistas africanos*, p. 30.

Cover of *Cabo Verde*

CAPE VERDEAN POETRY AND THE PAIGC

Russell G. Hamilton

It would be self-fulfilling prophecy to propose a relationship between Cape Verdean literature and the African Party of the Independence of Guinea and Cape Verde (PAIGC). A more valid undertaking would be to determine why this relationship exists and the extent to which Party policy and ideology have influenced Cape Verdean imaginative writing in its production, its internal structure, and its points of view.

To a greater or lesser degree, but without exception, the nationalist-independence movements of Lusophone Africa have drawn on the activities and membership of cultural and literary groups. Agostinho Neto, president of newly-independent Angola, first gained recognition as a poet who participated in cultural and literary organizations, many of whose members formed the nucleus of the Popular Movement for the Liberation of Angola (MPLA). The FRELIMO government of Mozambique counts among its present officials several literary figures, including short-story writer Luís Bernardo Honwana and poet Marcelino dos Santos (Kalungano). Under Portuguese colonialism literary expression was one of the few outlets for Africans' growing nationalist sentiments beginning in the early decades of this century.

Amílcar Cabral, founder, in 1956, of the PAIGC, and, from 1963 until his untimely death in 1973, leader of the armed struggle in Guinea-Bissau, took an active interest in Cape Verdean literary expression. Some of what Cabral wrote on the subject can give us some clues as to why cultural and literary groups have contributed to nationalist movements in Lusophone Africa.

In 1952, four years before the founding of the Party, Amílcar Cabral wrote "Apontamentos sobre Poesia Caboverdiana" ("Notes on Cape Verdean Poetry") in which he documented the birth of a "characteristic" Cape Verdean poetry in contrast to that which sang lyrically of far-off Europe. In acknowledging the importance of those poets who "planted their feet firmly on the ground," Cabral saw this poetry of the so called *Claridade* (a literary journal issued at irregular intervals from 1936 until 1960) phase as having mainly given impetus to a cultural transformation. Cabral was saying that the *Claridade,* and later the *Certeza* (another journal, of only two issues, published in 1944), poets, even though they wrote from within a Cape Verdean reality, constituted a small elite. Today, many Cape Verdean intellectuals have been touched, either directly or indirectly, by members of the *Claridade/Certeza* groups, some of whom taught in São Vicente's Gil Eanes Academy and served as mentors to young intellectuals and beginning writers. Thus in 1952 Cabral, himself a product of Gil Eanes, wrote that "these poets of the *Claridade/Certeza* groups were common men who have joined hands with the people and planted their feet firmly on the ground."[1] Toward the end of his article Cabral observes, however, that "the message of *Claridade* and *Certeza* had to be transcended."[2] What these messages were and why they had to be transcended offer some insights into issues that, in the early 1960s, began to divide Cape Verdean writers along political-ideological as well as cultural-aesthetic lines.

The *Claridade* and *Certeza* poets exalted a Creole ethos in Cape Verdean society. Their messages served notice to the rest of the Portuguese-speaking world, and to the world at large, that Cape Verde, in spite of its smallness and isolation (and in part because of these factors), was a unique cultural and racial amalgam within the Lusitanian family of widely scattered geographical regions and diverse ethnic and racial groups. To these proud, if somewhat defensive, sons of the islands, Cape Verde was a mixture of the African and the European—but more European than African. In a very real sense many Cape Verdeans of that and succeeding generations accepted Lusotropicology, an ideology that hails the Portuguese's supposed ability to create *sui generis,* acculturated societies in the tropics and to mix freely with the dark-skinned inhabitants of these regions. Generally speaking, the *Claridade* and *Certeza* intellectuals saw Cape Verde as a case of Romance regionalism even as they recognized the contribution of the African to the creation of a unique, Creole society.

Amilcar Cabral could justifiably speak of these poets as walking hand in hand with the people because much of their art relied on folklore and popular sources and did indeed reflect the archipelago's perennial social and economic problems: periodic drought and famine, chronic hunger and unemployment leading to mass emigration. In his poem "Crioulo" the *Claridade* writer Manuel Lopes speaks directly, and fraternally, to an abstract, flagelated Cape Verdean:

> Há em ti a chama que arde com inquietação
> e o lume íntimo, escondido, dos restolhos,
> —que é o calor que tem mais duração.
> A terra onde nasceste deu-te a coragem e a resignação.
> Deu-te a fome nas estiagens dolorosas.
> Deu-te a dor para que nela
> sofrendo, fosses mais humano.
> Deu-te a provar da sua taca o agri-doce da compreensão,
> e a humildade que nasce do desengano...
> E deu-te esta esperança desenganada
> em cada um dos dias que virão
> e esta alegria guardada
> para a manhã esperada
> em vão...[3]

(Within you burns the flame of restlessness/ and the intimate, hidden light of the crop stubble/ —which is the warmth that endures./ The land where you were born gave you courage and resignation./ It gave you pain so that/ in your suffering you became more human./ It let you sip from its cup of bitter-sweet understanding,/ and it gave you the humility that is born of disillusionment.../ And it gave you this disillusioned hope for/ in vain...)

Claridade poets, Manuel Lopes among them, established certain themes, and what distinguishes their verse from that of later poets are tone and point of view. The message in Lopes' above-quoted poem is one of acceptance of an unchangeable social and physical environment and of disillusioned hope tinged with humility. An overriding sense of resignation and melancholy evades the islands' endemic problems of poverty and mass emigration predicated on precarious economic conditions.

Jorge Barbosa, one of the best-known poets of the *Claridade* generation, wrote some appealing verse which confirms the prevailing attitude, tone, and posture of a "characteristic" literature. In his poem "Irmão" ("Brother") Barbosa celebrates Cape Verdean emigration in romantic, nostaligic terms:

> Cruzaste Mares
> na aventura da pesca da baleia,
> nessas viagens para a América
> de onde às vezes os navios não voltam mais.[4]

(You traversed Seas/ in the excitement of the whale hunt,/ on those voyages to America/ from whence ships often do not return.)

The Cape Verdean mariner is depicted as a heroic figure whose aggrandizement, along with the nostalgia attached to departing and never returning, mitigates the poet's lament of economic deprivation.

In another one of his poems, "Momento" ("Just for an Instant"), Barbosa expresses a kind of ineffable melancholy, peculiar to the islands:

> Quen aqui não sentiu
> esta nossa
> fina melancolia?
> . . . .
> Esta nossa
> fininha melancolia
> que vem não sei de onde
> Um pouco talvez
> das horas solitárias
> passando sobre a ilha
> ou da música
> do mar defronte
> entoando
> uma canção rumorosa
> musicada com os ecos do mundo.[5]

(Who here has not felt/ this our/ refined melancholy?/ . . ./ This our nicely refined melancholy/ that comes from I know not where./ A little perhaps/ from the soliary hours/ passing over the island/ or from the music/ of the sea beyond/ intoning/ a clamorous song/ instrumented with the echoes of the world.)

Like Lopes' poem, though less explicitly, Barbosa's "Momento" has a note of resignation, and the persona celebrates the islands' solitude and isolation. This compelling poem has, then, an ideological base which seems to complement much Cape Verdean literature of the period: putting it simply, Cape Verde is a group of forgotten islands whose inhabitants face their deplorable conditions with resignation and courage thereby giving proof of a unique inner strength projected, often with nostalgia (*saudade*) and melancholy, into the ethos of an autocthonous Creole, but static, society. This attitude, prevalent among members of the bourgeois elite, meant an identification with the people in their suffering and folk charm, but not in any manner that called for change through political action. It might well be argued that poetry is hardly the appropriate tool for political change. Be that as it may, we can still understand the desire, on the part of the committed, for an authentic poetry that would transcend the characteristic literature of the *Claridade/Certeza* groups and reflect the need for change.

When Amilcar Cabral called for a "new poetry in our land" he had in mind an authenticity based on a faithful expression of Cape Verde's reality as an African region where the forces of colonialism had brought about "decharacterization" and had exacerbated socioeconomic conditions, including patterns of emigration. In effect, the ambivalent motifs of "wanting to leave, having to stay," and "wanting to stay, having to leave" of some *Claridade* writers led to a form of evasion. Literally, evasion was the abandonment of the islands by a small elite seeking a more stimulating and comfortable life in the colonial metropolis. The poor went to the United States—before immigration restrictions—, to Brazil, to the plantations of the Guinea Gulf island of São Tomé, and in recent years to Portugal, France, and Holland. Significantly, because Cape Verde occupied the position of a supposedly highly acculturated society in the so-called "Portuguese Space," members of the petty bourgeoisie often served as minor administrators and civil servants in Guinea-Bissau and Angola. Mass emigration in itself was a form of evasion, not by the dispossessed, but by members of the island elite who evaded the contradictions of the colonial socioeconomic order that made "departing" a necessity.

Jorge Barbosa, who lived out his years on the islands, romanticized the early whalers of New Bedford, but the poor laborers of Massachusetts' cranberry bogs formed the bulk of Cape Verdean immigrants in the United States; and the contract workers on the plantations of São Tomé further brought the dilemma of immigration into focus.

Evasion became a politically charged term for those who called for a new poetry in the land. Paradoxically, many committed intellectuals abandoned the islands, not to seek a better material existence in Lisbon as members of a privileged group but as political exiles in cities like Algiers, Peking and Stockholm. On the other hand, some of the writers and intellectuals who steadfastly remained in Cape Verde were nevertheless labelled evasionists; the more militant accused them of not coming to terms with the people's problems and aspirations in any more than a lamenting, paternalistic, or folkloric way.

We might pause to consider that imaginative writing, and especially poetry, is unlike expository prose whose content can be easily abstracted from its form. To put it more precisely, it is the difference between language whose message is overtly political and language whose intent is to draw attention to itself. David Caute has rightly stated that "political language is dogmatic, assertive, exclusive. It regards language simply as a tool, a tool in the service of a Truth existing in complete independence of the language which expresses it. By contrast, literary language is open, exploratory, tentative, probing ambiguity and multiple levels of meaning, referrring back on itself, connotating more than it denotes."[6] Caute is talking here specifically about the language of fiction with reference to the excessivly "programmatic" novel or play that approximates political propaganda and thus ceases to be art, or at least loses its artistic advantages. Why does a committed person choose literature as a medium for his or her political message? One obvious answer is that the committed writer believes that art must serve to free mankind and be in itself a tool in the service of a truth. On a purely tactical level, art can engage an audience in a dramatic and emotional way and thus present its political message in a compelling wrapper or form. This is often the case with lyrical-combative poetry which, because it frequently says not what is but what ought to be, lends a special kind of emotive expression to identity-seeking and nationalism.

For the *Claridade* generation characteristic poetry was an emotive expression of unique regionalism that appealed to the bourgeoisie's sentiments of nostalgia and

Creole solidarity. By its very nature, this characteristic poetry, which bridged the gap between the bourgeoisie and the people, could only be intended for other members of the small elite.

An early indication of a different tone, which alters the nature of characteristic Cape Verdean poetry, appears in Aguinaldo Fonseca's "Sonho" ("Dream"), written around 1950. This different tone comes through most clearly in the following stanza:

> mamã
> este sonho meu
> é de nova vida
> é de outra terra dentro da nossa terra.[7]

(mother/ this my dream/ is of a new life/ is of another land within our land.)

By the early 1960s artistic and ideological differences among Cape Verdean intellectuals—the separation was in part generational—reached the level of a polemic predicated on the theme of evasion. Ovídio Martins' poem "Anti-Evasão" ("Anti-Evasion"), published in 1962, became a rallying cry for those intellectuals who openly or clandestinely supported the PAIGC. The persona of Martins' poem proclaims:

> Pedirei
> Suplicarei
> Chorarei
> Não vou para Pasárgada
>
> Atirar-me-ei ao chão
> e prenderei nas mãos convulsas
> ervas e pedras de sangue
>
> Não vou para Pasárgada
>
> Gritarei
> Berrarei
> Matarei
>
> Nao vou para Pasárgada.[8]

(I'll ask/ I'll plead/ I'll implore// I won't go to Pasargada// I'll throw myself to the ground/ and in my convulsed hands I'll clutch/ grass and stones of blood/ I won't go to Pasargada// I'll shout/ I'll yell/ I'll kill// I won't go to Pasargada.)

Pasargada, the sumptious capital of ancient Persia, represented hedonistic and lyrical escape for the contemporary Brazilian poet Manuel Bandeira.

In 1963 the Casa dos Estudantes do Império (The Student Empire House) in Lisbon published what was to become a controversial essay called *Consciencialização na Literatura Caboverdiana* (*The Process of Self-Awareness in Cape Verdean Literature*). The essay's author, Onésimo Silveira, a poet and short story writer of the post-*Claridade/Certeza* generation, modified Ovídio Martins' poetic reference into the defiant slogan "Esta é a Geração que não vai para Pasárgada" ("This is the Generation that will not go to Pasargada"). Without getting into the particulars of the controversy raised by the essay, Silveira's outspoken statements served notice that there was indeed an anti-establishment Cape Verdean literature based on African, not Romance regionalism, and dedicated to non-avoidance of the archipelago's social and economic problems.

Silveira himself exemplifies the paradox of anti-evasion, for in order to take a militant stance he had to go through a process of physical evasion which ultimately led him into voluntary exile in China and eventually Sweden. Ovídio Martins, the author of "Anti-Evasion," was also a political dissenter, and his poem reflects his militancy in its internal structure. We might note that his poem begins with three one-word lines composes of petitionary verbs ("I'll ask/ I'll plead/ I'll implore"), and it ends with verbs of a more demanding and violent denotation ("I'll shout/ I'll scream/ I'll kill"). All of the verbs are in the future tense, meaning that from now on "I shall be different;" and Silveira, in a poem called, significantly, "Um Poema Diferente" ("A Different Poem"), declares that

> O povo das ilhas quer um poema diferente
> Para o povo das ilhas:
> Um poema com seiva nascendo no coração da ORIGEM
> Um poema com batuque e tchabéta e badios de Santa Catarina
> Um poema com saracoteio d'ancas e gargalhadas de marfim![9]

(The people of the islands want a different poem/ For the people of the islands:/ A poem with a vigor born in the heart of ORIGINS/ A poem with drums and foot-stomping and hand-clapping and black folks from Santa Catarina/ A poem with swinging hips and ivory guffaws!)

Both Silveira's and Martins' poems share similarities of tone and point of view. In contrast to the *Claridade/Certeza* poets' lyricism and objectification of the Cape Verdean, younger poets wrote unadorned verse designed to issue forth protest and identify with the people in a subjective way. Silveira's persona, with references to origins and a "black way of being," approaches the unabashed celebration of an African essence found in much negritude poetry. The theme of Cape Verde as a case of African regionalism complements, in its defiant, celebratory tone, the anti-evasionist resolve of Martins' poem.

A number of poets who saw their works published in various, generally short-lived periodicals or in an occasional volume printed in Portugal, adopted the new tone while continuing to cultivate the established themes. Authenticity, or at least the search for this elusive quality, gained momentum in Cape Verdean poetry. The seed of defiance had been planted although the continuing colonial state of the islands, mitigated by a prevailing, and somewhat illusory, sense of self-determination on the part of the autochthonous bourgeoisie, channelled most protest into an occasional hortatory poem directed to a telluric African mother or to suffering contract workers in São Tomé.

By 1963 armed struggle had begun in Guinea-Bissau, and as a result of the Lisbon government's tighter censorship and more repressive measures in the colonies, committed writers in all of Lusophone Africa either wrote cryptically or for the desk drawer. In 1965 the PAIGC's Department of Information and Propaganda published, possibly in Algiers, *Noti (Night)*, a small volume of poetry by Kaoberdiano Dambara, pseudonym of Felisberto Vieira Lopes, a young lawyer of Santiago, Cape Verde. In a Creole as far removed from standard Portuguese as he could manage, Dambara fashioned what can be considered the first published Cape Verdean combative verse.

After the coup that on April 25, 1974 ended Portugal's right-wing dictatorship, a small corpus of militant Cape Verdean poetry appeared, mainly in periodicals and newsletters. Some of these poems had been composed before the change in the Lisbon government, and others were written just prior to or after Cape Verde's independence on July 5, 1975. A number of young poets, some bearing defiant Creole or Africanized *noms de guerre,* began to publish in Cape Verde and abroad. As a direct function of PAIGC policies many of these poems reveal a particular kind of tension arising from what can be termed an ideological crisis among members of the indigenous petty bourgeoisie, the class responsible for most Cape Verdean literary production. Amilcar Cabral wrote that this class can be divided into three groups as concerns their relationship to the liberation movement. According to Cabral, a minority, although they may have desired true self-determination, identified with the dominant colonial class and thus openly opposed the movement; another minority was hesitant or indecisive; and a third group participated in the liberation struggle. Concentrating on this third group, Cabral makes the point that although members of this autochthonous bourgeoisie played a key role in the development of the pre-independence movement, they did not truly identify with the culture and aspirations of the masses except on the basis of the struggle.[10] Poetry, as an emotional-ideological component of the independence movement, broadcasts an important aspect of this bourgeois crisis.

Cabral discusses the frequently-heard slogan "return to origins," which lies at the thematic, structural, and aesthetic heart of much pan-Africanist, negritude, and black nationalist literary expression. And Cabral sheds further light on the subject when he says.

> "But the 'return to origins' is not, nor can it be, an act of struggle against foreign domination (colonialist and racist), and it does not necessarily mean a return to traditions. It is the negation, on the part of the indigenous petty bourgeoisie, of the dominant group's supposed cultural supremacy over that of the subjugated people with whom the bourgeoisie must identify. 'Return to origins' is not a voluntary attempt but rather the only viable reaction to the irreducible contradictions which set the colonized society against the colonial force, the exploited masses against the foreign exploitative class."[11]

Writers, in their response to the irreducible contradictions of imperialism and colonialism compose poems that represent various levels of resolve and frustration as members of the bourgeoisie attempt to identify with the culture and aspirations of the people.

As a result of patterns of emigration several nuclei of Cape Verdeans in the "diaspora" contributed to the poetry of the *Nova Largada (New Departure).* As Amilcar Cabral observed, "it is not by chance that theories or movements like pan-Africanism and negritude (two pertinent expressions founded or postulated on the cultural identity of all black Africans) were conceived outside of black Africa."[12] In effect, many of the contributors to Cape Verdean literature have been students in Lisbon or civil servants in former colonial capitals like Luanda, Angola. This means that members of the indigenous bourgeoisie have had to transcend both temporal alienation from roots and spatial distance from a native cultural environment. We must also consider that the militancy and posturing in some contemporary Cape Verdean poetry have to be seen not only as the viable reaction to a set of irreducible contradictions but as an over-compensation on the part of those who did not take to the bush in the armed struggle in Guinea-Bissau.

In recent years Cape Verdean communities abroad have published newsletters that have become increasingly nationalistic in orientation and tone. Chief among these publications are, in Brazil, *Morabeza* (a Creole term meaning "affability"), in Holland,

Nôs Vida (Creole for "our lives"), and in Portugal, *Presença Cabo-Verdiana (Cape Verdean Presence)*. The latter is the official newsletter and cultural bulletin of the Cape Verde House in Lisbon. From its inception in January of 1973 until early 1974 the bulletin was called *Presença Crioula (Creole Presence)*. The ostensible reason for the change in title is that "Creole" does not pertain exclusively to Cape Verde; however, the alteration also carries some ideological and symbolic significance in that it was put into effect with the issue of April 1974, just in time to announce the end of the Salazar-Caetano regime in Portugal. Thus, the first use of the title coincided with an upsurge in nationalism among professionals and students residing in Lisbon. The new title speaks more authentically to Cape Verde as a geographic-political entity in contrast to the more romantic connotations of *Presença Crioula*.

A front-page editorial in the April 1974 issue of *Presença Cabo-Verdiana* states that when news of the coup came, work was suspended on the bulletin so that that particular number could reach the streets with the real truth, which until then could only be presented cryptically. In the fourteen issues published between April 1974 and August 1975 PAIGC policies exerted a discernible influence on the attitudes of Cape Verdean intellectuals living abroad. Nationalist sentiments quite naturally culminate in the combined July-August issue which commemorates Cape Verdean independence.

As one bit of proof that in pre-coup days editors of the bulletin had to keep a wary eye on the censor, the editorial states that they found it prudent not to print a poem that had been in their possession for several months. The poem in question, "Lar" ("Homeland") by Tacalhe (Alívio Vicente Silva), at the time a law student in Lisbon, does appear in the April 1974 issues:

> É acqui meu amor
> É aqui que fica
> O lar do nosso sonho
> Na boca vermelha desta espingarda...[13]

(Here my love/ Here is/ The homeland of our dreams/ In the crimson opening of the barrel of a gun...)

Superimposed on a full-page photograph of a smiling, female guerrilla with machine-gun in hand, this simple, explicitly combative poem, in which "less is more" (to quote architect Mies Van der Rohe), bears out Cabral's contention that members of the autocthonous bourgeoisie identify with the culture and aspirations of the people on the basis of the struggle.

Within the framework of the committed bourgeoisie's attempts to become one with the people we see variations on a few recurring themes in the seventeen poems published in *Presença Cabo-Verdiana* from April 1974 to August 1975. Sukre d'Sal (Francisco António Tomar), three of whose poems appear in the bulletin, joins Tacalhe in a kind of verse that consciously or unconsciously avoids the careful phrase and the well-worked image. A kind of committed *ars poetica*, Sukre's "Poema de Ordem" ("A Poem of Order") tells us what Cape Verdean poetry should be:

> Um poema
> de Acção
> para dinamizar a Transformaçao
>
> Um poema
> de Vigilância
> para aniquilar a reacção;

Um poema
de Luta
para acabar o obscurantismo;

Um poema
de Crítica e Autocrítica
para o progresso da revolução

Um poema
de Liberdade e Justiça
para garantir a Unidade;

Um poema
de Punhos Cerrados, confiantes
no futuro da África;

Um poema
de Amor e Cooperação
para a construção da felicidade.[14]

(A poem/ of Action/ to activate the Transformation// A poem/ of Vigilance/ to annihilate reaction;// A poem of Struggle/ to end obscurantism;// A poem of Criticism and Self-Criticism/ for the progress of the revolution;// A poem/ of Freedom and Justice/ To guarantee Unity;/ A poem/ of clinched Fists, confident in Africa's future;// A poem/ of Love and Cooperation/ to construct our happiness.)

This poem of revolutionary posturing, in which the word is a call to political action, has the urgency and immediacy of an exhortative speech in its rhythmic pattern and its pacing. Although the message calls attention to itself more than does the language, the poetic code supports the idea of order both figuratively and literally as well as structurally and thematically.

Corsino Fortes, an older poet (he was born in 1933, Sukre d'Sal in 1951), tempered his immediacy with a more mature sensitivity toward phrasing and imagery in the expression of the usual Cape Verdean themes. Two of Fortes' four poems in *Presença Cabo-Verdiana* also appear in his published volume *Pão & Fonema (Bread & Phoneme)*, a suggestive title in view of the ideological conflict inherent in the quest for identification with the people. "Bread," with all its staff-of-life connotations, combined with "phoneme," in its linguistic as well as its metaphorical meaning—and I take the latter to be sound as a call to action—lends a subtlety to the poems in the collection. The second part of Fortes' two-part poem "De Boca a Barlavento" ("Facing Windward") further enhances the collection's title:

Poeta! todo o poema:
      geometria de sangue + fonema
Escuto Escuta

Um pilão fala
      árvores de fruto
            ao meio do dia

E tambores
      erguem
            na colina
      um coração de terra batida

E lon longe
Do marulho à viola fria
  Reconheco o bemol
Da mão doméstica
  Que solfeja

Mar + monçào mar + matrimónio
Pão pedra palmo de terra
  Pão + património[15]

(Poet! the whole poem:/ geometry of blood + phoneme/ I listen you listen/ A mortar and pestle speak/ bountiful trees/ at midday/ And drums raise up/ on the hill/ A heart of beaten earth// And far off/ From the tumult like that of a cold guitar/ I recognize the flat note/ Of the domestic hand/ That runs down the scale/ Sea + monsoon sea + matrimony/ Bread stone plot of land/ Bread + patrimony)

The varied images give immediate sensorial impressions and collectively make a basic statement captured most explicitly in the first two lines which exhort poets to make combinations of sound and the life blood of reality. Fortes seems to want, in this poem, to cultivate the word in all its dimensions in order to make contact with at least the essence of Cape Verde's external reality.

Fortes has also written poems that celebrate the historical moment and event. Two such poems appear in *Presença Cabo-Verdiana:* "Guinea-Bissau e Cabo Verde," subtitled "unidade e luta ("unity and struggle"), and "P.A.I.G.C." Because Fortes has already been shown to be sensitive to phrasing and imagery, we get an idea of how he, as a member of the committed bourgeoisie, expresses the Party's emotional-ideological posture in an obvious political poem; the poet tells what the PAIGC *is:*

É a potência fálica da terra + a pontência famélica do povo
É o povo de coração em marcha sob a bandeira de Pidjiguiti
É a árvore de Boé + a proa do Arquipélago que abalroa

No umbigo da colônia
A caravela da opressão secular
É o tambor da história + o ovo da concórdia que devolve

A libertaria África
A dupla fatia de tal património
É o abraço do povo + o corpo da terra toda ela

De peito aberto, De pátria aberta
É a Estrela da manha
No sangue
Na alvorada
Na árvore,
  De todos Nós[16]

(Is the phallic might of the land + the famished might of the people/ Is the people with their hearts on march/ under the banner of Pidjiguiti/ Is the tree of Boé + the prow of the Archipelago that casts its grappling lines/ Onto the umbilical of the colony/ The caravel of age-old oppression/ Is the drum of history + the egg of concord that redeems// Libertarian Africa/ The slice of such a patrimony/ Is the people's embrace + the body of all the land// With sincerity, With a free land/ Is the morning Star/ In the blood/ In the dawn/ In the tree,/ Of us all)

The accumulation of ingredients presented in formulaic fashion (i.e., this *plus* that) makes for a unit based on the atavistic and telluric, in a virile image of fecundity, plus the negative turned positive in a legacy of hunger that leads to political, revolutionary consciousness. The poem has a historical perspective in which the past nourishes the present in preparation for the future. References to Pidjiguiti, Guinea where police massacred some fifty African strikers in 1959 and to Boé, also Guinea, where the PAIGC won a major military victory in 1969, help to establish the poem's in-group context.

We might term propagandistic poetry transient in that it depends so fundamentally on the immediacy of a given historical moment that once that moment has passed the rhetoric loses its reason for being. Perhaps this applies to much contemporary Cape Verdean poetry. But in order to make a point about literature of immediacy, let us consider that poetry composed specifically for the occasion of Cape Verde's independence. Several such poems invoke Amilcar Cabral's name, and two in *Nôs Vida* praise the "people's hero," whose death by assassination has made him something of a martyr. Tacalhe's "Canto Alegre para A. Cabral" ("Joyous Song for A. Cabral") and Natálio Spencer's "In Memoriam de A. Cabral" ("In Memory of A. Cabral") have more of the praise song that the elegy. The first stanzas of Tacalhe's poem portray the martyred hero as a telluric, unifying force:

> AMILCAR, Amilcar
> E das entranhas das nossas rochas
> Que o grito ressoa
>
> Amilcar, Amilcar
> E dos lábios brancos das nossas ondas
> Que o grito ressoa
>
> Amilcar, Amilcar
> E de dez bocas unidas
> Que a canção volatiliza[17]

(AMILCAR, Amilcar/ And from the depths of our land/ The cry resounds// Amilcar, Amilcar/ And from the white lips of our waves/ The cry resounds// Amilcar, Amilcar/ And from ten mouths at once/ The song rises like mist)

The invocation emits from "ten mouths at once," meaning the ten inhabited islands of the archipelago, as the land and the surrounding sea sing Amilcar Cabral's praises in this communal poem. The poem continues with a fourth stanza that goes from the past (Guinea-Bissau yesterday) to the present (Cape Verde today) to the future (perhaps the whole world tomorrow) in a celebration of Cabral as liberator. In his final stanza the poet makes use of the imperfect tense, with its sense of ongoingness, to cast Cabral as a tutelary hero whose name meant nourishment, whose shadow was protection, and whose name meant nourishment, whose shadow was protection, and whose word was peace. I mean to suggest that in spite of its immediacy and emotionalism this kind of poem can demonstrate a sensitivity dependent on its internal structure as well as its content.

The aesthetic value of poems like Tacalhe's becomes more meaningful when we take the following four factors into consideration: the sociopolitical and emotional-ideological context: the historical moment; the format in which they appear (in the case of a magazine like *Nôs Vida*, the material that precedes and comes after the poem); and the readers for whom they are intended. We have to assume that most readers approached the special issue of *Nós Vida* in an emotional frame of mind receptive to the euphoria and sentimentality that attended Cape Verde's independence under the aegis of the PAIGC and with Amilcar Cabral's legacy.

Now that political independence has come to Cape Verde, intellectuals must necessarily enter into a new phase in their efforts to identify with the people's culture and aspirations. During this post-independence period of nation-building writers will assist in the process of people-building and in the creation of a literature of universal appeal. In a very practical way Cape Verdean poetry and prose fiction will serve pedagogical ends, both in general education and literacy programs. In these functions poetry will undoubtedly regain some of its traditional communal dynamic: independence festivities in Cape Verde's towns and villages included poetry readings and recitations as well as the performance of traditional songs and dances.

A question that comes to mind is what will be the nature of Cape Verdean poetry during this transitional period? Sukre d'Sal, in his essay "A Poesia Caboverdiana: A Voz de Oswaldo Osório" ("Cape Verdean Poetry: The Voice of Oswaldo Osório"), sees post-independence literature as being of genuinely popular expression: "the people are consciously seeking to rediscover the path of their affirmation; the people want to be free. They must be themselves."[18] Sukre d'Sal thus affirms at least one intellectual's resolve to shun elitism and obscurantism although he certainly does not seem to be calling for a poetry of and *by* the people—in the words, a proletarian poetry. And remembering Cabral's words, to be the people's spokesman does not necessarily mean to identify with the people in any total sense nor does it mean a return to traditions. True, while telling the people that they comprise the sacred force of the nation and that their culture is valid, committed intellectuals are also telling the people that they must be educated to a new order.

Oswaldo Osório's collection of poems, in which Sukre's essay appears, bears the title *Caboverdeamadamente, Construção, Meu Amor,* based in part on a play on words that translates badly into English as *Capeverdelovingly, The Process of Building, My Love.* The author identifies the contents as "poems of struggle," and he divides the collection into "Caboverdearmadamente" (again literally and awkwardly translated as "Capeverdearmedly"), poems written clandestinely between 1967 and 1973, and "Caboverdeamadamente" ("Capeverdelovingly"), poems for after the struggle. In line with PAIGC policy, however, the struggle goes on in a continuing revolutionary process.

Osório seeks to combine the emotive impulse with the nation-building imperative. A poem that illustrates this combination is "Cantalutar" ("Singstruggle"). This poem consists of a series of combined words that rather defy translation but which in the original Portuguese project some of the tensions of the present phase of Cape Verdean literature:

> cantalutando caboverdeamamos
> caboverdeamadamente construimos a nossa terra
>
> cantalutando caboverdeamo os nossos sonhos descem às mãos
> a esse acto caboverdeamor
>
> cantaluta cantaluta cantaluta
> caboverdeamadamente[19]

(singstruggling we capeverdelove/ capeverdelovingly we build our land// singstruggling I capeverdelove our dreams come true/ in this act of capeverdelove/singstruggling
singstruggling singstruggling/ capeverdelovingly)

Osório's attempts to express a nationalistic sentiment may be a case of over-
reaching and his stylizations may be pretentious, but again, in the context of the
historical moment, his poem does hold emotional and aesthetic appeal for like-minded
intellectuals, and perhaps even for the people whose spokesman he intends to be.

Unable to go beyond certain themes and content in their quest for the
characteristic and the authentic, Cape Verdean poets, beginning with the *Claridade*
generation, with a few precursors, tried for regional flavor if not identification with local
culture. Language in all its dimensions, including sound, quite naturally aided writers
in this quest, and most understandably through the cultivation of Creole. Most contemporary Cape Verdean poets have composed works in both Portuguese and Creole
or in a combination of the two. Since the publication of Kaoberdiano Dambara's *Noti,*
mentioned several pages back, a number of collections of defiant Creole poetry have
appeared. And not just the poems content and themes convey militancy, the very use
of Creole is an act of defiance particularly when the writer has made an effort to
distinguish the language as much as possible from Portuguese. The letter "k" does not
belong to the Portuguese alphabet, but it does appear in many African languages.
Thus, committed Cape Verdean writers seem to have a penchant for the "k's" as in
Korda Kaoberdi (Awake Cape Verde) by Kwame Kondé, pseudonym of a Cape Verdean doctor who resides in Paris.[20]

Creole speech has had both a felicitous and problematic place in modern Cape
Verdean society. Most Cape Verdeans, whatever their social class, speak Creole.
Cape Verdean university students in Lisbon quite naturally converse in Creole among
themselves. In the former colonial metropolis Creole serves as a badge of distinc-
tiveness and a symbol of ethnic solidarity as well as a natural means of verbal communication for Cape Verdeans away from home; and on the islands the vernacular,
because of its acceptance and use on all levels of society, forms a link between the intelligentsia and the people.

Members of the intelligentsia have long debated Creole's appropriateness as a
literary language. Certain poets, including some of the *Claridade* generation,
cultivated popular Creole verse; and the debate has raged over whether "serious"
literature can or should be written in a language which for some retains the stigma of its
pidgin origins. Some writers have tried to "clean up" Creole by emphasizing its
similarities to standard Portuguese and by casting it in the mold of charming folk expression. Conversely, committed writers, especially those of the New Departure
group, emphasize that which might be unacceptable to those who see Cape Verde as a
case of Romance regionalism. These poets, besides using Creole as a tool in the service of sociopolitical concerns, also employ the language as one means of insisting on
an African presence in Cape Verde.

A literary piece written in Creole has a somewhat restricted audience. Most non-
Cape Verdean speakers of Portuguese cannot or will not read a poem or story in
Creole, and the spoken language is largely incomprehensible to most outsiders. Even
some middle-class Cape Verdeans who know Creole will not accept it as a literary
language. Thus, at this time in Cape Verde's development as a nation, Creole, as a
language of creative writing, reflects the committed bourgeoisie's efforts to attain that
real or imagined return to traditions and to identify with the people. When Oswaldo

Osório writes of the people's social alienation in "Kónde Lienacon Tava Mandá na gente" ("When Alienation Ruled the People"), he is also writing about the bourgeoisie's cultural alienation:

> nô ta bibé grogue
> pa nô skcé
> pa nô nimá
> 'lvantá spirte
> pa trá ess goste d'fel na boka
> nô ta toká violão
> pa sukdi tristeza
> ta sbi pa kabeça
> nô ta krê ser o knô ka era
> nô era tude lienóde[21]

(we drank rum/ to make us forget/ to cheer us up/ to raise our spirits/ to remove the bitter taste from our mouths/ we played guitars/ to chase away sadness/ it went to our heads/ we believed in what we weren't/ we were alienated)

Poets like Osório consider themselves to be bards who along with other writers of imaginative literature, as well as with artists and musicians, form a vanguard in search of national cultural authenticity.

In summary and in answer to the question posed at the beginning of this essay as to why a relationship exists between Cape Verdean poetry and the PAIGC, we can say that the philosophy of the latter does have something of a prescriptive influence on the former although there is no official policy that dictates what kind of literature and literary criticism must be produced. The *Claridade/Certeza* writers set a definitive direction for Cape Verdean literature by codifying and solidifying the ethos of an insular and relatively homogeneous society. Poetry, as the prime emotive expression of Cape Verdeanness, has been receptive to the nationalism of those who introduced the motif of anti-evasion into regional awareness. Since the mid-1960s committed writers have made poetry one of the principal products of anti-colonialism and nationalism under the banner of Amilcar Cabral's pronouncements on the indivisibility of culture and the liberation struggle.

With independence protest and combativeness became infused with the euphoria and rhetoric of nation- and people-building. Tensions of an ideological and artistic nature have attended the intellectual's search for identity and identification with perceived popular culture and aspirations. These tensions have determined the very aesthetic structure of much contemporary Cape Verdean poetry. "Art" poetry vs popular expression and Portuguese vs Creole underlie both the unadorned directness of poems by poets like Tacalhe and Sukre d'Sal as well as the experimentation and stylizations of poets like Corsino Fortes and Oswaldo Osório.

Poets and other writers will continue to align themselves with the growing political awareness of the heretofore exploited masses of the people. Besides its continuing emotive importance, imaginative writing will certainly serve during this transitional period, and perhaps for many years to come, as a pedagogical tool in the task of social and cultural reintegration.

Finally, lest my critical intentions not be fully understood, I should state that Cape Verdean poetry of this transitional period does deserve to be considered as poetry.

Without suspending critical judgments as regards poetry's intrinsic nature, we should alter our usual approaches, especially those dear to the hearts of academics, in order to emphasize the place of this poetry in its political and historical context. Pamphletary, political content and revolutionary posturing may at times overwhelm form and thus nullify the poem's value as poetry. These poems, however, like all imaginative writing, have their own aesthetic code. We cannot, and in most case we certainly will not, appreciate their aesthetic value if we read individual poems as soliloquys detached from social *praxis;* and a "literature of *praxis* is one which attempts an active role in mediating between the world and man's capacity to change it."[22] To speak, then, of the PAIGC and Cape Verdean poetry is not to determine how political ideologies may influence imaginative writing, it is also to delimit a historical period. The period is one of nation-building, and the poetry that serves and derives from this transitional phase can engage progressive readers everywhere on the basis of its artistic sensitivity and its social values ineluctably linked to a commitment to change.

Notes

[1]Amilcar Cabral, "Apontamentos sobre Poesia Caboverdiana," *Cabo Verde: Boletim de Propaganda e Informação,* No. 28 (1952), 7.

[2]Ibid., p. 8.

[3]Manuel Ferreira, *No Reino de Caliban: Antologia Panorâmica da Poesia Africana de Expressão Portuguesa* (Lisbon: Seara Nova, 1975), I (Cabo Verde e Guiné-Bissau), 105-106.

[4]Ibid., p. 91.

[5]Ibid., p. 99.

[6]David Caute, *The Illusion: An Essay on Politics, Theatre and the Novel* (New York: Harper Colophon Books, 1972), p. 72.

[7]*Cabo Verde: Boletim de Propaganda e Informação,* No. 15 (1950), 8.

[8]Ovídio Martins, *Caminhada* (Lisbon: Casa dos Estudantes do Império, 1962), p. 55.

[9]Onésimo Silveira, *Hora Grande* (Nova Lisboa: Colecção Bailundo, 1962), p. 34.

[10]Amilcar Cabral, "A Cultura e o Combate pela Independência," *Presença Cabo-Verdiana,* No. 17 (May 1974), 9.

[11]Ibid., p. 9.

[12]Ibid., p. 9.

[13]*Presença Cabo-Verdiana,* No. 16 (April 1974), 5.

[14]*Presença Cabo-Verdiana,* No. 27 (March 1975), 3.

[15]Corsino Fortes, *Pão + Fonema* (Lisbon: Oficina Gráfica, 1974), p. 10.

[16]*Presença Cabo-Verdiana,* No. 25 (January 1975), 5.

[17]*Nós Vida* (July 1975), 11.

[18]Sukre d'Sal, "A Poesia Caboverdiana: A Voz de Oswaldo Osório," in *Caboverdeamadamente, Construção, Meu Amor,* by Oswaldo Osório (Lisbon: Nova Aurora, 1975), p. 9.

[19]Ibid., p. 46.

[20]Kwame Kondé, Kordá *Kaoberdi* (Paris: Associação dos Caboverdianos em Franca, 1974).

[21]*Caboverdeamadamente, Construção, Meu Amor,* p. 17.

[22]David Caute, *The Illusion,* p. 46.

Cover of *Chiquinho* by **Baltasar Lopes**

BALTAZAR LOPES: CAPE VERDEAN PIONEER

Norman Araujo

Baltazar Lopes

Baltazar Lopes da Silva, known as "Baltazar Lopes" in the archipelago, resembles his colleague, Manuel Lopes, in several ways. He is a man of considerable formal schooling, possessing degrees in Law and Romance Philology. He writes in a variety of different genres, such as poetry, the short story, and the novel. A native of São Nicolau, where he was born in 1907, he has an added perspective on the islands, having spent his years of advanced study in Lisbon before becoming rector of São Vicente's Liceu Gil Eanes and later relinquishing that post to devote himself to teaching at the institution.

The similarities, in an artistic sense especially, are more apparent than real, however. Manuel Lopes, although less versatile intellectually than Baltazar Lopes, is artistically more gifted, more synthetic in his literary organization. Baltazar Lopes is at times more dense, more profound, but lacking, in his composition, the sustained esthetic development necessary to full achievement.

The first genre publicly cultivated by Baltazar Lopes— and in this he is similar to the other two *Claridosos* already considered—is the poetic. Appearing primarily in *Claridade*, under the pseudonym of Osvaldo Alcântara, this poetry neither pays homage to the Classical deity, like the first lyrics of Jorge Barbosa, nor suggests the frustration of insular confinement, like the verses of Manuel Lopes. Indeed, in its first phase, it is candidly optimistic, as witness "Rapsódia." This bright optimism is not only social but also esthetic, as reflected in poems like "Deslumbramento" (Fascination) and "Ignoto Deo," in which the poet seems to discover in poetry, in its expressive power and magical fascination, the proper antidote for the poisonous effect deriving from an incessant contemplation of the misery around him.[31]

Nevertheless, this poetry soon loses the gloss of great expectations and develops a somber tone, as is evident in "Poema do Rapaz Torpedeado" (The Poem of the Torpedoed Boy)[32] and "Brancaflor" (Blanchefleur).[33] The first of these two poems is especially indicative of Baltazar Lopes's disillusionment:

> Éramos vinte numa jangada,
> e o rapaz torpedeado connosco.
> Havia trinta dias
> que andávamos à tona da água
> e já não tínhamos comida,
> e já não tínhamos mais água.
>
> E o rapaz torpedeado contou a sua história.
>
> > "Uma vez um rapaz moço morreu
> > porque queria ver o mundo.
> > Mas o mundo queria
> > era sentir-se orgulhoso do seu poder.

31. Baltazar Lopes, "Deslumbramento," *Claridade*, No. 5 (September 1947), p. 12; "Ignoto Deo," p. 12.

32. Baltazar Lopes, "Poema do Rapaz Torpedeado," *Claridade*, No. 6 (July 1948), p. 1.

33. Baltazar Lopes, "Brancaflor," *Claridade*, No. 7 (December 1949), pp. 17-18.

> E o rapaz moço morreu
> porque queria ver o mundo."*

Unlike that of Jorge Barbosa, the poetic expression of Baltazar Lopes is indirect, suggestive. His disenchantment is not the exclusive product of his personal reverses but also the consequence of his sympathy with the plight of his fellow Cape Verdeans. In a series of poems called "Romanceiro de São Tomé" Baltazar Lopes treats the deplorable emigration to São Tomé: he commiserates in "Filho" (Son) with the father who sees his son return emaciated from the venture, his formerly excellent physique now completely destroyed; in "Grito" (Cry) there is the suicide of nhâ Vitória, whose husband perishes in the foreign land; in "Regresso do Paraíso" (Return from Paradise), the poet waxes ironic about the false notion of São Tomé as a paradise, when in reality those who go there are usually more than happy to come back.[34]

The poetic vision of Baltazar Lopes is not content, however, to skim the surface of Cape Verdean reality. His is a more subjective approach, an endeavor to penetrate beyond the material level and to sense the pulse of human reaction, to discover the way in which the Cape Verdean mind and heart react inwardly to the oppression of economic factors. In "Canção da Minha Rua" (The Song of My Street) the poet is attentive to the piano playing of his neighbor and speculates on how, through the magic process of music, she establishes contact with the outer world and travels about in it before returning to her present surroundings, to her "chão familiar" (home grounds):

> A vizinha chega ao seu chão familiar
> e vai poder olhar as estrelas que viu,
> sem receio de perder o equilíbrio.

---

* We were twenty on a raft, and the torpedoed boy was with us. We had been riding the surface of the water for thirty days and we didn't have any food, we didn't have any more water. And the torpedoed boy told his story. "One time a young boy died because he wanted to see the world. But what the world wanted was to feel proud of its power. And the young boy died because he wanted to see the world."

34. Baltazar Lopes, "Filho," *Claridade*, No. 8 (May 1958), p. 34; "Grito," p. 35; "Regresso do Paraíso," p. 38.

Depois que o piano se calou,
aparece enfim a sua e nossa canção,
a vizinha abre a porta
e certifica-se de que a rua está em paz absouta
antes de ir lá para dentro atender ao seu menino,
                    que choraminga.*

There is a bond between the poet and his neighbor: her "song"—the
non-musical song of her child crying—is also, in its implied symbolism,
the song of the artist who must in like manner return to the music
of reality after his poetic flights of escape.

Baltazar Lopes maintains this process of subjective identification
with the rest of his island world in "Aqui D'El-Rei" (Help!).[35] Again
the theme of piano music is present. The poet is at first disturbed by
the uncontrolled nature of his neighbor's piano playing. But suddenly
the music gains in precision and tells the sad story of the girl who lost
her virginity. This account establishes anew the bond between the
poet and his neighbor, for it voices a situation familiar to both, a common element of their general experience of life.

It is not only in music that Baltazar Lopes, himself a talented violinist,
discovers a medium of communication with the most intimate part
of his neighbors' subjective existence. It is also in the mysterious,
suggestive atmosphere of the night. In "Nocturno" Baltazar Lopes
meditates on the romantic yearning of the girl at the window, in the
moonlight, waiting for her lover to come.[36] The fact that the girl continues to dream of love, even when the lover does not appear, reveals
again, as in "Canção da Minha Rua" and "Aqui D'El-Rei," the curious
contrast between the dullness of the material or objective world and
the exciting richness of the subjective universe. There is also implied

* My neighbor reaches her home grounds and will be able to contemplate the
stars which she saw, without fear of losing her equilibrium. After the piano has
become silent, our song is finally heard; my neighbor opens the door to make
sure that the street is absolutely peaceful, before going inside to take care of
her child, who is crying.

35. Baltazar Lopes, "Canção da Minha Rua," "Aqui D'El-Rei," *Claridade*, No. 6,
p. 19.
36. Baltazar Lopes, "Nocturno," *Cabo Verde*, March 1, 1956, p. 6.

the relationship between the poet and his subject of study; the former is similarly caught between the harsh reality of his life and the poetic conceptions which, like the lover's visit, fail to materialize.

That Baltazar Lopes definitely intends this relationship is confirmed in the poem called "Serenata" (Serenade). Here he captures the atmosphere of the city at night, with a serenade floating in the air:

> É a hora que os poetas escolheram
> para a procura dos seus mundos perididos . . . *

Later, he associates these poets with romantic women and with children:

> Menina romântica, irmã
> das crianças e dos poetas . . .
> A tua janela, florida de esperanças,
> e um mistério que a cidade não entende.

Thus, to the extent to which they all share in this vision of a better world, be it the romantic vision of the girl, the wildly imaginative vision of the child, or the esthetic vision of the poet, all three are members of the same family. Baltazar Lopes has a further thought: each one may, at times, be lonely in his personal vision—like the girl, whom the city does not understand.

For Baltazar Lopes, therefore, the poetic form has largely the purpose of exploring the hidden life of the islands, that area of human thought and action which, because of its elusive and intangible quality, escapes the superficial viewer. In this the poet is quite distinct from his colleague, Jorge Barbosa. Whereas Barbosa endeavors to discern the surface poetic value of a commonplace situation on the islands, Baltazar Lopes is more concerned with the subtle circumstances in which this situation, banal and unattractive in and of itself, is made poetic by the tension between its static nature and the dynamic force of man's dreams and ambitions, his hope and imagination.

---

* It is the time that the poets have chosen for the pursuit of their lost worlds. Romantic maiden, sister of children and of poets . . . your window, abloom with hopes, is a mystery which the city does not understand.

The direct approach which Jorge Barbosa applies in poetry, Baltazar Lopes attempts to apply in prose. The attempt is rather successful in the short stories "Dona Mana"[37] and "A Caderneta" (The Booklet),[38] where the writer depicts realistically the ordeal of women forced for economic reasons to give themselves up to prostitution. Baltazar Lopes views the matter, in each case, not only from the personal vantage point of the people directly involved but also from the broadly social perspective, as both times society, through its medical institutions in "A Caderneta" and through its judicial officials in "Dona Mana," misinterprets the torment of the helpless victim.

The example of "A Caderneta" and "Dona Mana" notwithstanding, even in the short-story category Baltazar Lopes returns to the same artistic framework in which he placed his poetic contribution. One has only to analyse a short story like "Muminha vai para a escola" (Muminha Goes to School) to become aware of this.[39] The story, on the level of straightforward realism, is that of a student at the seminary who, because of his sickly frame, is tagged with an unfortunate nickname by his schoolmates, the latter never ceasing to make him the object of ridicule.

Beside the realistic portrayal of the maligned youth and the incisive grasp of juvenile psychology which this treatment reveals on the part of the writer,[40] there is still another important aspect of "Muminha vai para a escola." The story, by its characterization of the protagonist, lends further development to a theme which runs through the poetry of Baltazar Lopes—that of the basic contradiction between the negative, repressive force of the outside world, and the positive, progressive, idealistic vision which the individual nurtures within himself.

In "Serenata" this contradiction leads to the solitude of the girl, who is beyond the city's level of comprehension. In "Muminha vai para a escola," too, there is the solitude of the invalid youth, ostracized from the society of those who would normally be his closest associates, his best friends. His character is not without nobility, as evidenced

37. Baltazar Lopes, "Serenata," *Claridade*, No. 6, p. 21; "Dona Mana," pp. 2-8.

38. Baltazar Lopes, "A Caderneta," *Vértice* VII, No. 65 (January 1949), 114-122.

39. Baltazar Lopes, "Muminha vai para a escola," *Cabo Verde*, June 1, 1952, pp. 8-10.

40. Andrade, Alberto de, "Muminha de Baltazar Lopes," *Cabo Verde*, April 1, 1953, p. 7.

in his stalwart resistance to Zé Coimbra, the school bully. This display of courage is not capable of reversing the situation, however, and he continues in his lonely existence, an existence all the more bitter in its irony since what his schoolmates take to be effeminacy is simply the visible effect of his malady. The tragic suicide of Muminha in Lisbon, fatal fruit of his illness and the hostile treatment afforded him by his classmates, ends forever his noble impulses and personal aspirations.

Serving as a vehicle for the continued development of themes central to his poetry, the short-story genre is also used by Baltazar Lopes to express a certain *saudosismo*, a nostalgic reminiscence of his childhood days. In "Pedacinho" (Little Piece) he reviews this period of his life and sees it as a fabulous adventure, full of joy and fancy.[41] There were only vague echoes of a far-off World War I, and the writer spent his time scampering gleefully through a vegetation-filled countryside quite the contrary of the present-day barrenness.

Different in theme from the afore-mentioned short stories of Baltazar Lopes, "Pedacinho" would appear, at first glance, to stand apart in his writings. Yet it falls immediately into place when compared to a larger, much more substantial work very similar to it in tone, although written quite some time before. This work, the novel *Chiquinho* (1947), is not related only to "Pedacinho." It is also related to the other short stories already discussed and to the themes of Baltazar Lopes's poetry. *Chiquinho* absorbs every one of these elements; but unfortunately, as will be shown somewhat later, it does so in a loosely-knit and disorderly fashion.[42]

The realistic facet of *Chiquinho* recalls to mind the novels of Manuel Lopes and the problem of forced emigration. Lacking, nevertheless, is the dramatic role accorded to the forces of nature. Baltazar Lopes substitutes for this effect a laconic account of the gradually worsening conditions which eventually force the story's hero, Chiquinho, to leave the islands. This substitution does not in any way mean a total absence within the structure of the novel of artistic progression leading to a *dénouement*.

To prepare the way for his later departure, the narrator of *Chiquinho* tells us that his father left for America because of the drought of 1915

---

41. Baltazar Lopes, "Pedacinho," *Claridade*, No. 9, pp. 58-60.
42. Baltazar Lopes, *Chiquinho* (São Vicente, 1947).

and settled in New Bedford, from which he proceeded to send with
regularity letters containing anxiously-awaited money. Having established a *raison d'être* for his future duplication of his father's feat,
Chiquinho further prepares the reader by commenting soberly on the
drought presently devastating the islands:

> I had never seen the likes of that. This spectacle of life fleeing
> imperceptibly from people and from things was new to me. The
> moon specialists explained the cyclic fatality of the drought. Every
> twenty years there came that complete betrayal of the rain, which
> abandoned the islands for other places in the middle of the sea.
> I was used to the serene face of the routine life of my island . . .
> The want of other years had not prepared me for that cruel and
> all-embracing battle.

In the face of the frightful spectacle of this progressive liquidation
of life, it is not surprising that Chiquinho should consider following
in the footsteps of his father. Moreover, there are other considerations
weighing in favor of his leaving. No line of social endeavor offers
him the opportunity, should he stay, to provide for his personal security: agriculture, civil service, commerce, all the available occupa-
tions are paralyzed in the stagnant economy of the islands. On the
other hand, the letters he receives from America depict that country
in terms of wealth and boundless opportunity. He has every reason
to believe what he reads, for it is the money received from America
which has enabled his family to maintain a social position superior
to that of the extremely poor people around them.

Viewed in this light, it is perfectly understandable that Chiquinho
should not hesitate a minute when word comes from his father asking
him if he wants to go to America. The encouragement of his grandmother, Mamãe-Velha, and his uncle, Tio Joca, only serve to fortify
a previously favorable disposition. Unnecessary, therefore, are the
excruciating vacillations of a Quim unsure of his destiny and uncertain as to the proper setting for its evolution. Chiquinho departs
quietly in an atmosphere unmarked by great dramatic tensions.

The theme of forced emigration in *Chiquinho* is complemented by
the presence of other realistic elements which tend to give a natural,
authentic ring to the narrative. One finds, for example, a discussion
of Chiquinho's early education and a reference to his attendance at

the classes of José Martins in Praia Branca, a hamlet on his home island of São Nicolau. There his uncle, who had studied at the seminary with Cónego Coimbra and Cónego Silva, used to read to him. When the time comes to enter the seminary, Chiquinho senses the significance of the event with respect to his future career:

> For me a new life was going to begin. In the following school year I would be matriculated in the *liceu* course, in the seminary. With the good head which God had given him, it would have been a shame to have Chiquinho continue leaning on a shovel. The school was waiting for me with open arms to set me free. Thus I would later be able to talk down to those who had only completed the elementary course.

Indicating the respect which those of advanced schooling enjoy on the islands, *Chiquinho* focuses, at the same time, the folkloric aspects of Cape Verdean life. The novel speaks of the peculiar local customs of the people with reference to the treatment of ailments. Chiquinho relates how Mamãe-Velha preferred to the studied prescriptions of her doctors the application of a traditional homemade concoction of herbs, prescribed by one of the elders of the community.

Cape Verdean folklore is also viewed in its more fanciful aspects. As a child Chiquinho hears stories of *feiticeiros*, narrated in a chilling fashion by a friend of the family, nhâ Rosa Calita. These tales, more than simply a pleasant diversion, are for the young hero a source of eternal preoccupation. I can attest, from personal experience, that they continue to frighten many adults living on the islands at the present time.

By its realistic examination of various aspects of Cape Verdean life, by its conjunction of cultural and folkloric themes with the broad central line of forced emigration, *Chiquinho* contributes unmistakably to a better, more concrete knowledge of the archipelago. This contribution proceeds from an original angle, from the personal frame of reference of the narrator, who tells his own story. Yet it would be erroneous to dismiss *Chiquinho* as a simple documentary, written in the first person, on Cape Verdean matters. The novel has a far greater significance. It is the progressive destruction of the narrator's dream world of childhood, thus foreshadowing "Pedacinho." It is also the progressive intensification of the narrator's sense of solitude, thus previewing "Muminha vai para a escola" and the writer's poetry.

The very beginning of *Chiquinho* evokes the enchantment of the narrator's youth:

> I recall the little house in which I was born in Caleijão like one who hears a very sad melody. Destiny has led me to know houses very much bigger, houses in which there always seems to be tumult, but none would I change for our home, covered with French tile and roughcast on the outside with lime, which my grandfather constructed with money earned on the high seas. Mamãe-Velha always recalled with pride the honorable beginnings of our home. It is a shame that my grandfather died so young, without enjoying directly the fruit of his work.

For Chiquinho, a boy's home was really his castle, and the narrator's reference to music, in view of its employment in the poetry already studied, adds further to the wonderland atmosphere which radiates from this passage.

While this childhood wonderland may have included the house described as the center of its kingdom, its fascination was not limited to the family residence. Chiquinho tells with enthusiasm of the effect on his imagination of the exploits of Charlemagne and how they transformed the universe for him:

> The wars of Roland and the Twelve Peers swallowed up the obscure heroism of my people. And the sea was for me a battlefield where enormous giants struggled with one another to conquer the love of the sea maiden.

As Chiquinho mused imaginatively about the wonders of the sea and battles between giants, he speculated fancifully about life on São Vicente, which he and his little friends saw, too, as a land filled with soldiers, and with strange visitors from the world beyond the seas. A further subject of excitement for Chiquinho was the arrival at his own island of famous whaling ships such as the *Wanderer* and the *Charles W. Morgan*, the latter now permanently enshrined at the Mystic Seaport in Connecticut. With these ships came Cape Verdean sailors such as Chico Zepa, who thrilled the narrator with stories of his maritime feats, becoming in the eyes of the youngster a local hero.

This universe of make-believe had to come to an end. Chiquinho marks the start of his disillusionment with his trip to São Vicente.

There he does not discover the situation which he had conceived in his dreams but in its stead the misery of a port already in rapid decline and unable to offer any form of opportunity for economic stability to the thousands who look to it for help.

It is not exclusively in an economic sense, however, that Chiquinho is to suffer disillusionment. When he returns from São Vicente, he finds that the advanced schooling which he acquired there makes a difference in his social relations with the inhabitants of the island. First, it means that he is now above manual labor in the fields. But more important, it means that he is now regarded with suspicion and envy by those who do not share his high intellectual attainment, people typified by Mário Almeida, who, though he congratulates Chiquinho on his academic achievements, misunderstands their purpose and even warns him about being too haughty. As a final source of discouragement, Chiquinho is given a post as schoolteacher in a remote corner of the island, where his intellectual and moral solitude are now conjoined with geographical isolation. In this context, his eventual emigration possesses a significance far larger than that deriving solely from economic factors.

In addition to being a study of crisis conditions in Cabo Verde, and a personal treatment of the process of growing up on the islands, *Chiquinho* is also a partial treatise on art, an attempt—several years before the codifying fabric of Manuel Lopes's *Os Meios Pequenos e a Cultura*—to lay the basis for a new perspective on literary activity in Cabo Verde. In the very framework of the novel, the effort is made to transform theory into fact, and Chiquinho joins forces with a group endeavoring to found a review. The literary credo of the group is placed in the mouth of one of its members, Nonó.

> —We need to write things that could only be written in Cabo Verde, things that could not be written, for example, in Patagonia . . . Scandanavia and her fiords are not important to us. We are interested in the coal worker of São Vicente who has not worked for a long time.

As in the short stories of *O Galo Que Cantou na Baía*, there is here the constant compulsion, carried into the world of fiction, to demonstrate the need for a new literary orientation, a new way of composing literature in Cabo Verde with the avowed purpose of mirroring local phenomena. Both Manuel Lopes and Baltazar Lopes would seem to be in accord on this point, despite the more elaborate theorizing of the former and the evident difference of the genres used for this expression.

Yet the accord between the two writers is not absolutely complete. The attack which Manuel Lopes launches against the cult of *beleza* in *Os Meios Pequenos e a Cultura* and *O Galo Que Cantou na Baía* is forceful and unrelenting, as attested in the example of Eduardinho's jolting contact with reality. In *Chiquinho*, however, the campaign is waged with perhaps a more tolerant spirit, a greater degree of understanding evident in the episodes involving Sr. Euclides, a sort of fictional representation of José Lopes.

The treatment accorded Sr. Euclides is dual in focus. It involves, first of all, the perspective of his anonymous detractors who scorn and ridicule him because of his claim to be producing a great masterpiece, none of whose pages have ever been seen. The viewpoint of these observers might be said to symbolize the general opinion of the people of the island with respect to the old man. In the eyes of the majority, Sr. Euclides is not simply a mediocre man of letters; he is above all a fraud.

None the less, there emerges, at the same time, a more sympathetic, a more enlightened assessment of the man which grows out of the opinion which Chiquinho himself maintains. The narrator visits Sr. Euclides, listens patiently as the latter reads his ill-measured alexandrines and appreciates, if not their metric structure, at least their sincere religious fervor. Chiquinho further discovers that the poet has actually written a book condemning the fruit of his lifetime experience and intended to instruct the youth of the islands. As Chiquinho leaves the home of Sr. Euclides, his attitude is one of tacit understanding, reflected in the disapproval of his derisive friends, who find him excessively tolerant.

More conclusive proof of Chiquinho's feelings on the subject appears in his sharp censure of the unjust manner in which Sr. Euclides is exposed to ridicule. This censure does not come from the narrator himself: it is uttered, rather, by a friend of his, José Lima, with the silent approbation of Chiquinho:

—These men have the defect of never having seen a vaster horizon. They do not understand that everyone has a perfect right to experience in his imagination what ne cannot experience in reality. They are endowed with a capacity for derision which exceeds their experience. Why this old man is worth more than all of them put together. The others see only the rain not falling on their orchards and their cows dying for want of pasture. The old man has a more generous image of the world.

I do not find such a passage shocking when I recall that it was Baltazar Lopes who, after voicing his disagreement with the literary ideas of José Lopes, suggested that I go over to see the elderly poet.

Ironically enough, *Chiquinho* fails as a novel for being as poorly measured, with respect to the different esthetic ingredients which enter into its composition, as the inadequate versification which the novel's protagonist deplores in the poetry of Sr. Euclides. A loose blending of realism, childhood evocations, and broadminded reflections on the proper form and content of Cape Verdean literature, *Chiquinho* is an unorganized collection of different episodes rather than a *bona fide* novel in the truest sense. The first Cape Verdean novel by its unquestioned dedication to the Cape Verdean scene as such, it is stylistically unworthy of classification with the legitimate novelistic production of Manuel Lopes.

In the final analysis, *Chiquinho* is more a guide to the thought and sentiment of Baltazar Lopes the scholar and intellectual than it is a consecration of Baltazar Lopes the poet and novelist. Perhaps this can be said for the totality of the writer's literary production, although certain efforts, as observed in the poetry, often reveal a sensitive, if imperfect, artist. On the whole—curious though it may seem—Baltazar Lopes seems to stand in relation to his literary generation somewhat as José Lopes stands in relation to his. Both represent the pinnacle of formal intellectual development in the eyes of their colleagues. Both are the leading spokesmen for the doctrines of their respective groups and both are eager to rise in defense of their own. Both are conscious, Baltazar Lopes in less marked fashion than José Lopes, of their personal importance in the cultural and more specifically literary progress of the islands.

In purely literary terms the comparison would seem equally feasible. Both use literature more as a means of embellishing their lives than as a form of implementing an attitude which is *engagée*: José Lopes by poetic flights of the imagination in time and space; Baltazar Lopes by a subjective poetry in quest of the cherished dream in himself and others, or by a return in the novel or short story to the bliss of his youth. Both are cultured in their literary production: Baltazar Lopes by his subtle use of medieval symbolism, of legend, of history; José Lopes by his constant recourse to Classical mythology, by the broad reach of his information. Both, finally, are similar by their common inability to transfer their sensitivity and erudition to literature in a successful form: Baltazar Lopes because he cannot unify his artistic personality; José Lopes because his artistic personality rarely ever appears, subjugated as it is by the Classical importations that fill his poetry.

Lastly, José Lopes and Baltazar Lopes are alike in that they loom, on the islands, as giants to be emulated, as irrefutable proof of what the Cape Verdean is capable of achieving within the narrow boundaries of his archipelago. Because of this fact both are appreciated even by segments of the population considerably divided as to the category of their literary tastes.

THE REVIEW ENTITLED *CLARIDADE*

While Classicism was officially dethroned in Cabo Verde only in 1936, with the publication of the first number of the review *Claridade*, the new literary movement foreshadowed by Cardoso and Tavares had begin to gather momentum a few years earlier. Manuel Lopes, later a prominent *Claridoso*, wrote an article in 1931 for the *Notícias de Cabo Verde* entitled "A Mocidade Cabo-Verdiana" (Cape Verdean Youth), in which he urged the youth of the islands to champion the interest of their homeland.[1] Jorge Barbosa, another future *Claridoso*, answered in support of the article. Somewhat later, in 1933, a group including Manuel Lopes, the artist Jaime de Figueiredo, the prominent businessman Manuel Velosa, and the literary critic Quirino Spencer met on São Vicente with the intention of publishing *Atlanta*. This review, it was hoped, would illustrate the literary principles embodied in a manifesto which Spencer had just written denouncing the Classical style in Cape Verdean literature.[2]

These endeavors were isolated and abortive. The actual revolution did not come until 1936, when members of the group which had projected *Atlanta*, Manuel Lopes, Jaime de Figueiredo, and Manuel Velosa, joined by newcomers Baltazar Lopes da Silva and João Lopes, created *Claridade*.[3] Manuel Lopes was well disposed, by his demonstrated attachment to the cause of Cabo Verde, to participate in so significant an undertaking. Jaime de Figueiredo had for some time been distributing on the islands copies of the Coimbra review *Presença*, later to be discussed, which was a sort of continental counterpart to *Claridade*.[4]

---

1. Manuel Ferreira, "Consciência Literária Cabo-Verdeana: Quatro Gerações: Claridade—Certeza—Suplemento Literário—Boletim do Liceu Gil Eanes," *Estudos Ultramarinos: Literatura e Arte*, No. 3 (1959), p. 39.

2. Pedro da Silveira, "Relance da Literatura Cabo-Verdeana," *Cabo Verde*, August 1, 1954, p. 27.

3. Ferreira, "Consciência Literária Cabo-Verdiana," p. 38.

4. Luís Romano, "O Caso Caboverdeano na Moderna Literatura," *Vértice*, XIV, Nos. 131-132 (August-September 1954), 485.

PROPRIEDADE DO GRUPO "CLARIDADE"

Director: JOÃO LOPES - Editor: JOAQUIM TOLENTINO (com a habilitação legal) - Administração em S. Vicente, C. Verde

Composto e Impresso na Sociedade de Tipografia e Publicidade, L.da

S. VICENTE—TRAVESSA BRITES D'ALMEIDA, N.º 12

DEZEMBRO DE 1960

Cover of *Claridade* Magazine no. 9

Moreover, Figueiredo had produced sketches of types and motifs of Santiago, some of which had been duplicated on the pages of the Lisbon periodical, *Correio de Europa* (Letters from Europe).[5] Manuel Velosa had provided enthusiastic commercial assistance and permitted his office to be used for regular meetings of the team.[6] Baltazar Lopes da Silva had recently returned from Portugal where he had studied philology and laid the groundwork for his future opus, *O Dialecto Crioulo de Cabo Verde*. João Lopes had brought to the gathering the vigor of an alert and aggressive mind as gifted in matters of organization as in the study of Cape Verdean sociology.

From what I was able to discover on the islands, the name *Claridade* was applied to the infant review by Baltazar Lopes da Silva, after friction within the group had forced the withdrawal of Figueiredo. The artist had dissented from the majority intention of using the *Presença* format and had decided not to contribute the essay and sketch expected of him for the initial number. At the last minute, Manuel Lopes filled the gap with an article called "Tomada de Vista" (Taking a Stand). *Claridade* appeared in March of 1936 with contributions from Manuel Lopes, the poet Pedro Corsino Azevedo, Jorge Barbosa, and João Lopes. Later in 1936 a second number appeared and in 1937 a third, with basically the same contributing cast as that indicated above for the first. From 1937 to 1945 the publication of the review was interrupted, and when it appeared again in 1946 it displayed a different complexion. Now writing in *Claridade* were some of the young founders of another literary review, *Certeza*, namely such men as Nuno Miranda, Tomás Martins, and Arnaldo França. The fifth number of *Claridade*, materializing in 1947, revealed the participation of two new writers, Aguinaldo Fonseca and António Aurélio Gonçalves, the second of whom had been in Portugal during the early years of the enterprise. In the sixth number (1948), the ethnologist Félix Monteiro offered his first contribution, as did Gabriel Mariano with poems in Crioulo. No new names appeared in the seventh number (1949), but the eighth (1958) introduced to the Cape Verdean public the verses of Terêncio Anahory, the short stories of Virgílio Pires, and the work of another exponent 'of Crioulo poetry, Jorge Pedro. With the ninth

5. Pedro da Silveira, "Relance da Literatura Cabo-Verdiana," p. 28.
6. Romano, "O Caso Caboverdeano na Moderna Literatura," pp 487-488..

appearance of *Claridade* in 1960, poets Corsino Fortes, Ovídio Martins, and Sérgio Frusoni added their names to the literary roster.

As the dates of appearance suggest, *Claridade's* evolution was not always a smooth, ascendant one. The years of silence and inactivity between the third and fourth numbers and the checkered course which the review has pursued from then up to the present bespeak the irregularity and inconsistency of its development. The reasons behind *Claridade's* erratic growth are several and diversified; and most of them relate to the deterministic nature of the small island community which is Cabo Verde.

The archipelago's population of roughly 150,000 offers, first of all, a strictly limited capacity of literary consumption, the highly-touted literacy of the people notwithstanding. It must also be borne in mind that literacy is not to be confused with buying power, or the ability to read with the possibility of acquiring the literature desired. But in addition to the natural constringency of Cabo Verde with respect to its reading public and economic potential, the following factors are significant: the dispersal of the writers throughout the islands, the departure of some of them for the mainland, and the generally depressing effect of life in a remote corner of the universe isolated from the main stream of world activity. All of these causes have resulted in a weakening, if not a complete suspension, of the crusading spirit which launched *Claridade*.

*
* *

It would simplify matters considerably to be able to demonstrate that the founders of the movement which produced *Claridade* in 1936 had in their hands, as they discussed their new venture, copies of Cardoso's *Folclore Crioulo* and Tavares's *Mornas*. Reality, however, is more complicated. To be sure, the example set by the two pioneering writers was never far from the minds of the *Claridosos*. The *Claridade* group was later to tell an interviewer from Brazil that Cardoso and Tavares were the first poets to capture in verse the sentiment of Capeverdeanism.[7] Jaime de Figueiredo was to mention Tavares in the

7. Delfim de Faria, "Caboverdeanidade," *Boletim da Sociedade Luso-Africana do Rio de Janeiro*, No. 13 (April-June 1935), p. 114.

introduction to his *Terra de Sôdade* (Land of Nostalgia), where he explains the setting of his ballet on the island of Brava.[8] Manuel Lopes, in his lecture for the *Colóquios Cabo-Verdianos* (Cape Verdean Colloquia), was to distinguish Cardoso and Tavares from their unsuccessful imitators who failed to possess their high artistic accomplishment.[9] A later contributor to *Claridade*, Gabriel Mariano, was also to signalize the relationship of the poetic mentality of these two precursors to the review's literary message.[10]

If the *Claridosos* later recognized publicly their debt to Cardoso and Tavares, at the moment of the review's inception other influences played more heavily, or at least more consciously, upon their minds. One of these was the jolting effect of the revolutionary publication *Presença*. Circulated on the islands by Jaime de Figueiredo, *Presença* had first appeared in Portugal in 1927, founded by José Régio, Gaspar Simões, Branquinho da Fonseca, Edmundo de Bettencourt, Fausto José, and António de Navarro, with Adolfo Casais Monteiro and Miguel Torga as later directors.[11] Like *Claridade* on the islands, *Presença* represented in continental Portugal a violent dissociation from the then prevailing literary fashions.

The question of *Presença*'s new approach to literature and the relevance of this approach to the situation in Cabo Verde has succeeded in confusing the few critics who have addressed themselves to it. Some of these argue that the Cape Verdean *Claridosos* at first adhered to the *Presença* movement, then discovered that their real artistic calling lay in a more direct sensitivity to Cape Verdean realities.[12] Other critics imply that the Cape Verdean writers misunderstood the *Presença* undertaking and were influenced by it in ignorance of their fundamental

8. Jaime de Figueiredo, "Terra de Sôdade: Argumento de Bailado Folclórico em Quatro Quadros," *Atlântico*, Nova Série No. 3 (1947), p. 1.

9. Manuel Lopes, "Reflexões sobre a Literatura Cabo-Verdiana," *Colóquios Cabo-Verdianos* (Lisbon, 1959), p. 3.

10. Gabriel Mariano, "Inquietação e serenidade: Aspectos da insularidade na poesia de Cabo Verde," *Estudos Ultramarinos: Literatura e Arte*, No. 3, p. 58.

11. António José Saraiva and Óscar Lopes, *História da Literatura Portuguesa*, 2nd ed. (Porto, 1956?), pp. 429-430.

12. Henrique Teixeira de Sousa, "Cabo Verde e a Sua Gente: Palestra Lida na Liga Portuguesa de Profilaxia Social no Porto, em Novembro de 1954," *Cabo Verde*, October 1, 1958, p. 12.

divergence from its purpose.[13] What is stressed is the idealistic and introspective nature of *Presença* as contrasted with the social realism of *Claridade*.

In the particular context of Luso-Cape Verdean literary intercourse, the debate has assumed interesting proportions in the exchanges between continental Manuel Ferreira, a loyal friend of Cabo Verde, and insular Félix Monteiro. The former contends that the *Claridosos* were really *anti-presencistas* and consciously revolted from the review's guidance just as, according to him, the new generation of *Presença* writers—men like Mário Dionísio—rebelled against the tutelage of the old guard.[14] Monteiro replies that not only do the *Claridosos* owe a considerable debt to *Presença*, but that Jorge Barbosa and Jaime de Figueiredo even contributed to it.[15]

Complacent though it be, the truth would seem to lie somewhere between these extreme positions. A study of the *Presença* credo of the early stages of the review's existence reveals an attractive vagueness and ready susceptibility to a variety of interpretations. In the very first number of *Presença*, the following passage of José Régio appears:

> In art everything that is original has life. Everything that comes from the most virgin, the most authentic, the most intimate part of an artistic personality is original... As a general rule—I honor the exceptions—our artists have an inadequate mentality, a sensitivity at times intense but restricted, and a unilateral vision of life. Having exhausted their possibilities in two or three books, they repeat themselves painfully. And their progress is purely linguistic, superficial, and negative.[16]

This passage would seem, in large part, to justify an introspective view of the *Presença* credo. Yet, a number later, the same José Régio gives more breadth to his declarations:

> What is important is that an artist possess in himself and discover by himself his classicism.

13. Ferreira, "Consciência Literaria Cabo-Verdeana," p. 32.

14. Manuel Ferreira, "Breves Notas sobre a literatura caboverdeana," *Vértice* IV, no. 52 (November-December 1947), 493-498.

15. Félix Monteiro, Rectificação a proposito do Grupo Claridade, *Vértice* V, No. 58 (June 1948), 477-478.

16. José Régio, "Literatura Viva," *Presença*, No. 1 (March 10, 1927), pp. 1-2.

That is—the harmonious, vibrant conjunction of all of his creative faculties.
In view of the discussion of these general points and the conclusion arrived at, we must accept a timeless classicism...
Also I shall not strike out against the commonplace of considering classicism universalistic. The truth is that only inferior art is purely individualistic, that which neither directly nor indirectly succeeds in illuminating profound humanity, that which merely succeeds in revealing a case with no possibility of amplification. As bizarre as the sentiments, thoughts, sensations, and emotions of certain great artists may appear to us, they cannot refrain from revolving about the three or four exterior motives. What varies according to the times, the currents, the individual personalities is the way of feeling, of thinking, of interpreting these motives. If being individualistic is having and stubbornly following an individual personality, all the great artists are individualistic. All are also universalistic, if being universalistic is illuminating profound humanity.[17]

Certainly these words, especially those of the first paragraph, with their insistence on a personal, inner discovery of one's classicism, can be interpreted in the idealistic, introspective sense. And indeed José Régio's own works, like *Poemas de Deus e do Diabo* (Poems of God and of the Devil), *Biografia* (Biography) and *Jogo do cabra-cega* (Blindman's Buff) bear out this conclusion. Nevertheless, the reference here to "illuminating profound humanity," the flexibility of the genuine classical ideal, and the defense of universality are welcome features in the eyes of the *Claridosos*.

Furthermore, the very writers of *Presença* display a receptivity to such an interpretation of their master's declarations by the way in which they greet and encourage the efforts of *Claridade*. The publication of the island review's third number is hailed as the "first manifestation of an authentic Portuguese spirit of modernism outside continental Portugal." [18] The appraisal goes on to mention the successful conjunction, in the publication, of the particular Cape Verdean personality with a universal perspective. Thus *Presença*, in the historical context, acts not only as a positive source of orientation for the youthful literary movement on the islands but also as an enthusiastic

---

17. Régio, "Classicismo e Modernismo," *Presença*, No. 2 (April 10, 1927), pp. 1-2.
18. Ferreira, "Consciência Literária Cabo-Verdeana," p. 27.

assessor of the movement's sense of progress and direction. No wonder the *Claridosos* read it with extreme satisfaction.

In the exciting days of 1936 which preceded the *Claridade* explosion, the originators of the review were also absorbed in the reading of a somewhat different sort of literature, a literature different in the totality of its contexture and different also in the source of its provenance— the regionalistic works of the modern school of Brazilian writers. To understand the full impact of this literary importation from Brazil, it is helpful to recall the observations of one Brazilian author, Arnon de Mello, who was astounded, when visiting the islands in 1931, to discover their incredibly close kinship to his own country.[19] He speaks of the drought zones of Brazil as compared with São Vicente. He notes also the musical similarities, how Brazilian music is so willingly absorbed by the local population. He mentions, in addition, the surprising resemblance between Brazilian and Cape Verdean speech.

Of more significance for us is the fact that Mello marvels at the literary penetration of Brazil into Cabo Verde. He finds that modern writers such as Jorge Amado, José Lins do Rego, Amando Fontes, and Érico Veríssimo are well known on the islands. Excerpts from the works of these men, the observer states, are recited from memory, and enthusiastically, by the Cape Verdean populace.

That Mello's words contain little or no exaggeration becomes apparent when one examines the pronouncements of Cape Verdean writers themselves concerning the cultivation of Brazilian literature in the archipelago. Manuel Lopes, speaking of the lesson which this literature brought to the islands in the form of a vigorous protest against socio-economic conditions and an endeavor to express universality through regionalistic phenomena, mentions the following writers as those who most impressed him and his colleagues: José Américo de Almeida, Mário de Andrade, Jorge Amado, Manuel Bandeira, Ribeiro Couto, Amando Fontes, Gilberto Freyre, Jorge de Lima, Rachel de Queiroz, Graciliano Ramos, Marques Rebelo, José Lins do Rego, and Herberto Sales.[20] To this list other *Claridosos* or their followers have added the names of Raul Bopp, Luís da Câmara Cascudo, Euclides da Cunha, and Érico Veríssimo.

19. Arnon de Mello, *África* (Rio de Janeiro, 1941), pp. 68-88.
20. Manuel Lopes, "Reflexões," p. 16.

Of these myriad sources of Brazilian influence, the writer most mentioned by the Cape Verdean literati would seem to be José Lins do Rego, who died in 1957. Baltazar Lopes da Silva pays tribute to the late novelist with an article called "Adeus, José Lins" (Farewell, José Lins).[21] António Aurélio Gonçalves refers to him in another article, noting that he has read Lins do Rego's *O Menino de Engenho* (Plantation Lad), *Doidinho* (Daffy Boy), and *Banquê* (The Old Plantation).[22] Teixeira da Sousa, a staunch supporter of *Claridade* and an intermittent contributor to its numbers, relates the atmosphere of *Banquê* to that of his own island experience.[23]

After José Lins do Rego, the most influential of the Brazilian authors would appear to be Jorge Amado, whom Baltazar Lopes da Silva specifically indicated in one of his conversations with me, and, in the case of Jorge Barbosa, the poets Manuel Bandeira and Ribeiro Couto. Interestingly enough, it is the last-mentioned writer, Ribeiro Couto, who, in effect, places the seal of validity upon the notion of a strong Brazilian literary incursion into Cabo Verde when he writes, in the *Journal do Brasil* (Journal of Brazil), an essay called "Destino e poesia de Cabo Verde" (Destiny and Poetry of Cabo Verde), discovering in the literature of the islands an echo of his own land.[24]

Unfortunately, the repercussions of the Brazilian regionalistic movement on the literature of the Cape Verde Islands, a phenomenon frankly admitted by the Cape Verdean writers themselves and readily evident to perspicacious critics such as Couto, have been woefully exaggerated. The chief culprit in the matter is the Brazilian writer Gilberto Freyre. Lamenting the fact that Cape Verdean literature is so bound up with Brazilian, Freyre wishes that it could be more characteristic and extends his remarks to include even Jorge Barbosa, whom he particularly admires.[25] On another occasion, Freyre goes even farther, expressing his grave disappointment at the flagrant lack of originality in Cape

21. Baltazar Lopes da Silva, Adeus, José Lins" *Cabo Verde*, March 1, 1958, p. 6.
22. António Aurélio Gonçalves, "Algumas ideias sobre Lins do Rego," *Cabo Verde*, March 1, 1958, pp. 3-4. The translations of the Brazilian titles are from Fred P. Ellison, Brazil's *New Novel* (Berkeley and Los Angeles, 1954), pp. 45-79.
23. Teixeira de Sousa, "Lins do Rego e a Patologia Tropical," *ibid.*, pp. 4-6.
24. Faria, "Caboverdianidade," p. 113.
25. Manuel Ferreira, "Onde Gilberto Freyre fala de Cabo Verde," *Cabo Verde*, September 1, 1952, p. 16.

Verdean literature—a lack superseded only, in his opinion, by the shocking absence of universality.[26]

Fortunately, Freyre, whose supersonic jaunt through the islands, described in *Aventura e Rotina*, gave him little time to form anything but erroneous conclusions as to their literature, has not gone unanswered. In his report of an interview with the social scientist from Recife, Barbosa attacks him for his excessive considerations relative to the degree of Brazilian influence in Cape Verdean letters.[27] More than once, Manuel Lopes, while not referring exclusively to Freyre, scores those who see Cape Verdern literature as simply a pale reflection of Brazilian regionalism.[28] Even João Gaspar Simões, one of continental Portugal's critics most eager to discover Brazilian themes in Cape Verdean works, recognizes specific areas of literary development on the islands which owe nothing to the artistic emanations from Brazil.[29]

That Manuel Lopes and Jorge Barbosa should be so insistent on the restricted character of the Brazilian influence and that João Gaspar Simões should have perceived a certain element of originality, however inadequately defined, in the literary production of Cabo Verde, become eminently understandable when one consults the works of the Brazilian regional school with a prior knowledge of Cabo Verde and her literature. It is useful to consider, in this connection, two representative works of José Lins do Rego and Jorge Amado which are said to have exercised an appreciable influence on the artistic imagination of the archipelago's writers: *Menino de Engenho* and *Jubiabá*.

José Lins do Rego's *Menino de Engenho*, a story of the loss of innocence of a boy, Carlinhos, who grows up in the turbulent, depraved atmosphere of the sugar plantations of Brazil's Northeast, suggests, at first glance, the Cape Verdean scene. There is, at the outset, the proverbial factor of the environment as an oppressive, tyrannical element. Rainfall, causing the overflow of the Paraíba, drives the people from their homes—inhabitants of the *casa grande* (home of the masters) as well as the *senzala* (home of the slaves)—and obliges them to group

26. Virgílio de Lemos, Nós e Gilberto Freyre," *Império*, No. 14 (June 1952), p. 15.
27. Jorge Barbosa, "Crónicas de São Vicente," *Cabo Verde*, March 1, 1953, pp. 33-24.
28. Manuel Lopes, "A Literatura Caboverdeana," *Cabo Verde*, October 1, 1959, p. 8.
29. João Gaspar Simões, "A Antologia da Ficção Cabo-Verdiana," *Diário de Notícias*, January 1, 1961, p. 13.

together for common safety. In fact, the term *flagelados* (the flagel-lated ones) reminiscent of the novel by Manuel Lopes, is used to describe the fleeing masses.

In addition to the theme of natural forces and their destructive capacity, one finds the equally familiar emphasis on the stark poverty of the milieu, the depiction of children who become used to filth and wallow in it, without any standard of values compelling aversion or even reserve. The adult workers are portrayed at their overwhelming daily chores, reduced to a form of slave labor in the chain gang of José Felismino, the coarse foreman.

The novel further evokes the situation existing in Cabo Verde by its delving into the folkloric atmosphere of the people, specifically their particular brand of Christian beliefs tempered with vestiges of the African heritage. Through the eyes of the hero, Carlinhos, the people are shown as continually fearful of a meeting with the *lobisomem*, just as the Cape Verdeans dread a meeting with their own counter-part of the bogy man, the *feiticeiro*.

Finally, the outlook of resignation characteristic of the community examined parallels that of the Cape Verdeans. The people are pictured as not raising their arms in sign of revolt, as not even opening their mouths to utter imprecations at the cruel fate visited upon them. Much like the inhabitants of Cabo Verde, these folk are pacific and re-signed to the point of recoursing absolutely to passive faith in the benevolence of God and His eventual answering of their prayers. Lins do Rego also implies that the people do not perhaps measure correctly the extent of their misery, not having had a clear conception of life outside their immediate frontiers. Such is often the case in Cabo Verde.

Despite its many points of identity with the situation obtaining in the Cape Verde archipelago, *Menino de Engenho* reveals, upon closer examination, a wide range of divergence. If, indeed, the setting of the work recalls Cabo Verde in certain of its climatic, economic, and folkloric aspects, and even in certain psychological traits of its characters, it differs radically from the islands in its broad social complex and in its development of themes foreign to them. The society which unfolds in the novel is decidedly more primitive than the Cape Verdean, and the relationship of master to slave is virtually maintained in the mentality of descendants of the original slaves, who serve their bosses with the same obsequiousness that their forebears had displayed with the old-time slavery chieftains.

Furthermore, social relations are marked by a violence which— Manuel Lopes's *Os Flagelados do Vento Leste* notwithstanding—is totally untypical of Cabo Verde and her literature. The homicidal commencement of the narrative, with Carlinhos's father having killed the boy's mother, the later terror practised by the inexorable landowner António Silvino, and the scattered scenes of savage combat which run through *Menino de Engenho* are out of place in the usual progression of Cape Verdean life.

Also extraneous to Cabo Verde is the atmosphere of moral depravation which dominates the story. The young protagonist, Carlinhos, penetrates early into this perversity as he is schooled in sexual aberrations by a Negro servant girl, Luisa. Carolinhos is encouraged rather than dissuaded in this practice by the example of his uncle, Juca, who maintains a harem of mistresses and reads obscene books when he is away from them. So compelling is the dominancy of sex that it creates its own honor roll. Thus Carlinhos gains special prestige by his conquest of Zefa Cajâ, notorious throughout the community for her lust.

These characteristics of *Menino de Engenho*, radical in their departure from Cape Verdean reality, suggest that the lesson absorbed from it by the *Claridosos* was only partial. Obviously, the Cape Verdean writers did not forget the work's sharp cry of protest against the oppression of socio-economic factors, its realistic consistency with the actual problems involved, however disagreeable their nature, and even the writer's employment of a down-to-earth style divested for the most part of rhetoric and predicated on the language of the characters portrayed. As will later become more evident, however, the *Claridosos* complemented these borrowings, if quite imperfectly at times, with purely local ingredients and were not wholly subservient to the experience of *Menino de Engenho* and the novelistic mastery of José Lins do Rego.

Like *Menino de Engenho*, Jorge Amado's *Jubiabá* presents striking affinities with the real circumstances of Cape Verdean life. Here, too, there is the sense of socio-economic strangulation; the wretched childhood of the hero, António Balduíno, who is reduced in early adolescence to begging in the streets of Bahia, recalls to mind the boys of São Vicente and their lamentable mendacity. Here, too, is the folkloric element; Jubiabá is a sort of Cape Verdean *curandeiro* (quack doctor) who has office hours, or *consultas*, for the solution of the problems, medical and otherwise, of his clients. Here, too, is the problem of prostitution as an imposition of miserable living conditions—critical in the urban communities of Cabo Verde—as studied in the episode of the financially desperate Lindinalva. Here, too, is the theme of escape, occasionally reflected in the attitude of António Balduíno.

As in the case of *Menino de Engenho*, however, a keener assessment reveals substantial digressions from the normal pattern of social phenomena in Cabo Verde. The staple element of the novel is a theme absolutely unrelated to present conditions on the islands—the theme of violent, communistic class warfare conjoined with the problem of intense racial antagonisms. In this framework, the hero, Balduíno, is not the weak-spined individual crushed by the adverse factors of his circumambience. He is, rather, the heroic black man who leads the worker class to victory in a strike against the oppressor whites. Nor does he fear *feiticeiros*; he goes out looking for the *lobisomem* to wring his neck!

Just as Balduíno is not akin to the passive and resigned Cape Verdean, so Jubiabá is not germane to the typical *curandeiro* of the islands. His role in the novel far exceeds that of an ordinary medicine man, and he is treated symbolically, in opposition to Balduíno, as representing the passive form of resistance as against the active, strike-bound approach. His submission at the end to the victorious hero indicates the complete triumph of the latter conception—although it must be remembered that it was in the conclaves of Jubiabá that Balduíno first heard the exemplary stories of courageous revolutionaries.

Beyond the curious economic and folkloric modalities of Jubiabá, there are other contrasts with what is typically Cape Verdean. As in *Menino de Engenho*, the treatment of the sexual theme assumes its own particular characteristics in the vagabond promiscuity of the protagonist. The profusion of scenes of physical violence, even more pronounced here than in *Menino de Engenho*, contributes to an atmosphere largely removed from that of Cabo Verde. The very language of *Jubiabá*, sentimental at times when the writer evokes the stunning triumph of the strike, and fondly romantic when he depicts the circus scene, reflects a point of view characteristic only of himself, and a regionalism fitted specifically to the precise setting of the work—as it is viewed through the personal artistic prism of Jorge Amado.

In the case of *Jubiabá* as in that of *Menino de Engenho*, the Brazilian legacy to the *Claridade* movement was an ambivalent one—applicable to the extent to which it set attention not on *beleza* but on the immediate, concrete, palpable reality of social and economic conditions; inapplicable to the extent to which it conveyed meaning only in its own context, bound to that context as it was by the very concentration on what was typical, characteristic, local. The *Claridosos* were successful only because they proved themselves capable of making this distinction, of profiting from the Brazilian regionalistic venture without in effect succumbing to it. It was this capacity for discernment that enabled them to produce an original literature, a literature possible only in the Cape Verde Islands.

*
* *

As fruit of a threefold inspiration, flowing as well from the Cape-verdeanism of Cardoso and Tavares as from the incentive of the *Presença* movement and the revelations of Brazilian regionalism, the review *Claridade* assumes the form of a cultural rather than purely literary publication. It solicits, therefore, the collaboration of Félix Monteiro and the sociologist João Lopes, as well as that of a *pléiade* of poets, novelists, and short-story writers.

This general cultural penchant of *Claridade*, coupled with its limited and sometimes inferior literary content and sporadic appearance, raises, at first, the question as to how it could have survived as it did and been hailed as the prime instigator, on the islands, of a new flow of creative literary activity. It is helpful, at this point, to bear in mind the role of the *Almanach Luso-Africano* in the Classical period. Actually, the function of *Claridade* has proved far more significant than that of its predecessor, for it has been truer to its ideals. It has fixed attention squarely on Cabo Verde, her people, her customs, her language, and her literature. And this it has done always in the sense of establishing the intrinsic prestige of the Cape Verdean.

There emerges in *Claridade*, first of all, a serious study of the Cape Verdean as an individual distinct from his Portuguese brethren in Europe or in any of the other overseas possessions. Manuel Lopes, in "Tomada de Vista," sees him as being of dual make-up—on the one hand conscious of the limitations of his milieu and on the other steadfast in the love of his land.[30] While the writer criticizes the Cape Verdean for the sluggishness of his fight against the obstacles of his environment, he recognizes his *prudência* (prudence), his sensitivity to the advantages of the external world as compared with his own. Lopes goes farther: in a supplementary article with the same title he defends in this light the Cape Verdean's emigration to other lands and notes that, far from being a sign of weakness, such transplantation is proof of the island inhabitant's desire for action, his urge to progress.[31]

Manuel Lopes is not alone in concerning himself with the comportment of the Cape Verdean nor the only one to render a favorable appraisal. João Lopes, noting that Mário Ferro, a Cape Verdean lawyer, had observed the Cape Verdean's willingness to conform to adversity, his dying before warehouses and commercial establishments during periods of drought without any trace of revolt, undertakes to reply to the accusation. He emphasizes, in "Apontamento" (Note), that the so-called apathy of the Cape Verdean is excusable in the face of the demoralizing character of his living conditions.[32] The multiple crises which he has had to suffer have so debilitated him as to make vigorous reactions impossible.

The *Claridosos* not only rise to the defense of the Cape Verdean as a social or psychological entity; they justify him, too, on economic grounds. João Lopes explains the persistence of the African strains in Santiago as resulting from the peculiar economic system which developed there,[33] namely the *regime latifundário* (system of great rural properties of little productivity), which, in its creation of a feudal-type social structure, prevented the close mingling and hence intermarriage of Negro and white.

Likewise concerned with the economic aspect of the Cape Verdean, Teixeira de Sousa discusses, in *A estrutura social da ilha do Fogo em 1940* (The Social Structure of the Island of Fogo in 1940), the island's society as developing from a change in the financial status of the community. Stressing the economic rather than ethnic differences within the Foguetense society, he explains how the emigration process wrought

30. Manuel Lopes, "Tomada de Vista," *Claridade*, No. 1, (March 1936), pp. 5-6.
31. Manuel Lopes, "Tomada de Vista," *Claridade*, No. 3 (March 1937), p. 10.
32. João Lopes da Silva, "Apontamento," *ibid.*, p. 6.
33. João Lopes da Silva, "Apontamento," *Claridade*, No. 1, p. 9.

extreme changes in the social structure of the island.[34] Yet his main purpose is once again to evaluate favorably the Cape Verdean, to trace the rise of the mulatto against the background of declining white influence. Teixeira de Sousa demonstrates convincingly how, from 1925 on, the mulatto gradually ascended to his present position of dominance on Fogo.[35]

The attention which *Claridade* gives to the psychological and economic aspects of the Cape Verdean does not preclude its concern for the folkloric facet of his identity. Again, the analysis serves to enhance the Cape Verdean's prestige, to provide demonstrative proof of his high level of Europeanization as against the charge of his basically African primitivism. Baltazar Lopes da Silva presents two folk tales from Santo Antão, "A doutrina" (The Doctrine) and *O Cavaleiro e O Pão Quente* (The Horseman and the Hot Bread) and studies their religious content.[36] He uses this study as a basis for establishing the strong Catholic influence of the seminary and that influence's effect on the complexion of local folk tales.

Félix Monteiro, in his discussion of the folklore of Cabo Verde, is interested not only in a detailed explanation of such native customs as the *tabanca* (a term applied to popular festivities and rites on Santiago and to the mutual aid association organizing them), but also in suggesting that, despite the incontrovertible evidence of their African origin, these customs have become Westernized. He affirms in "Tabanca: uma lenda" (Tabanca: a legend), that in the *tabanca* ritual the erotic frenzy of the dancer never reaches the point of mysticism, there being no contact with the divine as in the case of the African version.[37] Monteiro further argues the European evolution of Cape Verdean folklore when he speaks of the late Ana Procópio, the last of the great *cantadeiras* (singer of folk songs) of Cabo Verde.[38] Studying the singer's

34. Teixeira de Sousa, "A estrutura social da Ilha do Fogo em 1940," *Claridade*, No. 5 (September 1947), pp. 42-44.

35. Teixeira de Sousa, "Sobrados, Lojas e Funcos: Contribuição para o Estudo da Evolução Social da Ilha do Fogo," *Claridade*, No. 8 (May 1958), p. 7.

36. Baltazar Lopes da Silva, "Dois contos populares da ilha de Santo Antão," *Claridade*, No. 7 (December 1949), pp. 30-32.

37. Félix Monteiro, "Tabanca; uma lenda," *ibid.*, p. 25.

38. Félix Monteiro, "Cantigas de Ana Procópio," *Claridade*, No. 9 (December 1960), pp. 15-23.

images, he concludes that most of them are European in origin and quite distinct from the African type. The very instruments used to accompany her singing were European also, the writer adds.

The general campaign designed to prove the solidly European culture of the Cape Verdean through an examination of all pertinent aspects of his existence takes on a further dimension with *Claridade's* probing of his linguistic nature. Baltazar Lopes da Silva, working with elements later to proffer the bedrock material of his *O Dialecto Crioulo de Cabo Verde*, dissects Crioulo in two articles entitled "Uma Experiência Românica nos Trópicos" (A Romance Experience in the Tropics). The main thesis of the writer is that Crioulo developed according to the natural linguistic laws for the development of that form of Portuguese—sixteenth-century language—which became isolated on the islands. He stresses that what often appears to be an African importation is in reality a modified Portuguese construction. The example given is that of the Crioulo expression *diaza* (some time ago), which is actually the Portuguese *dias há* found in Gil Vicente, the finest representative of the early Portuguese theater, and in Camões and other writers.[39]

Lopes da Silva proceeds to demonstrate the progressive sophistication of Crioulo, showing how, because of the democratic organization of Cape Verdean society, the more intellectual Cape Verdeans, speaking a more refined Crioulo, succeed in transmitting this refinement to their socially or intellectually less-advanced friends. The writer illustrates, in the meantime, the wide use of Crioulo even among the intelligensia, noting that there was a time when Cape Verdean women would sit around and discuss in the dialect the literature they had read.[40] Lopes da Silva terminates his argumentation with the observation —more political than linguistic—that the substance of Crioulo attests the depth of Portuguese colonization on the islands, for there have been Crioulos in the Portuguese Indies, but these have disappeared because of the rather superficial character of the Lusitanian settlement.

Like its nonfictional, more broadly cultural side, the literary side of *Claridade* endeavors also to illustrate the thesis that "the proper

---

39. Baltazar Lopes da Silva, "Uma Experiência Românica nos Trópicos II," *Claridade*, No. 5, p. 7.
40. Baltazar Lopes da Silva, "Uma Experiência Românica nos Trópicos I," *Claridade*, No. 4 (March 1946), p. 17.

study of Cape Verdean man is Cape Verdean man." The perspective, however, is somewhat different. There is no attempt to prove the Cape Verdean's degree of civilization, his social polish; the aim is rather to utter a loud protest against the conditions in which he lives, against the gloom and desperation of a miserable existence which propels him, quite often, out of his island habitat.

It is perhaps in the poetic content of *Claridade*, more significant than the selections in prose, that the cry of protest is most sustained and impressive. Jorge Barbosa, suggesting the new role of the poet in Cabo Verde as in close rapport with the people and reflection of their ills as well as his own, pours forth his dejection in "Não era para mim" (It was not for me).[41] The misery around him, of which he is acutely conscious, prevents his appreciating the local music and scenic beauty. Unlike José Lopes, he is led to ruminate more directly on the harshness of his fate rather than seek diversion in poetic flights of the imagination. In "Crianças" (Children) he again refuses to look away from the surrounding poverty. He notices the children:

> ...sem remédios
> sem escolas
> sem brinquedos

and points out that no one pays any attention to their want:

> Ninguém sabe
> Ninguém dá por isso.*

Lest the people assume that he is simply using their adversity as a purely poetic device, he reaffirms constantly his alliance with them, his sense of common identity, as in "Poema":

> Oh Caboverdeano humilde
> anónimo
> -meu irmão.

* ...without medicine, without schools, without toys. No one knows, no one notices this.[42]
Oh humble, anonymous Cape Verdean—my brother.[43]

41. Jorge Barbosa, "Não era para mim," *Claridade*, No. 5, p. 14.
42. Jorge Barbosa, "Crianças," *Claridade*, No. 8, pp. 24-25.
43. Jorge Barbosa, "Poema," *Claridade*, No. 1, p. 10.

Barbosa is not alone in his focusing of his people's suffering. Aguinaldo Fonseca, in "Perdida" (Lost), portrays the plight of the prostitute who, forced to sell her body to all buyers, has its youth and virginity "strangled" by their carnal desires.[44] Baltazar Lopes da Silva, in a series of poems called "Romanceiro de São Tomé" (Stories of São Tomé), depicts the horror of the emigration to the island in the Gulf of Guinea and tells of those who return emaciated, or do not return at all.[45] Terêncio Anahory's "Impermeabilidade" (Imperviousness) grows even more intrepid, implying that there is one who views the hardships of the people but is not moved.[46] The "one" is quite conceivably the governor himself.

Sensitive to the dour plight of their fellow Cape Verdeans, the poets of *Claridade* are also conscious of the world beyond, of the world seen as a concrete reality and not, in the manner of the Classical poets, as a basis for idle reverie. Manuel Lopes, in "Écran" (Screen), sadly contrasts the universe without and his own island prison, lamenting the fact that no ship will take him.[47] In *Rapsódia* (Rhapsody) Baltazar Lopes da Silva previews his coming escape from Cabo Verde and how much it will mean to him as an extension of his personality and improvement of his social status:

> vou ser
> chegador
> azeitador
> fogueiro
>
> . . .
>
> vou fazer serenata
> vou tocar violão
>
> . . .
>
> vou enganar o Governo
>
> . . .
>
> vou trabalhar em New Bedford.*

* I am going to be a machinist, a lubricator, a stoker...
I am going to serenade, I am going to play the guitar...
I am going to work in New Bedford.[48]

44. Aguinaldo Fonseca, "Perdida," *Claridade*, No. 7, p. 29.
45. Baltazar Lopes da Silva, "Romanceiro de São Tomé," *Claridade*, No. 8, pp. 34-39.
46. Aguinaldo Fonseca, "Impermeabilidade," *ibid.*, p. 32.
47. Manuel Lopes, "Écran," *Claridade*, No. 1, p. 4.
48. Baltazar Lopes da Silva, "Rapsódia," *Claridade*, No. 5, p. 13.

In contrast to Lopes da Silva, others, like Aguinaldo Fonseca, are infused rather with a deep pessimism, knowing that they will probably never leave the islands. In "Herança" (Inheritance), Fonseca can discover no hope of getting away from Cabo Verde.[49] He places his captivity, moreover, not only in the limited context of his own life span but rather in the broad spectrum of his family history. Recalling that his grandfather was a slave, he views himself as condemned to an equal slavery, as doomed to live and die on the islands.

While a sad and sometimes tragic note dominates the poetry of *Claridade*, as that poetry wrestles with the most crucial problems of Cape Verdean life, there is occasionally to be found a lighter tone, a less pessimistic outlook. This is certainly true of much of the poetry of Pedro Corsino Azevedo, discussed more fully in the next chapter; but it is primarily true of a group of poems written in Crioulo and representing in practice, as it were, the linguistic theorizing of Baltazar Lopes da Silva anent the respectability of the dialect.

Indeed, it may be said that this poetry in Crioulo, in its comic aspects, represents a popular reply to the grave issues raised by the more serious poets—an ability to laugh in the face of misfortune. Such is the case with Jorge Pedro's "Nha tabaquêro" (My Snuffbox):

> Nha tabaquêro
> ê cusa fino:
> pó di djacrandã
> co' prata tchuquido,
> Tampa midido
> qui câ tâ 'xâ frôxe
> força di lôro*

The poet goes on to treat of the extensive fame of his snuffbox and of the fallacy of those who, thinking they are dapper, do not realize that they lack this item indispensable to the completion of their elegance.

---

* My snuffbox is a precious thing: it is made of jacaranda with inlaid silver, having a top so fitted that the quality of the tobacco is sealed in.[50]

49. Aguinaldo Fonseca, "Herança," *Claridade*, NW. 8, p. 30.
50. Jorge Pedro Pereira Barbosa, "Nha tabaquêro," *Claridade*, No. 9, p. 76.

Of less comic resonance are the poems in Crioulo of Gabriel Mariano; yet they are considerably varied and far less dismal in tone than the Portuguese offerings already surveyed. "Dinhêro D'Ês Mundo" (The Money of This World) expounds the proverbial truth that money is not salvation.[51] "Bida'l Pobre" (The Life of the Poor Man) reflects the re-signed attitude of the Cape Verdean who sees the world as a large kettle into which he can place only the small spoon which God gave him.[52] "Casamento" (Marriage) warns of the perils of the conjugal existence. Finally, "Galo Bedjo" (The Old Cock) tells of a man, once a *galo rascom* (proud cock), who has now grown old and is but a *galo bedjo*, while, however, everything has remained static about him. In these poems Mariano has sought to rivet further attention on the rich folkloric life of the islands, featuring here local themes and tales of Santiago.

Unlike the poetic contribution of *Claridade*, its prose content runs a narrow gamut of topics. Unmitigated in its severity by any thread of humor comparable to that of the review's Crioulo poetry, it con-centrates exclusively on the Cape Verdean situation. One rediscovers the observer's fundamental sympathy for his compatriot, his frank exposition of the latter's reasons for despair. While the position of the writer vis-à-vis his object of study is the same, the points of empha-sis are different from those of the poetry, and so are, to a certain extent, the subjects discussed.

Virgílio Pires, in a short story called *Herança*, poses the problem of rainfall, but in a specific framework.[53] He is mindful not only of the vital importance of rain for the island economy but also of the grave fact that the eventual coming of rain does not suddenly remove all of the difficulties, all of the sources of desolation. Puxim, the central char-acter, is happy that "the land once again lives." But how about the death of Toco, of André, and now of Didi? They are not able, like the land, to come back to life again.

In "Recaída » (Relapse) António Aurélio Gonçalves sets his artistic gaze, like Virgilio Pires, on one aspect of Cape Verdean life.[54] He strives

---

51. José Gabriel Marinao da Silva, "Dinhêro D'Ês Mundo," *Claridade*, No. 7, p. 32.

52. José Gabriel Mariano da Silva, "Bid'al Pobre," "Casamento," "Galo Bedjo," *Claridade*, No. 6 (July 1948), m. 35.

53. Virgílio Pires, "Herança," *Claridade*, No. 8, pp. 55-56.

54. António Aurélio Gonçalves, "Recaída," *Claridade*, No. 6, pp. 22-25.

also to contribute a new facet to a common problem. Describing generally the dull existence of São Vicente, where people do not live but
pine away, he excerpts a man named Frank, who feels perhaps more
deeply than his neighbors the hollowness of his activity. Frank would
like to escape from the desperation of his lot, attain some sort of self-
fulfillment; but he is hopelessly trapped, his normal difficulties mul-
tiplied by the illness of his wife.

Thus in prose as well as in poetry, *Claridade* manifests its integral
attachment to the varied forms of the Cape Veredan drama. Having
demonstrated that the Cape Verdean is not only a social animal but
an advanced social animal, possessor of a secure European heritage,
the contributors to *Claridade* embark upon their task of illuminating
the realities of the *condition caboverdienne* with pride and frankness,
seeing in the epic struggle of the Cape Verdean a mark of heroism,
a spark of glory. It is interesting to reflect that the heroes, whom José
Lopes has to import into his literature from abroad or from the past,
the *Claridade* writers find at home, among the drought-beset farmers
and emigrants to São Tomé.

The dedication of the men writing in *Claridade* to their homeland
and its people is not new on the Cape Verdean scene, nor is it a legacy
received from continental Portugal or Brazil. It is already characteristic
to a large extent of Cardoso and Tavares, who wrote well before the
galvanizing impact of *Presença* and Brazilian regionalism. In much
the same way as their two precursors, the contributors to *Claridade*
have a nativistic attitude, a primary concern for the people of Cabo
Verde and a direct and unremitting involvement in the archipelago's
paramount issues.

Yet *Claridade* marks an important advance over the local founts
of inspiration. Its writers, if they are still conscious of their European
background and indeed eager to evince it, are, nevertheless, keenly
aware of their original characteristics and loathe to worship false gods,
be they social or purely literary. Moreover, they do not fragment
their explorations; they confront simultaneously the folklore and the
psychological substructure of their island folk. They are all-embracing
in their emphasis.

Perhaps, in effect, the very expanse of the emphasis contributes to
the partial vagueness and unevenness, the characteristic undiscipline
of *Claridade* as an organ of literature. Nowhere among its pages does

one discover a word of purely esthetic signification, comparable to the passages of José Régio quoted earlier. Nowhere does one encounter a word of literary criticism, an endeavor to orientate the production of the collaborating writers. Nowhere does one find, in short, an expression, in terms of literature, of a certain sense of direction. These are among the reasons for the oft-mentioned poverty of the movement, its repetitious nature and limited production. Be this as it may—and the matter will be discussed later in greater depth—*Claridade* served, from the very outset, as a stimulus to the literarily-gifted in Cabo Verde and is inseparable from whatever artistically creative efforts have been realized in the archipelago since the review's genesis.

Norman Araujo

Cover of *O Galo Cantou na Baía* by Manuel Lopes

NEW DIRECTIONS IN CAPE VERDEAN LITERATURE? THE FIRST NUMBERS OF *RAÍZES*

Norman Araujo

Raízes, whose first number was published officially in January 1977, follows in the heroic tradition of Cape Verdean literary reviews, such as *Claridade, Certeza,* the *Boletim dos Alunos do Liceu Gil Eanes,* and the *Suplemento Cultural de Cabo Verde,* which have struggled valiantly against the constringencies of an impoverished land merely to stay alive. It is to be hoped that the publication of *Raízes* will know neither the irregular cadence which afflicted *Claridade* nor the ephermerality of *Certeza,* which appears but twice. Certainly such would not be the case if everything depended on the zeal and dedication of the editor of *Raízes,* Arnaldo França. Yet I must report that the review's second number begins with an apology for not keeping to the intended quarterly pace of publication due to "technical reasons," and the third number, the last which I have seen, renews the apology, claiming that a variety of factors conspired to prevent its coming out by the originally scheduled date.

What do the first three numbers of *Raízes* tell us, if anything, about the future orientation of Cape Verdean literature? The question is by no means gratuitous because the review addresses itself consciously, if not self-consciously, to this very matter. On the inside cover of the first number, the ideal which animates the contributors to the publication is clearly set forth as "uma condição caboverdeana, africana e de cidadania do Mundo; uma autenticidade nascida da liberdade dessa condição; uma independência assente nas comuns *Raízes.*" Granted, the ideal so set forth remains simply that: there is no specific indication of a cultural or literary program for the review. But the contours of that program emerge with progressive clarity as we turn to two prose pieces published in *Raízes,* both involving, significantly enough, the collaboration of Mário de Andrade. It might be remembered that in their compilation of the first collection of African poetry of Portuguese expression in 1953, he and Francisco José Tenreiro had decided to exclude Cape Verdean poets because the latter, with very few exceptions, did not convey the sense of *négritude* which in their view was at the very core of black poetry. The first prose piece is the lead article of the maiden number of *Raízes,* an article composed by Andrade and Arnaldo França and entitled "A Cultura na Problemática da Libertação Nacional e do Desenvolvimento, à Luz do Pensamento Político de Amílcar Cabral." The article develops Cabral's axial belief that the war of liberation for the Cape Verdean people, as for all African peoples, is a struggle to affirm the native culture, a struggle which becomes, in its very essence an "act of culture."[1] Indeed, Cabral refines on this concept, demonstrating how the "acto de cultura" is also a "factor de cultura," in that the struggle results in the enrichment of the native culture, endowing it with a scientific dimension and at once universalizing it.[2] To the extent to which the affirmation of the national culture in Cabral's eyes, is synonymous with the affirmation of the national identity, one can already start to deduce the implications of Cabral's thought for the possible future direction of Cape Verdean literature, or, more broadly, Cape Verdean cultural inquiry.

But what is only implied in the framework of the aforementioned article is explicitly elaborated in the second prose piece to which I alluded earlier, the "Jornal" of the third number of *Raizes,* in which are included sections of Andrade's "Literatura Africana e Consciência Nacional," a lecture given in September 1977 at the Liceu Domingos Ramos in Praia. Andrade goes directly to the matter at hand in these excerpts, asking what the role of literature is in the national reconstruction and proceeding to answer his own question. Situating the issue necessarily within the context of ideology, although he recognizes that the *PAIGC* is averse to what he terms "sociologia policial" in the realm of the arts, Andrade appears to echo Cabral when he speaks of the constant struggle for national identity, first defined in these terms then enlarged to Guinean-Cape Verdean identity; he appears to echo both Cabral and editor of *Raizes* when he speaks of the universal projection of this identity through the *critical* assimilation of values of other cultures. Andrade's recommendations are more precise, however, and, in a word, more programmatic. He asks for a critical study of the national heritage, a revaluing of the forms of oral literature, the rehabilitation of the popular instrument of expression, Crioulo, together with the study of African literature in its entirety.[3]

However we sift the complementary or contrasting emphases of the ideal articulated in the first number of *Raizes* and the two articles just discussed, their common thrust seems to be the affirmation of Cape Verdean identity stripped of its colonialist distortions, rich in its African roots yet open to the universal scale of values. The question is then how the contributors to *Raizes* have thus far reacted to the asserted program of cultural self-identification, or, rather, anticipated it, since, as has been observed, Andrade's program comes only in the third number of the review, and, at that, in this number's final pages. Time does not allow us to pursue this question in anything other than its literary framework, although we might mention in passing that certain articles or notations in the three numbers of *Raizes* display the writers' sensitivity to the significance of the issues raised by França and Andrade in their broadly theoretical or cultural ramifications. Dulce Almada Duarte's "Uma Nova Pedagogia do Ensino do Português em Cabo Verde" embodies the author's recognition that a curious and crucial problem exists in the islands due to the coexistence of Portuguese, the "língua oficial," and Crioulo, the "língua nacional."[4] The novel approach prescribed here to the teaching of Portuguese in the archipelago is perhaps conceived with Cabral's observations on the subject in mind, observations which lead França and Andrade to argue that Portuguese must become, in Cape Verde, a "língua de utilização," whereas it has been but a "língua de recurso."[5] The same constructive spirit appears to inform Félix Monteiro's criticism of António Carrera's *Migrações nas Ilhas de Cabo Verde,* as the critic pays tribute to the historian's study of spontaneous and forced emigration from the islands.[6] A like inspiration guides França's critical comments on Manuel Ferreira's *Literaturas Africanas de Expressao Portuguesa,* in the course of which França exalts a little-known Cape Verdean cultural hero, L. Loff de Vasconcelos.[7]

But our main concern is the literary production features in *Raizes.* At first glance this literary production seems to fall far short of the program formulated by Andrade. We are treated to the Portuguese love poetry of Mário Fonseca, to his "Amour de la langue française," to his "Dans le silence de cette nuit," to his adaptation of medieval French a la François Villon with "Ballade des Compagnons du Temps Jadis," and finally to his vague, Frenchified poetic evocation of Cape Verde called "Iles."[8] We are treated to the erudite love poetry of Jorge Carlos Fonseca incorporating a reference to the French poet Rimbaud, and then we are introduced to the Cape Verdean poet's admiration for French surrealisme in Fonseca's direct tribute to André Breton's *Manifeste*

du surrealisme, a piece of prose poetry entitled "Beija-me, Palavra.[9] We are treated to
the antique poetic allusions of Arménio Vieira in "Parábola," where Oedipus, the
Sphinx, and the city of Thebes are evoked, to Vieira's "Canto do Crepúsculo," with its
introductory quotation from Shakespeare's *Richard III* and its allusions to Zeus and
Oedipus, to Herod and John the Baptist, to Cain and David.[10]

A glance at the prose of these first numbers of *Raízes* is only slightly less disap-
pointing. It is true that we are not now treated to passages in French, or generous
doses of classical mythology. But if the texts offered to us are more identifiably Cape
Verdean, their Cape Verdeanness, upon examination, does not seem appreciably
original, nor truly in harmony with the prescriptions of Andrade. Despite some local
color, the three stories of Osvaldo Osório furnished in the first number of *Raízes* could
for the most part have been set almost anywhere.[11] Much the same might be said for
Arménio Vieira's surrealist screen play, "Descrição de Um Pesadelo."[12] The prose contributions of Baltazar Lopes, António Aurélio Gonçalves, Teixeira de Sousa, and
Virgílio Pires are more characteristically Cape Verdean, but on the whole they explore
facets of Cape Verdean life already examined in more or less the same fashion in
previous works.[13] Lopes' "Nocturno de D. Emília de Sousa" deals with childhood
memories, a theme cultivated in the author's earlier prose, such as the novel *Chiquinho* and the short story, "Pedacinho." Childhood remembrances are prominent
also in Pires' "Histórias da Velha Simôa." Death, drought, and rainfall are deadly
serious themes, and are invested with an ominous significance in the light of Cape
Verde's tragic history of deprivation. Yet whatever newness of perspective is lent the
treatment of these themes in Teixeira de Sousa's "Nhâ Caela," or in Maria Margarida
Mascarenhas' "Nhâ Vicência, Paciência!" or in Virgílio Pires' "História da Velha
Simóa," this newness of perspective is not sufficiently original or revealing, in my opinion, to be regarded as a particularly valuable contribution to the illumination of the
Cape Verdean identity as suggested by the announced ideal of *Raízes* and the programmatic recommendations of Andrade.[14] This I maintain with all due sympathy to
the poignant delineation of Chinoi's personal tragedy in Pires' short story.[15] My sentiments are similar with respect to Gonçalves' two connected short stories, "Biluca"
and "Burguesinha," in which the character of the young girl Biluca, though fascinating
by its contradictory components, is not enough to confer special value on a work which
otherwise continues to attest the author's recognized gift for social realism.

But there are works in the three numbers of *Raízes,* poems to be precise, which do
reflect the new spirit of Cape Verdean literature or at least point in the new direction.
Oliveira Barros' "Trilogia Eventual do Tempo Proibido," set in a time preceding Cape
Verdean independence, shatters the long-standing mythology of Portugal's ideological
supremacy and, in the process, the particular myth of Lisbon as a dreamland and that
of Cape Verdean cultural uniqueness as totally separated from the African example:

> Assim comecou
> o que Portugal vem chamando
> nossa cultural diferente
> —Em tempos dessa remota subjacência
> cabo verde cantou a adjacência. . . [16]

In "De Boca Concéntrica na Roda do Sol" Corsino Fortes implies an African fraternity
in symbolic but unmistakable language, and Jorge Carlos Fonseca, in a rare moment,
dreams of "angola próspera/apartheid aniquilado," of "operários americanos em
luta," of "palestina candando."[17]

The African definition of Cape Verdean reality, and the association of that reality with the universal struggle of oppressed peoples is of course conjoined, in these poems, with the joyous contemplation of Cape Verdean cultural independence, and the excitement generated by the thought of a people at long last in control of its destiny. In a poem appropriately entitled "Raíz" and written in Crioulo, Luís Romano sings the joy of this newfound freedom, the Cape Verdean's freedom to be himself, to go where his native capacities will take him, to raise his eyes proudly to the heavens.[18]

More expansive still, in his poetic exuberance, is Ovídio Martins, who, in the prose poem "Ilha a Ilha," writes of the reconstruction of the Cape Verdean *nation* with all the effusive confidence of one who views his fellow countrymen as complete masters of their destiny: "Não tentaremos comover os deuses, pela simples razão de sermos nós os deuses." Toward the end of this work, Martins uses concepts and language reminiscent of the article composed by França and Andrade in tribute to the ideas of Cabral and specifically the notion of the "homen novo" resulting from Cape Verdean independence:

> O nosso destino, estamos a cumpri-lo: dar a Cabo Verde outro mar,
> outro céu, outro homen. Devagar, vamos conhecendo o sabor do sal da
> terra.[19]

Even as Martins exults in the gradual emergence of the new Cape Verdean, wonderfully vibrant in the authenticity of his liberated personality, so another poet, Oliveira Barros, delights in the imagination of a Cape Verdean future which will repudiate the dreary postulates or conclusions arrived at in the writings of the *Claridosos* or their disciples. He imagines better things happening to the likes of Baltazar Lopes' Chiquinho, or Gonçalves' Xandinha, or Jorge Barbosa's hungry children.[20] But if Barros' allusion to the *Claridade* movement is significant as a measure of the fresh optimism propelling the exponents of a new Cape Verdean literature, the allusion is also signficiant as an intimation of the lasting impact of *Claridade,* and, finally, as a point of departure for the overall assessment of the examples of new poetry discussed here.

It is of no small significance, in my view, that the *Claridade* movement has left such a large imprint on these first three numbers of *Raizes.* I am not now merely referring to the remarks of Barros, nor even to the collaboration of Baltazar Lopes, Teixeira de Sousa, and Gonçalves. I am alluding to the affectionate homage rendered Jorge Barbosa and the publication of some of his poetry, with a recognition of the latter's *relevance;* I am alluding to the tribute paid Jaime de Figueiredo, and the publication of his study on António Nunes.[21] To my mind these testimonials are more than simply *pro forma* reflexes dictated by a combination of good taste and superficial sensitivity. They are rather an indication, perhaps in certain cases unconscious, of a feeling of literary indebtedness, the vague realization that, whatever the final form—if final form there ever is—of the new Cape Verdean literature, it cannot represent a complete divorce from the principles and practices of the *Claridosos* and their emulators. The impossibility of such a divorce becomes all the more apparent when one recalls that the basic orientation of the *Claridade* movement was nativistic, even if the nativism cultivated was incomplete, superficial, or hedged with political considerations imposed by the exactions of a dictatorial regime. Even so, the *Claridosos* dared to explore the question of African roots, and if the exploration was not sufficiently extensive or intensive, it nevertheless represented a beginning, and helped, however haltingly, to prepare a climate propitious for the pursuit of an African heritage sensed earlier by António Nunes. The *Claridosos,* in short, viewed the Cape Verdean as an individual, and the current ambition to penetrate more deeply the Cape Verdean's personality, to clearly establish his identity, is but the extension and intensification of the earlier investigation in a social, political, and economic atmosphere now purified of its colonialist pollutants.

A study of the first three numbers of *Raízes* has shown that the new Cape Verdean literature as conceived by Mário de Andrade is barely beginning to emerge, indeed is all but submerged in the review by the prolongations of the *Claridade* idiom or the promptings of a sophisticated literary curiosity reaching out to other lands and other tongues. It would be unfair, however, to judge these early numbers of *Raízes* with severity. Cape Verde's independence is a recent acquisition, and the reorientation of Cape Verdean literature cannot come about overnight, especially given the material poverty of the archipelago, which, even with independence, does not allow a writer the luxury of being able to pursue his craft full-time. Moreover, it would be dogmatic to regard Andrade's program as truly prescriptive, whatever its excellent points, and to demand its exact and immediate enactment. Whatever the social or ideological determinants, literature never develops automatically in response to a preconceived set of rules. Andrade himself appears to acknowledge this, when he characterizes the policy of the *PAIGC* as being compatible with the expression of the writer's originality, *hoping* all the while that such originality will work in accordance with the national ideology.[24] For my part, I am confident that in the future Cape Verdean writers will artistically illuminate the authentic Cape Verdean identity beyond the modest but praiseworthy beginnings of the first three numbers of *Raízes.* Furthermore, I dare to hope that they will do so without feeling the compulsion entirely to forsake the cultivation of literary ideas and forms emanating from other cultures, preferring rather to fuse these ideas and forms with their own in the progressive enrichment of Cape Verdean literary expression.

Notes

[1]Cabral, quoted in Mário de Andrade and Arnaldo França, "A cultura na Problemática da Libertação Nacional e do Desenvolvimento, à Luz do Pensamento Político de Amílcar Cabral," *Raízes,* No 1 (January-April 1977), p. 9.

[2]Ibid., p. 11.

[3]Andrade, Quoted in "Jornal," *Raízes,* No. 3 (July-September 1977), pp. 81-82.

[4]Dulce Almada Duarte, "Uma Nova Pedagogia do Ensino do Português em Cabo Verde," *Raízes,* No. 2 (April-June 1977), pp. 3-19.

[5]Andrade and França, "A Cultura," p. 18.

[6]Félix Monteiro, "Crítica," *Raízes,* No. 2 (April-June 1977), pp. 99-106.

[7]Arnaldo França, "Crítica," *Raízes,* No. 3 (July-September 1977), pp. 77-80.

[8]Mário Fonseca, "Vai-Se a Cor Fica o Dor (e o Amargor)," *Raizes*, No. 1 (January-April 1977), pp. 76-77; "Amour de la langue française," p. 78; "Dans le silence de cette nuit. . . ," *Raizes*, No. 3 (July-September 1977), pp. 61-64, "Ballade des compagnons du temps jadis," p. 64, "Iles," pp. 64-65.

[9]Jorge Carlos Fonseca, "Polivitamina de Meus Sonhos," *Raizes*, No. 2 (April-June 1977), pp. 85-86; "Beija-Me, Palavra," *Raizes*, No. 3 (July-September 1977), pp. 66-67.

[10]Arménio Vieira, "Parábola," *Raizes*, No. 1 (January-April 1977), p. 82; "Canto do Crepúsculo," *Raizes*, No. 2 (April-June 1977), pp. 88-89.

[11]Osvaldo Osório, "3 Histórias de Amores de Rua," *Raizes*, No. 1 (January-April 1977), pp. 63-66.

[12]Vieira, "Descrição de Um Pesadelo," *Raizes*, No. 2 (April-June 1977), pp. 73-76.

[13]Baltazar Lopes, "Nocturno de D. Emília de Sousa," *Raizes*, No. 1 (January-April 1977), pp. 59-62; António Aurélio Gonçalves, "Biluca," *Raizes*, No. 1 (January-April 1977), pp. 31-58, "Burguesinha," *Raizes*, No. 3 (July-September 1977), pp. 41-54; Teixeira de Sousa, "Nhâ Caela," *Raizes*, No. 2 (April-June 1977), pp. 53-56; Virgílio Pires, "Histórias da Velha Simôa," *Raizes*, No. 3 (July-September 1977), pp. 36-40.

[14]Maria Margarida Mascarenhas, "Nhâ Vicência, Paciência!" *Raizes*, No. 2 (April-June 1977), pp. 65-72.

[15]Pires, "Histórias," p. 79.

[16]Oliveira Barros, "Trilogia Eventual do Tempo Proibido," *Raizes*, No. 2 (April-June 1977), p. 81.

[17]Corsino Fortes, "De Boca Concêntrica na Roda do Sol," *Raizes*, No. 1 (January-April 1977), p. 74; Jorges Carlos Fonseca, "Poema de Amanhã," *Raizes*, No. 1 (January-April 1977), p. 87.

[18]Luís Romano, "Raíz," *Raizes*, No. 2 (April-June 1977), p. 98.

[19]Ovídio Martins, "Ilha a Ilha," *Raizes*, No. 1 (January-April 1977), p. 70.

[20]Barros, "Trilogia," pp. 79-80.

[21]Jorge Barbosa, "Expectativa-Contadores de Histórias," *Raizes*, No. 2 (April-June 1977), pp. 77-78, "Demografia," p. 78; "Jornal," p. 111; Jaime de Figueiredo, "Um Poeta do Quotidiano Crioulo," *Raizes*, No. 1 (January-April 1977), pp. 20-30.

PART TWO

Essays and Articles
(in Portuguese)

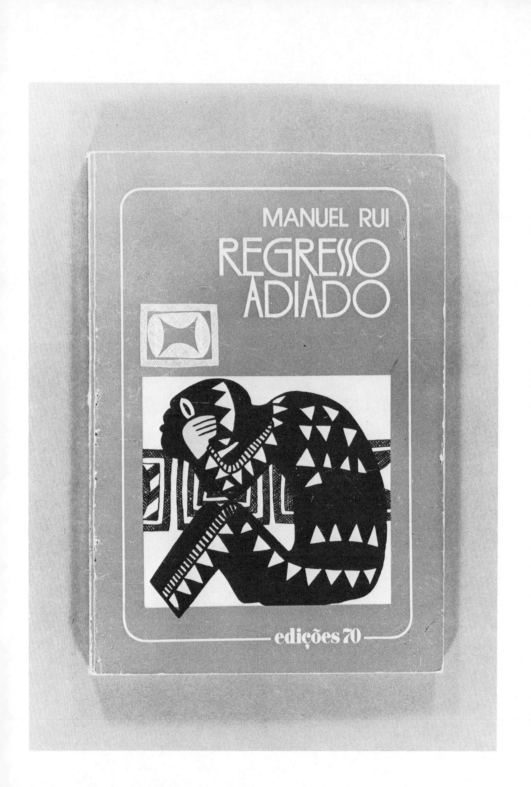

Cover of *Regresso Adiado* by Manuel Rui

MANUEL FERREIRA
DA DOR DE SER NEGRO
AO ORGULHO DE SER PRETO
[On Being a Negro and the Pride of Being Black]

The theme of color has existed in Portuguese African literature from the mid-nineteenth century to modern times. The poetry of the Angolan José da Silva Maia Ferreira, published in 1849, implies that the mulatto writer is culturally alienated, for whiteness is the standard by which beauty is measured. Other poets of the nineteenth century, including J. Cándido Furtado and Cordeiro da Mata, also reflect the insecurity of the black man who feels a need to relate to white standards of beauty.

With the writing of Caetano da Costa Alegre, the San Tomesian poet of the late nineteenth century, the theme of the suffering of the black man is introduced into Lusophone African literature. Although Costa Alegre seems to accept the concept of the "physical" inferiority of the black man, he totally rejects the idea of African cultural or moral inferiority.

In the twentieth century Portuguese African poets, Francisco José Tenreiro in particular, exalt their negritude. A poetry of revolt, of a fraternal bond uniting oppressed black people throughout the world, manifests a strong opposition to colonial, cultural and political domination. Other poets such as José Craveirinha of Mozambique and António Jacinto of Angola have not only spoken with pride of blackness; they have also written of a society in which both the white man and the black man are equals. Whereas lusophone African writers a little over a century ago viewed their blackness as a source of inadequacy and grief, modern writers, filled with self-respect, use blackness not as a sign of inferiority but rather as a prideful assertion of mental decolonization.

Cover of Voz de Prisão *A Aventura Crioula*

Covers of Literaturas africanas de expressão portuguesa by Manuel Ferreira

Da dor
de ser negro
ao orgulho
de ser preto

por **Manuel Ferreira**

Referente dominante umas vezes, de circunstância outras, a cor da pele vem percorrendo o longo e acidentado rio da poesia africana de expressão portuguesa desde as origens até aos nossos dias.

África, espaço violentado, os homens aí divididos em dois grupos — negros e brancos, dominados e dominadores, envolvidos numa espessa teia de relações sociais, económicas —, cedo o Negro foi animalizado e logo também coisificado. A sua «antropomorfização» não poderia dar-se por outra via que não fosse a de avançar pelos caminhos que o identificassem, tanto quanto possível, com o Branco. E esses caminhos seriam os da obtenção de poder económico ou os da assimilação cultural. O que praticamente só se tornou viável, e para uns tantos, a partir do século XIX. Algumas famílias terminaram por se constituir numa burguesia mestiça ou negra cuja ascensão social teve como preço a alienação, uma vez que quanto cada um mais se integrasse nos esquemas europeus mais se apartava e se opunha aos seus irmãos de raça. Com efeito, a instalação do prelo em meados do século passado completa as condições *sine qua non* para o exercício da actividade literária. Na generalidade, a relação que os poetas negros estabeleciam com o mundo africano era idêntica à que estabeleciam os europeus radicados e integrados ou os euro-africanos.

A DILUIÇÃO DO MENOSPREZO

Os primeiros indícios do tópico da cor detectam-se logo no mais remoto poeta africano de língua portuguesa: o angolano mestiço José da Silva Maia Ferreira (*Espontaneidades da Minha Alma*, 1849). No poema «A Minha Terra» [Benguela], em louvor da sua pátria, muitas são as virtudes de

Angola de «palmeiras de sombra copada» (p. 13) e onde «[...] percorre afanoso, / A zagaia com força vibrando, /O Africano guerreiro e famoso» (*ibid.*). Mas, adiante, «Não tem Virgens com faces de neve», embora tenha «[...] donzelas de planta mui breve, / Mui airosas, de peito fiel» (*ibid.*). Este, o primeiro sinal de aristocratização da cor branca: «Não tem Virgens com faces [cor] de neve». Implícita a negação da cor negra. O que significa o registo, em espaço literário, da primeira manifestação de *alienação racial*. É verdade que o sujeito da enunciação contrapõe afirmando que a sua terra «Tem donzelas de planta mui breve, / Mui airosas, de peito fiel» e que o «Seu amor é qual fonte de prata / Onde mira quem nela s'espelha» (p. 14). Porém, do mesmo passo se diz que «Suas galas não são afectadas» (*ibid.*) e o «Coração todo o amor lhe palpita» e «Suas juras não são refalsadas» (*ibid.*). Dá-se ênfase aos predicados morais, mas minimizam-se os valores culturais: «Sabe amar! — Mas não tem a cultura / Desses lábios de mago florir» (*ibid.*). Seja, depois de nobilitar a mulher negra, volve, por comparação, à mulher branca, a mulher europeia, a detentora duma cultura superior, e assim à alienação racial se associa a *alienação cultural*.

Isto em 1849. Em 1864, J. Cândido Furtado incorpora novos traços significativos, ajudando a melhor definir o eixo semântico deste tema.

> *Qu'importa a cor, se as graças, se a candura,*
> *Se as formas divinais do corpo teu*
> *Se escondem, se adivinham, se apercebem*
> *Sob esse tão subtil, ligeiro véu?*
>
> *Que importa a cor, se o ceptro da beleza*
> *Co'o mesmo enleio e brilho nos seduz?*
> *E se o facho d'amor reflecte e esparge*
> *Ou no jaspe, ou no ébano, igual luz?*

(«No Álbum de Uma Africana», in Almanach de Lembranças Luso-Brasileiro, 1864, p. 116)

Para este português, radicado por longos anos em Luanda, a beleza é suprema, o amor universal. E na necessidade de recorrer ainda à compensação, ele outra coisa não faz que não seja, apenas, diluir a *subestimação da cor:* «É menos bela, acaso, a violeta / Porque o céu lhe não deu nevada cor?» (*ibid.*). A cor é um dado real e com um peso conotativo que não pode ser disfarçado, porque ele está jacente ou subjacente em todos quantos se entretecem nas malhas duma sociedade colonial. Aqui, porém, o discurso poético de J. Cândido Furtado pontua um avanço na valorização da mulher africana. E fá-lo por intermédio de subentendidas antinomias telúricas, cósmicas, que, pelo facto de o serem, transportam a força da evidência: «Não tem encantos mil a noute escura» e, no entanto, «Não deleita então mais o rouxinol?» (*ibid.*), acentuado o facto pela utilização duma redundância («noute *escura*»), banalizada nos nossos dias, mas cujo emprego naquele poema, e naquele tempo, nos parece pertinente.

Vinte anos depois, em 1884, portanto, o negro angolano Joaquim Dias Cordeiro da Mata, também na mesma publicação, *Almanach de Lembranças* para 1884, numa composição intitulada «Negra!», avança deste modo:

> *Negra! negra! como a asa*
> *do corvo mais negro e escuro,*
> *mas tendo nos claros olhos*
> *o olhar mais límpido e puro!*   (p. 124)

Aqui se entra no jogo semântico de J. C. Furtado, reduzindo o menosprezo dado à cor negra, e pelo mesmo recurso à absolutização da beleza («mas, linda, mimosa e bela», *ibid.*), todavia ainda sob um novo e paradoxal processo, que já referimos: o da «valorização da subestimação». Subestimação que se acentua e degrada numa outra estrofe do poema II sob a mesma epígrafe («Negra!»): «branca que ao mundo viesses, / serias das filhas d'Eva / *em beleza, ó negra, a prima!...*» (ibid). E neste balanceio lírico-sentimental, neste rodopio entre duas forças, uma centrípeta, lançada para o universo europeu, outra centrífuga, orientada para o universo negro, J. Cordeiro da Mata — por certo aplaudido na época —, hoje, numa visão diacrónica (injusta, convenhamos!), abunda no próprio absurdo e deixa a descoberto a sua inconsciente alienação:

> *s'elevar-te ao sexo frágil*
> *temeu o rei da criação;*
> *é qu'és, ó negra criatura,*
> *a deusa da formosura!...*
>
> (*Ibid.*)

— porquanto admitindo que ela, a *Negra!*, uma certa e determinada mulher negra, seja a «deusa da formosura!...», aceita de igual modo que não seja classificada de autêntica mulher, pelos vistos categoria só alcançada pelo dom da pele branca.

Contemporâneo de Cordeiro da Mata é o poeta são-tomense Caetano da Costa Alegre. Deslocamo-nos no espaço e não no tempo, já que alguns dos seus versos são datados de 1882 a 1889, embora o seu livro *Versos* tenha sido dado à estampa, postumamente, em 1916 [1]. Escritos a maioria deles em Lisboa e todos em Portugal, onde o poeta viveu desde muito novo (morreu com 25 anos de idade), se não há uma inversão no tratamento do tema — e não há —, entretanto o problema tende a facetar-se e a ganhar uma nova configuração, em alguns aspectos, pelo menos.

A DOR DE SER NEGRO

Vimos que os poemas se organizam, em regra, numa relação entre o *eu* e o *tu,* entre o poeta e a mulher negro-africana, sendo o referente a cor da pele. Vimos ainda como os citados poetas angolanos transmudaram o seu lirismo amoroso numa confessada alienação, mal suspeitando, sobremodo os de pele negra, do exercício de subserviência racial e cultural a que se entregavam. Pois bem. Que sucede com este solitário poeta são-tomense? Variadas e significativas coisas. A primeira questão a considerar é que ele vivia numa cidade europeia, ao contrário dos poetas angolanos. Outra é que o seu interlocutor não é a mulher negra, mas a mulher branca. Diremos então que a situação do discurso, o contexto e o acto de enunciação são

---

[1] Reeditado em 1951, por iniciativa dum sobrinho do autor, Norberto Cordeiro Nogueira Costa Alegre, de São Tomé [Lisboa, Liv.ª Ferin].

outros. Equivale a que, sendo a referência predominante a cor da pele, as oposições não se ordenam em branco vs. negro ou na identificação negro- -negra, mas sim em preto vs. branca.

> *A minha cor é negra,*
> *Indica luto e pena;*
> *É luz, que nos alegra,*
> *A tua cor morena.*
> *É negra a minha raça,*
> *A tua raça é branca,*
> *Tu és cheia de graça,*
> *Tens a alegria franca,*
> *Que brota a flux do peito*
> *Das cândidas crianças.*

(p. 47)

Inclusive, e ainda no mesmo poema: «Tu és a luz divina, / Em mil canções divagas», enquanto «Eu sou a horrenda furna / Em que se quebram vagas!...»

Eis, assim, a manifesta declaração do sentimento de inferioridade perante a pessoa branca. Se a mulher branca «É luz, que nos alegra», a expressão da «graça», da candura, ou, como noutro poema se diz, «Tu és o dia» (p. 26), o enunciador, prisioneiro duma cor que «Indica luto e pena» (p. 47), declara: «Todo eu sou um defeito», «a horrenda furna», «a noite espessa» *(ibid.)*, enquanto tu «És a luz, eu a sombra pavorosa» (p. 26), «és o dia».

Tudo se resume a este articulado primário: cor branca = graça, beleza, luz, felicidade; cor negra = fealdade, tristeza, desgraça («Todo eu sou um defeito»).

Duas componentes semânticas ganham dramática intensidade neste poeta: o sentimento aristocratizante conferido à pele branca, à raça branca, e o sofrimento enquanto ente negro, sujeito de pele negra — e a isto chamaríamos a *dor de ser negro*. «Uma das desditas que mais o alanceava era ser negro. Ouvi-lhe mesmo algumas poesias em que esse desgosto ressaltava duma maneira tão viva que confrangia» (Cruz de Magalhães, Introdução a *Versos, 1916*).

Obsessivamente, a linguagem de Costa Alegre, mesmo quando a mensagem não decorre dessa oposição mestra que atravessa o texto — preto/ branco —, é dominada pela ideia da cor branca: «o vosso ebúrneo colo» (p. 19), «almas de leite e rosas» *(ibid.)*, «límpida onda alabastrina e pura» (p. 21), «loura criatura» (p. 22), «dois trementes sóis em miniatura» *(ibid.)*, «outrora foste neve» (p. 24), «despontar do dia» (p. 25), «Na branca mão artística e pequena» *(ibid.)*, «asas brancas» (p. 28), «nevada coroa» *(ibid.)*. Repete-se em toda a estrutura do enunciado o recurso obsessivo a signos, sintagmas, versos completos, figuras de retórica: «[...] o sol, a estrela vespertina» (p. 29), «A lua cintilante, alvíssima, argentina» *(ibid.)*, «pérola nevada!» (p. 40), «ó minha branca fada!» *(ibid.)*, «[...] no teu seio, ó virgem linda! / Tão branco como o seio da virtude» (p. 42), «espuma alvinitente» (p. 48), «Com fúlgido clarão duma fatal aurora!» (p. 59).

Uma outra característica do seu processo estilístico é o das antíteses, num jogo de significações obtidas através de agrupamentos do que é «branco» e do que é «negro»: «Branca a espuma e negra a rocha» (p. 62), «Nem sempre o dia é claro e a noite escura!» (p. 65), «Nos olhos cor da noite mais escura, / Fulge, cintila o olhar da cor do dia» (p. 115). A obsessão é de tal monta que a virtude é branca («E talvez no teu seio, ó virgem linda! / Tão branco como o seio da virtude», p. 42), incorrendo o poeta no comum delito da utilização de noções criadas e exploradas pelo colonialismo e pelo racismo, como, por exemplo, a de «um negro de alma branca», numa «espécie de incorporação por destruição» (*canibalismo*).

Somente que Costa Alegre, cativo declarado dessa alienação racial, já o não é da alienação cultural, e liberto se manifesta do complexo de inferioridade cultural. E neste ponto se afasta e enobrece em relação aos irmãos coevos angolanos. De que modo? Por norma, através da antítese, da compensação. Vamos ver como.

> *És a luz, eu a sombra pavorosa,*
> *Eu sou a tua antítese frisante,*

(p. 26)

E logo, pendularmente:

> *Mas não estranhes que te aspire formosa,*
> *Do carvão sai o brilho do diamante.*

Estamos assim no plano da desmontagem das aparências, donde sobressai o intento da reabilitação da cor negra, na atitude orgulhosa de a situar ao mesmo nível da cor branca. Uma espécie de «impulso do eu» no investimento de autodefesa.

> *Ah! pálida mulher, se tu és bela,*
> *Eu não sou menos belo em minha essência,*
> *E, se amas entre as nuvens uma estrela,*
> *Ama o belo também nesta aparência!*

(p. 61)

Ou ainda:

> *Não me fujas assim, mulher feita de espuma!*
> *Eu sou ébano; tu, rainha das donzelas.*
> *Mas, olha, a noite é negra e tem milhões de estrelas,*
> *O dia é belo e branco e tem apenas uma.*

(p. 79)

Recorde-se: nos poetas angolanos o esforço de identificação fazia-se através de oposições telúricas e os atributos exaltados eram os que dizem respeito ao corpo. Em Costa Alegre a sua lei é a da utilização da antítese de ordem moral e intelectual. E nisto estará o ganho significativo e, inclusive, a mudança do traço semântico da compensação. Ele aceita a humilhante situação de infelicidade do homem negro, enquanto sujeito físico, mas já não aceita a suposta inferioridade que releva da cultura, da moral, da essência. O homem é o que forem os seus predicados morais, culturais, as suas qualidades intelectuais. O homem é a sua essência. E para Costa Alegre a «essência» do negro não é diferente da «essência» do branco. É a partir desse conceito de essência, matriz primeira da valorização da pessoa, independentemente da cor da pele, que ele tece o seu dramático diálogo, que é um apelo, introduzindo, para além do *eu* e do *interlocutor*, um novo elemento: o *mim*. Tudo isto pela necessidade real e premente de se libertar do sentimento de inferioridade racial (= étnica) no interior dum mecanismo de compensação, chegando mesmo a perguntar, a perguntar-se — e perguntando e perguntando-se como que o *eu* responde ao *mim*, afirmativamente, quando pela alegoria diz que a noite pode ser mais brilhante que o dia. Sim, ela, a mulher branca, seria a «graça», «a alegria franca», e ele, negro, a «horrenda furna», mas, se a manhã pode ser irmã da noite, porque não poderão ser irmãos o preto e o branco? — pergunta Costa Alegre, como se pretendesse, deste jeito, ultrapassar o jogo de relações contraditórias:

> *Porém, brilhante e pura,*
> *Talvez seja a manhã*
> *Irmã da noite escura!*
> *Serás tu minha irmã?!...*

Todavia, esta ponte interrogativa, esta esperança, não o liberta do drama que o texto demasiadamente evidencia, parecendo autopunir-se num complexo de culpabilidade por um crime que não cometeu, como se desejasse mitigar a sua dor, na exploração sucessiva e aprofundada do seu próprio sofrimento, lembrando a filosofia masoquista renovada e intensificada na *Menina e Moça* de Bernardim Ribeiro, texto que, aliás, também recorre à antítese, como recentemente notou Helder Macedo (*Do Significado Oculto da «Menina e Moça»*, Lisboa, 1977).

A estas formas de tratamento poético dum conteúdo específico, formas que provêm da condição do homem negro num espaço conflitual e traumatizante, mas quando ainda se não vislumbra, com relevo, um suporte desalienador, daríamos um nome. Por similaridade histórica, a exemplo do que nas primeiras décadas deste século sucedeu com os movimentos haitiano (*indigenismo*) e cubano (*negrismo*), rotulá-lo-íamos, para o espaço de língua portuguesa, não de indigenismo ou negrismo, mas simultaneamente de *negrismo-indigenismo*, discurso em que a precariedade ideológica não permite respostas de expressão criativa às solicitações reais da História.

Um vazio na literatura angolana (e são-tomense) de algumas décadas se interrompe em 1932 com o português, por décadas radicado em Angola, Tomás Vieira da Cruz. Em período florescente duma literatura colonial, a que exalta o Branco e diminui o Negro, aquele poeta, pelo menos ao nível afectivo, furta-se ao enleio imperial e estrutura um enunciado que se enobrece, em parte, pela sua «lira mulata». Na representação da mulata que idealiza nas «Saudades de duas raças / que se abraçaram no mundo!» (*Quissange*, 1971, edição global de três obras suas, p. 15), Tomás Vieira da Cruz derrama toda a sua generosa dádiva humana: «Os teus defeitos são graças / que mais me prendem, querida... / Mistério de duas raças / que se encontraram na vida» (p. 13). Mais do que a negra, a mulata é o centro motivador da empatia com forte conotação erótica. «Teus beijos são tiranias, são como espinhos de rosas...» (p. 14). Conotação erótica que já se patenteia em outros produtores de textos poéticos angolanos do século XIX — e é o caso de J. Cordeiro da Mata: «Viam-se-lhe a descoberto / — com arte bem modeladas — / (e que eu mirava de perto) / umas formas cinzeladas». Tomás Vieira da Cruz, exaltando a mulata, fá-lo, portanto, num envolvimento fraterno que exclui a distanciação racial. (Diremos, à guisa de parêntesis, que o tópico da mulata é mais tarde enriquecido pelo contributo de vários poetas moçambicanos ou angolanos, como Rui Knopfli, José Craveirinha, António Cardoso, Costa Andrade, Viriato da Cruz, Ernesto Lara Filho e outros mais, cada um dando a sua achega pessoal e semanticamente assaz diversificada.) Alguns anos depois (1944), com Geraldo Bessa Victor, mestiço angolano, o interlocutor pode ser a mulher negra, a mulata, mas pode ser também o homem negro, o menino negro. O campo semântico tenderá agora a alargar-se, no desenvolvimento, sobretudo, de tensões sociais.

A DESALIENAÇÃO / O DISCURSO DA REVOLTA

A mudança da visão racial de África surge com o poeta Francisco José Tenreiro. Contribuição verdadeiramente transgressiva (revolucionária): «Negro / para quem as horas são sol e febre / que colhes / nesse ritmo de guindaste. // Negro / para quem os dias são iguais / que respeitas teu patrão e senhor / como água que mexe o engenho. //

> *Negro!*
> *Levanta os olhos pra o sol rijo*
> *e ama tua mulher*
> *na terra húmida e quente!*

> (*Ilha de Nome Santo*, 1942, p. 34)

A «Exortação», título do poema, incita à rebeldia contra o Branco e a fecundação para que a raça se procrie e fortaleça. Com F. J. Tenreiro se introduz o conceito de *negritude,* dez anos antes proclamado e exaltado, em Paris, pelo grupo de Senghor, Aimé Césaire e Léon Damas, e se ultrapassam, pelos conteúdos ideológicos do texto, as formas incipientes do *negrismo* ou *indigenismo.*

> *Segue em frente*
> *irmão!*
> *Que a tua música*
> *seja o ritmo de uma conquista!*
> *E que o teu ritmo*
> *seja a cadência de uma vida nova!*

> (*Obra Poética de F. J. T.*, 1967, p. 62)

— tema que Amílcar Cabral, alguns anos depois, havia de retomar no poema «Segue o Teu Rumo, Irmão».

Em Tenreiro o interlocutor deixa de ser a mulher africana, ou a mulher europeia, tónica do discurso do negrismo-indigenismo. Curiosamente, quanto à biografia, a sua situação é paralela à de Costa Alegre. São-tomense, vivendo em Lisboa desde muito novo, e não sendo negro, é, contudo, mestiço. Mas o corte na perspectiva social e da sua representação é absoluto. À humilhação de Costa Alegre, à imploração, por assim dizer, de C. Alegre, sucede a altivez, a conscientização libertadora de Tenreiro.

Metodologicamente cingidos, tanto quanto possível, à exploração do tema — a cor da pele — que nos propusemos, num contexto complexo

onde vários outros temas e motivos ou *topoi* (Curtius) nele se imbricam (exploração económica, Mãe-Negra, protesto anticolonialista, negritude, etc.), não nos é permitido alargarmo-nos sobre a extraordinária importância desta mensagem inovadora, que incorpora não o Negro apenas são-tomense ou angolano ou moçambicano, mas o Negro de todo o mundo, o Negro escravizado por séculos e por todo o planeta: «Libéria! Libéria!», «Brasil», «Cabo Verde», «Em Lisboa?», «Na América?», «Harlem! Harlem!», vivendo assim a sua universal odisseia, escarniado ou chicoteado.

Mensagem exaltante, a iniciar de vez o *discurso da revolta,* que só dez anos após irrompeu em Angola e em Moçambique. Discurso conotado pelo humor e pela ironia, o que se tornou, posteriormente, um traço característico de todas as literaturas negras, desde Césaire a Ferdinand Oyono ou a Mongo Beto, e que, sendo uma forma de destruição do paternalismo do senhor, termina por se revelar veículo da revolta. Ironia bem evidente nesta «Canção do Mestiço» *(Ilha de Nome Santo)* que, pela sua natureza, nos parece — e, agora, sim — perfeitamente a carácter na progressão da nossa proposta:

Mestiço!

Nasci do negro e do branco
e quem olhar para mim
é como se olhasse
para um tabuleiro de xadrez:
a vista passando depressa
fica baralhando cor
no olho alumbrado de quem me vê.

Mestiço!

E tenho no peito uma alma grande
uma alma feita de adição
como 1 e 1 são 2.

Foi por isso que um dia
o branco cheio de raiva
contou os dedos das mãos
fez uma tabuada e falou grosso:
— mestiço!
a tua conta está errada.
Teu lugar é ao pé do negro.

Ah!
*   Mas eu não me danei...*
e muito calminho
arrepanhei o meu cabelo para trás
fiz saltar fumo do meu cigarro
cantei do alto
a minha gargalhada livre
que encheu o branco de calor!...

Mestiço!

Quando amo a branca
*   sou branco...*
Quando amo a negra
*   sou negro.*

Pois é...

(Ilha de Nome Santo, pp. 19-20)

Assim se introduziu na poesia uma outra categoria: a do mestiço. O conceito de bivalência racial (não no sentido freudiano: amar e odiar) prolonga-se e reparte-se por um lastro mais profundo: social, cultural, linguístico. Porque o mestiço, o mulato, não o é apenas pela fusão de sangues, mas sim, e sobretudo, pelo sincretismo de culturas. E daí transformar-se naquilo a que alguns teóricos chamam o homem de dois mundos: o Africano moderno, mais ou menos aculturado (há quem prefira «desaculturado», citemos M. Pinto de Andrade; e, sob um certo ponto de vista, muitas vezes com razão) — daí a sua bipolaridade, a sua dual condição cultural, e o falar-se da sua natureza de indivíduo «problemático» (designação que, se correcta, caberia bem a Costa Alegre). Portanto, em desequilíbrio? Instável ou estável? Ou pura invenção dos sociólogos? [2]

Na «Canção do Mestiço» de Tenreiro, como em poemas doutros autores que mais tarde se fizeram eco do mesmo tema, a ironia e o humor que atravessam o texto, de princípio ao fim, são uma exemplar afirmação da personalidade do sujeito de enunciação. Retenha-se ainda o salto qualitativo obtido na poesia africana de expressão portuguesa com a intervenção de Tenreiro.

A ironia, o sarcasmo desabusado e acutilante, ácido e virulento, eis o recurso estilístico doutro poeta de São Tomé e Príncipe, Marcelo da Veiga — amigo de Almada Negreiros, Mário Eloy, Hernâni Cidade, Mário Domingues —, homem duma geração anterior à de F. J. Tenreiro, mas cuja poesia só mais tarde veio a ser verdadeiramente conhecida (*Poetas de S. Tomé e Príncipe*, 1963, de Alfredo Margarido).

> *Sou preto — o que ninguém escuta;*
> *O que não tem socorro;*
> *O — olá, tu rapaz!*
> *O — ó seu merda! ó cachorro!*
> *O — ó seu filho da puta!*
> *E outros mimos mais...*

(apud No Reino de Caliban, II, 1975, p. 464)

Ou, noutro texto:

> *O preto é bola,*
> *É pim-pam-pum!*
> *Vem um:*
> *— Zás! na cachola...*
> *— Outro — um chut — bum!*
> *«Aqui d'el-rei!!!»*
> *Grita ele louco...*
> *Vem o da lei,*
> *Diz-lhe — «inda é pouco!»*

(Ibid., pp. 465-466)

---

[2] Antropólogos como Balandier, M. Collin Turnbull e Malinowski não partilham esta opinião. E intelectuais africanos como Erick From, Abraham Kardiner, Cheik Hamidou Kane, Ezequiel Mphahlele contestam a teoria e reivindicam a sua qualidade de serem «autenticamente». Por sua vez, Chinua Achebe, prestigioso romancista nigeriano, faz a este respeito um gracioso comentário: «Outro dia fui à minha aldeia natal para participar nos funerais dum vizinho. Estava profundamente tocado pelo ritmo violento do *ekwwe*, do *ogene* e do *oyo* produzidos pelos músicos amadores da aldeia. Quando voltei a Enugu, pude deliciar-me ouvindo o concerto de piano meu favorito, de Schumann. E teria podido, quando a noite veio, jantar à maneira europeia mais refinada e na noite seguinte comer com as minhas mãos o doce de inhame e a sopa amarga de folhas verdes. [...] É espantoso, na verdade, como transmitimos assim com uma facilidade incrível duma cultura para a outra. Eis porque os nossos observadores construíram o mito do homem de dois mundos, o homem que sofre os conflitos internos intoleráveis e susceptíveis de o levar a abandonar as suas próprias educação e civilização em cada momento crítico» (in *Spear*, Lagos, Dezembro de 1963, p. 13, cit. por Sunday O. Anozie, *Sociologie du Roman African*, 1970, p. 49).

Na transição da década de 40 para a década de 50, a moçambicana Noémia de Sousa, no poema «Negra», datado de 1951, e publicado na *Mensagem* (Luanda, 1952), zomba das «Gentes estranhas com seus olhos cheios doutros mundos» que «quiseram cantar teus encantos / para elas só mistérios profundos, / de delírios e feitiçarias... / Teus encantos profundos de África», numa alusão implacável (e necessariamente felina) à visão exótica, folclórica, dos Europeus, que, «em seus formais e rendilhados cantos, ausentes de emoção e sinceridade», outra coisa não fizeram do que diminuir e degradar a imagem da mulher negra, mascarando-a de «[...] esfinge de ébano, amante sensual, / jarra etrusca, exotismo tropical, / demência, atracção, crueldade, / animalidade, magia... / e não sabemos quantas outras palavras vistosas e vazias».

Era o tempo duma nova poesia em Moçambique, cuja contribuição, deste ponto de vista, no século XIX, fora inexistente. O tempo da real medida da personalidade africana, o tempo duma poesia inserida num espaço agora percorrido pela consciente oposição colonizado/colonizador. O tempo da valorização do verdadeiro real moçambicano. É assim que, com Virgílio de Lemos, se retorna ao lirismo amoroso do século XIX continuado no período de 1930-1940 mas, tal como nesta última data, projectado na mulher mulata. Com uma diferença, porém: agora é total a nobilitação da mulata, recolocada na sua verdadeira condição de mulher e de africana: «Amo a seiva do teu corpo», «Amo a resignação da tua carne / Rosa Maria / tua humilhada resignação quotidiana», «Amo-te Rosa Maria / nesta ou na manhã futura / dos dias com e sem poesia» (*Poemas do Tempo Presente*, 1960, pp. 84-86).

Esta identidade de cada um com a globalidade africana, fruto duma consciência que sobe do lastro fecundo da História e que aponta para a reabilitação do humilhado povo colonizado, tendendo a esbater ou a eliminar de vez as barreiras da cor, é tal que os próprios poetas brancos nascidos ou não em África infringem todo o sistema cristalizado e procedem a uma revisão humanista em suas mentes colonizadas. A dilucidação, neste caso, vem de Moçambique, com o poema «Um Igual a Um», datado de 1952, de Manuel Filipe de Moura Coutinho (*Direito de Cantar*, 1956, pp. 15-18):

> *Pois é verdade, conheci o negro que há em mim*
> *E senti os açoites*
> *Que durante sete dias e seis noites*
> *Lhe infligiram os Ku-Klux-Klans*
>
> (p. 16)

E neste mundo-cão do negro

> *Na pátria do negro o branco ladrão*
> *Mandou*
> *Que eu fosse um homem e ele fosse um cão*
>
> (p. 17)

Mas

> *Pelo canto que nos guia*
> *Nós podemo-nos de novo abraçar;*
> *Pelo canto que nos guia*
> *Hoje o negro é meu irmão*
>
> (p. 17)

> Conheci hoje o negro que há em mim
> E que vive no meu peito ignorado
> Sob uma pele branca de europeu.
> Aquele negro que se dá ao Jorge Amado
> E hoje se me deu

(p. 18)

Tal identificação real e irreversível, já interiorizada, tornada fundamento da acção participante na «pátria do negro», transparentemente surge no angolano António Jacinto, que deste modo resolve a ambiguidade entre dois códigos culturais diferenciados e que se pretendia contraditórios:

> O meu poema sou eu-branco
> montado em mim preto
> a cavalgar pela vida fora

(Poemas, 1961 p. 41)

Por complementaridade, a significativa correspondência vem do poeta moçambicano, já mencionado, Noémia de Sousa. Rejeitando o exclusivismo racial, elide a barreira da cor na ponte fraterna dum humanismo integral:

> Companheiro branco
> de sorriso de abraço,
> de olhos claros de esperança,
> Não queremos que te fiques no caminho...
> vencido e cansado, sem um carinho...
> Que tu mesmo nos ensinaste
> que o Povo é sempre Povo, em qualquer pedaço do mapa!

(Poetas de Moçambique, 1962, p. 86)

Ainda aqui interfere a pele como significante. Agora para ser destruído, na acentuada consciência de que a oposição entre os homens (brancos e negros) não depende de dados circunstanciais, mas de algo mais profundo, ancorado na História. Desmitificam-se assim, pelo canto, os acidentes da cor da pele; pela suprema manifestação da linguagem se procede, simultaneamente, à dessacralização do «Branco» e do «Negro».

O ORGULHO CONQUISTADO

Pedra basilar da construção dos impérios coloniais, sujeito à quotidiana humilhação da sua cor, escarnecido na sua própria natureza física, o Negro acaba por ser ele próprio a libertar-se dos anátemas e mitos europeus, atitude personificada em José Craveirinha no poema «Manifesto», onde canta os seus «belos e curtos cabelos crespos», os seus «olhos negros», «olhos enormes», as suas «maravilhosas mãos escuras como raízes do cosmos», a sua «boca de lábios túmidos, /cheios da bela virilidade ímpia de negro», a sua «face altiva», os seus «dentes brancos de marfim», o seu «corpo flexível», o «cálido encantamento selvagem» da sua «pele tropical»:

Ah, Mãe África no meu rosto escuro de diamante
de belas e largas narinas másculas
frementes haurindo o olor florestal
e as tatuadas bailarinas macondes
nuas
na bárbara maravilha eurítmica das negras ancas sensuais
e no bater uníssono dos pés descalços.

Oh! e meu peito da tonalidade mais bela do breu
e no imbondeiro da minha inaudita esperança gravado o tótem do Mundo
e minha voz estentórea de homem do Tanganhica
do Congo, Angola, Moçambique e Senegal.
Ah! Outra vez eu chefe zulo
eu zagaia banto
eu lançador de malefícios contra as pragas insaciáveis de gafanhotos
eu tambor, eu seruma, eu negro suaíli
eu Tchaca
eu Mahazul e Dingana
eu Zichacha na confidência dos ossinhos mágicos do Tinlholo
eu árvore da Munhuana
eu tocador de presságios nas teclas das timbilas chopes
eu caçador de leopardos
eu batuque
e nas fronteiras de água do Rovuma ao Incomáti
eu cidadão dos espíritos das velhas luas
carregadas de anátemas de Moçambique.

(*Chigubo*, 1964, pp. 5-7)

Repare-se no contraste: Costa Alegre, no último lustro do século XIX, autoflagelando-se na sua própria natureza física: «Todo eu sou um defeito», «Eu sou a horrenda furna» — como que envergonhadamente desculpando-se de ser negro; José Craveirinha, na segunda metade do século XX, subvertendo orgulhosa e altivamente, no espaço cultural africano, o conceito de beleza europeu que, por certos níveis sociais africanos, havia sido adoptado, e glorificando o Negro não só na sua qualidade de portador duma cultura milenária como também nos atributos físicos com que a Natureza o dotou. No trânsito da dor de ser negro, em Costa Alegre, para o consciente orgulho de ser preto, em José Craveirinha, se edifica, no espaço lírico, o discurso da descolonização mental e se organiza o *corpus* da libertação racial e cultural.

Linda-a-Velha, 15-8-77.

NOTA DO AUTOR

Ignorámos Cabo Verde no decurso deste artigo, porque o tópico da cor é praticamente inexistente na poesia e até na ficção cabo-verdianas — facto que constitui uma excepção nas literaturas africanas de língua portuguesa.

Precis

MARIO ANTONIO
PARA UMA PERSPECTIVA CRIOULA
DA LITERATURA ANGOLANA
[Towards a Crioule Perspective
in Angolan Literature]

The unpublished volume of J.D. Cordeiro da Matta's Repositório de Coisas Angolenses (usos, costumes, tradições, lendas e anecdotas) Compilation of Angolan Things (uses, customs, traditions, legends and anecdotes) *in the 19th century enables us to see and to understand the crioule perspective in Angolan culture and literature. This work of over six hundred handwritten pages includes many notes of Cordeiro da Matta particularly in the areas of linguistics and history. His knowledge of Kimbundu and the etymologies of Portuguese regionalisms spoken in Angola enabled him to study "angolanisms" with scholarly confidence. An analysis of the contents of the study permits us to define the themes of "crioulidade" and to appreciate the participation in the historic process of Angola by the crioule society.*

PARA UMA PERSPECTIVA CRIOULA DA LITERATURA ANGOLANA

MÁRIO ANTÓNIO

Decidimos rever a aprendizagem de um tempo que afinal é apenas de ontem, não obstante a lembrança-aviso de um poeta que decorámos, Afonso Duarte: *O voltar ao passado é sempre um resto / ou pior / Uma falta de saúde.* Ora, foi já na consciência desse risco que, rapazes, começámos a dedicar o tempo que nos sobrava da actividade profissional à frequência da biblioteca da Câmara Municipal de Luanda — a referência serve para chamar as atenções, possivelmente ainda não despertas, para certas riquezas únicas, iniciais, com que a dotaram os herdeiros do Dr. Alfredo Troni, cuja fotografia, então, como supomos que hoje, presidia à sua utilização pelos ensimesmados leitores habituais —, desorientados nos primeiros passos, recompensados depois pela alegria da descoberta de pequenas coisas, essas pequenas coisas que nos conduziram a uma perspectiva que se nos afigurou a mais adequada ao entendimento de uma condição social de que participávamos e, consequentemente, condicionava, por maior ou menor consciência que dela tivéssemos, a expressão literária de que fôssemos capazes. Só mais tarde, e ao contacto com a particular incidência do termo no campo linguístico, encontrámos a designação apropriada a essa perspectiva, usando-a para título de um livro que, no entanto, apenas implicitamente a defendia: *Luanda, Ilha Crioula* (Agência-Geral do Ultramar, Lisboa, 1968). Reunia esse livro textos escritos ao longo de um decénio, em diversas circunstâncias e latitudes, o que de certo modo compensava a ausência de esquema e a irregularidade metodológica por um percurso biográfico cumprido.

Os primeiros factos que dessa pesquisa do passado colhemos consubstanciaram-se numa história de vida, erguida de forma não comum, pois se baseara na leitura de jornais, sem as habituais averiguações de documentação ainda existente, mas com a sedutora vantagem de uma imagem social, aquela por que se reflectiu a personalidade de Joaquim Dias Cordeiro da Matta — em escritos próprios que foram desde o livro ou artigo ao anúncio, e em alheios — na sociedade do seu tempo. O título da comunicação que fizemos e, dépois, publicámos, reflectia essa imagem: *A Sociedade Angolana do Fim do Século XIX e um seu Escritor* (Luanda, Editorial Nós, 1961).

Já essa comunicação que, significativamente, terminava por sugestões, não por conclusões, assinalava insatisfação relativamente ao que de limitante continuaria a subsistir se apenas se preenchessem as anteriores zonas de desconhecimento da cultura crioula angolana pelo arbítrio das «geneologias» literárias, documentadas nas escassas manifestações que era possível encontrar. Tanto como a personalidade do escritor, interessava-nos o que nela era herança comum de uma sociedade. E supomos que assim ganhavam o esclarecimento dos problemas que essa personalidade nos punha e a reconstituição de elementos básicos da cultura que representava.

É curioso como um interesse que de início se tinha desenvolvido afectivamente, procurando reparar a injustiça imerecida do olvido de um escritor que morrera jovem e longe da glória que pretendera — na inconfidência de Chatelain —, cedo se transformou na urgência de identificação por alguma gente sentida necessária, o que aparece demonstrado em algumas das repercussões que suscitou. No entanto, é verdade que se trata de escritor mais em esboço de grandeza que em realização dela. Das várias alíneas por que, desde a nossa referida comunicação, fazíamos o escorço da sua personalidade literária, resultavam um poeta cujas primícias estão longe de poder justificar a aproximação de um patamar de notoriedade mesmo na circunstância de atraso da sociedade envolvente; um cronista documentado em algumas tantas linhas de prosa leve e humorada, espalhadas por vária Imprensa; um jornalista incluído na equipa redactorial de um órgão de Imprensa e com qualidades efectivadas em colaborações; um pedagogo revelado na atitude francamente positiva em face dos problemas como no esforço para a sua solução; um filólogo apenas apetrechado pelo ensaio de dicionarização que ficou marcando um ponto importante no, até hoje, pouco frequentado e menos ainda servido campo dos estudos linguísticos do grupo banto angolano; um folclorista detentor de método adequado, com obra recolhida valiosa, de que a parte inédita parecia, contudo, sobrelevar o importante volume que teve tempo de editar; um historiador simplesmente anunciado no que nos parecia obra preparatória, uma *Chronologia de Angola*, por vários autores utilizada ⸲ desaparecida da biblioteca da Câmara Municipal de Luanda antes de 1960.

Numa apreciação a que a distância da descoberta consente maior objectividade, supomos poder dizer hoje que de personalidade menor se trata, ainda em comparação com outros casos locais, em todos os referidos aspectos, com excepção do relativo ao folclore; mas mesmo neste sujeita à proximidade de um trabalho pioneiro e até hoje inultrapassado: o realizado pelo suíço Chatelain, seu companheiro de interesses.

Gostaríamos de ter chegado a conclusão diversa e alimentámos durante largo tempo a esperança de podermos encontrar a colectânea, porventura anotada, de *114 contos angolanos* que, no início do decénio de 40 deste século, passaram pelas mãos do falecido Padre António Moreira Basílio. Em 1968, quando nos foi dada a oportunidade de trabalharmos, por algum tempo, no Arquivo Histórico de Angola, reacendeu-se-nos essa esperança, à vista de um maço de papéis que haviam pertencido ao referido padre, mas foi desfeita ao fim da consulta que fizemos do seu conteúdo. Nesses papéis encontrámos, contudo, mais uma revelação de original desaparecido, uma *Autobiografia*. Um documento deste tipo, da autoria de personalidade tão característica de uma sociedade crioula africana no século XIX, teria um valor certamente único e esclarecer-nos-ia sobre muitos dos problemas que o estudo dessa sociedade nos põe.

Esse era o quinto original desaparecido — um romance, uma recolha folclórica, uma cronologia, uma crónica social foram os outros — que assinalávamos de autor cujo nome nos surgia impresso em número idêntico de livros: um de poemas, um dicionário, uma recolha folclórica, uma iniciação à leitura e uma tradução da Bíblia. Lamentávamos que herdeiros (ou quem a isso se arrogou) tivessem feito o «auto-de-fé monumental» que, em altura de desespero, Cordeiro da Matta prometera realizar com os seus papéis, descrentes já de encontrarmos laudas preenchidas pela sua letra, cuja perfeição caligráfica apenas conheceramos das assinaturas apostas aos volumes numerados do seu dicionário, quando, quase por acaso, nos veio parar às mãos um volume com seis centenas de páginas cuidadosamente manuscritas por J. D. Cordeiro da Matta, o *Repositório de Coisas Angolenses*, propriedade do Museu de Angola e motivo da comunicação que agora encontramos a ocasião de divulgar.

A primeira impressão com que ficámos, antes da leitura das páginas copiadas e arrumadas em volume por J. D. Cordeiro da Matta, foi a do reencontro de um rosto, na ausência, até hoje, do conhecimento de qualquer das fotografias que abundantemente deve ter tirado esse coetâneo do aparecimento da máquina e das técnicas fotográficas na cidade onde viveu, na segunda metade do século XIX, em África. Através da sua caligrafia estendida por seis centenas de páginas, vimos desenhar-se a figura desse jovem surpreendido por contemporâneos no seu estudo isolado, rodeado de livros, pois, antes de mais, de apontamentos de estudo se trata. E é esse o seu particular valor: permitem compreender a *démarche* intelectual de que os livros dão pálida imagem, de toda uma geração que haveria de firmar orgulhoso marco na vida angolana.

O volume tem o título seguinte, escrito pela mão de J. D. Cordeiro da Matta: *Reportório / de / Coisas Angolenses / (Usos, costumes, tradições, lendas e anedotas)*. O parênteses dá evidência do espírito minucioso do compilador, como a si próprio se chama, adequadamente, em muitas páginas, Cordeiro da Matta, e a discriminação que apresenta aponta acertada escolha de matérias, para quem, como já escrevemos noutro lugar, assumira o empenho de valorização cultural em relação à sociedade que era a sua. Contém o volume 665 páginas, aparentemente consideradas concluídas, das quais, no entanto, faltam, vitimadas pela degradação que parece ter perseguido os manuscritos de Cordeiro da Matta, as seguinte: 31 a 67, 75 a 114, 163-164, 177-178, 459-460. A partir da página 422, surge a numeração com a rubrica *J. D. C. Matta* em todas as páginas pares. As transcrições são numeradas até «173 — Distrito de Icolo e Bengo», seguindo as restantes sem numeração. Em todo o volume, no alto das páginas ímpares, aparece escrito o título do documento transcrito e, nas pares, *Repositório de Coisas Angolenses*. O papel usado é do tipo almaço, com 35 linhas.

Que é o volume? Destiná-lo-ia o compilador à publicação? O *Repositório de Coisas Angolenses* é uma colectânea de documentos vários, transcritos de outras publicações e anotados pelo compilador. A arrumação que deles faz J. D. Cordeiro da Matta pode levar a supor que almejasse a sua publicação, mas talvez seja mais crível que, numa sociedade onde esse desiderato era ainda difícil, apenas entendesse ter um adequado instrumento de trabalho, utilizável também por outros dos seus companheiros de aventura intelectual. Se relacionarmos essa colectânea documental com o facto de o autor ter escrito também uma *Chronologia de Angola*, que não chegou a ser publicada, veremos nesta a ossatura de um trabalho histórico que aquela ajudaria a preencher. Com efeito, o primeiro historiador angolano que depois surgiria, Francisco Castelbranco, cita algumas vezes elementos da *Chronologia;* talvez tivesse também conhecido o *Repositório* que, no entanto, não cita. Ficamos com a ideia, à vista do grosso volume de transcrições do *Repositório*, que J. D. Cordeiro da Matta estaria apto à realização de trabalho de envergadura maior do que aquela de que foram capazes os seus imediatos sucessores.

Uma deficiência apresenta essa recolha: os documentos são transcritos, muitas vezes, sem indicação de origem. Algumas vezes esta surge, contudo, o que, com o reconhecimento que realizámos de outras, nos leva a supor que principalmente utilizadas foram as fontes impressas. Destas, destacam-se a série não oficial do *Boletim do Conselho Ultramarino, o Almanach de Lembranças,* de que Matta foi, no seu tempo, o principal colaborador angolano, e órgãos da Imprensa luandense, designadamente, *O Cruzeiro do Sul, O Pharol do Povo* e *O Futuro de Angola.* Cremos não errar supondo que algumas, poucas, transcrições foram feitas a partir de documentos manuscritos, não tanto por notarmos a ausência de indicação de fonte — pois, em muitos casos destes, fácil nos foi a sua referência a publicação conhecida —, mas por sabermos a importância que a tradição manuscrita assumia como meio de comunicação cultural na época de Matta, em Angola.

Associavam-se, assim, o saber que fora recuperado na Metrópole sobre o Ultramar, principalmente através do Conselho Ultramarino reconstituído, umas décadas antes, e o que da tradição local se tentava fixar. No primeiro movimento, de resto, se haviam incluído contribuições locais, valorizada a experiência vivida em face do aprendido nos livros. É típico o caso das memórias escritas por autoridades, a solicitação do Ministério e Secretaria de Estado da Marinha e Ultramar, com emendas sobre os *Ensaios de Estatística*, de Lopes de Lima. Essas autoridades eram ou residentes de longa data ou naturais, uns como outros representantes da cultura crioula local, pois, como e óbvio, a crioulidade, produto do contacto de culturas, é recíproca na sua realização. Do segundo, foram pontos altos secções como «Usos e Costumes» e «Apontamentos para a história de Angola», de *O Pharol do Povo* e *O Cruzeiro do Sul*, cuja reedição, há dez anos, apontávamos como valiosa.

A contribuição anotada de J. D. Cordeiro da Matta reparte-se pelos sectores que mais cultivou: a Linguística e a História. No primeiro aspecto, entenda-se Linguística como era possível o seu cultivo por um autodidacta em África no século XIX, anteriormente, portanto, às experiências europeias que abriram os caminhos da florescente ciência que hoje é. Teve, porém, Matta o benefício do convívio de Chatelain, que foi quem pôs o conhecimento do Quimbundo no pé em que, infelizmente, até hoje ficou, e isso se reflecte na segurança da sua grafia, adiantada em relação à de quantos anteriormente tentaram escrever aquela língua, o que propícia as correcções, que quase sempre tem de fazer, das palavras quimbundas que surgem nos textos transcritos. Essas correcções são, por isso, sempre justificadas. Dá também, nalguns casos, as etimologias de regionalismos do português falado em Angola — angolanismos — com segurança. Assim, a página 456: «chinguilador, *é vocábulo aportuguezado; em Kimbundo se diz* xingiri *derivado do verbo* Ku-xingila». As observações feitas às anotações de João Vieira Carneiro sobre os *Ensaios* de Lopes de Lima dão também exemplo do grau do seu conhecimento. Duas notas a página 474: 1) Nzéke *e não* nzegue, *costumo ouvir dizer*. 2) *Vieira Carneiro, apesar de ter sido exacto em algumas regras das suas observações, não o foi porém a respeito de* Canzele *ou* Canzelele, *por nenhum desses lugares ser o a que se refere Lopes de Lima:* Anzele *ou* Nzele; *conforme a índole da língua angolense, é o lugar denominado* Ndondo-á-Nzele, *no sobado de* Malambu, *jurisdição do Icola e Bengo* (...)

Num caso, a menção humilde do testemunho da experiência própria; no outro, a condenação da crítica fácil a que são dados muitos pseudo-especialistas... Há também várias notas propondo traduções discordantes.

Quanto à História, surgem aqui e ali elementos quase sempre complementares da informação do documento transcrito. Um exemplo é o da página 662, sobre a trascrição que faz de um artigo de Luís Augusto

Rebello da Silva, relativo à «Recepção do Infante D. Luiz na cidade de Loanda»: *El-Rei D. Pedro V, de saudosa memória, na abertura da sessão ordinária do anno legislativo de 1860-61 (4 de Novembro de 1860) proferiu as seguintes palavras: «Cabe-me a satisfação de agradecer aos habitantes da capital d'aquella província as manifestações de jubilo com que receberam meu muito prezado irmão o serenissimo infante D. Luiz, na sua viagem à África Ocidental».*

São notas modestas as do compilador, e se supomos por elas se acrescentar valor ao *Repositório*, permanecem, sem dúvida, secundárias. Mais importante nos parece o que do *Repositório* traduz ou pode traduzir o percurso mental não apenas do compilador, mas da sua geração.

Já sobre isso algo ficou dito, ao apontarmos de onde foram recolhidas as transcrições, fontes por isso mesmo consideradas importantes por J. D. Cordeiro da Matta. Supomos, porém, que uma análise do seu conteúdo poderá permitir-nos uma hipótese sobre a consciência cultural crioula, que julgamos pertença colectiva de uma sociedade.

O lugar que a História ocupa entre as transcrições dos *Usos, costumes, tradições, lendas e anedotas*, que J. D. Cordeiro da Matta quis reunir no seu *Repositório* aponta-nos um primeiro aspecto da definição cultural do homem crioulo: sentindo-se uma das resultantes de um processo histórico, tinha a necessidade do seu conhecimento.

Que essa característica é generalizável, sentimo-lo comprovado no espaço que ocupa a História nos produtos literários da sociedade crioula, particularmente na Imprensa que criou e manteve nos últimos três decénios do século XIX, em Angola.

Há também uma incidência muito particular nas transcrições do *Repositório*, sobre temas definidores de crioulidade, que nos parece não justificado considerar ocasional, antes traduzir um esforço de autodefinição. Com efeito, no *continuum* por que se podem alinhar as realidades sócio-culturais susceptíveis de serem definidas como crioulas, encontramos, desde, num extremo, transcrições várias ocupando-se dos «pretos calçados» a, noutro, as respeitantes a europeus africanizados. As formas de sincretismo cultural são também motivos de preferência de J. D. Cordeiro da Matta: e delas se apresentam exemplos desde as missas de sufrágio e os óbitos às regras de sucessão e às diversões.

Importante também para esta autodefinição é a incidência de transcrições sobre o papel que, no processo histórico angolano, a sociedade crioula parece ter desempenhado. Desde Lopes Sequeira, que merece uma das anotações de Matta, até mais recentes representantes dessa sociedade crioula, abundam as transcrições comprovando um sentido de participação no processo histórico angolano. São significativas, a esse respeito, as de textos da autoria de crioulos, como Joaquim António de Carvalho e Menezes que, actuando na primeira metade do século XIX, permanece vivo na segunda, como defensor da sociedade crioula, pois o seu livro *Demonstração Geographica* conheceu frequentes transcrições na Imprensa angolana dos fins do século XIX; ou D. Ana Joaquina dos Santos Silva, numa carta para o barão de Santa Comba, naturalmente escrita com a assistência de advogado, personagem que não deve ter dispensado essa mulher de tão largos voos com o comerciante; ou contemporâneos de Matta, como Ignácio Pinho e José de Fontes Pereira.

Outro aspecto definidor de mentalidade crioula é a transcrição de documentos relativos à coisa pública — a «diplomacia» do sertão, a instrução, a moeda, a administração, etc. —, de que tão próxima se achava por vocação. Isto tem que ver com um dos sentidos da sua tendência elitista, que não teve apenas a caracterizá-la aspectos positivos, como os que lhe granjearam um papel de relevo na administração de Angola, pois também se lhe associou um sentido «etnocêntrico», que pôde fazer com que alguns dos seus representantes subscrevessem generalizações abusivas a respeito dos negros, de que abundam as transcrições de Matta. Uma das transcrições corrobora essa presunção, pois que de artigo do próprio compilador — autotranscrição, portanto —, tirado de páginas do *Almanach de Lembranças*, de 1888, com o título «O Matabicho n'África». Vale a pena reproduzi-lo de páginas 68-69 do *Repositório:*

«Entre a gente boçal do continente africano, exerce o *matabicho* uma tão grande influência, que não é possível imaginar-se o ponto a que pode atingir.

«A espórtula que deve dar-se em retribuição d'um serviço valioso, é em África o contrário. Por qualquer trabalho, ainda que seja insignificante, pede-se matabicho! Sem elle o *monangamba* (carregador) não faz nada. O *matabicho* é, por assim dizer o motor do *monangamba;* sem elle parece que perde a força physica e moral! Quando por esquecimento deixa de ser gratificado, ouve-se logo a ladainha do costume: — «Então, senhor, o matabicho!» — A pessoa a quem se pede, zangada às vezes, diz — «Que diabo de bicho é esse que estão constantemente a *matar* e que nunca *morre!*» — E o *monangamba*, com toda a seriedade replica: — «*O bicho*, senhor, nunca morre: só morre quando. a gente deixa de viver! ...».

«Quem não dér o *matabicho*, por qualquer trabalho, a começar de Loanda até o sertão, não póde contar com um bom serviço do indígena inculto d'Africa. Dir-se-hia concentrar este povo somente no *matabicho* a sua alma, a sua vida! ...

Oh! povo africano, em quanto o *matabicho* vos predominar e a aguardente electrizar-vos sempre, jamais saireis do estado do embrutecimento em que jazeis.»

É importante este texto pela visão que patenteia de um problema maior do século XIX angolano — o do carreto — que motivou algumas das mais notáveis páginas da literatura ultramarina, como as do preâmbulo da, também constante do *Repositório*, Portaria de 22 de Setembro de 1858, subscrita por Sá da Bandeira, em que se contraria a ideia-feita da relutância do negro ao trabalho, utilizando o método comparativo para evidenciar a sua relação com comportamentos condenáveis *— e é seguramente da lembrança dos actos que os chefes e negociantes praticaram, e do receio de que se repitam que provém essa relutância dos districtos centraes a sujeitarem-se ao serviço do carreto.*

Esse sentido algo «etnocêntrico» é elemento definidor da sociedade crioula, cuja literatura — que por alguns vem sendo entendida como de protesto — tem de ser vista também à luz desse fenómeno. Entre as boas intenções? — que as houve — e as realidades, interpôs-se uma consciência cultural — e a desse tempo estava, na sociedade crioula, muito longe de a isentar em relação a problemas que já haviam sido condenados pelos mais lúcidos cultores da problemática ultramarina.

MÁRIO ANTÓNIO

ANEXO

Parece-nos oportuna a transcrição de algumas páginas do *Repositório*. Apresentamos, seguidamente, três exemplos: de anotação da «pequena história» dos governadores, o primeiro; de homenagem a personalidades crioulas, o segundo; de registo de memórias de contemporâneos de acontecimentos relevantes, o último.

Mário António

Precis

JOSÉ MARTINS GARCIA
LUANDINO VIEIRA: O ANTI-APARTHEID
[Luandino Vieira: Anti-Apartheidist]

Luandino Vieira, noted equally for his stylistic audacity and his portraits of life in and around Luanda, is not primarily concerned with the question of race in his stories. His are tales of confrontation, of social conflict in which sexual relationships frequently play an important part. Such confrontations between man and woman, colonialist and native Angolan, cannot deny the existence of the other on the present stage of history. Through the interactions of different worlds we can see that Luandino Vieira's vision is contrary to the view of social or artistic apartheid in which different communities are developed independently of one another.

Cover of *Macandumba* by José Luandino Vieira

Luandino Vieira:
o anti-*apartheid*

por **José Martins Garcia**

Nenhum autor pode criar uma língua. Um sistema linguístico situa-se a um nível tão profundo como o da mundividência que lhe é inerente. Um sistema linguístico é necessariamente colectivo. Por mais reduzida que seja a comunidade que o utilize, o sistema fundamenta-se nas marcas diferenciadoras, características que o opõem aos outros sistemas.

Nenhum autor, por mais inventivo, se pode dar ao luxo de criar *do nada*. As transformações, aberrações, violentações que impõe ao sistema em que se encontra integrado constituem derivações das potencialidades desse sistema, ou herança de línguas faladas num dado solo (substratos), ou empréstimos linguísticos devidos a fenómenos socioculturais, ou aquisições causadas por línguas que tentaram sobrepor-se (superestratos), etc.

O autor, enquanto criador, inventa o seu «discurso» (ou fala). Não inventa a «língua». Mas a História diz-nos que, em certas épocas, em certas condições sociais e políticas, o papel dalguns autores foi importante para a estabilização duma língua. Assim, na conjuntura específica da Itália pré-renascentista, Dante surge como o «pai» da língua literária florentina, cuja designação (florentina, toscana, italiana?...) forneceria pretexto para polémicas seculares.

Dante, independentemente do génio poético, não inventou essa língua. Chamar-se-lhe «pai» do florentino não passa de metáfora.

Dante aproveitou o sistema linguístico que vigorava em Florença, decidindo acerca dalgumas questões de «norma», apoiando-se no uso tido por mais culto, o uso duma camada letrada. O resto, a medida do seu génio, respeita às peculiaridades do seu discurso poético.

Metaforicamente, Luandino Vieira é o «pai» duma língua de Luanda. Uma análise da sintaxe, da semântica, do léxico dessa língua mostra-nos que se trata dum caso de interpenetração a um nível profundo. Tanto ao nível da complementação como ao das propriedades sémicas, das várias categorias morfológicas, da derivação vocabular, estamos perante uma transformação do sistema português, a qual, assimilando processos da língua (ou línguas?) subjacente, muitas vezes acaba por dificultar, ou até tornar impossível, a compreensibilidade, por parte do leitor português.

O resto, a elaboração artística que Luandino Vieira impõe a essa língua, é da exclusiva responsabilidade do A.: a exploração da sonoridade, a manipulação ao nível lexical, a ordenação rítmica aproveitando as potencialidades sintácticas, o sentido transformado pela criatividade deste discurso.

A linguagem de Luandino Vieira é, no âmbito da literatura de expressão portuguesa (ou derivada), o maior desmentido à teoria do «reflexo», a radical negação de que um sistema de tipo filosófico esgote as coordenadas culturais dum tempo ou dum espaço. A linguagem de Luandino Vieira é o exemplo linguístico mais acabado de como tudo se move internamente, na interpenetração dos sistemas linguísticos. A linguagem de Luandino Vieira é a negação da cristalização, do «academismo», da norma imposta por pruridos culturais que já não correspondem às necessidades duma comunidade. Por tudo isto, Luandino Vieira ficará na História da Literatura Angolana como a principal vítima da audácia linguística, ciente, como o foi desde *Luuanda,* de que a função referencial da linguagem é discutível e mesmo invalidável, dado que o recorte representativo que o falante executa no mundo empírico transporta inerentemente a ambiguidade. Por ser assim, por ter trocado as categorias às partes do discurso, por ter transformado semanticamente os verbos, por ter posto os conectivos a funcionar de acordo com um novo sistema relacional, nunca Luandino Vieira caiu, nos seus livros, na execução mecânica dum programa político. Para ele, a explicitação política foi a vida, a prisão, o Tarrafal. De resto — já o ouvimos insistir neste ponto — os seus livros são primordialmente «obra de arte».

Os textos de Luandino Vieira abrem-se a uma dupla forma de injustiça: a literária e a política. Literariamente, eles podem ser atacados em nome duma norma imposta pelos espíritos fechados em gabinete. Politicamente, eles só poderiam requerer a seguinte alternativa: ou se sabotavam pelo silêncio; ou se proibiam. Malograda parcialmente a primeira hipótese (graças, principalmente, ao «escândalo» de 1965), restava reprimi-los materialmente. Alguém pressentiu, mesmo sem conselheiro linguístico, que a linguagem de *Luuanda* era uma reivindicação de autonomia.

★

Da interpenetração linguística, presente na obra de Luandino Vieira, resultam relações inovadoras, das quais nos parece justo destacar as que respeitam a uma «animização» do ambiente e as que revelam, pelo choque das personagens, o conflito social.

Grande parte do fascínio decorrente deste discurso reside, é certo, nas aproximações sonoras que, desde *Luuanda* [1] a *No Antigamente na Vida* [2], se vão acentuando a ponto de ganharem, nesta última obra, uma extrema densidade. Mas tais processos são ricos em matéria de significação, não apenas pelo virtuosismo fónico, mas também por corroborarem a animização do ambiente, da natureza excessiva dos quadros evocados, onde se movimentam, numa espécie de diluição, as personagens. Concorre para este efeito (a que apetece chamar *mágico*) a circularidade da técnica narrativa do A., a qual faz corresponder a cada informação, ao nível da peripécia, uma digressão que veicula as observações de tipo histórico, económico, social, político.

Desde a primeira narrativa de *Luuanda,* deparamos com exemplos de interpenetração do mundo e do ser humano. Afirmar-se que «[...] esse calor mau secava as lágrimas ainda lá dentro dos olhos [...]» (p. 20) significa que o *choro reprimido* encontra, na mundividência do A. (aliás identificada com a da sua criatura), uma interpretação física, transposta da experiência exterior, do mundo onde o calor seca as fontes e os rios.

Este processo aproxima-se, por vezes, da simples peculiaridade estilística. «O cheiro bom do café ria na lata [...]» (*Velhas Estórias* [3] p. 18) será disso exemplo. Mas «[...] discutir com seu mestre

---

[1] Utilizamos a 3.ª edição, de Edições 70, Lisboa, 1972.

[2] José Luandino Vieira, *No Antigamente na Vida,* Lisboa, Edições 70, 1974.

[3] Luandino Vieira, *Velhas Estórias,* Lisboa, Plátano Editora, 1974.

pode chamar chapada» (*id.,* p. 25) exemplifica como a acção, expressa pelo infinitivo verbal, é encarada como sujeito animado, o único compatível com o verbo *chamar.* Outras vezes, este processo resulta na identificação: «[...] os verdes xaxualhos das folhas da bandeira eram agora a alegria da tarde» (*id.,* p. 30). Outras vezes, a adjectivação testemunha de análoga animização: «[...] acendendo a *sobrevivente* cigarrilha holandesa» (*id.,* p. 86 — sublinhado nosso). Outras vezes ainda, ao fenómeno natural atribui-se vontade; note-se, neste exemplo, a crescente animização da chuva: «Aí se sentiu a chuva *quebrar* seu cair, *desistir* de chover a tarde toda, *dar licença* de vir ainda resto dum sol [...]» (*id.,* p. 100 — sublinhados nossos).

Não nos admira que o A., ao evocar a infância em *No Antigamente na Vida,* nos fale, por exemplo, da areia *viva*: «E sempre a demais constante areia viva: parada, se a gente estávamos calados; cada palavrita nossa, terráquea, que desatava mexer nos pés, caía, puxava corpo para fora da alma» (p. 44). «Corpo para fora da alma» talvez seja a melhor síntese do processo em causa. Exemplo tão elucidativo que dispensa mais comentários.

A esta interpenetração do homem e do cosmos, harmonia lembrada e simultaneamente projectada, opõe-se, em toda a obra de Luandino Vieira, o mundo social, conflituoso, multifacetado, percorrido por forças antagónicas, dilaceração da harmonia e, consequentemente, múltipla guerra.

Desde *Luuanda* que se nos patenteia a aberração que consiste na condenação do ser humano «sem culpa formada». Nessa estória que inicia o primeiro livro do A., intitulada «Vavó Xíxi e Seu Neto Zeca Santos», a suspeita basta, aos olhos do «senhor», para justificar o castigo. O fenómeno «terrorismo», criando apreensões nos detentores do poder — do poder económico, do poder político — é a mola que faz explodir as contradições do colonialismo. Vavó Xíxi Hengele — note-se, paralelamente, como os nomes das personagens, presentes nos títulos da estória, assinalam a coexistência de duas gerações, de dois estratos antroponímicos e de duas mundividências —, não podendo compreender como o terrorismo despertou o ódio, comenta: «Um branco como sô Souto, amigo de João Ferreira, como é ele ia ainda bater de chicote no menino só porque foi pedir serviço? Hum!»

Esse branco *decente* e protector do amigo, quando o conflito ainda não estalara, é, todavia, quem nega trabalho ou ajuda, dado que a cor da pele, problema até aí de segundo grau, ganha uma nova grandeza quando o terrorismo eclode. O conflito racial, no fundo um desvio em relação ao conflito real — o económico, o da exploração do homem pelo homem — irrompe quando os explorados organizam a luta. Sem essa quebra nas tradicionais relações, nas quais a exploração colonialista se revestia de benévolo paternalismo (Vavó Xíxi monologa, interrogando-se como é possível que um branco seja injusto), sem essa contestação da dependência aceite com a sua máscara «civilizadora», a consciência do colonizado estagnaria na submissão.

Desde essa primeira estória de *Luuanda,* as implicações político-sociais dos textos de Luandino Vieira denunciam, com maior ou menor explicitação, o conflito, o choque das etnias e das respectivas culturas, a interpenetração de vários sistemas simbólicos, o diálogo, em certo ponto necessariamente violento, da Europa com a África.

O chamado «terrorismo», essa forma de os colonizados quebrarem a ancestral surdez europeia, reaparece mais algumas vezes nas páginas de *Luuanda.* O problema da assimilação — no fundo um fenómeno de aculturação, se encarado do pólo oposto ao do colonizador — é posto com acuidade na estória intitulada «Estória do Ladrão e do Papagaio». As diferentes concepções do amor e da propriedade vêm ao de cima através da paixão dum defeituoso nativo por uma nativa já parcialmente europeizada. Mas essa fábula singela alcança uma outra dimensão: a enxovia, as arbitrariedades policiais, a incapacidade destas no entendimento do mundo africano, etc. são outros tantos círculos desenhados em torno do núcleo eventual. E uma concepção social da diferença impõe-se à consciência das personagens, para além da cor da pele: «No coração estava ainda ferver um bocado da raiva da queixa, mesmo que tinha visto bem aquela cara de arrependido e triste do Lomelino quando entrou, não ia comer com um bufo» (p. 147).

Mas falemos de *Velhas Estórias,* que, como o título indica, vão aproveitar contradições mais recuadas no tempo, ou melhor, latentes sob a capa da estabilidade social.

A primeira estória, intitulada «Muadiê Gil, o Sobral e o Barril», incide na oposição capital-trabalho. Mais uma vez, e à semelhança do antagonismo denunciado em *Luuanda,* as decisões do patrão são arbitrárias na medida em que desrespeitam os costumes tacitamente implantados entre exploradores e explorados. A narrativa em questão acentua que só uma das partes tem o poder de modificar o direito consuetudinário, enquanto a outra, ainda desorganizada — se bem que um elemento conheça alguns pontos da interdita reflexão sobre a economia — se limita à expressão duns princípios de vago humanitarismo.

A segunda estória, intitulada «*Manana, Mariana, Naninha*—, será das mais ricas do ponto de vista duma informaçao histórico-cultural. Accaretando seus mitos e suas contradições, seus preconceitos e seus missionários, os colonos revelam-nos as próprias fraquezas: «*Dom Francisco Inoncêncio Vaz-Cunha, resumido nome público de quem que gozava, legal e privilegiadamente, oito outros assim nobres e honrados . . .* » (p. 81). Dom Francisco e seus familiares «*não iam nas missas e confissôs, mas nunca que tiravam os donativos que, com a graça de Nossenhor e a protecção da Serenissima Senhora do Carmo, prosperavam sua freguesia, se afamavam suas procissões oráguicas . . .* » (p. 84). Dom Francisco, colono decadente, tem un filho que cobiça a nativa Mariana, ou Manana, ou Naninha, cujo nome se vai transformando de acordo com o escalãa social. Há oposição ao amor de ambos—como é corrente nas fábulas ditas ocidentais e cristãs. E o diálogo de Manana com o mundo europeu assimila, de facto, dois motivos essenciais do triangulo amoroso: hipocrisia e adulterio; sem que ela deixe, pois, de virar contrar o colono as armas que este lhe forneceu. Do ponte de vista religioso, esta estoria envolve toda a problematização da partenogenese, que tão profundas marcas deixou na cultura europeia. E «*os corpos ondulam aquele riso tão novo que dá berrida na humidade toda do quarto com seu livre calor*» (p. 101). Assimilados os termos do inverosimil genético, resta a santificação da transgressão, como sintese das culturas e das crenças e possibilidade do «*livre calor*».

Semelhante conflito nos apresenta a terceira narrativa, «*Estória da Menina Santa*» A poligamia, costume colonial tão praticado por que invalida, em sua mente, o casamento civil: «*Nem que foram na igreja, nem nada. Na administração só ué! Isso é amiganço, não m'intrujam só!*» A poligamia, costume colonial tão praticado por quem cristãmente jurava fidelidade eterna à carne da sua carne, suscita o confronto entre as inclinações amorosas e a engrenagem repressiva, apanágio da civilização: «*Viviam assim, no Makutu, mais muitas mulheres de um homen só*» (p. 128)—remata o Autor. Um patriarcado excessivo, costume atribuido ao negro, mas tão ao gosto do branco poderoso.

Se *Velhas Estórias* nos denuncia o conflito latente num contexto colonial de adultos, *No Antigamente na Vida* opera idêntica denúncia no que respeita ao mundo da infância. Evasão, sonho, solidariedade, conflito, amor, ciúme, contestação e crime percorrem esses «*miúdos*» que, apesar da curta experiência, já transportam os germes dos conflitos futuros. A reivindicação da dignidade humana põe em causa os valores gerados pela interpenetração cultural. A solidariedade do branco-de-segunda com o negro contestatário é uma certeza: «*nunca nos deixaremos domesticar, juro!*» (p. 140).

* * *

Neste mundo—tanto dos adultos como das crianças, tanto de pretos como de brancos e mestiços, tanto de exploradores como de explorados—neste mundo tecido de História e de sangue, violações, adultérios, atropelos, superstições, religiosidades conjugadas, almas-penadas, feitiços, chicotadas e prisão, terrorismo e fome, neste mundo arquitectado por Luandino Vieira a partir daquilo que foi e é a sua pátria, reconhece-se a milenária injustiça da existência do senhor e do escravo. Mas, igualmente, a consciência do laço imprescindível que, unindo-os, os revela mutuamente como seres à face da Terra.

* * *

Da subserviente concepção de Vavó Xixi—para quem, em sua mente colonizada, o branco representa quase a justiça divina—até à rebeldia daquele «*nunco nos deixaremos domesticar*», vai todo um caminho de apropriação do real, caminho da consciência, do apelo à luta, da reivindicaçao dos direitos humanos.

O lugar que as lutas sociais ocupam na obra de Luandino Vieira, lutas denunciadas pelo sistemático confronto de situações, deixa em segundo plano a questão da cor da pele. *O apartheid* é, como se sabe, o desenvolvimento independente de duas comunidades de pigmentação diferente, na ignorância voluntária das relações que o trabalho estabelece entre essas comunidades. E o *apartheid* que a obra de Luandino Vieira não consente. As propostas de Luandino Vieira vão todas no sentido duma confrontação que, mesmo manifesta pela violência, não pode negar ao *outro,* ao antagonista, a presença activa na cena da História.

EDIÇÃO DA CASA DOS ESTUDANTES DO IMPÉRIO — LISBOA

Cover of *Chigubo* by José Craveirinha

ONÉSIMO SILVEIRA
CONSCIENCIALIZAÇÃO NA
LITERATURA CABOVERDIANA
[Consciousness Raising in Cape Verdean Literature]

The writers of the thirties and forties were inadequate and insufficient, for instead of being rooted in Cape Verdean culture as they were claiming, they were elitists, inspired by European traditions. The New Generation of writers, in harmony with colleagues throughout Africa, is committed both to pointing out social and political problems and actively seeking solutions to these problems. The younger writers, exponents of a literary African regionalism, raise the cause of African consciousness by deriving their inspiration from the black world.

Pedro Cardoso, who belonged to an earlier generation than the Claridade *writers of the thirties, is a valid precursor of the New Generation, for he gave crioule literature a sense of dignity and importance. Contemporary writers such as Ovidio Martins in his poem "Anti-Evasion" not only repudiate a political system that is unjust, but also refuse to find solace in idealistic revery; they shout and protest, for they will not accept foreign domination.*

consciencialização na literatura caboverdiana

ONÉSIMO SILVEIRA

SUMÁRIO

I

INVIABILIDADE DO PROSSEGUIMENTO ÉM CABO VERDE, DO MOVIMENTO CLARIDOSO:

a) Caracterização geral do Movimento Claridoso;

b) Inadequação do Movimento às realidades sociais do Arquipélago.

II

APARECIMENTO DE UMA LITERATURA DE REI-VINDICAÇÃO PARA-AFRICANA:

a) Integração dos problemas de Cabo Verde na problemática geral africana;

b) O surto de uma consciencialização autêntica e sua manifestação literária: Novos Rumos.

I

Não foi, de modo algum, em vão que escolhemos para tema do nosso ensaio o da consciencialização na literatura caboverdiana. Justificamo-nos: o surto de actividades culturais que parcelam aquilo a que hoje se vai chamando, com insistência, literatura angolana, levar-nos-ia a trazer à tona um complexo de circunstâncias relativas à actividade cultural em Cabo Verde, por julgarmos conter esta algo de útil para a definição de uma literatura angolana, tomada no sentido concreto da palavra, e não no seu sentido abstracto e geral, como infelizmente vem sucedendo.

A trajectória da literatura caboverdiana, com ponto de partida situado na década de trinta e definido pelo Movimento Claridoso, impõe-nos a nós os mais modernos cavadores da literatura insular, o problema de definir, em palavras claras e insofismadas, e através de uma literatura verdadeiramente funcional, uma consciencialização com raízes no húmus étnico-social caboverdiano. Esta conscienciálização, e só ela, pode, quanto a nós, situar regionalmente a mesma literatura e atribuir-lhe merecimento para comparticipar, ainda que muito modestamente, no amplo ressurgimento que caracteriza o dobrar da primeira metade deste século, com uma parcela ideológica autêntica e actual.

Partindo do princípio, tão fundamental quanto axiomático, de que nenhum empreendimento à escala mundial pode dispensar um elevado sentido de responsabilidade por parte dos seus comparticipantes, é evidente que toda a literatura do nosso tempo terá de ser, em todas as suas dimensões, consciente para que corresponda à referida funcionalidade.

Demonstraremos, ao longo deste trabalho, que a literatura caboverdiana, estando profundamente ferida de inautenticidade, não traduz nem produziu uma mentalidade consciencializada e daí se ter tornado, como não é difícil verificar, em título de prestígio da elite que a vem encabeçando e não em força ao serviço de Cabo Verde e suas gentes.

Ora, hoje que é mais do que nunca imperativo definir-se, numa terra como Angola, uma consciencialização autêntica, étcnica e culturalmente, temos para nós que uma literatura de exportação como a criada pelo Movimento Claridoso, pode, pelos efeitos enganosos que comporta, constituir séria e fecunda advertência a quantos, aqui, se dedicam à missão literária pensando ùnicamente em si mesmo e postergando, em consequência de tal pessoalismo, as aspirações irreversíveis dos povos que compõem a paleta social desta terra africana.

Uma das raízes do Movimento Claridoso é a que o liga ao processo social geral a que as Ilhas sempre estiveram submetidas e ao aspecto particular e lógico da instrução como elementos do referido processo.

O Seminário-Liceu de S. Nicolau, estabelecimento escolar mais preponderante em Cabo Verde até ao primeiro quartel deste século, infundindo nos componentes desse grupo uma cultura fortemente europeia e europeízante, será, ao mesmo tempo, a génese do Movimento e a longo prazo a causa da sua falência. A erudição aí ministrada era mais literária que científica. Na parte literária mais atendia ao estudo do formalismo gramatical e da estilística das línguas que aos pensamentos de que estas são depositárias. Esta preocupação, junta ao estudo de uma filosofia cristalizada é incompatível com o aprendizado de critérios de livre exame, conduzia a uma mentalidade retoricista, de comprazimento em subtilezas verbais, de que não viriam a estar isentos até os elementos mais bem dotados.

Assim imbuídos duma erudição que não tinha em conta as realidades sócio-culturais do Arquipélago, foram-se distanciando das massas de que inicialmente faziam parte e impregnando-se de um complexo de sedimentos de saberes que, pela sua força de expansividade e correlativas possibilidades de aceitação, muito contribuiriam para esse afastamento do povo, embora se servindo deste para as suas criações literárias de fundo pretensamente telúrico.

Tal distanciamento é, quanto a nós, um dos aspectos «contraditórios» da chamada ascensão do mestiço, à qual se liga uma concepção egotista do saber que deste faz mais um ornamento e um motivo de êxito individual, que instrumento posto ao serviço da colectividade, na acepção real do termo.

Por isso é que o enraízamento tentado pelos componentes do grupo resultou numa atitude literária inoperante. Isto, em consequência de não se terem esses homens apercebido de que o enraízamento da literatura caborverdiana era impossível sem a consciencialização, entendida esta como intervenção no processo social, quer no momento da criação literária quer no momento da acção prática. Ao tratar aspectos da vida caboverdiana, tinham uma sensação ilusória de cravar as unhas na realidade circundante, mas jamais outra coisa fizeram senão raspar à superfície dos problemas do ilhéu.

Uma das notas dominantes da literatura criada por este Movimento, quer na poesia quer na novelística, foi o evasionismo. Com esta atitude espiritual propuseram-se os componentes do Movimento exprimir uma dada situação de existência do povo caboverdiano, decorrente do condicionamento geográfico e telúrico do arquipélago, e que conceberam como o drama da evasão do ilhéu. Esta expressão, cunhada pelos claridosos, viria a tornar-se moeda corrente nos meios lisboetas dedicados ao estudo de problemas de Além-Mar. O drama da evasão pretendeu ser a tradução intelectual do problema da emigração do ilhéu. Mas, conquanto fosse um dos principais tópicos do seu programa, em parte não expresso, esses homens não lograram tomar e manter, no plano literário e no da acção prática, as posições necessárias à denúncia desse problema em termos positivos. Focando o drama da evasão, a dualidade «querer partir e ter que ficar» ou «querer ficar e ter que partir» — conforme e filosofia evasionista de cada um — acabaram por simplificar, arbitràriamente, este complexo problema e por oferecer uma imagem estereotipada do homem caboverdiano, renunciando conscientemente a buscar as raízes psicológicas e sociais do facto emigratório.

Propondo-se exprimir essa situação, faltou no entanto aos claridosos o verdadeiro sentido do povo, isto é, aquele grau de comunhão emocional e intelectual que leva espontâneamente à identificação da consciência individual do escritor com a consciência colectiva das massas. Isto pode ser comprovado, tanto pela análise do contúdo das suas obras como pelo confronto de suas posições literárias com as que, divergentemente, e até contraditòriamente, adoptaram no seu dia-a-dia social. Aquela análise revela que o evasionismo é muito menos uma interpretação do drama real do povo, acossado pela imposição migratória, que o caso individual e subjectivo do escritor avassalado pela frustração resultante do desejo irrealizado de conhecer e viver em meios mais fortemente ocidentalizados que o meio caboverdiano. Esta nossa observação coincide com observação semelhante de Manuel Ferreira quando diz: «Que estará reservado ao anónimo escritor caboverdiano, lá longe, só , ele só, nas «grades da sua prisão»... e na distância lobrigando os barcos na rota do mar alto, comunicando-lhe um desejo profundo de querer partir, tendo de ficar?!»

Tanto assim que só se reflecte nas obras dos claridosos o facto da emigração para as Américas e jamais a emigração degradante para terras como S. Tomé e Príncipe, coexistente com aquela, mas que eles escritores nunca desejariam para si mesmo. Só recentemente, um deles, Baltazar Lopes, se mostrou preocupado com o tema desta última emigração, em seu ciclo poético intitulado «Romanceiro de S. Tomé», o qual, não obstante a expressão formal por vezes bela, apresenta uma intenção social bastante difusa.

Torna-se-nos necessário focar que, se é Baltazar Lopes quem no Movimento Claridoso faz uma discreta denúncia do problema da emigração, no seu aspecto especial para S. Tomé, Teixeira de Sousa é contudo aquele que procura manter uma linha coerente de estudo sério sobre aquela emigração, com realce para as suas incidências técnicas, nosológicas, económicas e sociais principalmente. Aliás, quanto a nós, essa coerência está intimamente ligada à dissidência que representa a presença de Teixeira de Sousa adentro do grupo, pela matriz ideológica definida de que ele se nutre.

Efectivamente, a sua atitude contrasta com a do «pontífice» do evasionismo, que é o «sacrossanto» Jorge Barbosa. Este poeta, preocupado com uma descrição típica das realidade insulares, jamais fez senão exportar um retrato social esbatido do caboverdiano de quem, aliás, nunca ofereceu outra coisa que um enganoso e romântico estereotipo. A evolução deste poeta desnuda sua atitude essencial. Da fase espontânea de livros como «Ambiente» e «Arquipélago», passa à fase decadente de «Caderno de um Ilhéu», em que o leitor exigente é decepcionado pela convencionalidade do tema e o artifício da forma poética. Estamos então perante o que se poderia denominar ultra-evasionismo, esvaziado até daquelas qualidades mínimas que pudesse ter inicialmente

Outra das notas dominantes da literatura criada por esse Movimento é o seu realismo paisagístico.

Não se depara com a preocupação de pesquisar, no plano literário, as coordenadas sociais e o comportamento real do homem caboverdiano como ser traumatisado pelas mesmas coordenadas. Na novelística e na poesia oferecem-nos esses escritores não os dados essenciais da problemática caboverdiana com as suas múltiplas imbricações e sim alguns momentos mais ou menos cristalizados do que é, lògicamente, realidade na sequência das intenções que sempre animaram o Movimento; aqueles momentos são, por isso, meros dados paisagísticos flutuando num solo ideológico de relevo incaracterístico.

Esta selecção de elementos pinturescos perante uma realidade eivada de problemas básicos e de importância decisiva para o destino do homem caboverdianno como tal, traduziu-se, em última análise, numa verdadeira fuga à mesma realidade, em que, programàticamente, se propuseram enraízar a literatura das Ilhas. Nisto consistiu sua inautenticidade. Não poderia ser enraízamento nem a descrição dos plácidos e «felizes» jogadores de «ouri», nem a descrição do caboverdiano que sonha com terras distantes ao contemplar o barco de louça que lhe serve de cinzeiro.

A nova geração não pode, por conseguinte, silenciar o facto altamente comprometedor que resulta da atitude estéril dos claridosos perante as grandes crises que, na década de quarenta, trouxeram a morte a milhares de caboverdianos. Agrava esta indiferença o não existir sequer uma cobertura literária desse longo enterro, ainda que, contemplativamente, à laia do cortejo descrito por Aurélio Gonçalves, levando Nha Candinha Sena à sua última morada. E tal facto é tanto mais surpreendente quanto é cer'.o que a referida década coincide, de algum modo, com o período de desenvolvimento e consolidação do grupo. Não invalidam a atitude indiferentista a que nos referimos nem «Chiquinho» de Baltazar Lopes, nem «Os flagelados do Vento Leste» de Manuel Lopes. Naquele romance encontramos escassas páginas finais que relatam um esboço de motim ocorrido em período de crise, mas a análise literária nos mostra que o facto narrado não logra inserir-se na tecitura e concepção do romance. «Os Flagelados do Vento Leste» enquadra-se num realismo puramente descritivo, de que está ausente uma intenção social reformista, o que se torna manifesto no carácter derrotista dos ingredientes seleccionados para a composição da personagem colectiva central do romance, que é a família de José da Cruz.

A favor de Manuel Lopes ressalvamos, porém, essa

sua obra singular, que é «Chuva Braba», romance de intenção social clara, tanto pelo criticismo pertinente à sociedade santantonense, como pela luz que seu epílogo traz à decantada questão evasionista. Esta é pela primeira vez posta, não como uma fatalidade e sim como uma razão forte, deparada a certa altura do processo geo-social do ilhéu, traduzindo uma situação cuja gravidade outros escritores deformaram, pela implícita solicitação de fuga às raízes do problema emigratório.

O mesmo realismo despreocupado encontramos no enfoque de meios urbanos, como o mindelense. «Pródiga» de Aurélio Gonçalves, pretende ser uma réplica realista ao idealismo ético da parábola bíblica. Se o leitor inquieto logra encontrar, através dos dados da narrativa, uma razão de ser social do comportamento da personagem central da novela, é porque Aurélio Gonçalves se mantém, em seu realismo puramente descritivo ou analítico, fiel aos elementos psicológicos individuais. No fundo, o comportamento daquela personagem não é mais que o resultado de traumatismos decorrentes dos males sociais duma cidade que, sustentada em bases económicas precaríssimas, acabou por se tornar um viveiro de falhados. Falta à novela, por isso, o enquadramento mais complexo de psicologia social que lhe conferisse uma mais completa validade, pela justificação articulada do gráfico que representa o comportamento de Xandinha.

Portanto, não chegou a realizar-se o tópico do programa claridoso que, recentemente, Aurélio Gonçalves assim reformulou: «Necessidade de protestar e de dar o alarme perante uma crise económica, causada pela estiagem, pelo abandono do Porto Grande de S. Vicente, pela sufocação proveniente do encerramento da emigração para a América do Norte».

Uma literatura assim inautêntica, oferecendo ao povo, em vez dos caminhos duma resolução do seu problema, alguns dados só propícios à romantização do mesmo, não pode, lògicamente, conduzir à conscien-

cialização, sem a qual todo o povo se sujeita sempre
à perda de sua dignidade, por enfeudalização e consequente omissão dos seus anseios, manifestados em
reivindicações justas e adequadas à sua participação
no concerto universal dos povos.

Em abono da tese que vimos esplanando, anotamos
que o Movimènto Claridoso nasceu e desenvolveu-se
sem que dentro de si fosse possível o despontar duma
actividade crítica que propiciasse uma antítese das
posições assumidas, evitando até seu claro ambiente
arcádico de elogio mútuo. Faltou ao «grupo» uma síntese de ideias, no sentido hegeliano do termo.

Falando de actividade cultural caboverdiana, alguém houve já que nos assinalasse, com intenções crí-
ticas, a inexistência duma arte caboverdiana, traduzida
plàsticamente em pintura e escultura. Se em alguns
momentos nos faltou justificação cabal para vácuo tão
eloquente, hoje, porém, a análise que vimos fazendo à
literatura claridosa, leva-nos a atribuir tal facto não
à carência de elementos inspirativos para consumação
plástica, mas ao que insistimos em caracterizar como
ausência de consciencialização na cultura intelectual
caboverdiana. Assim, se é relativamente fácil impres-
sionar o leitor estranho às Ilhas pelo descritivo pito-
resco, este processo concerteza não traria os mesmos
êxitos, adaptado à arte plástica, muito mais susceptí-
vel como é de conduzir a uma análise mais próxima
das fontes e por isso uma análise mais exigente. Os
motivos, humanos ou paisagísticos, tão gratos aos
escritores que fundaram a revista «Claridade», não
seriam de molde a possibilitar aquele devaneio analítico no fundo do qual se originou a justificação de
seus êxitos.

A omissão do homem do grupo de ilhas geogràfica-
mente denoiinado de «Sotavento», que não sendo pro-
positada será de qualquer modo significativa, denuncia só por si a inexistência de identificação que o Movimento pretendeu realizar com a terra caboverdiana.
Atendendo a que as ilhas desse grupo são as menos

ocidentalizadas, cremos haver razão lógica bastante para atribuir aquela falta de representação ao que se poderia chamar, com toda propriedade, o «barlaventismo» da literatura claridosa, isto é, a atenção quase exclusiva aos aspectos da realidade caboverdiana que, por haverem sofrido uma maior lusitanização, permitiam uma imediata coincidência entre a mentalidade saturadamente europeia dos claridosos e a matéria de observação e anotação literária. Embora Félix Monteiro e Baltazar Lopes se possam considerar destacados etnólogos do grupo, as suas actividades circunscrevem-se, no aspecto ora visado, a pequenos estudos de folclore das Ilhas de Santiago e Fogo. Estudos esses em que não emerge, como não poderia deixar de acontecer num retrato fiel, o drama social de que aquele folclore mesclado jamais deixou de ser um reflexo nítido. E, por estranho que pareça, permanecem um compartimento quase estanque adentro da actividade criadora do grupo, e os elementos deles resultantes não alicerçaram a elaboração consequente de um pensamento ideológico, não diremos expresso, mas vivo e actuante. Caso não tivessem abandonado o esforço de acertar o passo com um mundo mais largo, teria esse pensamento proporcionado ao grupo razoáveis possibilidades de se integrar no movimento das ideias que hoje, directa ou indirectamente, influenciam todo e qualquer intelectual africano.

Particularmente, a clave de denúncia e protesto a que sem dúvida obedeceram os trabalhos como os que integram o n.º 8 de «Claridade», editado em 1959, não resultaria desgarrada no conjunto da revista como tentativa tardia de coerência programática; antes sua virtual eficácia encontraria inteira realização pela inserção no desenvolvimento de uma constante ideológica.

Fora, aliás, na busca dessa actualidade que o Movimento se apercebeu do conteúdo do modernismo brasileiro. Este, contudo, não foi de modo algum a génese do Movimento, como já se tem aventado, apesar de nele ter deixado influências palpáveis.

Uma certa similitude entre o mestiço caboverdiano (em especial o de Barlavento) e o mestiço brasileiro — o nordestino, principalmente — pela comunhão de flagelos sociais idênticos, trouxe sem dúvida aos escritores caboverdianos uma possibilidade de situação do problema ilhéu, nas mesmas coordenadas em que no Brasil, escritores como Jorge Amado, Lins do Rego, Gilberto Freyre, Graciliano Ramos e outros definiam, numa cobertura literária autêntica, o estádio do homem brasileiro.

Todavia, ainda que os problemas do ilhéu tivessem de situar-se nas mesmas coordenadas das do homem brasileiro, nada nos leva a crer que os claridosos pudessem alcançar êxito nessa caminhada, já que o clima de expressão no Brasil não conhecia as restrições com que se deparava em Cabo Verde. Mais ainda: a mestiçagem que no Brasil revelaria, pela novidade de tema sociológico que implicitava, um destacado número de estudiosos, não poderia, de modo algum, determinar, em Cabo Verde, um paralelismo de directrizes, já que no Arquipélago o mestiço, sem dúvida em percentagem expressiva, jamais gozou do complexo de condições como as que derivavam do facto de o mestiço brasileiro há muito estar entregue ao seu próprio destino.

Isto explica por que da lição dos mestres brasileiros apenas apartaram o realismo pinturesco ou paisagístico e não o realismo profundo ou de estrutura. É que havia um desfazamento acentuado entre a elite brasileira e a elite caboverdiana: enquanto já havia aquela superado ou, pelo menos, vinha superando a fase de artificiosa aristocratização, condicionada pelo complexo de inferioridade, a elite crioula ainda se achava em plena busca dessa aristocratização; quando no Brasil floresciam movimentos culturais que limitavam o impacto do europeísmo literário a seus aspectos legítimos, em Cabo Verde ainda se estava em pleno processo de europeízação literária.

II

Os jovens que viriam a fundar a revista «Claridade» tiveram, como já dissemos, uma formação exclusivamente europeízante. Em suas preocupações literárias extra-escolares seriam levados a contactar com escritores e estudiosos integrados numa cultura mesclada como a brasileira, que sendo europeia nos métodos de investigação científica e filosófica e descrição estética da realidade, não o era já na matéria interpretada e na experiência humana.

Eram, porém, demasiado espessos os estratos de europeísmo na mentalidade dessa geração, para que, repetindo a façanha dos modernistas e regionalistas brasileiros, rompessem as cadeias do inibitivo complexo de inferioridade e atentassem substancialmente nos componentes negróides da cultura caboverdiana. Tal complexo nutria, pois, como terra gorda a referida formação intelectual. Uma mentalidade assim estruturada determinaria que esses homens centrassem seu interesses — no sentido psicológico da palavra — sobre a Europa, inconscientemente deslumbrados com as luzes brilhantes da civilização tecnológica do Ocidente, enquanto África era era um eco distante de valores humanos e de cultura. Aurélio Gonçalves reconheceu expressamente o facto que acabamos de apontar, quando disse que em Cabo Verde «existe efectivamente uma tentativa de civilização, muitas vezes gorada pela intervenção de elementos da elite intelectual caboverdiana, nas suas tentativas de europeízação, de magnificação».

Focando este fenómeno, apresentou Manuel Lopes um esquema interpretativo segundo o qual seria a literatura caboverdiana uma compensação — na acepção psicanalítica do termo — das frustrações materiais do povo ilhéu. Suscita-nos este esquema alguns comentários que reputamos fundamentais:

1 — Além de acusarem, como já dissemos, uma nítida fuga aos componentes negróides da cultura caboverdiana, há outro aspecto importante e correlacionado

do problema, que se pode e deve pôr, das relações entre o povo e os criadores da moderna literatura caboverdiana;

2 — Posto o problema e analisando-o, quer do ponto de vista das obras literárias criadas pelos escritores, quer do ponto de vista das atitudes que eles como meros cidadãos adoptaram no terreno das questões práticas, constatamos que se porventura ocorre algo semelhante ao fenómeno de compensação, foi o mesmo condicionado muito mais (senão exclusivamente) pelas frustrações pessoais dos indivíduos suportes dos escritores, que por qualquer vivência sincera e profunda das frustrações colectivas. A pretensa identificação mesmo em termos compensatórios seria inconciliável com a referida fuga aos elementos negróides da nossa cultura. Tanto uma coisa como outra mostram que a literatura criada pelos claridosos muito aquém ficou de realizar a identificação entre escritor e povo;

3 — Por conseguinte, o esquema aventado por Manuel deve ser tão sòmente referido à literatura claridosa que não à literatura caboverdiana em geral, porquanto a moderna geração, como adiante melhor esclareceremos, vem construindo uma posição à qual é inteiramente inadequado esse esquema, tomado de per si ou com acrescentos correctivos, pela razão de que o problema crucial que a nova geração se pôs, foi a denúncia das causas económicas e raízes psicológicas das frustrações colectivas e não a mera contemplação destas. O esquema psicanalítico de Manuel Lopes só conduz, projectada a literatura claridosa no plano colectivo em que deve ser situada como movimento de ideias, à sofisticação do problema de sua compreensão sociológica. Não só o realismo paisagístico era a atitude intelectual que de acordo estava com a aludida fase de aristocratização, mas também escolhendo o ofício de escritor sentiam-se e julgavam-se dispensados de intervir no processo de mudança social, o que se ajustava à mentalidade conservadora, pseudo-reformista, aquela que tinha terreno para germinar

na conjuntura em que surgiu o Movimento. Não é outra coisa que justifica o favorável acolhimento que este teve nos círculos dirigentes.

A enorme desorganização com que se depara ao primeiro golpe, numa anatomia do Movimento, poderá, até certo ponto, encontrar suas raízes no terreno económico de que o mesmo emergiu. Todavia, não podemos (nem sequer devemos) admitir a inabilidade dos homens do «grupo», a quem sobretudo se impunha, como primeiro passo para uma consciencialização radical, injectar um húmus ideológico autêntico em tal terreno, opondo deste modo uma negação dialéctica, única via conducente ao advento do condicionamento favorável a uma colheita condigna no porvir.

Para os homens da geração claridosa, «a convicção de uma originalidade regional caboverdiana» significava, no fundo, que é Cabo Verde um caso de regionalismo europeu. Este modo de conceber a realidade cultural e social das Ilhas comporta, no entanto, duas básicas restrições:

1 — Não existiam e hoje, decorridos mais de vinte e cinco anos sobre o advento do Movimento, não existem ainda estudos exaustivos de etnografia, geografia humana, antropologia social e economia, que em seu conjunto constituam uma análise espectral do Arquipélago;

2 — O esfacelamento dos contributos negróides da nossa cultura, de que não restariam, segundo assevera Baltazar Lopes, em «Cabo Verde visto por Gilberto Freyre», mais que meros vestígios insignificantes, não tinha por certo o carácter duma imposição pura e simples da natureza, de efeito de cataclismo ocorrido no mundo físico, e sim é o resultado dum processo social bem definido através da história das Ilhas.

Entendemos que o problema decisivo não é o de saber quais as contribuições humanas que predominam nas Ilhas, mas, diversamente, o de tornar o homem comum caboverdiano consciente de seu destino africano e possibilitar-lhe os meios que conduzam à realização autónoma do mesmo destino.

Os jovens da nossa geração pensam que Cabo Verde é um caso de regionalismo africano. Esta inversão dos termos do problema decorre do influxo do renascimento africano, que revitaliza todos os campos de actividade e todos os momentos de espiritualidade do homem negro ou negrificado. Este vem passando da velha atitude de negação de si mesmo para a nova atitude de auto-aceitação integral; esforçando-se por renunciar à mentalidade dolorosamente forjada em cadinho de limitações e imposições que ignoravam sua condição de pessoa humana, procura hoje encontrar as vias do modo de ser autêntico que Sartre definiu no ensaio «Orfeu Negro». A nova geração vem participando deste movimento de ideias, que no fundo envolve um conflito de humanismos. Têm os seus comparticipantes a consciência de que só passando antitèticamente pela revalorização do homem negro ou negrificado e sua dimensão cultural, é possível construir-se uma imagem do homem universalmente válida e elaborar-se um humanismo consequente e autêntico. Porque a essa revalorização se acha dinâmicamente ligada a emancipação económica e social das massas para si mesmas inoperantes, é o igualitarismo postulado da nova ética social e da convivência humana a qualquer escala.

A moderna geração vem-se alimentando nesta matriz ideológica, e por isso sabe bem distinguir entre as elites feridas de inautenticidade — floração efémera duma sociedade decrépita — e as massas depositárias das verdadeiras aspirações da colectividade.

Estruturada uma nova mentalidade em cadinho de martírios silenciosos e de não pequenas frustrações, teriam de ser novas suas manifestações. Uma nova filosofia da vida determina novos tipos de preocupação intelectual e novos modos de concepção estética da realidade e de integração do homem na literatura como forma particular de linguagem.

A fidelidade ao homem caboverdiano, em suas circunstâncias naturais e dimensões espirituais, levada às últimas consequências, resulta na atitude de reconstrução do enraízamento da cultura intelectual em bases profundas e coerentes. Propõem-se os «novos» fazer da arte literária uma projecção intencionalmente combativa da problemática do ilhéu, em relação a quem se sentem investidos de uma missão que transcende seu destino individual. Porque partem da convicção de que o artista é apenas o homem-cidadão em determinado momento de sua existência total, procuram manter uma coerência monolítica entre as atitudes de alcance prático e as posições assumidas ao nível da criação literária. Esta, de ofício gratuito e sem consequências éticas, torna-se em processo de auto-vinculação em face de valores corporizados cujo respeito se impõe quotidianamente. Esclarecemos, porém, que para nós, é meramente relativa a ilegitimidade da arte desinteressada; entendemos que no presente estádio de evolução do homem caboverdiano (dominado por pesados lastros materiais) não pode o intelectual representante entregar-se à actividade lúdica em que consiste essa arte. Infelizmente não chegou ainda a hora do jogo diversivo.

A integração do homem caboverdiano numa literatura caboverdiana segundo critérios de fidelidade estreme, implicou o problema da utilização literária do principal idioma falado nas Ilhas, ou seja a transposição integral do crioulo que não apenas de seu estilo ou «sabor». A falta ou insuficiência do aproveitamento literário do crioulo vem gorando a expressão artística dos caracteres irredutíveis do homem caboverdiano como realidade singular, sabido como a língua não é só instrumento da vida de relação, de comunicação do pensamento mas também um quadro lógico e emocional de organização da experiência específica decorrente de determinada ambiência física e cultural.

Recentemente, Baltazar Lopes publicou essa obra monumental de linguística científica, que é «O dialecto crioulo de Cabo Verde». E na «Mesa redonda sobre o homem caboverdiano», que, em Julho de 1956, Almerindo Lessa organizou em S. Vicente, demonstrou as possibilidades expressionais do crioulo, fazendo comentários decisivos, dos quais destacamos os seguintes: «O crioulo é uma língua suficiente». «Todos nós que ensinamos português no liceu verificamos que o crioulo já oferece hoje aos alunos possibilidades expressionais. Eu já ouvi à saída de exercícios de matemática e até de filosofia os alunos a discutirem sobre o exercício em crioulo».

Embora tendo dado fundamentação científica ao prestígio de que o crioulo, para desagrado de alguns, goza em Cabo Verde, no entanto mantém-se Baltazar Lopes numa posição puramente teórica, que não se enriquece e dinamiza com realizações práticas, as únicas que, na ordem dos factos, modificam as perspectivas do futuro literário do crioulo.

Só hoje compreendemos a grandeza dos propósitos desse esclarecido patriota que foi Pedro Cardoso, pertencente à geração anterior à dos escritores claridosos. Seu esforço de dar dignidade literária ao crioulo e libertar seus conterrâneos do complexo de inferioridade ligado ao mesmo e aos componentes negróides da cultura caboverdiana, traduz já, ainda que embrionàriamente, a mesma inquietação de autenticidade que domina os da nossa geração. Por isso devemos considerá-lo um verdadeiro precursor, na medida em que, não obstante a incompreensão consciente das elites e o condicionalismo social adverso, teve coragem para defender e praticar seu pensamento e manter com ele a coerência que então era possível.

Pensamos que de tudo quanto esplanamos, resulta que, para a moderna geração, a consciencialização é, em todas as suas manifestações, incluída a literária, a tomada por parte do caboverdiano da consciência activa do processo histórico geral que nesta conjuntura o envolve em largo amplexo. Tal consciência apresenta dois momentos essenciais e correlacionados: a) O impulso inicial para se buscar a si mesmo como realidade étnica e cultural perdida no abismo da alienação;

b) A reivindicação do condicionamentno absolutamente necessário para que comece a realizar-se o encontro autónomo consigo mesmo.

Só a autenticidade é a lei lógica e ética que rege a génese e desenvolvimento dessa tomada de consciência. Recordamos aqui esta reflexão de J.-P. Sartre: «Se convirmos que o homem é uma liberdade em situação, conceberemos fàcilmente que esta liberdade possa definir-se como autêntica ou inautêntica, segundo a escolha que ela faça de si própria na situação em que surge. A autenticidade, é evidente por si, consiste em tomar uma consciência lúcida e verídica da situação, em assumir as responsabilidades e os riscos que tal situação comporta, em reivindicá-la no orgulho ou na humilhação, às vezes no horror e no ódio».

Estudando as manifestações literárias dos «novos», se encontramos alguns que ainda se situam dentro do campo gravitacional do Movimento Claridoso, mercê do enorme prestígio que este grangeou, vai-se, porém, formando e consolidando um grupo verdadeiramente representativo do que, neste trabalho, chamamos «Moderna Geração». Aqueles, embora não apresentem uma perfeita filiação ao Movimento Claridoso, enquanto afloram em suas criações instantes reivindicativos e procuram no terreno das questões práticas atitudes menos contemplativas que as dos claridosos, no entanto ainda estão afastados do grau de coerência pensante e actuante que caracteriza os elementos do último grupo.

Partindo da legitimidade dum critério de amostragem, passamos a considerar e a apreciar algumas das composições poéticas publicadas pelos novos.

O poema «Regresso» de Terêncio Anahory ilustra a mentalidade dos novos que ainda não conseguiram de todo libertar-se da enorme influência da órbita claridosa:

Deixem-no passar, por favor;

Ele vem cansado,
O seu caminho foi longo...

Desde manhã cedo
As aves que cantam
O sol e o prado
E a brisa do mar
Trouxeram com eles
O teu cartão de visita.

Mas eu não queria visita anunciada...

Podias entrar sem bater
Beber da minha água
E comer da minha comida.

Descansa!

...E enquanto adeja
Em volta de nós
Este sossego tranquilo
De um retorno desejado
Vou contar-te histórias
Para embalar o teu sono
Afugentar do teu pensamento

Roças, secas, sol ardente,
Fuba,
Terra-longe!

O final do poema mostra, sem grande esforço de análise, um convite dirigido ao contratado caboverdiano para se refugiar no esquecimento de amarguras ligadas ao facto emigratório, cujas consequências o poeta reflecte na descrição do seu poema. Encerra este uma contradição que outra coisa não é senão a erupção literária espontânea duma posição ideológica que não leva a observação e análise dos factos às últimas consequências.

Para ilustrar um pensamento consequente e uma

posição sem suspensões em seu desenvolvimento cora-
josamente dinâmico, escolhemos o poema de Ovídio
Martins, intitulado «Anti-Evasão»:

Pedirei
Suplicarei
Chorarei

Não vou para Pasárgada

Atirar-me-ei ao chão
E prenderei nas mãos convulsas

Ervas e pedras de sangue
Não vou para Pasárgada

Gritarei
Berrarei
Matarei

Não vou para Pasárgada

Este poema não só traduz uma atitude de activo
inconformismo e de repúdio de situações decorrentes
de uma ordem injusta, mas também é a denúncia da
atitude contemplativa e idealista que constitui a essência da poesia evasionista e se sublima no «Itinerário
de Pasárgada» de Osvaldo Alcântara (Baltazar Lopes). O final de «Anti-Evasão» é a vinculação à ácção
consciente e reivindicativa com a aceitação total das
consequências que ela implica, mesmo as havidas con-
vencionalmente por ilegítimas.

Este cotejo permite-nos ver o problema da emigração de ângulos claramente distintos, que revelam,
quando mais não seja, diferentes graus de intencionalidade agente num e noutro.

Mas não é só o evasionismo que oferece campo para
se estabelecer um contraste extremado de posições.
A vivência da problemática caboverdianna, entendida
como conjunto dos problemas da organização da socie-

dade insular, em todos os seus sectores e níveis de vida, e que vêm afligindo pelo sofrimento na própria carne as sucessivas gerações, é vasto campo onde a posição consequente e desmistificadora do grupo liberto das influências claridosas, não se confunde com a daquelas que, embora de boa fé, ainda se deixam seduzir pelo canto da sereia. A estes últimos advertimos de que ainda é tempo de repensarem com coragem a tão falada actualidade do ideário claridoso. Espanta-nos que ainda se não tenham apercebido do que há de autêntica actualidade e consciência perfeita da necessidade da nossa participação no processo histórico envolvente, em criações do quilate de «Quando a vida nascer» de Mário Fonseca, «Hora» e «Cantá nha Povo» de Ovídio Martins, ou na poesia de Felisberto Vieira Lopes.

A síntese de consciencialização e a totalidade de força expressiva que Ovídio Martins encerrou em «Hora», poema formalmente tão curto, quase pirular, mostram definitiva tomada de posição e o grau de maturidade espiritual alcançado pelo grupo que caracterizamos com a expressão «Nova Geração».

Esta geração, a cujas fileiras esperamos se venham juntar valores como Gabriel Mariano, Aguinaldo Fonseca e Terêncio Anahory, pela razão da evolução crescente que acompanha a temática de sua poesia no sentido de uma consciencialização mais perfeita, dispõe já dum escol onde ressaltam nomes-promessas como os de: Abílio Duarte, Corsino Fortes, Rolando Martins, Amiro Faria, Dulce Almada, Dante Mariano e outros.

ESTA É A GERAÇÃO QUE NÃO VAI PARA PASÁRGADA.

Angola, 1963

BIBLIOGRAFIA

Antologia da ficção caboverdiana contemporânea: Introdução de *Manuel Ferreira;* Comentário de *Aurélio Gonçalves*

Ambiente — *Jorge Barbosa*

Arquipélago — *Jorge Barbosa*

Boletim «Cabo Verde» — *Imprensa Nacional de Cabo Verde*

Cabo Verde visto por Gilberto Freyre — *Baltazar Lopes*

Caderno de um ilhéu — *Jorge Barbosa*

Caminhada — *Ovídio Martins*

Chiquinho — *Baltazar Lopes*

Chuva Braba — *Manuel Lopes*

Claridade — N.º* 1 a 9 (S. Vicente — Cabo Verde)

Consciência literária caboverdiana — *Manuel Ferreira,* in *Revista de Estudos Ultramarinos n.º 3*

Enterro de nha Candinha Sena — *António Aurélio Gonçalves*

Itinerário de Pasárgada — *Osvaldo Alcântara,* in *Revista Atlântico* (edição SPN)

Os flagelados do vento leste — *Manuel Lopes*

Orfeu Negro — *Jean-Paul Sartre*

Pródiga — *António Aurélio Gonçalves*

Quando a vida nascer — *Mário Fonseca,* in «Cabo Verde» *n.º 126*

Reflexões sobre a questão judaica — *Jean-Paul Sartre*

Seroantropologia das Ilhas de Cabo Verde — Mesa Redonda sobre o homem caboverdiano — *Almerindo Lessa e Jacques Ruffié*

Suplemento Cultural N.º 1 do Boletim «Cabo Verde»

Temas caboverdianos — *Manuel Lopes,* in *Revista de Estudos Ultramarinos n.º 3.*

PART THREE

Brief Essays on Six Journals
(by Manuel Ferreira, in Portuguese,
with English précis)

Cover of *Africa*/5 (M. Ferreira, ed.)

Cover of *Africa*/6 (M. Ferreira, ed.)

Precis
MENSAGEM—A VOZ DOS NATURAIS DE ANGOLA
[Mensagem—The Voice of the Angolan People]

In July of 1951 the journal Mensagem appeared in Luanda. The rising national and cultural consciousness of young Angolan intellectuals found expression in a "New Culture, of Angola and for Angola." Here was foreshadowed the idea of national independence. The wide feeling of African culture was further affirmed by social contact with fellow artists from Mozambique. Mensagem only partially fulfilled its goal. It did open new doors not only in the short story but also in poetry; for instance "a Terra," the land, the country, the earth, became a central theme in the writings of Alda Lara and Viriato da Cruz. The land was not understood merely as territory but as a prodigious living force fulfilling itself only through union. With only two issues published, Mensagem was a beginning, a point of departure that was continued in the review Cultura, in the collection of "Overseas Authors" published by the Casa dos Estudantes do Império, and also in various anthologies.

MENSAGEM

«A VOZ DOS NATURAIS DE ANGOLA»

Em Julho de 1951 surge em Luanda a revista *Mensagem*. E com ela e nela convergem e ganham impulso ideias, projectos, iniciativas isoladas ou colectivas anteriormente esboçadas, de natureza cultural e literária.

«*Mensagem* será, — nós o queremos! — o marco iniciador de uma Cultura Nova, de Angola e por Angola, fundamentalmente angolana, que os jovens da nossa Terra estão construindo.»

Isto se dizia no primeiro número. E mais se dizia: «E a Cultura de Angola, somatório dos nossos esforços; a Cultura de Angola, forte como é forte o nosso desejo de vencer; verdadeira, como a verdade do nosso Querer; pujante, como a pujança da nossa Mocidade; humana como a humanidade que lhe imprimirá a auscultação dos nossos problemas, a compreensão do nosso Povo e a vontade que a todos nos irmanará, de nos compreendermos e sermos compreen-

---

(¹) Luanda, Departamento Cultural da Associação dos Naturais de Angola, 1951/1952. Quatro números, os três últimos num só caderno. Colaboradores literários *angolanos:* Agnelo Paiva, Antero Abreu, António Cardoso, A. Leston Martins, Agostinho Neto, Alda Lara, António Jacinto, António Neto, Bandeira Duarte, Ermelinda Pereira Xavier, Herberto da Silva Andrade, Humberto da Sylvan, João Jeremias, José Mensurado, Lília da Fonseca, M. A. M., Manuel José Jeremias, Maria Joana Couto da Silva, Mário António Fernandes de Oliveira, Mário Pinto de Andrade, Maurício Gomes, Orlando Távora [pseudónimo de António Jacinto], Óscar Ribas, Tomás Jorge, Viriato da Cruz; *moçambicanos:* José Craveirinha, Noémia de Sousa; *portugueses:* António Mendes Correia (com muitos anos de Angola), Augusto dos Santos Abranches (durante vários anos radicado em Moçambique).

didos, impor-se-á na amplidão de nossos horizontes.» O seu projecto vasto e ambicioso: «Urge criar e levar a Cultura de Angola além fronteiras, na voz altissonante dos nossos poetas e escritores; na paleta e no cinzel seguro dos nossos artistas plásticos; ao som dos acordes triunfais da nossa música que os nossos músicos e compositores irão buscar aos férteis motivos que a nossa Terra, grande e maravilhosa, lhes oferece.»

Com efeito, nos dois cadernos publicados *Mensagem* adquiriu a fisionomia original, qual seria a de tornar-se a expressão literária e cultural da angolanidade e de ser a primeira voz de uma cultura regional autêntica das áreas do continente africano de influência portuguesa. O primeiro número abre com um poema de Ermelinda Pereira Xavier, intitulado «Mensagem», apelo lançado a todos os angolanos numa hora em que a consciência nacional começa por definir-se em termos inequívocos: «Avante, irmão, demos as mãos/ recomecemos a nossa jornada:/ vamos buscar os outros irmãos/ que hesitam em dizer sua mensagem.»

Nesse tempo, longo era já o percurso no domínio do debate sobre a criação literária e artística afro-negra ou, mais concretamente, da *negritude*. A Angola (e de admitir também a Moçambique), haviam chegado os ecos directos ou indirectos de uma poesia afro-americana; os ecos directos ou indirectos de uma poesia africana de expressão francesa; a sombra de Guillén, de Wat Whitman, de Langston Hughes, Countee Cullen; ou a voz de Francisco José Tenreiro que, em 1942, tinha publicado na colecção coimbrã do «Novo Cancioneiro» um livro que se alimentava substancialmente de motivações da negritude: *Ilha de nome santo*.

De notar ainda que os jovens intelectuais de Luanda iniciavam-se no momento em que as ressonâncias e as terríveis consequências da guerra eram ainda bem vivazes, e quando por via disso mesmo se agitava a problemática das culturas negras, e se começava, por outro lado, a aceitar a sua firme decisão de conquistar o lugar a que tinham direito. Sentiam, por isso, a irreversível necessidade de revitalizar os caminhos percorridos pela actividade cultural angolana no sentido de uma radicação sem concessões: «o marco de uma Cultura Nova, de Angola e por Angola». Aqui se pré-anuncia a marcha para a ideia da independência nacional.

O Movimento dos Novos Intelectuais de Angola propunha: Vamos descobrir Angola: Descobrir implicava redifinir e daí partir para a valorização dos dados fundamentais da caracterização cultural e não apenas continuar limitados ao prolongamento de uma perspectiva viciada ou inconsequente.

Mensagem é o porta-voz ou, antes, a expressão desse movimento que se traduz não só na criação desta revista, como numa actividade cultural e literária que se pretendia ampla e intensa: «concursos literários», «exposições de artes plásticas», «início de uma larga campanha para a alfabetização», «publicação periódica da Revista *Mensagem*», «edição de obras de autores angolanos», «realização de palestras, conferências, recitais, divulgação artística, literária ou científica», «fundação de escolas primárias, médicas e técnicas e profissionais, para a valorização e aperfeiçoamento do nosso operário», «criação de bibliotecas».

Mensagem na verdade não pretende ser apenas um órgão literário. A sua ambição é a de tornar-se num verdadeiro orgão cultural, desbordando pelo conto, poesia, ensaio linguístico, sociológico, crítico, folclórico, etc. «E nós queremos que a cultura seja acentuadamente como caminho livre: todos transitarão. Assim, a cultura que surge em Angola é mensagem que, dum determinado ponto do globo, nós dirigimos à juventude de todo o mundo, certos de que a juventude de todo o mundo poderá compreender os nossos anseios, as nossas aspirações e as nossas esperanças» (n.º 2/4, 1952). O sentido amplo de cultura nacional afirma-se pelo convívio com os companheiros da outra costa do Índico, Moçambique, tais como Noémia de Sousa, José Craveirinha, do metropolitano, ali radicado, Augusto dos Santos Abranches, um homem da geração coimbrã neo-realista e mais concretamente do «Novo Cancioneiro» e que em Moçambique se tornou um dos mais activos impulsionadores de uma poesia e cultura moçambicanas, quer no *Itinerário,* quer no «Sulco» ou no «Ātrio», estes dois últimos suplementos literários que ele próprio fundou e animou.

Mensagem, porém, só parcialmente se cumpriu. Deu o sinal da partida apenas. Nesses tempos difíceis houve de ficar-se pelo número colectivo 2/4. Reafirme-se, porém: fixou um momento importante da cultura angolana. E abriu caminhos novos não só ao conto como também, e sobretudo, à poesia. Pois a despeito de mal lhe ter sido dado oportunidade para uma expressão momentânea, ali em *Mensagem* se definem algumas das linhas mais importantes da nova poesia de Angola. Por um lado, a Terra, espaço geográfico, teatro e fundamento de uma realidade que amavam quase messianicamente: «Oh Terra! Oh Terra, oh nossa Mãe Terra...». (Viriato da Cruz). Terra que amavam na plenitude e cujo apelo encontrava eco profundo nas suas almas. «É a Terra que nos chama.../ E é tempo companheiros!/ Caminhemos...» diria mais tarde Alda Lara. Terra não entendida apenas como territorialidade, ou como imanência telúrica, mas como força humana prodigiosa que só na união se realiza. Não teria sido ainda a floração de uma poesia da totalidade das vivências autóctones. Os poetas aqui como que fazem uma profissão de fé e lançam as raízes dos pré-requesitos de uma poesia necessária. Revolucionária para além mesmo do que lhes era permitido. «Ó poetas do novo cancioneiro,/ cantai, espalhai, pelos sulcos da terra,/ as sementes do poema novo!» (Humberto da Sylvan). E clamam. «Já não há luar porque a noite morreu./ Chorai vós, poetas/ que eu canto o Sol no apogeu!» (António Jacinto). É uma anunciação. Não é ainda a ressurreição. Não é ainda a torrente úbere do universo angolano a caminho da sua libertação. Isso virá depois. Com os anos, a cultura, com uma mais aguda e generalizada consciencialização. Mas já se detectam elementos radicados na consciência de uma fisionomia social múltipla, complexa, original. Um exemplo poderá ser Mário António de uma fase que abandonaria. «Minha avó negra, de panos escuros/ Da cor do carvão./ Minha avó negra, de panos escuros/ que nunca mais deixou// Andas de luto/ toda és tristeza(...)./ Se pudesses,/ talvez revivesses/ as velhas tradições!». Ou ainda um Viriato da Cruz: «Na noite de breu/ ao quente da voz/ de suas avós,/ meninos se encantam/ de contos bantus.../ «Era uma vez, uma corça/ dona de cabras sem macho.../ ... Matreiro, o cágado lento/ tuc... tuc... foi entrando/ para o conselho animal...». Ponto de partida, definido, decisivo que em *Cultura* se continuará e na Colecção Autores Ultramarinos da Casa dos Estudantes do Império, nas antologias e em vários outros volumes encontraria a sua expressão acabada.

Precis

CULTURA—*A VOZ QUE SE PROLONGA*
[Culture—A Continuing Voice]

With thirteen issues over four years (1957-61), the literary and cultural review Cultura's singular vitality provided a market place for the dissemination of Angolan poetry, fiction, criticism and essays on cinema, music, linguistics and social themes. A manifestation of a fecund period of intellectual investigation comparable to that of the last quarter of the nineteenth century, the publication of Cultura coincided with sundry conferences, debates, and cultural sessions taking place in such cities as Lobito, Sá da Bandeira, Malange, Nova Lisboa and Mocámedes. Some of the contributors to Cultura had collaborated on Mensagem and other publications produced at secondary schools including O Estudante (Luanda, 1933-1953) and Padrão (Huila, 1950-1952). New writers too participated in Cultura, among them the poet Arnaldo Santos. António Cardoso, Costa Andrade, Tomás Jorge and Luandino Vieira were significant voices of denunciation, of protest and of hope. The experience of Mensagem was continued in Cultura. However, the formation of an active resistance to the Portuguese resulted in political trials and the suppression of such cultural and literary activity as Cultura.

Cover of *When Bullets Begin to Flower*

PROPRIEDADE E EDIÇÃO DA SOCIEDADE CULTURAL DE ANGOLA – LUANDA NOVEMBRO DE 1957

CULTURA (II)

A VOZ QUE SE PROLONGA

Treze números, em quatro anos, de uma publicação exclusivamente literária e cultural, e de dimensões razoáveis, é uma expressão de vitalidade singular no espaço africano, só ultrapassada pelo *Itinerário*, de Lourenço Marques e de certo modo pelo «Artes e Letras» de *A Voz de Moçambique*. Mas nem o *Itinerário* nem o suplemento de *A Voz de Moçambique*, este ainda em publicação, se revestem de uma tão marcada regionalidade actuante, característica de *Cultura*(1). No n.º 1 se acentuava:

«Não nos cabe esboçar um plano. Cumpre-nos, isso sim, propiciar, como homens honestos e conscientes, fazendo parte de um mesmo

---

(1) Luanda, Sociedade Cultural de Angola, 1957/1961. Treze números. [De 1945 a 1951 foram publicados, em Luanda, dezanove números de uma outra publicação intitulada também *Cultura* (I). Trata-se de uma fase incaracterística do ponto de vista da angolanidade. No entanto, num ou noutro número, sobretudo nos últimos anos, já se dá conta 'e um certo tipo de colaboração que prenuncia uma nova época cultural. Aparecem assim em *Cultura* (I) os nomes de Cochat Osório, Geraldo Bessa Víctor, Agostinho Neto, Humberto da Sylvan, e o de Mário António Fernandes de Oliveira a subscrever um artigo].

Colaboradores (poetas ou ficcionistas, ensaístas ou críticos): *angolanos:* Africano Paiva (Costa Andrade), Agostinho Neto, Andiki (Henrique Lopes Guerra), Angolano Andrade (Costa Andrade), Antero Abreu, Benúdia (Mário Lopes Guerra), Carlos Ervedosa, Costa Andrade, Ermelinda Pereira Xavier, Fernando Mourão, Helder Neto, João Abel, José Graça (Luandino Vieira), Mário António, Oscar Ribas, Samuel de Sousa, Tomás Jorge; *sã-tomenses:* Tomaz Medeiros: *portugueses radicados em Angola:* Amélia Veiga, Henrique Abranches, Leonel Cosme, Garibaldino de Andrade; *radicado em Moçambique:* Manuel Filipe de Moura Coutinho.

aglomerado, os meios pelos quais hão-de tomar forma, ganhar relevo e conteúdo, as expressões de todos aqueles que são efectivamente capazes de escrever verso ou conto, de estudar ou analisar, de criticar ou equacionar, os diferentes problemas de toda a ordem que se põem em Angola». Na certeza de que «múltiplos e complexos são os problemas culturais de Angola. Problemas que, tendo como base questões económicas e sociais, se ligam aos mais variados problemas da vida e dela são resultantes. Pode dizer-se que, enquanto estes problemas não forem resolvidos, toda a acção cultural há-de pecar por defeito».

Não lhes cabia esboçar um plano. Mas o plano seria, como se deixa entrever, predominantemente o da angolanidade. A angolanidade dentro de todos os condicionalismos possíveis e imaginários, os maiores de todos sendo a Censura e a repressão policial — e que terão de se ter sempre presentes quando se analisa o fenómeno cultural da África e as generosas iniciativas aí rasgadas ao futuro.

Diga-se porém que nenhum órgão cultural, com excepção para alguns números de *Mensagem* (C.E.I.), teria ido tão longe e logrado uma tão exemplar preocupação de tratamento autóctene, como a revista *Cultura*. Os mais variados aspectos da actividade cultural angolana: ficção, poesia, cinema, artes plásticas, crítica, temas sociais, música, linguística, nela foram objecto de análise ou referência com uma dignidade e um saber que honra uma geração.

Ali se definiram conceitos sobre arte e literatura angolanas, ali se revelaram ou confirmaram valores da poesia e da ficção ou da crítica, ali se chamava a atenção para os importantes problemas culturais, humanos, sociais de Angola, em artigos na sua maioria assinados por angolanos. E mesmo quando subscritos por portugueses ou outros se enquadram numa linha de vigilante exigência crítica e dinâmica.

Ao percorrermos cuidadosamente estes treze números fica-nos a convicção de que em Angola, por essa época, despontaram inteligências lúcidas e criadoras, empenhadas na construção de uma cultura inserida nas realidades específicas nacionais, como o tentaram fazer os homens do último quartel do século XIX, consideradas obviamente as alterações de estrutura de pensamento que as longas décadas agora impunham. E fica-se ainda com o conhecimento de uma inquestionável actividade que hoje talvez mal se possa cuidar. Colóquios, conferências, debates, sessões culturais não apenas de poesia, de literatura em geral, mas outrossim de música, artes plásticas, organização de bibliotecas, problemas postos sobre a música africana, linguística, folclore, cinema, etc. e isto se alargando às cidades de Lobito, Sá da Bandeira, Malange, Nova Lisboa, Moçâmedes e outras, nomeadamente através das secções da Sociedade Cultural de Angola, organismo a que estava radicada a revista *Cultura*. É um período fecundo, que se reflecte sadiamente nas páginas deste órgão e que, em rigor, nem foi ultrapassado nem sequer igualado.

Alguns dos seus colaboradores eram dos que haviam sido revelados em *Mensagem* (Luanda), para não citarmos outras publicações, incluindo as liceais, por exemplo, o caso d'*O Estudante* (Luanda, 1933-1953) e *Padrão* (Huíla, 1950-1952), que definem mais um aspecto interessante da actividade cultural de Angola, por essa altura. Mas alguns deles foi em *Cultura* que puderam, com efeito, dar uma ideia mais acabada do seu talento, enquanto outros mais novos encontraram ali oportunidade para a sua autêntica iniciação literária, como Arnaldo Santos, uma voz repousada, expectante: «E sinto como que o sopro melódico/ De uma canção cruel/ Perpassando na paisagem silenciosa.»; mas nele, também, serena e firme, a esperança: «...os pássaros voarão/ E o mundo encher-se-á de suas penas». Por vezes a intencionalidade reflexiva e crítica vem num tom magoado: «Como o meu bairro mudou...» (Aires de Almeida Santos). O tom altivo, carregado de significações, releva de António Cardoso, na forma interrogativa: «Quando será que este cacimbo nos abandona/ e o Sol virá sorrir próximo do meu telhado?» — ou na recusa, sem apelo: «Cada um de nós/ lance a lenha que tiver/ mas que não chore/ embora tenha frio./ Se choramos aceitamos, é preciso não aceitar.» É uma poesia determinada, implantada na própria terra e no próprio momento. Agressiva, até, não poucas vezes: «Ouve.../ Não te cales sob a violência/ nem grites a tua inocência» (João Abel). O drama marginal do mulato, integra-o Costa Andrade na soberana expressão universal: «Mas sou apenas Homem./ Igual a ti irmão de todas as europas/ e a ti irmão que transpareces as áfricas futuras», enquanto se faz eco das «Mensagens de/ um mundo novo/ que da sombra das acácias/ se derrama»; outros acreditam nesse «mundo novo» através da fraternidade original perdida: «Quando a terra se cobriu de frutos/ e os frutos amadureceram/ os homens não lutavam (...)» e «sem gestos contraídos/ sem ódio sufocados/ foram homens/ e amaram-se/ E com o Amor dos homens/ a verdade foi mais clara/ e o sol mais brilhante.» A barreira da cor, naturalmente um tema dominante da poesia africana, exprime-a aqui Costa Andrade, no plano do amor: «Chamar-te: Amor!... Amor!... Amor!...// Chissola!... e não poder fazê-lo// Chissola! florimos junto sob as acácias/ Oh, drama do branco nascido em África.» Tomás Jorge porém alonga o sonho da multirracialidade: «Menina mulata/ E mais crianças/ Negras e brancas/ No jardim da esperança.» Poetas urbanos e na maioria dos casos feitos na experiência social de Luanda, a cidade forjada ou forjando-se sob a presença de vários grupos étnicos e crescendo ao ritmo das mais insuspeitadas contradições — ela própria, heterógena, complexa, percurso histórico de fundas mutações, nela mergulham os poetas e a interrogam, e se interrogam: «Luanda onde está» «Sorrindo/ as quindas no chão/ laranjas e peixe/ maboque docinho/ a esperança nos olhos/ a certeza nas mãos/ mana Rosa peixeira/ quitandeira Maria/ Zefa mulata/ — os panos pintados/ garridos/ caídos/ mostraram o coração:/ — Luanda está aqui!» (Luandino Vieira). De todos se repercute uma vigilância atenta à terra e ao homem. É um momento em que os poetas angolanos pensam e repensam os seus problemas cingidos a um espaço definido: a terra de Angola. Com todas as limitações impostas, a adesão histórica é evidente. Adesão que nem os poetas metropolitanos querem enjeitar. Também eles, ali radicados, se integram, e dela fazem sua terra de adopção. O caso, por exemplo, de Amélia Veiga: «Angola,/ não serás terra do meu berço/ mas és terra do meu ventre!» e «Das entranhas da terra/ irrompe um vento alucinado/ que varre... varre... varre/ as folhas secas do mundo...». Quiçá por tudo isto, o angolano Antero Abreu fazia esta confissão anos antes na *Mensagem:* «Vejo a flor desenhar-se em fruto/ E quer ela o dê, quer não dê,/ É esse o fim por que luto.»

São muitas as vozes de denúncia, de protesto, de esperança ou de reflexão reunidas em volta deste órgão de cultura. Algumas limitaram-se a uma presença fugidia, como seja o caso de Henrique Abranches que, no entanto, se sagra em várias páginas de *Cultura* como um antropólogo de sérios recursos, limitando-se a subscrever apenas um poema (?), embora venha a publicar em 1961 um excelente livro de contos, *Diálogo*. Por sua vez, Helder Neto assina aí um poema e alguns contos, e como que desaparece da cena literária, para o reencontrarmos numa antologia de poesia africana de expressão portuguesa, em tradução inglesa, *When bullets begin to flower,* 1972, da autoria de Margaret Dickson, representado no poema *We shall not mourn the dead,* escrito durante a luta de libertação nacional, já que ele, tal como Henrique Abranches, é militante do M.P.L.A.

Mas outros nomes há a assinalar: Samuel de Sousa, Ernesto Lara Filho, Henrique Guerra. O primeiro reaparece, mais tarde, concretamente no início desta década, em páginas literárias angolanas. E de poeta da humilhação em 1958 («Mamãzinha/ a minha face é a face amarela/ dos mortos esbofeteados») se transfere para o poeta da esperança, em 1973: «Não há fronteiras na distância/ nas nossas bocas a ânsia/ da nova idade/ e nos corpos as angústias da fecundidade». Henrigue Guerra encarna a natureza do ente angolano branco alienado: «Que me interessa saber a língua de Voltaire,/ De Goethe e Shakespeare,/ (...) Se não sei o dizer dos marimbeiros,/ Os tocadores de tchingufos e kissanjis/ Quando entro calado pelos quimbos?» Ernesto Lara Filho, também angolano branco, realizada a comunhãc existencial com o mundo negro, de que aliás a sua obra é reflexo inegável (chega a afirmar: «Eu gostava de ser negro») é ainda um poeta da anunciação: «Os nossos filhos/ Negra/ Serão os construtores, os engenheiros, os médicos, os cientistas do Mundo que vem».

A experiência de *Mensagem* continua-se em *Cultura*. E não só em *Cultura* (II), é a ocasião de o dizermos. Há que prestar uma cuidada atenção a um órgão de periodicidade muito irregular (de semanal, depois quinzenal, mensal, terminou por sair quando calhava) que desempenhou papel importante na divulgação da cultura angolana no período que decorre entre 1953 e 1963. Trata-se do *Jornal de Angola* da Associação Regional dos Naturais de Angola (ANAN-GOLA) (¹). Surgindo pouco depois de extinta a *Mensagem*, apesar de não ser um órgão exclusivamente de cultura, mesmo assim dispensou-lhe uma esmerada atenção. E no que respeita à poesia, ao conto e até à crítica ou ao comentário crítico é folgada a colaboração e frequentemente marcada pela novidade. Ali vamos encontrar quase todos os nomes representativos de *Mensagem* e os que entretanto levaram por diante o projecto de *Cultura* que, aliás, veio a coexistir com o *Jornal de Angola*.

Em 1953 havia sido fundado o Partido da Luta Unida dos Africanos Angolanos e, em 1956, este e outras organizações políticas formaram o Movimento Popular de Libertação de Angola (M.P.L.A.), no qual terminaram por ser incorporadas outras formações políticas que surgiram posteriormente. Daí que «o ano de 1958 tivesse sido particularmente marcado por uma grande actividade política. Por meio de panfletos, programas de acção, proclamações de luta anticolonialista, através de centros clandestinos, a agitação das massas angolanas cresce e inquieta os portugueses». E a 5 de Dezembro de 1960 «o Tribunal Militar de Luanda empreendeu a mascarada dum julgamento de vinte nacionalistas angolanos que se reclamavam do M.P.L.A. e outras formações políticas» (in Mário de Andrade, «Le Nationalisme Angolais» — *Présence Africaine*, n.º XLII, 3.º trimestre, 1962). Eis porque não se pode desligar a actividade cultural e literária deste período dos anseios políticos que tomavam forma e expressão. As forças de repressão sabiam-no e sufocaram o jornal *Cultura* (II) como já haviam sufocado outras iniciativas e outras mais haveriam de sufocar nos longos anos que se seguiram. Afinal, em vão.

Em 1960, com o afastamento de Luanda do director do jornal, cria-se um problema de legalização da revista. E por isso ou porque o poder político se interpôs — e deve ter sido isso —, *Cultura* desaparece. Em 1961 ainda se dá pelo número 13, duas páginas apenas para «garantia do título», como se diz no Editorial, prometendo-se um próximo número de dezasseis páginas. Até hoje. E hoje sabe-se porquê.

(¹) Luanda, 21.11.1953-1965. 127 números. Pelo menos na Biblioteca Nacional de Lisboa o último número da colecção é o 127.

Precis

M. FERREIRA
CONVIVIUM — UM INOFENSIVO GESTO
[Convivium — An Inoffensive Gesture]

With the conviction that Angolan culture was a subsidiary extension of a European perspective, the literary review Convivium did not correspond to socio-political realities. Led by Filipe Neiva, who also edited five poetry anthologies, Convivium was an inoffensive gesture that did produce some good poetry by Angolans and Portuguese whose chose to make Angola their home.

CONVIVIUM

UM INOFENSIVO GESTO

Motivada por Filipe Neiva (português desembarcado em Angola por volta de 1963), em boa verdade não se poderá dizer que esta iniciativa tenha ido além de um voo raso. Orientada a partir de uma perspectiva europeia que entendia a cultura angolana como um prolongamento subsidiário da cultura portuguesa, *Convivium* (¹), na sua qualidade de revista de cultura literária, de modo nenhum correspondeu, ainda considerando todos os condicionalismos sociais e políticos, àquilo que o momento requeria. Isto mesmo se aplica (de um modo geral, claro!) às cinco antologias de poesia editadas por Filipe Neiva. Quer na revista quer nas antologias, aí se trouxeram à superfície alguns nomes que pouco ou nada adiantaram para a poesia angolana. Ao cabo e ao resto, *Convivium* sagrou-se num inofensivo gesto de quem não pretendia levantar problemas. Porém, ainda nas coisas que não são importantes, é sempre possível nelas descortinar algo que por si se impõe e injusto seria esquecê-lo. E é o que acontece em relação a alguns colaboradores, dentre eles uns tantos poetas que não se furtaram a dar a sua colaboração. Uns já considerados, por óbvias razões, em capítulos anteriores, e essa a razão porque não são agora tomados em linha de conta, outros por talvez não se enquadrarem na orientação que vimos equacionando, mas que merecem aqui o registo do seu nome: Leiria Dias e Artur Queiroz. Três poetas, então, nos restariam: Fernando Alvarenga, Carlos Gouveia e Jofre Rocha. Preferíamos, no entanto, reservar os nomes de Fernando Alvarenga e de Jofre Rocha para capítulos ulteriores.

E diríamos que em Carlos Gouveia, nascido em Portugal, mas desde tenra idade vivendo nos meios pobres de Benguela («Eu andei brincando com todos os meninos da cidade,/ Figa na mão/ Comendo mangas verdes, jogando pião»), o referente da sua poesia é lá onde a sua vida se joga, entre «Mana Josefa/ Velha Margarida/ Comadre Neli/ Mais o Zeca Cambuta/ filho do sapateiro/ E o tio Monteiro/ Todos». É assim, como noutros mais, produto de uma aculturação, mas em sentido inverso daquela em que normalmente é entendida em África: transitando, por consciente opção, do europeu para o africano.

(¹) *Convivium* — boletim cultural. Benguela, 1971-1972. Nove números. Colaboradores — *angolanos,* entre outros: Arnaldo Santos, João Abel, Jofre Rocha; Jorge Macedo; *portugueses radicados:* António Cordeiro da Cunha, Artur Queiroz, Carlos Gouveia, Fernando Alvarenga, Filipe Neiva, Leiria Dias.

Precis
VECTOR—*AINDA A PREDOMINANCIA EUROPEIA*
[Vector—Still European Predominance]

A little after the appearance of Convivium, *a new journal was launched in 1971 in Nova Lisboa. Directed by three Portuguese writers living in Angola, Bellini Jara, Jorge Huet Bacelar and Fernando Alvarenga,* Vector *resembled* Convivium *far more than it did* Mensagem *and* Cultura, *for its poetry did not reflect an authentic Angolan identity.*

VECTOR

AINDA A PREDOMINÂNCIA EUROPEIA

Pouco depois do aparecimento de *Convivium*, Bellini Jara, de colaboração com Jorge Huet Bacelar e Fernando Alvarenga, lança, em Nova Lisboa, a revista *Vector* (¹), dedicada à poesia. Sublinhe-se que *Vector* nada tem a ver com o parentesco da política oficial que, no fundo, presidia à direcção de *Convivium*.

Os três responsáveis são homens radicados em Angola, embora Bellini Jara trouxesse de Moçambique a permanência de muitos anos. Por sua vez, Fernando Alvarenga quando chegou a Angola levava já na sua bagagem um livro de poemas publicado. Dá-se conta que também não era da vocação destes cadernos seguir a tradição de uma autenticidade angolana proposta pela *Mensagem* e pela *Cultura*. Certo é também que dois ou três colaboradores de *Vector* contrariam a regra sem que, no entanto, influam na dominante traduzida por uma poesia de desvinculamento regional. Mas, à semelhança do que dissemos para *Convivium*, esses são poetas ou já agrupados anteriormente ou a agrupar no fecho desta articulação. Ficam-nos, assim, Fernando Alvarenga, Jorge Huet Bacelar e Bellini Jara.

Fernando Alvarenga denota um esforço para uma integração regional e, naturalmente que, dada a sua ainda curta permanência em Angola, não lhe seria fácil a apreensão segura de um referente cuja complexidade e riqueza para ser dominado exige a um europeu demorada vivência. Mas na sua poesia dessa data já se dá por uma adesão significativa: «Em ti mais entro para ter cá fora/ teu canto nas raízes do meu canto/ e em nosso canto sacudido agora/ a mulher feita de áfrica chorando», adesão que depois se foi acentuando em *Hoje na madrugada*.

Jorge Huet Bacelar, por sua vez, tocado de um lirismo existencial («É minha a hora adiada,/ Minha a força nocturna/ Que erra em meus desertos»; ou «Dói com certeza muito/ na matriz do Absurdo»), em poema inédito comenta, satiricamente, aquilo que ele considera a «receita» para a construção de «cultura angolana», embora «Da cultura africana nem saber»: «Uma vóvó qualquer, de preferência/ Muito velha e negrinha»; ou «Benguela é indispensável/ E um versito em quimbundo é magistral». Se haverá que dar-lhe razão, considerando o artifício de algumas tentativas (gratuitas) na elaboração de uma poesia angolana, a verdade é que não podemos partilhar desse desdém se ele envolver a recusa da legitimidade de uma participação angolana ao nível poético por parte de europeus radicados. É que se, por um lado, havemos de compreender a sua reserva, porque filiada numa atitude de consciente opção, não menos rigoroso será reconhecer o honesto esforço de muitos para se despirem da ganga europeia e se tornarem cidadãos e poetas penetrados do devir histórico do povo africano.

Não será esta a posição de Bellini Jara, embora a maioria da sua poesia (publicada) se mantivesse veiculada a uma substância europeia. De qualquer modo diríamos que, para além do que separa ou aproxima os poetas dos últimos anos, uma coisa os identifica: o terem dentro de si o peso do silêncio. «As agulhas do silêncio/ doiem/ por dentro do silêncio/ corredores e arestas/ espiam-nos por dentro/ contra a pedra/ doiem/ as carnes em silêncio» (Bellini Jara). Silêncio que todos, afinal, procuravam quebrar, mas amarrados continuavam ao medo, ao medo nesse tempo inseguro que todos vivíamos, «cerrando os dentes» cantando ou chorando.

(¹) *Vector*. Nova Lisboa, 1971-1972. Três números. Colaboradores — *angolanos:* Cochat Osório, Fernando Ferreira de Loanda (radicado no Rio de Janeiro desde 1936), João Abel, Tomás Jorge; *sã-tomenses:* Carlos Alberto Carvalho Jordão; *portugueses radicados:* Alberto de Oliveira, António Bellini Jara, Artur Queiroz, David Mestre, Fernando Alvarenga, Jorge Huet Bacelar, José Fialho.

CLARIDADE
OU A REDESCOBERTA DAS RAIZES
[Claridade or the Rediscovery of Roots]

In 1956 Baltasar Lopes remarked that the purpose of the journal Claridade, which first appeared in 1936, was the study of Cape Verdean roots. Essentially literary in its first three issues, Claridade also studied social characteristics of the archipelago as well as its particular dialect. In fact, in the initial two issues, poems written in crioulo appeared on the cover. For the first time in Lusophone Africa, there was a regional poetry, a poetry of roots. The values of traditional popular culture were the source of a rediscovery of the Cape Verdean ethos. But the journal also presented a tragic drama of isolation, drought, and suffering, where to live is in itself a heroic act.

In its second phase, Claridade incorporated values of succeeding generations, enriching itself with many neo-realist poets. It continued to be a proud organ of crioulo culture.

CLARIDADE
OU A
REDESCOBERTA DAS RAIZES

Em 1936, na cidade do Mindelo, publicava-se o primeiro número de revista *Claridade*.[1]
Que representa *Claridade* para Cabo Verde? Como surgiu essa revista? Oiçamos, em 1956, Baltasar Lopes: « Há um pouco mais de vinte anos, eu e um grupo reduzido de amigos começámos a pensar no *nosso problema*, isto é, no problema de Cabo Verde. Preocupava-nos sobretudo o processo de formação social destas ilhas, o estudo das raízes de Cabo Verde.» (*Cabo Verde visto por Gilberto Freyre*, 1956).

Era precisamente pela altura em que, na cidade da Praia, encabeçado por Aimé Césaire, Leopold Sédar Senghor e Alioune Diop, se concretizava o movimento de *negritude,* que reclamava a necessidade e o dever de os intelectuais africanos afirmarem e defenderem a sua cultura.

Quer nos Estados Unidos da América do Norte quer em Cuba, e sobretudo nas Antilhas, diversas manifestações haviam já ocorrido no propósito de afirmarem a cultura negra, com o objectivo de a libertarem da categoria de subproduto a que os europeus ou os homens de cultura ocidental a haviam relegado. Mas é por esta época que se consubstanciam todas as tentativas anteriores e se dá corpo e consciência a um verdadeiro movimento tendente à revelação dos valores humanos, sociais, literários e artísticos do homem afro-negro.

No entanto, esta tomada de consciência passou despercebida aos intelectuais cabo-verdianos e em nada teria influído no processo literário das ilhas crioulas. Além de que a estrutura social de Cabo Verde, específica no quadro dos valores africanos, não se mostraria muito receptiva, pelo menos nessa época, a um movimento com as características do que eclodiu em Paris. Pois se a negritude se caracterizava por uma acção cultural, literária e sociológica, o certo é que política era a sua contextura, já que se propunha reivindicar o direito de colocar em pé de igualdade com a cultura branca os valores culturais afro-negros, ao mesmo tempo que, no plano dos direitos humanos, reclamava um estatuto comum dos povos africanos e europeus. Não se punha ainda o problema de autodeterminação das colónias francesas ou inglesas, fenómeno decorrente do pós-guerra. O acto revolucionário naquele momento traduzia-se na exigência de preroggativas e liberdades, ao nível da Comumidade, e neste caso mais em relação às colónias francesas. Em jogo, sobretudo, uma questão de ordem cultural, associada à desafronta étnica e racial, e todos estes problemas, em força, se tornaram a substância corrente quer do panfleto político quer do ensaio quer de poesia.

Ora este tipo de problemas não era de molde a alcançar um certo acolhimento ou só mui delidamente o poderia ter sido em Cabo Verde, ainda mesmo que os intelectuais se tivessem dele apercebido. Larga miscegenação étnica e cultural, no seio do Arquipélago, permitiu que o cabo-verdiano de há muito viesse apropriando-se do processo interno das suas estruturas sociais, e por isso a Africa, em termos raciais, étnicos ou em termos de Terra-Mãe, ali não se punha. E, embora se não subestimassem os *apports* africanos, a verdade é que também se não valorizavam. O que nessa fase da evolução cultural crioula se colocava era a redescoberta dessa própria realidade, já se disse vincadamente original, e até então por inteiro ignorada, com excepção para os criadores populares ou para um Eugénio Tavares, nas suas mornas em crioulo, nos estudos de um Pedro Cardoso ou na poesia lírica de língua portuguesa de um Pedro Corsino Azevedo. A tarefa imediata estava no abandonar os padrões europeus e os temas inspirados numa poesia lisboeta. O que se impunha era pensar «o nosso problema», isto é, o problema de Cabo Verde.

Eis que, para tanto, havia um país que poderia dar uma ajuda. Um país semelhante nas estruturas, semelhante na sua formação social, semelhante no seu contexto racial. Esse país outro não era que o Brasil—e nessa altura já com vários romancistas, poetas, sociólogos capazes de servirem de catalizadores às energias acumuladas pelos intelectuais cabo-verdianos mais atentos e dispostos à reformulação cultural.

«Ora aconteceu que por aquelas alturas nos caíram nas mãos, fraternalmente juntas em sistema de empréstimo, alguns livros que considerámos essenciais *pro domo nostra*. Na ficção, o José Lins do Rego do «Menino de Engenho» e do «Banquê», o Jorge Amado do «Jubiabá» e do «Mar Morto», o Amado Fontes de «Os Corumbas», o Marques Rebelo do «Caso de Mentira», que conhecemos por Ribeiro Couto; em poesia foi um 'alumbramento' a «Evocação do Recife, de Manuel Bandeira (. . .).»

«A vinte anos de distância, teimo em considerar essas reacções nossas como autênticas. Esta ficção e esta poesia revela-nos um ambiente, tipos, estilos, forma de comportamento, defeitos, virtudes, atitudes perante a vida, que se assemelhavam aos destas ilhas, principalmente naquilo que as ilhas têm de castiço e de menos contaminado.»

Entretanto, vieram os sociólogos e os etnólogos: «Nestes (. . .) deu-se a revelação. Da revelação era grandemente responsável um livro magnífico—a «Casa Grande e Senzala», de Gilberto Freyre, ao lado dos volumes, densos de investigação e interpretação, do malogrado Artur Ramos.»

Isto foi importante, mas por si só não teria sido bastante se outros factores não tivessem intervindo. Se outros factores não tivessem realizado a levedação de um estado de espírito em potência.

Estamos numa época de crise, o colapso americano afectando o aparelho económico do mundo inteiro, o Porto Grande de São Vicente ultrapassado tecnicamente pelo de Dakar, com efeitos desastrosos para a economia de São Vicente; o nazismo e o fascismo europeus como formas violentas e virulentas de reaccionarismo em choque com as necessidades de afirmação nacional e individual. Por outro lado, a importância que em Portugal adquiriu a querela do modernismo, através da revista *Presença,* conhecida em Cabo Verde, defendendo a predominância do subjectismo na criação literária, mas reclamando a liberdade de criação do ponto de vista formal, atacando uma literatura insípida de fim-de-século, reflectindo e estruturando todo o impacte saudável do *Orfeu*, em suma, proclamando a necessidade de modernidade, de sinceridade, de valorização da literatura nacional. Enfim, um conjunto de circunstâncias, algumas apenas aqui afloradas, contribuíram para que, em 1936, se tornasse um facto esse movimento que, por milagre, em terra tão minguada, deu a *Claridade.*

Essencialmente literária nos seus três primeiros números, nem por isso deixam de nela aparecer notas que apontam não só às características sociais de Cabo Verde mas também às suas razes humanas e telúricas, conferindo ao dialecto de Cabo Verde uma presença de honra. Com efeito, logo nos dois primeiros números se publicam na página de rosto poemas em crioulo, um, de carácter popular, outro, uma morna de Xavier Cruz: «Venus!... Oh astro di nhâ pensamento,/ Pamó qui bô há-l dixám morrê...» (primeira quadra). Não são, sejamos rigorosos, não são os elementos culturais africanos que adquirem importância, mas sim os elementos crioulos, o produto de uma aculturação, já sem conflitos, que ganham um fundo valor nos propósitos dos claridosos: « Enquanto o crioulo tem um sentido profundo da terra-mãe e por ela sente irremessível apelo quando emigrante, o negro americano liberta a sua esperança de desforra social nas estridências do *Jazz*, na nostalgia dos *blues* ou em poemas de afirmação reivindicadora, como o de Langston Hughes—*I too am America*» (João Lopes).

Isto se passava na primeira fase de *Claridade,* constituída pelos seus três primeiros números. E neles aparecem três poetas: Osvaldo Alcântara (Baltasar Lopes), Jorge Barbosa e Manuel Lopes, que precisamente formavam o núcleo dinamizador da revista, embora a estes três juntemos um outro tardio colaborador, Pedro Corsino Azevedo, mas já de há muito com poemas na gaveta.

A modernidade poética cabo-verdiana poderá não nos ter sido dada somente pela *Claridade* (março de 1936) porque, em dezembro de 1935, Jorge Barbosa tinha feito já a sua estreia literária com *Arquipèlago.* Como quer que seja, é legítimo conferir à *Claridade* o mérito da renovação poética cabo-verdiana, porque é nela que se vive a diversidade que enriquece a unidade, e tanto mais que o livro de Jorge Barbosa precede o primeiro número daquela uns escassos três meses. E mais. Esse libro traz a chancela de Edições Claridade, o que, para o caso, é bastante revelador.

Estes poetas, pela primeira vez na bistória da literatura culta de Cabo Verde, arrancam do próprio húmus. Pela primeira vez nas terras africanas de influência portuguesa se experimenta uma poesia de raiz. Uma poesia de raiz predominantemente telúrica e social. E por isso, se não era directamente protestária e militante, era com certeza de denúncia: « Ai o drama da chuva,/ ai o desalento,/ o tormento/ da estiagem// Ai a voragem/ da fome/ levando vidas!/ (...a tristeza das sementeiras perdidas...)// —Ai o drama da chuva!» (Jorge Barbosa). Os poetas cabo-verdianos pela primeira vez se reconciliavam com a terra-mãe, como que envergonhados de uma longa jornada de abandono: « Mamãe-Terra,/ venho rogar uma oração ao pé de ti.../ Teu filho vem dirigir suas súplicas a Deus Nossenhor» (Osvaldo Alcântara). Os valores da tradição cultural popular sobem à flor da consciência numa redescoberta amorosa: « Terreiro de trapiche,/ aromas adocicados do melaço/ pontado na chieira dos tachos./// Volteiam os bois na roda intérmina da almanjarra...// —Vira boi/ —volta boi/ quero uma noiva bonita/ como as sereias do mar!// ai tâmara/ ai figo/ de Portugal!» (Osvaldo Alcântara). Ou como Pedro Corsino Azevedo, no seu poema, escrito em 1929, *Galinha Branca:* « Galinha/ Branca/ Que anda/ Por casa/ De gente/ Catando/ Grão/ De milho./ E mais./ E mim/ E bô/ E Carlos/ E Valério/ E Fêdo.» Terra fechada, cercada pelo mar, o drama da insatisfação insular, avivando os sonhos, embalando o ser no doce e saudoso desejo da evasão, tema, como tantos outros, repetido ao longo do percurso poético cabo-verdiano, é dado aqui por Manuel Lopes: « E fico mudo/ ouvindo o vento a cantar na penedia,/ olhando as ondas que não param nunca,/ o horizonte sempre igual,/ e este sulco branco que umas hélices deixaram no mar/ (onde se desfazem os ùltimos esgares duma longa ironia/ e no extremo do qual/ flutua ainda/ o perfil dum vapor que não me quis levar)...». Mas uma coisa será o desejo de evasão, de raiz intelectual. Outra será a necessidade de emigração, de raiz económica. Dilema dramático esse que amarra o cabo-verdiano: querer-partir-e-ter-de-ficar—ou, querendo-ficar, ter-de-partir. De qualquer modo, luta secular de sobrevivência, tragédia contínua numa terra flagelada pelas estiagens, onde viver é um acto heróico. « Cruzaste Mares/ na aventura da pesca da baleia/ nessas viagens para a América/ de onde às vezes os navios não voltam mais./ O teu destino. . ./ o teu destino/ Sei lá!/ Viver sempre vergado sobre a terra,/ a nossa terra/ pobre/ ingrata/ querida!// Ou outro fim qualquer/ humilde/ anónimo/ Oh Cabo-Verdiano humilde/ anónimo/ meu irmão!» (Jorge Barbosa).

A originalidade desta poesia está ainda no facto de que, por esse tempo, em Portugal continuavam predominantes os padrões da *Presença*. Por isso a poesia de Cabo Verde só teria a sua correspondência aqui, em Portugal, a partir de 1939, com o surto neo-realista, embora este enriquecido por uma visão dinâmica do mundo, dada pelo materialismo histórico, e que faltava ao espírito de *Claridade*.

Na segunda fase, aquela revista foi incorporando valores de sucessivas gerações, alargando-se assim na expressão estética das estruturas sociais e enriquecendo-se com novos poetas, muitos deles neo-realistas da *Certeza* e do *Suplemento Cultural,* e outros que se revelaram marginalmente, deste modo continuando, embora a tão longo prazo, a constituir-se em órgão soberano da cultura crioula.

---

[1]Mindelo, São Vicente, 1936-1960, nove números; 1936, dois números; 1937, um número; 1947, dois números; 1948, 1949, 1958 e 1960, um número em cada um destes anos.

Colaboradores: Aguinaldo Brito Fonseca, António Aurélio Gonçalves, Arnaldo França, Artur Augusto da Silva, Baltasar Lopes, Corsino Fortes, Félix Monteiro, Francisco Lopes, Francisco Mascarenhas, Gabriel Mariano, Henrique Teixeira de Sousa, João Lopes, Jorge Barbosa, Jorge Pedro, Manuel Lopes, Manuel Serra, Mário Macedo Barbosa, Nuno Miranda, Onésimo Silveira, Osvaldo Alcântara, Ovídio Martins, Pedro Corsino Azevedo, Pedro de Sousa Lobo, Sérgio Frusoni,Terêncio Anahory, Tomaz Martins, Virgílio Avelino Pires, Virgínio Melo, Xavier Cruz; metropolitano: José Osório de Oliveira.

Precis

CERTEZA OU A ALELUIA DESLUMBRANTE
DOS DEZOITO ANOS
[Certeza or the Dazzling Halleluja of 18-Year-Olds]

Organized by students in the last two years of the Gil Eanes high school, including such authors as Arnaldo França, Certeza was in a certain sense a continuation of Claridade. *But unlike its predecessor, Certeza was committed primarily to ideological rather than regional truths. There were only two published issues of this neo-realist journal, which first appeared in 1944. A third issue was prohibited from being printed by the censors. Although the review did not produce a great poet, it did manifest the preoccupations of eighteen year old students dedicated to critical objectivity. Such articles as Orlanda Amarilis' essay on woman and her role, and Eduino Brito's study of the poet Jorge Barbosa, made Certeza a journal that celebrated the dazzling hallelujah of its youthful contributors.*

Certeza

Fôlha da Academia

REDACTORES: Nuno Miranda, José Spencer, Arnaldo França, Silvestre Faria, Guilherme Rocheteau, Filinto Meneses e Tomaz Martins

DIRECTOR: EDUINO BRITO SILVA
EDITOR: JOAQUIM RIBEIRO

COMPOSTO E IMPRESSO NA Tipografia "Minerva de Cabo Verde" Avenida Andrade Corvo — Praia

POEMA DE AMANHÃ

de
António
Nunes

Mamãi!
    sonho que, um dia,
em vez dos campos sem nada,
do êxodo das gentes nos anos de estiagem
deixando terras, deixando enxadas, deixando tudo,
das casas de pedra a vila fumegando do alto,
dos meninos espantalhos atirando fundas,
das lágrimas vertidas por aquêles que partem
e dos sonhos, aflorando, quando um barco passa,
dos gritos e maldições, dos ódios e vinganças,
dos braços musculados que se quedam inertes,
dos que estendem as mãos,
dos que olham sem esperanças o dia que há de vir,

— Mamãi!
    sonho que, um dia,
estas leiras de terra que se estendem,
quer sejam Mato Engenho, Dàcabalaio ou Santana,
filhas do nosso esfôrço, frutos do nosso suor,
serão nossas.

    E, então,
o barulho das máquinas cortando,
águas correndo por levadas enormes,
plantas a apontar,
trapiches pilando,
cheiro de melaço estonteando, quente,
novas seivas brotando da terra dura e sêca,
vivificando os sonhos, vivificando as ânsias, vivificando a Vida!...

Número de Junho   **2**   *S. Vicente de Cabo Verde. 1944*

CERTEZA

OU A

ALELUIA DESLUMBRANTE

DOS DEZOITO ANOS

Organizada por Nuno Miranda, José Spencer, Arnaldo França, Silvestre Faria, Guilherme Rocheteau, Filinto Menezes e Tomaz Martins, todos alunos dos dois últimos anos do Liceu Gil Eanes. E é aos seus condiscípulos que Arnaldo França se dirige: «Amigo cabo-verdiano, camarada jovem dos bancos do liceu, se pensas iniciar uma literatura viva e humana em que traduzas bem, ou mal, as angústias e as esperanças dos teus irmãos de raça, o teu jornal é este.»

De algum jeito aqui estão os continuadores de *Claridade*. Mas só de certo jeito. *Claridade,* como se deixou dito, apontava, essencialmente, às raízes crioulas. O ponto de partida era a redescoberta da realidade social e psicológica das ilhas. Os seus componentes não perfilhavam uma ideologia comum. No sentido rigoroso da expressão, alguns deles tê-la-iam? A sua ideologia, fundamentalmente, relevava de uma ideia única: a *cabo-verdianidade*. A revelação da sua terra. E da sua gente. Uma reacção contra a subserviência europeia dos modelos, dos temas, dos processos. O grupo de *Certeza* (¹) dir-se-ia pensar mais em termos ideológicos do que em termos regionais. O regional aflorava por pressão ideológica. Que tipo de ideologia os impulsionava? A mesma que justificara o movimento neo-realista português. Na verdade, *Certeza* não teria sido possível, pelo menos naquela data, sem o neo-realismo. Redol, Carlos de Oliveira, Manuel da Fonseca, Soeiro Pereira Gomes, Joaquim Namorado, Vergílio Ferreira, Namora, Afonso Ribeiro, Mário Dionísio, Sidónio Muralha foram ali conhecidos, comentados, até colectivamente, e ajudaram à construção de uma certa forma de encarar a vida. E, se os promotores de *Certeza* nada tinham contra a *Claridade,* a verdade é que os animava a consciência orgulhosa de a terem ultrapassado nesse aspecto. Haviam saído três números de *Claridade,* os dois primeiros, em 1936, e o terceiro, em 1937. Portanto oito anos eram passados e *Claridade* não dava mais

---

(¹) Mindelo, São Vicente, 1944. Dois números. O n.º 3 chegou a ser impresso, mas a Censura proibiu a sua saída da tipografia; anos depois a edição foi destruída.

Colaboradores: Arnaldo França, Eduíno Brito, Guilherme Rocheteau, José Spencer, Nuno Miranda, Orlanda Amariles, Teixeira de Sousa; metropolitanos: Maria Guilhermina, Manuel Ferreira (ou Luís Pinto); e Luís Terry (goês).

notícia de si. Ora os promotores de *Certeza* teriam apenas oito, nove anos na altura em que foram publicados os dois primeiros números daquela revista. Mal a conheciam quando começaram a interessar-se pela literatura. Tanto que dois ou três anos antes de *Certeza* todos eles faziam o seu exercício poético nos moldes tradicionais. A sua grande sombra era ainda a do poeta José Lopes e um pouco menos a de Januário Leite. E só compreenderam o acto revolucionário de *Claridade* depois de apetrechados culturalmente. Faltou-lhes então o fôlego necessário para, ao nível estético, com ela ombrearem. Mas alargaram-na ao nível ideológico.

É António Nunes, vivendo em Lisboa, e dos mais adestrados entre eles, e perfeitamente sintonizado com o espírito do grupo, que dá o tom em nota alta: «Mamãe! / Sonho que um dia, / estas leiras de terra que se estendem, quer seja Mato Engenho, Dàcabalaio ou Santana, / filhas do nosso esforço, frutos do nosso suor, / Serão nossas,» — e define assim o ideário colectivo. Com efeito, os fundadores da revista consciencializavam (pode ser que ainda imaturamente — mas consciencializavam) «as novas seivas brotando da terra dura e seca» e a orgulhosa descoberta dos falsos mitos: «Oh, esse momento d'oiro / em que tombaram, um por um, os falsos deuses!» (Nuno Miranda). O tema da evasão, com fundas influências de Jorge Barbosa, ali perpassa, é verdade: «Partir / deixar a ilha tão pequena / que o vento nómada / bafeja / e as ondas do mar / rodeiam» (Arnaldo França) — mas a integração ecuménica na odisseia universal do homem, reflectida no desespero da destruição moral, ali se ergue também: «E fica-nos a certeza / de que há um 'front' em toda a parte» (Guilherme Rocheteau), a definir uma consciencialização dinâmica da vida.

Para além de poesia, nos dois números de *Certeza* encontra-se a colaboração de Teixeira de Sousa: *Da Claridade à Certeza;* um artigo sobre as condições socioeconómicas do estudante cabo-verdiano (Nuno Miranda); outro sobre a mulher e o seu papel participante (Orlanda Amariles); e ainda outro sobre Jorge Barbosa (Eduíno Brito); questões locais, notas de reflexão sobre a actividade literária insular; um conto (José Spencer); alguns instantâneos pertinentes, de Arnaldo França. Tudo isso não será matéria excepcional, mas traduz as preocupações de objectividade crítica desses jovens que pensavam já em termos de intervenção intelectual.

É verdade que *Certeza* não formou um grande poeta da literatura cabo-verdiana. Arnaldo França, por exemplo, poderia ter-nos impedido de fazer esta afirmação. Mas, de qualquer forma que seja, o marco ali ficou. Aliás pressentido não só no título mas também nas últimas linhas do número 1: «O nosso jornal é uma lápide. Uma lápide que contará tudo aquilo que nos animou na aleluia deslumbrante dos nossos dezoito anos.»

SELECTED BIBLIOGRAPHY

GENERAL

BURNESS, Donald

Fire: Six Writers from Angola, Mozambique and Cape Verde. Afterword by Manuel Ferreira. Washington: Three Continents Press, 1977.

"Lusophone African Literature." Paper presented at Translation '74. Columbia University, New York, N.Y., Dec. 1974.

"Chinua Achebe and Luandino Vieira: Paths to the Understanding of Anglophone and Lusophone African Literatures." Paper presented at African Literature Association Meeting, Gainesville, Florida, April 1980.

"The Literature of Cape Verde, São Tomé and Príncipe." *Zeitschrift für Kulturaustausch* (Stuttgart, West Germany). no. 2, 1979. pp. 183-188.

"Literary Opposition in Angola, Mozambique, Cape Verde, Guiné-Bissau and São-Tomé e Príncipe During Portuguese Colonial Time." Paper presented at Third International Janheinz Jahn Symposium, Mainz, West Germany, May 1979.

"Portuguese-African Literature and the English Reader." *Kunapipi* (Aarhus, Denmark), vol. 2, no. 1, 1980.

CESAR, Amândio

Parágrafos de literatura ultramarina. Lisbon: Sociedade de Expansão Cultural, 1967.

Novos parágrafas de literatura ultramarina. Lisbon, 1971.

DATHORNE, O.R.

The Black Mind: A History of African Literature. Minneapolis: University of Minnesota Press, 1974. 1974.

FERREIRA, Manuel

No Reino de Caliban—vol. I and II. Lisbon: Seara Nova, 1975-76. Vol III scheduled for publication soon.

Literaturas Africanas de Expressão Portuguesa. vol. I and II. Lisbon: Instituto de Cultura Portuguesa, Biblioteca Breve, vol. 6-7, 1977.

"Da Dor de Ser Negro ao Orgulho de Ser Preto." *Colóquio-Letras,* no. 39, September 1977, pp. 17-29.

With Gerald Moser. *Bibliografia Africana de Expressão Portuguesa.* Soon to be published by the Imprensa Nacional in Lisbon.

HAMILTON, Russell

Voices From an Empire. A History of Afro-Portuguese Literature. Minnesota: University of Minnesota Press, 1975.

HERDECK, Donald

African Authors: A Companion to Black African Writing, 1300-1973, vol. 1. Washington: Black Orpheus Press, 1973.

KLIMA, Vladimir and ORTOVA, Jarmili

Moderní Literatury Subsharské Afriky. Prague: Universita 17 Listopadu V, 1971, pp. 110-132.

MARGARIDO, Alfredo
"Incidences socio-économiques sur la poésie noire d'expression portugaise." *Diogène*, no. 37. Paris, January-March 1962, pp. 53-80.

Negritude e Humanismo. Lisbon: Casa dos Estudantes do Império, *1964.*

MARTINHO, Fernando J.B.
"O Tema da Esperança na Poesia Africana de Língua Portuguesa." *Colóquio-Letras*, no. 39, September 1977, pp. 5-16.

MOSER, Gerald
Essays in Portuguese-African Literature, Pennsylvania State Studies no. 26, University Park, Penn.: The Pennsylvania State University, 1969.

A Tentative Portuguese-African Bibliography: Portuguese Literature in Africa and African Literature in the Portuguese Language. University Park, Penn.: The Pennsylvania State University Libraries, 1970.

"How African is the African Literature Written in Portuguese?" In "Black African." *Review of National Literature*, vol. 2, no. 2, Jamaica, Long Island, N.Y., Autumn 1971, pp. 148-166.

"The Changing Image of the African in Portuguese-African Writing." *Neo-African Literature and Culture — Essays in Memory of Janheinz Jahn*, Mainzer Afrika-Studien. Wiesbaden: B. Heyman, 1976, pp. 196-219.

"Relações das Literaturas Lusófonas de Africa com a Asia e as Americas." *Colóquio-Letras*, no. 39, September 1977, pp. 38-41.

"The Lusophone Literatures of Africa since Independence." Paper presented at African Literature Association meeting, Boone, North Carolina, April 1978.

"Nationalliteratur in Angola und Mozambik." *Zeitschrift für Kulturaustausch* (Stuttgart, West Germany). no. 2, 1979. pp. 189-196.

PALLISTER, Janis L.
"Island Imagery in the Poetry of São Tomé, Cape Verde, Madagascar and Mauritius." Paper presented at African Literature Association meeting, Boone, North Carolina, April 1978.

PINTO BULL, Benjamin
"Regards sur la poésie africaine d'expression portugaise." *L'Afrique*, no. 2. University of Dakar, 1972, pp. 79-117.

PRETO-RODAS, Richard A.
Negritude as a Theme in the Poetry of the Portuguese-Speaking World. Humanities Monographs Ser. No. 31. Gainesville, Fla.: University Press of Florida, 1970.

RIAUSOVA, Helena A.
As Literaturas da Africa de Expressão Portuguesa. Moscow: ed. Nauka, 1973.

SYLVAN, Fernando.
A Lingua Portuguesa no Futuro da Africa, Braga, Editora Pax, 1966.

TORRES, Alexandre Pinheiro
O Neo-Realismo Literário Português. Lisbon: Moraes Editores, 1976.

ZELL, Hans, editor; Bundy, Carol; Burness, Donald; Coulon, Virginia: assoc. editors.
A Reader's Guide to African Literature, 2nd ed. London: Heinemann, 1981.

CAPE VERDE

ARAUJO, Norman
   A Study of Cape Verdean Literature. Boston: Boston College, 1976.

FERREIRA, Manuel
   A Aventura Crioula. 2nd ed. Lisbon: Plátano Editora, 1973.

   "O Círculo do Mar e o *Terra-Longismo* em *Chiquinho* de Baltasar Lopes." *Colóquio-Letras,* no. 5, January 1972. pp. 66-70.

GÉRARD, Albert
   "The Literature of Cape Verde." *African Arts/Arts d'Afrique,* vol. 1, no. 2, Winter, 1968, pp. 66-70.

GONÇALVES, António Aurélio
   "Alguns Poemas de Osvaldo Alcántara. *Cabo Verde,* no. 80, May 1956, pp. 9-13.

HAMILTON, Russell
   "Cape Verdean Poetry and the PAIGC." Paper presented at African Literature Association meeting, Madison, Wisconsin, March 1977.

LOPES, Baltasar
   O Dialecto Crioulo de Cabo Verde. Lisbon, Imprensa Nacional, 1957.

MACEDO, Donald
   "The Need for the Standardization of Cape Verdean Orthography." Paper presented at African Literature Association Meeting, Gainesville, Fla., April 1980.

NUNES, Maria Luisa
   "Cape Verdean Oral Traditions and Contemporary Oral History." Paper presented at African Literature Association Meeting, Gainesville, Fla., April 1980.

   The Phonologie of Cape Verdean Dialects of Portuguese. Lisbon: Centro de Estudos Filológicos, 1963.

SILVEIRA, Onésimo
   Consciencialização na Literatura Cabo-verdiana. Lisbon: Casa dos Estudantes do Império, 1963.

GUINÉ-BISSAU

BARROS, Marcelino Marques de
   "O Guineense." *Revista Lusitana,* vol. II, pp. 166-168; vol. V, pp. 174 and 271; vol. VI, p. 300; vol. X, pp. 306-310.

MARTINHO, Fernando, J.B.
   "The New Poetry of Guinea Bissau." Paper presented at African Literature Association, Boone, North Carolina, April 1978.

MOSER, Gerald
   "Amilcar Cabral, the Poet." *Research in African Literatures,* vol. 9, no. 2, Fall, 1978, pp. 176-197.

   "Os jovens Poetas de Bissau." *Colóquio-Letras,* no. 52.

SÃO TOMÉ E PRÍNCIPE

MARGARIDO, Maria Manuela
   "De Costa Alegre a Francisco José Tenreiro." *Estudos Ultramarinos,* no. 3. Lisbon, Instituto Superior dos Estudos Ultramarinos, 1959.

RIBAS, Tomaz
"O Tchiloli ou as Tragédias de São Tomé e Príncipe." *Espiral*, vol. I, no. 6-7, 1965, pp. 70-77.

ANGOLA

ANON.
Reflexões Sobre o Estudo das Linguas Nacionais. Cadernos da Frente Cultural. 4 Serie. No. 1. Luanda: Conselho Nacional de Cultura, 1977.

ANTÓNIO, Mário
"Angolan Poetry Since Independence." tr. by Irwin Stern. Paper presented at African Literature Association Meeting, Bloomington: University of Indiana, March 1979.

"Literatura Angolana e Expressão Portuguesa." Paper presented at Second International Meeting on Modern Portugal. Durham: University of New Hampshire, June 1979.

Luanda, 'Ilha' Crioula, Lisbon: Agência-General do Ultramar. 1968. (Essays on Oscar Ribas, Tomaz Vieira da Cruz, *António de Assis Junior*, Cordeiro da Matta).

"Para Uma Perspectiva Crioula da Literatura Angolana." *Gil Vicente,* 1974, pp. 1-15. (on Cordeiro da Matta).

ANDRADE, Costa
"L'Angolanité de Agostinho Neto e António Jacinto." *Présence Africaine,* no. 42. 1962, pp. 76-91.

ANDRADE, Mário de
"Littérature et Nacionalisme en Angola." *Présence Africaine,* no. 41. 1962, pp. 91-99.

BURNESS, Donald
"The Short Stories of Geraldo Bessa Victor." *Ba Shiru,* vol. VI, Fall 1975.

"Angolan Writing: an Arm of Liberation." Paper presented at African Literature Association meeting, Madison, Wisconsin, March 1977.

"L'Optimisme dans la Littérature de l'Angola." Paper presented at 7e Colloque de l'Association Canadienne des Etudes Africaines, Sherbrooke, Québec, Canada. May 1977.

"Nzinga Mbandi and Angolan Independence." *Luso-Brazilian Review,* vol. 14, no. 2, Winter, 1977, pp. 225-229.

"Arlindo Barbeitos and the Voice of Silence." Paper presented at African Literature Association meeting, Boone, North Carolina, April 1978.

CUTLER, Charles
"The Proletarian Figures in the Early Fiction of Luandino Vieira and Jorge Amado." Paper presented at African Literature Association meeting, Boone, North Carolina, April 1978.

DAVID, Raul
Interview. *Lavra e Oficina.* no. 13, October 1979, p. 12.

DIAS, Eduardo Mayone
"O Elemento de Confrontação na Poesia de Angola." *Hispania,* vol. LIV, no. 1, March 1971, pp. 54-61.

DORIA, Alváro
"Um Poeta da Negritude." Guimarães, 1966; reprint from *Gil Vicente,* August 1966, pp. 119-129, (on Geraldo Bessa Victor).

FERREIRA, Eugénio
"Literatura e Herança Cultural." *Lavra e Oficina,* no. 13. October 1979, p. 5.

FIGUEIREDO, António de
"The Children of Rape." *The New African*, vol. 4, no. 9. London, 1965, pp. 203-211. (on Luandino Vieira).

GARCIA, José Martins
"Luandino Vieira: o anti-apartheid." *Colóquio-Letras*, no. 22, November 1974, pp. 45-50.

JACINTO, Tomás
"The Art of Luandino Vieira." *Ba Shiru*, vol. 5, no. 1, Fall, 1973, pp. 49-58.

LOURENÇO, Manuel
"Is Sagrada Esperança Modern?" Paper presented at African Literature Association meeting, Boone, North Carolina, April 1978.

MARTINHO, Fernando
"Nzoji de Arlindo Barbeitos—Ars Poetica e Ars Combinatoria." Paper presented at African Literature Association Meeting, Gainesville, Fla., April 1980.

MESTRE, David
"Carta de Angola—uma Profunda Relação Dialéctica entre História e Literatura." *Colóquio-Letras*, no. 39, September 1977, pp. 42-47.

MOSER, Gerald
"Queen Nzinga in Fact and Fiction." *Neo-African Literature and Culture—Essays in Memory of Janheinz Jahn*, Mainzer Afrika-Studien, Wiesbaden: B. Heyman, 1976, pp. 220-242.

"Oscar Ribas' Careeer as a Writer of Angolan Stories." Paper presented at African Literature Association meeting, Madison, Wisconsin, March 1977.

"Re-Africanization in Recent Angolan Publications." Paper presented at African Literature Association Meeting, Gainesville, Fla., April 1980.

MOURÃO, Fernando Augusto Albuuerque
A Sociedade Angolana através da Literatura. São Paulo: Atica, 1978.

NETO, Agostinho
On Literature and National Culture. Cadernos Lavra e Oficina, no. 20. Luanda: Union of Angolan Writers, 1979.

RASSNER, Ronald
"Colonialism and the Fiction of Luandine Vieira." Paper presented at Conference on Interdisciplinary Perspectives on Colonial and Néo-Colonial Africa, Northern Illinois University, Dekalb, Illinois, June 1975.

DOS SANTOS LIMA, Manuel
"Itinerário e Perspectivas da Literatura Angolana." paper presented at African Literature Association meeting, Boone, North Carolina, April 1978.

STERN, Erwin
"Luandino Vieira: Linguistics and Politics." Paper presented at African Literature Association meeting, Boone, North Carolina, April 1978.

TORRES, Alexandre Pinheiro
"Propedéutica à 'Trilogia de Camaxilo' de Castro Soromenho." *Colóquio-Letras*, no. 39, September 1977, pp. 30-37.

TRIGO, Salvato
"A 'Fala' Poética Luandina como Resultado de Várias 'Falas'—O Logotetismo." Paper presented at African Literature Association Meeting, Gainesville, Fla., April 1980.

Introducão à Literatura Angolana de Expressão Portuguesa. Colecção Literaturas Africanas. no. 1. Porto: Brasilia Editoria, 1977.

VIEIRA, Luandino
   "O Escritor na Sociedade Angolana." *Lavra e Oficina,* no. 9-10, 13. October 1979, p. 4.

MOZAMBIQUE

BURNESS, Donald
   "Interview with Luís Bernardo Honwana." *Pacific Quarterly Moana* (Hamilton, New Zealand), vol. 6, no. 3, 1981.

CORTEZ, Maria de Lourdes
   "Uma Leitura d'Arca, texto de Grabato Dias." *Colóquio-Letras,* no. 12, March 1973, pp. 34-40.

HONWANA, Luís Bernardo
   The Role of Poetry in the Mozambican Revolution." *Lotus,* no. 8, Cairo, Egypt, 1971, pp. 148-166.

HUGHES, Heather
   "Protest Poetry in Pre-Independence Mozambique and Angola." *English in Africa,* vol. 4, no. 1. March 1977, pp. 18-31.

LEMOS, Virgilio de
   "Le Sens Anti-Culturel da la Politique Coloniale Portugaise." *Remarques Africaines,* no. 249, September 1965, pp. 11-18.

MOSER, Gerald
   "Luís Bernardo Honwana's Place among the Writers of Mozambique" in *A Celebration of Black and African Writing,* eds. Bruce King and Kolawole Ogungbesan. Oxford: Oxford University Press, 1975, pp. 189-203.

   "Moçambique: outra república de poetas." *Colóquio-Letras,* no. 51, September 1979, pp. 60-62.

TURNER, Doris
   "The Stories of Luís Bernardo Honwana." Paper presented at African Literature Association Meeting, Bloomington: University of Indiana, March 1979.

JOURNALS*

África—edited by Manuel Ferreira, Rua de Alcantara 53, Lisbon, Portugal.

África—Centro de Estudos Africanos. University of São Paulo, São Paulo, Brazil.

Colóquio-Letras—Fundação Calouste Gulbenkian, Lisbon, Portugal.

Lavra e Oficina, Box 2767-C, Luanda, Angola.

Raizes—C.P. no. 98, Praia, Santiago, Republic of Cape Verde Islands.

*These journals contain many articles on Lusophone African Literatures. I have cited a few individual articles in *Cóloquio-Letras,* which is devoted to literatures from throughout the Portuguese speaking world. Manuel Ferreira's triannual journal, *Africa,* the first issue of which appeared in July 1978, offers by far the richest storehouse of criticism. Because so many articles and reviews have been published in *Africa,* I have chosen not to list them individually. The very existence of *Africa* and the success that it has had is ample evidence of the recent effulgence of Lusophone African literary criticism.

*There are several bibliographies of Portuguese African writing and criticism. The most complete and up-to-date reference is the soon-to-be published *Bibliografia africana de expressão portuguesa* by Gerald Moser and Manuel Ferreira. Among other outstanding sources are the bibliographies included in Russell Hamilton's *Voices from an Empire* and Manuel Ferreira's *Literaturas africanas de expressão portuguesa* as well as Gerald Moser's *A Tentative Portuguese-African Bibliography*. This selected bibliography of critical writings on Lusophone African literature is limited in scope; perhaps its most useful contribution is the inclusion of scholarly papers that have been presented at recent conferences.

STOP PRESS ADDITIONS

CARDOSO, Antônio
> Interview. *Lavra e Oficina*. no. 16. January, 1980, pp. 4-5.
> "A Revolução de Outubro e a Literatura." *Lavra e Oficina*. no. 14. November, 1979, pp. 6-7.

EDIÇOES 70
> *Luandino–José Luandino Vieira e a Sua Obra* (a collection of critical essays on the work of Luandino Vieira by 16 scholars, selected by the publishing house Edições 70). Lisbon, 1980.

FERREIRA, Eugénio
> *A Crítica Neorealistia.* Cadernos *Lavra e Oficina*. no 27. Luanda, Angolan Writers Union, 1980.

HAMILTON, Russell
> "A Literatura Escrita e a Integração Culturel." In two parts. *Lavra e Oficina*. nos. 16 and 17, 1980.

JACINTO, Antônio
> "Reflexões sobre Cultura, Cultura Popular, Cultura de Masas." *Lavra e Oficina*. no. 14. November, 1979, p. 9.

NETO, Maria Eugénia
> Interview. *Lavra e Oficina*. no. 14. November, 1979, p. 3.

NOTES ON CONTRIBUTORS

Mário António (Mário António Fernandes de Oliveira), an Angolan, currently living in Lisbon, is the author of many books of poetry and short stories including *100 Poemas* (1963) and *Mahezu* (1966), and numerous articles on Angolan culture and literature.

Norman Araujo, an Associate Professor of Romance Languages and Literature at Boston College, is the author of *A Study of Cape Verdean Literature* (1966) and *In Search of Eden: Lamartine's Symbols of Despair and Deliverance* (1968).

Donald Burness, Professor of English at Franklin Pierce College in Rindge, New Hampshire, has written *Shaka, King of the Zulus, in African Literature* (1976) and *Fire: Six Writers from Angola, Mozambique and Cape Verde* (1977).

Ray Duarte de Carvalho is an Angolan cinematographer, poet, and short story writer. His published works include *A Decisão da Idade, Como Se o Mundo Não Tivesse Leste* and *Exercicios de Crueldade*.

Manuel Ferreira, who teaches African Literature at the Instituto de Estudos Africanos in the Faculty of Letters of the University of Lisbon, has written *A Aventura Crioula* (1967), various novels including *Hora di Bai* (1962) and *Voz de Prisão* (1971), and has edited the two volume *No Reino de Caliban: Antologia panorámica de poesia africana de expressão portuguesa* (1975/76); he most recently published *Literaturas Africanas de Expressão Portuguesa Vol. I and II* (1977).

José Martins Garcia of the Departmento de Linguistica of the University of Lisbon has contributed critical essays to *Colóquio-Letras* and other journals concerned with Lusophone African writing.

Henrique Guerra of Angola is the author of various books including *O Circulo de Giz de Bombôand Angola: Estrutura Económica e Classes Sociais.*

Russell G. Hamilton, a Professor in the Department of Spanish and Portuguese at the University of Minnesota, is the author of *Voices from an Empire: A History of Afro-Portuguese Literature* (1975) and numerous articles on African literature.

Tomás Jacinto has studied at the University of Wisconsin and after a personal interview in Lisbon with Luandino Vieira, published in *Ba Shiru* his article on the Angolan story teller.

Gerald Moser, Professor Emeritus of Portuguese and Spanish at the Pennsylvania State University, has authored numerous articles and published two books on African subjects, *Essays in Portuguese-African Literature* (1969) and *A Tentative Portuguese-African Bibliography* (1970).

Richard A. Preto-Rodas, Professor of Spanish and Portuguese at the University of Illinois, has written *Negritude as a Theme in the Poetry of the Portuguese-Speaking World* (1970), *Dialogue and Courtly Love in Renaissance Portugal* (1971) and co-edited *Crónicas Brasileiras: A Portuguese Reader* (1978).

Onésimo Silveira, a Cape Verdean poet and essayist from the island of São Vicente, who has studied in Sweden, has appeared in many literary anthologies including *Resisténcia Africana* (1975) and has authored *Toda a Gente Fala: Sim Senhor* (1960) and *Consciencialização na literatura caboverdiana* (1963).

Uanhenga Xitu (Agostinho Mendes de Carvalho), the governor of the State of Luanda, is one of Angola's outstanding prose writers. Among his published works are a novel *Mañana* and a collection of stories *'Mestre' Tamoda e Outros Contos.*

Critical Perspectives on Lusophone Literature From Africa

Recent years have witnessed a burgeoning interest in the literatures of Lusophone Africa. The struggle for liberation culminating in independence has produced a vigorous body of work, innovative in theme and language.

This collection of essays accompanied by over thirty illustrations and photographs offers a variety of critical perspectives on national literatures, as well as such individual writers as Luandino Vieira, Agostinho Neto, Cordeiro da Matta, Castro Soromenho and Baltasar Lopes. Though no essay specifically treats of women writers, such poets as Alda do Espirito Santo, Maria Manuela Margarido and Noémia de Sousa, are dealt with in several of the essays.

This literature by Africans, black, white and mestizo, expresses the values, traditions and aspirations of their societies. The inclusion of this volume in the *Critical Perspectives Series* attests to the growing need to recognize Lusophone African writing not only in the African context, but in world literature.

The Editor

Donald Burness is Professor of English at Franklin Pierce College in Rindge, New Hampshire, U.S.A. He is the author of numerous articles and two books, *Shaka, King of the Zulus, in African Literature* and *Fire: Six Writers from Angola, Mozambique and Cape Verde,* both published by Three Continents Press, Washington, D. C. Burness also enjoys his role as Assistant Basketball Coach.

LC No: 80-53348; ISBN: 0-89410-015-7 (Cased); –016-5 (Pbk)